HEROIC MEN, GREAT SHIPS, AND
EPIC BATTLES OF THE AMERICAN NAVY

ON SEAS
OF GLORY

JOHN LEHMAN

THE FREE PRESS
New York London Toronto Sydney Singapore

THE FREE PRESS
Rockefeller Center
1230 Avenue of the Americas
New York, New York 10020

DESIGNED BY LISA CHOVNICK

Manufactured in the United States of America

1   3   5   7   9   10   8   6   4   2

Library of Congress Cataloging-in-Publication Data

Lehman, John F.
On seas of glory : heroic men, great ships, and epic battles of the
American Navy / John Lehman.
p.   cm.
Includes bibliographical references and index.
1. United States—History, Naval.   2. United States. Navy—History.
3. United States. Navy—Biography.   4. United States—History, Naval—Anecdotes.
5. United States Navy—History—Anecdotes.   I. Title.
E182.L47 2001
359'.00973—dc21   2001042840
ISBN: 0-684-87176-9

To Barbara,
Sasha, John III
and Grace

The Navy . . . acts on an element strange to most writers, as its members have been a strange race apart, without prophets of their own, neither themselves nor their calling understood.

ALFRED T. MAHAN

CONTENTS

INTRODUCTION

THE GRANDEUR OF THE American naval tradition is best found in its people, fighting sailors, technical innovators and inspiring leaders. In turn, the physical embodiment of that spirit is to be found in great warships, and the people and ships together have shaped history in epic sea battles from the Revolution through the Cold War.

My exposure to naval persons aloft and alow, from history, to hearing the stories of my father's service in World War II, to my own many years as a naval reserve aviator, to my six years as Secretary of the Navy, has convinced me that those who have made their profession upon great waters in ships of war are deeply changed by the experience, and some in every era deeply change the experience for all those who follow. This has been true of those who have served only a few years as well as those who have devoted their lives to naval service.

The sea is utterly unforgiving of inattention, negligence or ineptitude. Add to this perpetual conflict with the elements the dimension of mortal combat, and we have a unique crucible. Through American history the Navy has drawn men of all types. Then it has put those men together in close quarters in wooden—and now steel—containers and sent them off for years at a time to deal with ferocious storms and deadly enemies. Those who return are still individuals, but common patterns of temperament are discernible. These patterns have shaped the service, and through it, America.

In my view, naval personalities fall into three general categories. There are the daring warriors who live for glory and for battle: John Paul Jones, Stephen Decatur, Jr., and William B. Cushing come immediately to mind. Such men, as once was said in a fitness report on General Patton, "are invaluable in war but a disruptive influence in peacetime." Then there are sailors who are equally courageous but more prudent—less dramatic leaders in both war and peace. John

Barry, David Farragut and James Forrestal would fall in this category. The last and largest category is made up of reluctant warriors who leave their civilian professions to go to sea in time of war. They bravely—and often brilliantly—do their duty, then like Cincinnatus return to civilian life. Because they do not stick around to achieve high rank, they are rarely celebrated in conventional accounts. But these officers and seamen are the largest source of naval greatness. Fourteen-year-old Samuel Leech, at the height of the battle in *Macedonian*, spoke for them all: "To give way to gloom, or to show fear would do no good, and might brand us with the name of cowards, and ensure certain defeat. Our only true philosophy, therefore, was to make the best of our situation, by fighting bravely and cheerfully."

As the subtitle of this book implies, the narrative is divided among stories about men, ships, and battles. There are in the traditions of the Army and the Air Force great and classic weapons that are a part of service history: the M-1 rifle, the Sherman tank, the P-51 Mustang, and the F-86 Saberjet, for example. But there is nothing quite the same as the relationship between seamen and their ships.

Sailors live for months and years inside their weapons. And their weapons last a very long time. Three of the original six great superfrigates built before 1800 were still in active service when the Civil War began. The battleship *Wisconsin* was nearly fifty years old when it went into combat in Desert Storm, and remains in the reserve fleet at this writing. Not unlike automobiles, buildings and airplanes, some rare warships achieve a perfect balance of efficiency and combat effectiveness—and beauty. Included here are stories of some of the most significant and unusual American warships, like Joshua Humphreys' superfrigates and the *Iowa*-class battleships, both near-perfect instruments of naval warfare.

There is also in the sea service—far and away the most superstitious of professions—a deeply held belief that there are certain lucky ships just as there are unlucky ships. I have thus tried to tell stories of both types: the lucky, like *Fair American* and *Constitution*, and the distinctly unlucky, like *Chesapeake* and *Porter*.

Naval shipbuilding today continues to benefit from the tradition of the great ships that are described in this book. It is a design philosophy formed from the hard lessons of those ships and their battles. Quite the opposite of the criticism by some that the Navy has always been resistant to change, the tradition of American naval shipbuilding is one of innovation. From *Fair American* through the superfrigates, the *Monitors*, the *Dreadnoughts* and nuclear aircraft carriers, American naval ships have led the world in speed, survivability and firepower. In recent years smaller American combatants have been attacked with mines, cruise missiles and enormous suicide bombs and have survived every attack. The tradition continues.

The final strand of the book is made up of tales of the battles that defined the Navy. There are many books about the most important naval battles in our history, and my list of battles is not intended to be definitive. I chose battles that I find of particular interest because they illustrate the flexibility, adaptiveness and ferocity of the American naval culture. There are some that would be on all lists—like the battles of Virginia Capes, New Orleans and Midway—and others that are little known, like those of Valcour Island and Ironbottom Sound.

A word of warning to the reader. This book is not yet another survey history of the U.S. Navy. It is a selection of stories on people, ships and battles of the American Navy set in historical context. So while the reader can expect to find here a chronological history of American naval power from the Revolutionary War through the Cold War, the book is not a comprehensive canon. It is deliberately selective and subjective. The list of whom and what I find to be of significance leaves out much that would demand inclusion in an official history or biographical dictionary, and includes much that would never make it into the same.

My opinions also frequently differ from the opinions of many professional historians, and the historians of the Navy itself. Some of my judgments in the book, such as on the importance of privateers in winning American independence, or of gunboats to Union naval victory, or of lessons from the Vietnam War, are not shared by many authoritative texts.

It is hoped that these accounts of great people, in their ships, during their battles, set in the context of the flow of naval history, will give the reader an understanding of America's naval tradition. Thomas Jefferson disliked the Navy because he thought it was elitist. Through much of its history it was; punctilious courtesy, tailored uniforms and silver napkin rings have coexisted at times with bigotry like that suffered by the Jewish Commodore Uriah Philips Levy, and racial inequality that endured even into the 1970s. From its founding until 1900, only one percent of midshipmen at the Naval Academy were from working class families. But a tradition of elitism based on real merit is the true legacy of the story told here. The genuine color-blindness of the naval service today is more a part of naval tradition than the practice of discrimination that at one time the Navy shared with the rest of the nation.

There is another tradition: of aggressive forward strategy, and ferocious prosecution of war once started. It is what Alfred Thayer Mahan described in his writings as offensive defense. The greatest victories of this naval tradition have been not the wars recounted here but the wars that were never fought because American seapower was so strong that to challenge it would be foolhardy. If we let it, the strength of that tradition will continue to underwrite peace in our land.

I

THE
REVOLUTIONARY
WAR

THE BRITISH COLONIES established in North America in the 17th and 18th centuries were maritime enterprises. Their principal industries (other than agriculture) were cod fishing and whaling, and to that they soon added shipping, becoming major exporters of tobacco and foodstuffs to Britain. All of the major cities were trading ports: Boston, Newport, New York, Philadelphia, Baltimore, Norfolk, Savannah and Charleston. There was also much shipping to Europe direct from hundreds of smaller ports located on the bays, sounds and rivers of the East Coast. Trade among the colonies was overwhelmingly done by river and sea.

It is not surprising that such an economy would rapidly develop a large and sophisticated industrial base for building, repairing, supplying, outfitting, investing in and operating seagoing vessels. Because of unlimited supplies of the finest timber for the construction of sailing ships—yellow pine for masts, cedar for planking, oak and the specially valuable native live oak—builders could make first-class ships at low cost. (For similar reasons, furniture- and cabinetmaking attracted fine craftsmen from Britain and elsewhere in Europe.) By the mid-18th century, American merchant ships were recognized as some of the finest in the world. Yankee schooners and brigs had come to dominate the North Atlantic and Caribbean trade. They were the best in the business.

The British Admiralty generally did not allow the production of major combatants, frigate size and larger, to be built outside of Britain. Yankee shipbuilders built two exceptional Royal Navy frigates, *Boston* and *America*, in the 1740s and 1750s, and many smaller combatants and schooners, so that by the time of the American Revolution there were numerous shipyards in America quite experienced in building warships. They had moreover applied a Yankee culture of innovation to their art. Without the bureaucracy of admiralty oversight, they had long been competing one with the other to build the fastest and best all-around ships for discriminating shipowners. They had drawn on and improved techniques and designs from France, Holland and Britain, while inventing a good many of their own.

When war broke out Britannia did not yet rule the waves to the extent that she did during the War of 1812. Nevertheless she was one of the world's great sea powers (with France, Holland and Spain). At the time she had in commission about a hundred ships of the line, seventy frigates and hundreds of smaller combatants. But this great fleet was stretched across the oceans of the world. Britain had to protect her growing interests in India and its sea commerce; protect its allies in the Mediterranean; maintain its power in northern Europe to balance France, Prussia, Holland and Sweden; maintain its extremely valuable trade and possessions in the Caribbean and Sugar Islands; and project power in North America. Rampant corruption throughout the British naval establishment further diluted the readiness of the fleet. And after the Seven Years' War many ships had been laid up or sold and their mariners dispersed. Britain had far more commitments than her fleet could meet.

The colonies had less sea power, but they had it at hand. While they did not have the capability to deploy a battle fleet of ships of the line, they could raid commerce like no one else. Deployed almost immediately in the form of privateers, naval militias and eventually a Continental Navy, this sea power became a decisive factor in winning independence.

The ships of the Continental Navy were sailed by a different sort of man than those who fought opposite it. While the colonies had thousands of experienced mariners and captains, some with extensive experience as privateers in the Seven Years' War, they had virtually no trained professional naval officers. The sole prominent exception was Nicholas Biddle.

CAPTAIN NICHOLAS BIDDLE: AMERICA'S FIRST NAVAL HERO

When the American colonies declared their independence Britain's Navy encircled the globe. Indeed, after the successful struggle for independence John Paul Jones asked whether it was "proof of madness in the first corps of sea officers to have at so critical a period launched out on the ocean with only two armed merchant ships, two armed brigantines, and one armed sloop?" Even among the quarter of the American population that stood firmly in favor of complete independence and separation from the mother country, there were those who turned down offers of a commission in the fledgling Navy, remarking that "they did not choose to be hanged."

One who thought otherwise was Nicholas Biddle of Philadelphia. Born in 1750 to a prominent Philadelphia family, Biddle's maternal grandfather, Nicholas Scull, had been surveyor general of Pennsylvania. His father, William, did not match his father-in-law's accomplishments in business. He died leaving nine children including Nicholas, aged 6, and very little of the monies or property that had come his way, including his wife's considerable dowry.

As with so many other men who have been drawn by the sea, Nicholas Biddle felt the tug when he was a youngster. At age 14 he gained a position as cabin boy aboard a merchant ship owned in part by his brother-in-law. Within a few years he had experienced a shipwreck off the east coast of Central America and the responsibility of leading survivors many years his senior as they waited and hoped for rescue.

By 1771, with rising tensions between England and Spain over the Falkland Islands, Biddle, with the help of an older brother, secured a commission as a midshipman in the Royal Navy. One of Nicholas's older brothers, Edward, recommended Nicholas to Benjamin Franklin, then the American colonies' representative in London, in a letter that explained, "The Navy under the prospect of war, is the first object of his wishes."

Biddle would have to wait. For the time being he joined *Seaford*, a sixth rater of 20 guns, in June 1771 and later transferred to the larger *Portland*, involved in the final stages of the search for accurate measurement of longitude that concluded the following year when George III insisted that the £20,000 prize be awarded to John and William Harrison. Biddle took great interest in the expedition, but was ultimately dissatisfied.

In a letter to his brother Charles, Nicholas wrote that, "I have too little duty. This situation I liked well enough with the expectation of a War. But as that prospect is past I cannot bear to think of murdering more of my time."

As revolution approached in America, Biddle looked for adventure abroad, securing a position aboard *Carcass*, one of two ketches bound for a polar expedition with another enterprising and ambitious young officer six years his junior: Horatio Nelson. The future hero of Trafalgar was the only shipmate mentioned by Biddle in retrospect. When trapped in ice in the northern latitudes during July 1773 Nelson had gone exploring and attacked a polar bear with the butt of his gun, which had fired without effect. Fortunately, the captain ordered one of the ship's guns discharged to frighten off the irritated bear. Had this not succeeded, Biddle may have had considerably more to report. And Prime Minister William Pitt the Younger—who thirty-two years later announced the decisive victory over the French fleet at Trafalgar to George III—might have had considerably less.

Returning to London to seek a new ship word reached Biddle of the December 1773 Boston Tea Party and he promptly resigned his Royal Navy commission and headed back to Philadelphia.

In America, through the influence of his elder brother Edward, one of Pennsylvania's representatives, Nicholas received command of one of thirteen row galleys that the Pennsylvania legislature's Committee of Safety had contracted for building. But the Pennsylvania Navy was small, weak and overtaxed even to supply such necessities as winter quarters. The second Continental Congress's dawning realization that some kind of naval force was indispensable to success in arms resulted in the purchase of several ships to be converted to armed naval vessels. Edward Biddle's influence was again sufficient to have Nicholas assigned to one of the brigs, *Andrew Doria,* that would carry fourteen 4-pounders. The young captain resigned his commission in the Pennsylvania Navy and joined the Continental Navy.

But nepotism produced less capable leaders than Nicholas Biddle. The commander of the new Continental Navy was Esek Hopkins, the brother of the naval committee chairman, Stephen. On January 5, 1776, Hopkins was ordered to take the new squadron to sea to relieve the blockade of Norfolk and Charleston. Hopkins was slow in readying his command. Finally on February 17, 1776, the little squadron including *Andrew Doria* set sail from Philadelphia with orders from the naval committee that gave him the flexibility . . . "your best Judgment shall Suggest to you as most useful to the American cause, and to distress the Enemy by all means in your power." He decided instead of working the Virginia and Carolina coasts to attack Nassau, New Providence Island, in what are now the Bahamas.

The landing of some 300 men supported by naval gunfire was a success, capturing seventy-three cannon and copious ammunition and small arms for Washington's army.

This first amphibious assault in American history had some related minor actions. On Saturday April 6, 1776, Biddle's *Andrew Doria* caught sight of a 20-gun British frigate, *Glasgow.* The British ship exchanged fire with *Cabot* and *Andrew Doria* as the other Continentals maneuvered to bring their guns to bear. Biddle led the chase as *Glasgow* put on sail and held to a northerly course. But Hopkins called off the attempt to further engage *Glasgow,* fearing that following her could lead to a duel with other significantly more powerful enemy ships.

Biddle was angered by Hopkins's passivity. He wrote his brother Charles about "the Shameful Loss of the *Glasgow.* A more imprudent ill-conducted Affair never happened." By June, Congress had also had enough. Hopkins and two other of his subordinate commanding offi-

cers—each related by marriage to a member of the marine committee—were recalled to Philadelphia "to answer for their conduct."
Command devolved to Biddle as the senior officer along with Congress's admonition to "take no steps" until further orders arrived. But
if Hopkins failed on account of too little initiative, Biddle was the polar opposite.

Biddle returned to sea on *Andrew Doria* and completed a cruise that
netted six prize ships before the end of the summer 1776. After a short
leave, he reported to Philadelphia in mid-October to assume command
of the newly built frigate *Randolph* (32).

After considerable difficulties manning his new command, Biddle
took *Randolph* to sea in February 1777. After some routine convoy duties, Biddle negotiated with John Rutledge, president of the South
Carolina Privy Council, to exchange *Randolph*'s services against
blockading British warships for financial support that would produce
the recruits needed to man the ship. When Biddle arrived on station
off the South Carolina coast, there were no enemy ships to be found.
He set a new course to place himself athwart the trade route between
Jamaica and New York.

In those waters, *Randolph* found a group of British merchantmen
escorted by an armed sloop. Although the smaller enemy vessel opened
fire once its guns came into range, Biddle refused to make the course
change that would allow a broadside. Had he done so, the merchant
ships would have used the interval to escape. He bore *Randolph* down
upon the enemy ship until it was within hailing distance and fired a
single shot from a forecastle gun. *True Briton* struck her colors, and Biddle was able to capture, as well, three of the convoy's laden merchants.

The young captain returned to an enthusiastic welcome at
Charleston, and the additional satisfaction of a tenth of the value of the
prizes, whose worth was calculated at £90,000. Recruiting would not be
a problem again.

While *Randolph* was being scraped of worms and prepared for her
next mission, the relationship deepened between Biddle and Rutledge, based on the former's need for crew members, dockyard labor
and materiel; and the latter's need for a naval presence to keep the port

of Charleston open. The marine committee sent Biddle orders to sail to transit the Atlantic and use French ports to prey upon British shipping, but from Biddle's correspondence with the marine committee, it seems that he never received these orders. Biddle accepted orders from Rutledge to form a small squadron with vessels supplied by South Carolina and destroy the threat posed by enemy warships to the state's seaborne trade. Biddle, however, asked Rutledge, "if it ever becomes necessary you justify me in the eyes of Congress." There is no further evidence and the reader is left to speculate whether the lure of prize money led Biddle to ignore Congress's orders. I believe that Biddle simply felt he could do more good for the cause keeping Charleston open and "turned a blind eye" to Congress.

Biddle made out a will on January 12, 1778, perhaps because of the considerable fortune earned in prizes he had accumulated and because he wanted to provide for his fiancée, Elizabeth Baker, the South Carolina woman to whom he had recently been engaged. In any event, his biographers like to ascribe the timing of the event to his premonition of death.

Randolph was accompanied by four smaller combatants, including the privateer *Fair American*, about which more will soon be heard. She cleared the Charleston bar on February 14, 1778. The little squadron's mission was to destroy British warships on blockade duty before the port, but none was found. Biddle headed again for the Caribbean shipping lanes, meeting several neutrals as he progressed. A small British schooner out of New York bound for Grenada was captured when she mistook the American squadron for a British one. Biddle decided to use her as tender.

Three days later on March 7, off the east coast of Barbados, a sail was sighted to the north. Changing course to intercept, Biddle ordered his squadron to follow. In the failing light of a tropical late afternoon, the stranger maintained her course. To intercept as the lead ship, *Randolph* took in sail, preparing to await the enemy ship. The American vessel closest to *Randolph*, *General Moultrie*, was the first to realize that their opponent was a powerful two-decker, *Yarmouth* (64 guns), with twice the armament of *Randolph*.

As *Yarmouth* passed within hailing distance of *Randolph*, she told the American ship to identify herself or face the consequences. Biddle opened fire, and *Yarmouth* returned it immediately. *Moultrie* emptied three broadsides at *Yarmouth* before her commanding officer became convinced that he might be firing into *Randolph*. Biddle's training paid off, an eyewitness noting that *Randolph* was firing four or five broadsides to one of *Yarmouth*'s. But *Yarmouth*'s broadsides meant more.

For fifteen minutes the two ships poured fire into one another separated by less than fifty yards. Biddle was injured in the thigh and, refusing to be taken below, had the surgeon brought up from his usual duty station deep in the ship to attend him on the quarterdeck. The surgeon went to work on Biddle in a chair while the patient urged his men in their labors. Then suddenly *Randolph* was disintegrated by an enormous explosion that threw debris down in small and great pieces on *Yarmouth*'s deck.

Four days later *Yarmouth*, in pursuit of new quarry, passed close to the position of the engagement. There she found four young survivors whom the explosion had blown clear and who had fashioned a floating platform from the wreck's debris. Of Captain Biddle and the rest of the crew or their vessel, nothing was ever again seen. The cause of the explosion remains a mystery.

The 27-year-old's death in the face of a larger and more powerful enemy produced an immediate and glamorous romantic hero for the colonies, but denied their Navy of its most promising leader and only trained professional naval officer.

THE ROYAL NAVY'S PRESENCE on the North American station had been a major factor contributing to the movement to independence. There was resentment among the powerful shipowner merchants that the Royal Navy did little to protect its commerce from French raiders during the Seven Years' War. More importantly they were furious with the Royal Navy's role in enforcing the mercantilist acts after the Seven Years' War. In 1775 Parliament passed four successive Restraining Acts intended brutally to force the colonists into line through crippling the New England maritime economy. After the Boston Tea Party, the Royal Navy closed the port of Boston, infuriating all of the colonists.

The Continental Army was established in 1775 with George Washington as its commander and was ordered to the relief of Boston. It was from this operation that the Continental Navy was born. On August 11, 1775, John Adams, Silas Deane and John Langdon were named to a new naval committee of the Continental Congress charged with finding a way to intercept arms and ammunition en-route by sea to the British forces gathering at Boston and to attempt to obtain them for General Washington's use.

As will be seen, many people have been called the father of American naval power; if there is a true father, it is surely John Adams. He was a vigorous proponent of building naval power before war broke out and maintained a strong pressure throughout the war for using seapower to support General Washington's efforts. After independence was gained he was a tireless advocate for the establishment of a Navy for the new United States, and when he became president vigorously pursued the policy of naval expansion.

By the end of the year, armed American schooners of George Washington's fleet had intercepted or captured several British supply ships off New England and supplied Washington with muskets, gunpowder and shot. The actions forced the Royal Navy to begin to transport all arms in well-armed ships, which of course reduced their ability to blockade. As the war progressed, the rapidly growing numbers of American privateers and naval vessels forced the Royal Navy to convoy all of its supply ships.

In a resolution of October 13, 1775, Congress voted to acquire the first two warships of the Continental Navy. That date is currently celebrated by the U.S. Navy as its birthday. In fact, the naval effort by the colonies ran its full course during the war and was then abolished before the establishment of the United States, so the date has more to do with Pentagon politics than historic validity. A more accurate birthday would be March 27, 1794, when the United States Navy was established by act of the United States Congress.

The U.S. Navy took its procedure unabashedly from the Royal Navy. John Adams in November 1775 drafted the "Rules for the Regulation of the Navy of the United Colonies," lifting them wholesale from those of the Royal Navy. (These were resurrected with the Navy in 1794.)

The first ship to be commissioned into the Continental Navy was *Black Prince*, bought from Philadelphian Robert Morris and renamed *Alfred* (24 guns) in honor of the founder of the Royal Navy. It was swiftly followed by *Columbus* (20), *Andrew Doria* (14), negligently named for the great Venetian admiral Andrea Doria, *Cabot* (14), *Providence* (12), *Hornet* (10), *Wasp* (8) and *Fly* (8). Adams hired Joshua Humphreys, the leading Philadelphia ship designer, to supervise the converting of these ships into warships.

On December 11, 1775, Congress authorized the construction of thirteen frigates to form the battle fleet of the Continental Navy. Under Adams's guidance it was a wise decision to build fast frigates rather than ships of the line. The frigates could operate singly to evade the blockade, capture enemy merchantmen and disrupt their convoys. Schooners and sloops were too small, ships of the line too big. The strategy was well put by Robert Morris, the first among naval commissioners of the Congress: "Forcing the British to defend their extensive possessions at all points is of infinitely more consequence to the United States of America than all the plunder that can be taken."

It is fashionable today to lament the growth of "pork-barrel" spending in defense, but it has in the United States an ancient history. The construction of the first thirteen frigates was directed by Congress to be spread around for political reasons: four to be built in Pennsylvania; two each in Massachusetts, New York and Rhode Island; and one each in Connecticut, Maryland and New Hampshire.

In February 1776 the new Navy undertook its first major operation in taking Nassau, described above. As a result of this success the British Admiralty decided to shift its strength to North America and the Caribbean and greatly reduce its presence in the Mediterranean and northern Europe. This would have far-reaching consequences later in the war as France and then Holland took advantage of the power vacuum.

By the end of 1777 the Royal Navy had eighty-nine men-of-war on the North American station armed with 2,576 guns, nearly half of the entire Royal Navy's inventory of active warships, 80 percent of its frigates and about one-third of its total firepower. Facing it, the Continental Navy at this time deployed only fourteen vessels with 332 guns.

On American shipping and its overmatched Navy, the British exacted a steady toll.

HMS *JERSEY:* SHIP OF MARTYRS

In Brooklyn, New York, there stands a monument to martyrs. Erected in Fort Greene Park, it is dedicated to the Revolutionary War soldiers and sailors whose lives were lost aboard British prison ships anchored in the East River's Wallabout Bay, adjacent to the Brooklyn Navy Yard. The impressive 145-foot, fluted granite Doric shaft stands above a hidden crypt containing twenty large slate coffins that actually hold the bone fragments of the fallen. They had been collected over the years of the 19th century as each tide washed up the remains of prisoners whose bodies had been slipped over the side of the hulks or hastily buried ashore when they died. The monument is engraved with a promise that "They Shall Not Be Forgotten."

But history has forgotten that more Americans lost their lives aboard His Majesty's prison-ships than on the battlefields from Concord to Yorktown. Over twice as many Americans were lost as prisoners in British hands than as combatants against them. Some 4,435 Americans died in battle, over 11,000 in captivity. In every other war, deaths among prisoners have been a tiny fraction of deaths in battle.

In the wake of the Battle of Long Island and the capture of New York City in August 1776, thousands of American prisoners fell into British hands. Soon all available jails and makeshift confinement facilities such as churches, warehouses and sugar factories in the city were

overflowing with captive soldiers, sailors and anyone suspected of being a traitor to the crown. Royal Navy ships were also seizing American
privateers and their crews, and sending them into New York.

The prisoner question was a complicated one. Washington's army,
always on the run, could not deal adequately with British prisoners.
The British should have been eager to exchange them because their
manpower otherwise had to be tediously imported from abroad, but
they were not. Partly this stemmed from the fact that the stiff-necked
British officers saw the rebels only as traitors and not true combatants
eligible for parole or exchange under oath, and partly from an evil
troika of men who profited through Americans' captivity: David
Sproat, naval commissary; Joshua Loring, commissary of prisoners; and
Captain William Cunningham, the provost marshal of New York.

By regulation, each of their prisoners was supposed to receive half
the daily ration issued to one of King George's tars, but these three
scoundrels conspired in a scam as old as the Roman legion. They traded
edible rations for garbage to feed the prisoners, sold rations outright on
New York's thriving black market and continued to keep dead prisoners'
names on the rosters of the living in order to draw their rations. They
soon earned a macabre reputation for feeding the dead and starving the
living. There is some indication they may have even poisoned the bread
issued to prisoners on the verge of being exchanged. In any event, it was
to their collective and profitable advantage to keep as many prisoners in
New York as possible, and they successfully did so to the very end of the
war, with Sproat bragging that he had done away with more rebels than
the entire British Army. After the war, back in England, these rogues
came to bad ends, with Sproat hanged for other crimes.

Faced with their ever-growing prisoner population, the British were
desperate to find confinement of any type. Some prisoners were
shipped to England and to faraway crown colonies in Asia for safekeeping, but there was not enough sealift to transport the growing numbers.
The British turned to a decrepit surplus of ships found in the backwa-
ters of the Royal Navy and converted at least sixteen unseaworthy
hulks into prison-ships, the most infamous of the lot being HMS *Jersey.*

Jersey was a 64-gun ship of the line when launched on June 14, 1736, with a length of 144 feet and beam of 42 feet. From her commissioning to 1740 she served in the Mediterranean and Channel fleets. In 1741 she was in the West Indies and took part in the unsuccessful attack on Cartagena. According to an admiralty report, "On 28 July 1745 *Jersey,* Capt. Charles Hardy, when near Gibraltar, fell in with the French seventy-four guns *St Esprit* and after an action which was very severe and lasted from 6.30 until 9 in the evening, both ships were crippled and the French bore away for Cadiz, having lost her foremast and bowsprit, and with 20 men killed."

During the Seven Years' War, in June 1759 *Jersey* was off Toulon and got badly beat up chasing two French frigates into a heavily fortified bay. Two months later, on August 18, 1759, *Jersey* was one of the British fleet in action against the French off Lagos, when an 80-gun and a 74-gun ship were burned and two 74s and a 64 were taken.

From 1763 to 1775 she spent most of her time cruising in the Mediterranean, with time out for refits.

Jersey was converted to a hospital ship in 1775 and in 1777 sailed to the American station where she served as such until 1779, anchored in the East River. That winter she was converted to a prison ship and stripped of anything useful to the fleet's carpenters. Gone were her figurehead, rudder, masts and spars. Naked except for a flagstaff, bowsprit and wooden crane for boarding supplies, her once rakish silhouette looked bottom-heavy and grotesque. Further marring her beauty, her gunports and portholes were nailed shut and pierced with twenty-square-inch air holes cross-barred with iron. Her hatches were battened down and cross-barred, too. Padlock hasps were installed on her gratings.

"She was by this time a dismasted hulk," recorded one prisoner, "with four other hulks as consorts, but *Jersey* was the receiving ship. She was first anchored near the city of New York, but the terrible conditions on board bred ship fever and other diseases. Instead of disinfecting the hulk, the authorities moved her to Wallabout Bay to prevent the contagion spreading to the city." There she was unceremoniously chain-cabled into permanent mooring about 110 yards off the sandy Brooklyn shoreline.

Manned by an over-the-hill captain and a complement of equally old Royal Marines, *Jersey* was soon jam-packed with over one thousand prisoners. The dying began immediately, on average five to eight men per day.

Because of this horrific death rate, the once-worthy *Jersey* soon earned a new sobriquet: the "Floating Hell." Without exception, horrible hulks like *Jersey* were vermin-ridden pestholes of disease. Amoebic dysentery led the list, followed by yellow fever, malaria and typhus. The most deadly was smallpox, and prisoners often "borrowed pus" from recovering comrades with a pinprick to inoculate themselves. Still, these diseases, aided by a starvation diet, combined to make the death rate aboard British prison-ships more than twice that of the notorious Andersonville prison camp during the Civil War.

As in Andersonville, the prisoners received little food, and the pittance they did receive was loathsome in the extreme: rancid oil, dried peas, wormy bread, weeviled oatmeal, rock-hard salted beef that was nevertheless often rotten and no fresh fruits or garden vegetables of any kind. The pallid, lean-jawed and starving prisoners made it all into "burgo," a stewed mush concocted of anything they could get their hands on, including rats, candle tallow and shoe leather, that often led to food poisoning.

Several ex-prisoners of war who survived *Jersey* wrote about their captivity. Personal American accounts of imprisonment tend to be justifiably bitter, subjective and written with invective, because all prison experiences, whether in *Jersey*, Andersonville or the Hanoi Hilton are remarkably similar. Most *Jersey* accounts are of this POW genre; one account, however, written forty years after the fact, stands out from the rest.

Captain Thomas Dring, in and out of the Continental Navy and a prisoner aboard more than one of the infamous ships, recorded that a typical day aboard *Jersey* started shortly after sunrise, when a well-breakfasted British NCO would bellow down into the hold, "Rebels, turn out your dead!"

Those cheerful words began another twenty-four-hour fight for life in the miasmic air of the Floating Hell's hold. Upon hearing this command, the prisoners would haul their departed mates topside, all stripped of any usable garments. With rigor mortis setting in, the skeletal corpses were stacked, tied and winched over the side and into a waiting boat like contaminated cordwood. A working party of volunteer prisoners under guard escorted the bodies ashore to bury them in a long two-foot trench dug above the waterline on the beach. The trench's length depended upon the number of bodies to be laid head-to-foot in the unmarked grave. After the war, melting snows, ebbing tides and rains uncovered these patriot bones for years.

Shocking as it all is, what happened aboard *Jersey* was not atypical. Conditions were similar throughout the Revolutionary War aboard other prison ships like HMS *Prince of Wales*, the ironically named HMS *Good Hope* and the more suitably named HMS *Scorpion*.

Not all of the blame can be laid at the feet of the British authorities and Cunningham and his ilk. The Continental Congress was supposed to provide money, rations in kind, and health and comfort items to American prisoners but failed miserably to do so. In fairness, there are also many credible accounts of British prisoners, especially loyalist Americans, being brutalized. But even the most horrific British accounts do not approach anything like the scale of suffering sustained aboard *Jersey* and her consorts.

Well-intentioned but feeble American efforts to investigate and correct the problem predictably came to nothing; as a result, American prisoners continued to die on *Jersey* at the same awful rate to the bitter end.

When the British abandoned New York on November 25, 1783, the last prisoners were set free, and *Jersey* soon settled a few fathoms to the muddy bottom, the greater part of her hull still above the water line. There she sat, a visible but unattended navigation hazard for years, detectible in darkness by her rank smell. No one dared board and fire her for fear of contracting disease. Time, worms and weather finally did their inevitable work, and her deck disappeared, her timbers weakened and her planks rotted away, giving the once proud man-of-war an entirely appropriate skeletal appearance. In the end, her decayed bottom gave way, and she slowly disappeared beneath the waves of Wallabout Bay, where presumably she still remains.

THE BRITISH HOPE for winning the Revolutionary War lay not in the steady attrition of her prison ships but in her naval blockade, now greatly strengthened. The British blockade "would soon make them tired of war," proclaimed the first lord of the admiralty in 1777. But as historian Robert Love has observed, "This contest for the control of American coastal waters, geography and the indigenous economy favored the patriots. No single port dominated American trade, there were no vital choke points through which rebel shipping had to pass, and New England's rugged coast line offered an abundance of harbors and sheltered anchorages."

Along this coast a doughty little Navy was coming together. On December 22, 1775, Congress had appointed the first eighteen officers of the Continental Navy with Esek Hopkins as "Commander-in-Chief of the Fleet." Three captains were named in addition to Nicholas Biddle: Dudley Saltonstall, Abraham Whipple and Esek's son, John Hopkins. There were also five first lieutenants, the most senior of whom was 28-year-old Scotsman John Paul Jones. In March 1776, another captain was appointed by the Congress, John Barry, the most successful captain of the Revolution.

CAPTAIN JOHN BARRY: HERO OF LAND AND SEA

Born in Ireland around 1745, the son of a poor tenant farmer, John Barry, like the more famous John Paul Jones, went to sea as a cabin boy. Barry ended up in Philadelphia at the age of 15 in 1760 and continued to live there until his death in 1803.

No welterweight in size like fellow Celt Jones, the ruddy-complexioned Barry grew to a strapping 6 feet 4 inches in stature and rivaled even George Washington in presence. Known to be kindly in his dealings with men, Barry nonetheless had a volcanic temper and was a firm but fair disciplinarian when the need arose.

Barry's feats of arms are not quite as dramatic as those of his little colleague. They are nevertheless remarkable, both in their audacity and in their cumulative total. Barry captured the third British prize ship of the war in 1776 and was victorious in the war's last sea engagement in 1783. In the seven critical years between these two signal events, he fought endless battles, on both land and sea.

Like Jones, the young Irishman first commanded a merchant ship at age 21, the schooner *Barbados,* sailing out of Philadelphia in 1766. Plying to and fro in the West Indies trade, he made at least nine round trips without a serious mishap. In doing so, "Big John" earned substantial wealth and a fine reputation within the merchant community for his maturity, steadiness and judgment. Returning from London in another, larger merchant, *Black Prince,* in 1775, he set an 18th-century sailing record, covering 237 miles in 24 hours, averaging 10 knots, all by dead reckoning.

The Continental Congress purchased *Black Prince* on November 4, 1775, renamed her *Alfred* and fitted her out as a 24-gun man-of-war. She was the first ship in the Continental Navy. But she was not to be Barry's. He was commissioned a captain in the Continental Navy on March 14, 1776, and given command of *Lexington,* named after the first battle of the Revolution fought in April of that year. Originally an old brigantine christened *Wild Duck,* "she was a tight vessel, a fast sailer, and pierced for 16 guns." Thirty years old, the burly, personable and handsome Irishman embarked with *Lexington* on his remarkable naval career, leaving Philadelphia on March 26, 1776.

At the time, things were not going well for the colonies. Congress was broke. Tories were raising hell. British warships had ports, harbors and bays bottled up. Washington had been chased off Manhattan Island and up to White Plains by Sir William Howe and then over into New Jersey. His bedraggled troops were in dire need of everything from socks to cannons, not to mention tents, food and pay. Washington was also dealing with more than one French nobleman who had washed ashore expecting a general's commission, a command and a carriage. And as far as being an American bluejacket went, it was much more profitable and less dangerous for a colonial lad to sail with a privateer, and share the profits brought from prizes on the high seas, than in the fledgling Continental Navy.

Barry provided a morale booster just four months after taking command of *Lexington*. On May 5, 1776, he eluded and frustrated the powerful British frigate *Roebuck* (44) in the dangerous lower reaches of Delaware Bay. A week later, on April 7, 1776, he saw an opportunity further south and boldly took it. After a hot one-hour fight, he captured the British sloop tender *Edward* (6), making it among the very first prizes taken by the Continental Navy. *Edward* was a tender assigned to support the frigate *Liverpool* (32), whose captain was furious that a Yankee upstart would snatch up one of the Royal Navy's commissioned ships and its valuable cargo, almost from under his nose. Barry escorted *Edward* to Philadelphia, arriving in his jubilant hometown four days later, April 11.

Barry was then given command of *Effingham*, a 32-gun frigate then under construction in Philadelphia and not completed until the spring of 1777. While he waited, he served as a volunteer in the Continental Army. His soldierly duties also included serving in a Marine company and then as an aide-de-camp to General John Cadwalader, the Philadelphia militia commander. Later, Washington picked Barry as his trusted courier to Lord Cornwallis and made him responsible for safely shepherding wounded British POWs through enemy lines under a flag of truce. Returning to Philadelphia, he was apparently approached by a party who offered him a substantial bribe, a King's commission and command of a Royal Navy ship, if he could somehow deliver *Effingham* into British hands. He turned the offer down, of course, but later in 1777, he was forced to scuttle her when a British assault on Philadelphia was imminent.

Lacking a man-of-war in early 1778, Barry proceeded to amass a miniature armada of seven stout little craft, including longboats, rowboats and barges. Manned with volunteers of his choosing, Barry set out on March 6 to raise havoc on a hit-and-run mission against British ships and transports coming up the Delaware River, shortly after navigation opened in the spring. He successfully surprised and captured an armed schooner, *Alert,* and two British transports near Reedy Island, while demolishing three other ships and damaging two more that tried to bear down on him. During this audacious foray, he burned a large British cavalry hay forage and captured large quantities of valuable supplies and equipment bound for the redcoats. Barry's exploits once again bolstered the flagging Continental morale, and he received a personal letter of commendation from Washington, wishing that "a suitable recompense always attend your bravery."

Later in 1778, Barry was given command of *Raleigh,* a 32-gun frigate, and ordered to break the British blockade. Setting out in her for the first time on the morning of September 25 from Boston, two strange sails were spotted on the horizon around noon. Not looking for a fight on his shakedown cruise, Barry tried to tack safely away, but was soon being harried by an aggressive pair of British frigates: *Unicorn* (20) and *Experiment* (50). The marathon chase went on for almost sixty desperate hours, when Barry finally thought he had lost the unrelenting twosome off the coast of Maine, only to have them reappear when the fickle wind ebbed.

The gallant but uneven contest thus began. *Unicorn*'s first broadside took down *Raleigh*'s foretop and her main topgallant masts, rendering her almost immobile. But Barry refused to strike colors and fought into the night. Finally, to avoid the dismasted *Raleigh* falling into British hands, he ran her on the rocks of a coastal island. He ordered his ship burned, but was foiled by a traitorous seaman; *Raleigh* ended up flying the Union Jack.

Meanwhile, Barry and eighty-five of his crew escaped via boats to the mainland and made their way back to Boston two weeks later, having lost twenty-five men, killed and wounded in the fight the prudent commander had tried to avoid. A board of inquiry found his actions without fault, and he was subsequently given command of a 36-gun frigate, *Alliance.*

Barry's finest hour on the high seas came on May 29, 1781, when

Alliance took on HM sloop *Atalanta* (16), and her consort, the brig *Trepassey* (14). After the challenges were made and returned, the drums rolled, the colors hoisted and the seesaw battle began. About an hour after the first shots were fired, *Trepassey*'s captain was killed, but the desperate fighting continued. With the wind ebbing into doldrums, the smaller and more maneuverable British ships gained tactical advantage over their more powerful Continental adversary. Then "Captain Barry received a wound by grape shot in the shoulder. He remained, however, on the quarterdeck until by the much loss of blood he was obliged to be helped to the cock-pit."

With her skipper below, *Alliance* took a hit and her colors were shot away. Seeing this, the British tars climbed their shrouds and gave three huzzahs of victory across the water. Then, much to their dismay, they saw Barry's bluejackets hoist their colors up a jury-rigged mizzen and try to carry on. Soon, however, the situation looked truly unsalvageable, and the first officer went below to ask Barry for permission to strike their colors.

The stubborn skipper said no, arose from his bloodstained crib, climbed back on deck and rallied his crew. A fresh breeze then filled *Alliance*'s tattered sails, enabling her to maneuver into position to bring her superior firepower to bear. She fired a broadside into each of her enemies, they both struck, and now Yankee hurrahs crossed the water.

Barry's fighting career ended in the last naval action of the Revolution. Still in command of *Alliance*, Barry was responsible for transporting 100,000 Spanish-milled dollars to fill the empty coffers of Congress. Sailing out of Havana with *Duc de Lauzun* (20), which carried the gold, Barry wanted to avoid British warships and get to Philadelphia as soon as possible. Nevertheless, while northbound under full sail off the coast of Florida, he spotted hostile ships at dawn March 10, 1783. They were the frigates *Alarm* (32) and *Sybil* (28), and *Tobago* (16), a sloop.

Alliance, with her copper-sheathed hull, could have easily outdistanced these three, but Barry had no choice but to protect the slower-sailing *Duc de Lauzun*. Heaving to, he cut back between *Duc de Lauzun* and her immediate pursuer, *Sybil*, who hailed and challenged *Alliance*.

According to a poet of the time, Phillip Freneau, Captain Barry boomed back, "This is the United States ship *Alliance,* saucy Jack Barry, half Irishman, half Yankee. Who are you?" Within 45 minutes of this supposed rejoinder, Barry's hustling gun crews proceeded to reduce *Sybil* to a silent and barely floating wreck. With that, *Alarm* and *Tobago* appeared on the scene, and Barry was forced to withdraw.

Ironically, at the outset of this final engagement, one of Barry's lookouts reported a 50-gun French man-of-war headed their way. With its help, he could have possibly captured all three British ships, but such was not to be. The French skipper stood off, instead, and became a spectator. When the smoke finally cleared, Barry had some warm and salty words for the Frenchman, who had some surprising words for him, too. Saucy Jack and the British skippers did not know that hostilities with King George had officially ended more than a month before.

In his post-Revolutionary War days, Barry was recalled to active duty in 1794 and appointed "Senior Captain," with commission number one, the leading billet in the Navy. He was given the nominal title of "commodore," although that rank did not become official in the Naval Service until the Civil War. In this capacity, he supervised establishment of the U.S. Navy, as we know it today, and assumed command of *United States* (44). He directed and oversaw West Indies operations from 1798 to 1801.

Barry returned to Philadelphia where he remained in charge of the Navy, until he passed away from a prolonged case of asthma on September 13, 1803.

LONG BEFORE BARRY had first achieved success with *Alliance,* and before the unnecessary trouncing of *Sybil,* the Continental Congress had appointed a captain whose fame would go on to eclipse that of his more senior colleague. That man was John Paul Jones.

JOHN PAUL JONES:
THE HEROIC PIRATE

As every schoolboy knows, John Paul Jones said, "I have not yet begun to fight," and, as every midshipman has heard, Jones was quite a ladies' man, his conquests including Catherine the Great. Theodore Roosevelt called him the father of our Navy and Jones's mythic image has since been enhanced by more than thirty biographies and forty novels, including James Fenimore Cooper's *The Pilot*, Alexandre Dumas' *Le Capitaine Paul*, Herman Melville's *Israel Potter* and several Hollywood movies. In the preview of one 1959 film the narrator invites viewers to "Range with him from George Washington's Virginia to Louis XVI's Versailles; from Jamaica's burning shores to Russia's frozen steppes— as this fighting leader and fiery lover conquers in battle and boudoir."

Jones never met Washington face-to-face, but was briefly presented, with others, to Louis XVI at Versailles. As to "Jamaica's burning shores," in 1764, Jones was a 17-year-old third mate aboard a British slave ship, *King George*, out of Kingston, Jamaica. "Russia's frozen steppes" are far from where Jones did all his fighting for the Russian Navy in the Black Sea, and when Jones first met Catherine the Great in 1788, she was a 60-year old, overweight woman, with swollen legs and wooden dentures, hardly a cameo role for Bette Davis, who played her in the 1959 movie.

Nevertheless, the facts of his life are exciting enough.

He was a Scot by blood, born July 6, 1747, at Kirkcudbright, his father a gardener, his mother a domestic servant. Named John Paul, he joined the British Merchant Marine and went to sea at 13 as a cabin boy on *Friendship*, a brig out of Whitehaven bound for Virginia, where his older brother, William Paul, ran a tailor shop in Fredericksburg, on the Rappahannock. He remained aboard *Friendship* for several years until it was sold, whereupon he shipped in the slave trade. By age 20, he had quit the slave trade in disgust and got the first of his many providential breaks. A fellow Scot, Samuel McAdam, happened into Kingston in his new 60-ton brig, *John*, and offered John Paul passage home. While underway *John*'s master and mate both died of fever, and he was found to be the only one aboard who could navigate. He took command and saw her safely home to Kirkcudbright, where the delighted owners made him her master at 21.

From 1769 to 1770, John Paul proved to be a shrewd trader, but also had the first of his major problems with discipline on the high seas. He had a certain incompetent ship's carpenter, one disobedient Mungo Maxwell, flogged with a cat-o'-nine-tails (all in keeping with the law of the sea). Although Maxwell transferred to another ship in apparent good health, he died while homeward bound, and his father, a prominent local in Kirkcudbright, filed murder charges. The charges were dismissed, but the death-by-flogging sea story followed John Paul to the end of his days.

In 1773, a far more serious incident occurred in Tobago. John Paul was cornered by the ringleader of a mutinous crew; he ran the man through with a quick sword thrust. This stopped the mutiny but killed the ringleader, a native of Tobago. Fearing he could not get a fair trial there, and not wanting to wait in prison to see, he fled across the island to escape in a friend's vessel, leaving all his worldly goods behind. The authorities declared him a fugitive pirate.

For the next twenty months, John Paul went on the lam, apparently in Virginia. While there, he seems to have had an affair with Ms. Dorthea Dandridge, who later wed Patrick Henry, governor of the Old Dominion, in 1777. During this mysterious time, John Paul also took an alias, Paul Jones.

When war with King George broke out in 1775, Paul Jones made his way to Philadelphia, where, with the help of Joseph Hewes, a North Carolina delegate to the Second Continental Congress, he was commissioned a first lieutenant in the Continental Navy. With characteristic bravado he declared, "I wish to have no connection with any ship that does not sail fast, for I intend to go in harm's way." In 1776, he got his first command in *Providence* (12), achieving brilliant success, winning his promotion to the rank of captain on October 10, 1776. After further success commanding *Alfred*, he took command of the sloop of war *Ranger* (18) and sailed her to France the following year. Franklin instructed Jones to sail to the British Isles for the purpose of "distressing the enemies of the United States by sea, or otherwise."

He proceeded to make daring raids in the British Isles, terrorizing coastal inhabitants and sinking assorted vessels, and gaining a popular image in the British press as a swashbuckling pirate. Jones's famous raid on Whitehaven Harbor, on the Solway Firth, while useless from a military point of view had an immense impact in providing ammunition to the antiwar faction in Parliament including Wilkes, Fox and Burke, and "immeasurably undermined Parliament's confidence in Lord North's government."

As a result, Jones's reputation soared in Paris, and Louis XVI gave him command of a heavily armed East Indiaman, which he promptly renamed *Bonhomme Richard* in honor of his new mentor, Ben Franklin, who was then serving as U.S. ambassador to France, where *Poor Richard's Almanack* had become a bestseller.

Once outfitted, Jones returned brazenly to the British coast. Cruising off the Yorkshire coast in hopes of catching the Baltic convoy, Jones beheld a cloud of sail on the morning of September 23, 1779. Driving in to cut out some valuable prizes, *Richard* was intercepted by the convoy's escort, the far more powerful 44-gun two-decker, *Serapis*, under the command of Captain Richard Pearson.

Serapis was not one of a successful class of ship. While delivering a powerful broadside, it and its mates were slab-sided and unweatherly. In any stiff breeze, in fact, the lower deck gunports had to be closed. But *Richard* was no better a sailer and this day the water was calm. While local citizens crowded Flamborough Head to watch the fight just offshore, *Serapis*'s broadsides soon reduced *Richard* to wreckage. In desperation, Jones skillfully maneuvered a collision and grappling hooks made fast the two ships, Pearson all the while pouring in broadsides at point-blank range. With *Richard* sinking fast, and all but three of her guns silenced, the British captain hailed Jones, asking if he had struck his colors, to which Jones responded with words that have been simplified into the immortal "I have not yet begun to fight."

And indeed Jones and his men fought on, with sharpshooters clearing the *Serapis*'s deck; Jones personally fired one of the last remaining guns. One of these bluejackets may have decided the battle. He was sitting on *Richard*'s main course yardarm with a basket of grenades directly over *Serapis*'s quarterdeck. His rain of explosions cleared the British quarterdeck. He finally got one down a hatch, which ignited powder on the gundeck with a flash explosion killing fifty tars. Finally, after three and a half hours of desperate carnage, with nearly 150 killed and wounded in each ship, Pearson surrendered. Despite massive efforts to save her, *Richard* sank the next day.

In the Navy Museum at the Washington Navy Yard may be seen a handsome silver service inscribed to Captain Pearson by the grateful merchants of London for sacrificing his ship and thereby saving the Baltic Convoy from plunder by Jones. King George made Pearson a knight, causing Jones to remark "Let me fight him again and make him a lord!"

After this great capture Jones was demonized in London papers and lionized in Paris. His military bearing, personality and temperament bloomed. Descriptions of him vary, but he was a small, wiry man, standing between 5 feet 5 inches and 5 feet 7, and weighing around 140 pounds. In speaking, his voice was reportedly soft, but on the quarterdeck, electrifying; although he consciously tried to lose his Scottish burr, it came out in times of stress.

During his Parisian days of triumph, he sat for a life-size marble bust by Jean-Antoine Houdon, Europe's leading sculptor. During my tenure as secretary of the Navy, I kept the striking bust outside my office in the Pentagon. Despite his receding hairline, he eschewed the fashionable wigs of that day, and his hair is pulled back neatly over his close-tucked ears into a tight queue. Houdon has brilliantly captured the very essence of the great captain.

When Jones came home he was given command and supervised construction of his new warship, *America* (74), a true ship of the line. It was not completed until after the peace, whereupon a penniless Congress gave it to France. This along with other affronts from the new government, including denying him a medal recommended by the Continental Congress, refusing to make him an admiral and ignoring

Houdin's famous bust of John Paul Jones, the most audacious, fearless and colorful captain in the Continental and Russian navies. He never became an American
citizen. *U. S. Naval Academy Museum*

his thoughtful and prescient recommendations for the organization of a proper Navy, left him a deeply alienated man.

With no real ties to a new nation now at peace, and still seeking an admiral's flag, Jones accepted the offer of Catherine the Great to help her win the second Russo-Turkish war. Commissioned "Kontradmiral Pavel Ivanovich Jones"—or rear admiral—he was promised overall command of a fleet, but ended up commanding a squadron. Although victorious in several engagements with Ottoman Turks in the Black Sea, he was outmaneuvered by a cabal of Russian rivals and was beached by Potemkin, the commander in chief, in October 1788, never to set foot on a quarterdeck in combat again.

Returning under a cloud of scandal to Paris in 1790, Jones, only 42, became what Emerson observed in other retired great men of the sword: "a bore at last." He spent his days writing voluminous letters, trying to right old wrongs that had been done to him, seeking awards he felt he deserved and coveting renewed recognition. A bachelor to the end, but without a mistress, he died on July 18, 1792.

He was buried in Paris's only Protestant cemetery, his body sealed in a lead coffin engraved with his name, filled with alcohol for preservation purposes, paid for by the French Legislative Assembly. The unmarked grave was soon forgotten by all except General Horace Porter, who actively searched for the location of Jones's burial. The site was eventually discovered when the cemetery was dug up to make way for a new Paris suburb in 1905. The body was so well-preserved when found that an autopsy was performed, establishing that Jones died not of syphilis as some had written, but of hepatitis, nephritis and pneumonia—in short, of poverty.

But Jones's story does not end there.

Upon learning that Jones's body had been disinterred, then-President Theodore Roosevelt found it the perfect public-relations opportunity for his campaign to build a Navy to command the seas. Declaring Jones to be the "Father" of the Navy, he dispatched *Brooklyn* and three other cruisers to bring the body back in triumph.

On April 24, 1906, in a long commemorative ceremony at Annapolis, featuring Roosevelt as the keynote speaker, John Paul Jones's remains were interred in an elaborate twenty-one-ton sarcophagus centered on a rotunda in the crypt beneath the Naval Academy chapel. A gift from France, the beautiful sarcophagus was sculpted from precious black and white Royal Pyrenees marble and resembles that of Napoleon's in the Invalides.

Roosevelt used the occasion to the fullest.

> Every officer in our Navy should know by heart the deeds of John Paul Jones. Every officer in our Navy should feel in each fiber of his being an eager desire to emulate the energy, the professional capacity, the indomitable determination and dauntless scorn of death which marked John Paul Jones above all his fellows.

There are several candidates for the paternity of the U.S. Navy. George Washington viewed John Barry as first among the revolutionary captains and treated him accordingly. In the early 19th century Stephen Decatur was considered the father, but was gradually eclipsed by Thomas MacDonough, the hero of Lake Champlain. Since TR, though, Jones has held fast. But with his claim resting on one dazzling raid, one brilliant fight and a very grand tomb, the true and final father of the Navy may yet be unnamed.

Valcour Island:
The Naval Battle of Saratoga

In the early years of the Revolutionary War, John Barry and John Paul Jones provided heroes, but what were really needed in 1776 were ships, men and arms. Without these, however great the individual heroics, independence was still a long way off.

Here again, one individual, though he would go down in history for something other than his naval achievements, used a small amount of sea power, mustered in the right time and place, to brighten America's murky future. In the fall of 1776, Brigadier General Benedict Arnold commanded in one of the most important if somewhat bizarre naval battles of the war.

Arnold was ordered by Washington to attempt to block the British invasion by Sir Guy Carleton down the Hudson River through Lake George and Lake Champlain. Calling on the help of New England shipbuilders, Arnold hastily built a fleet on Lake Champlain. It included the sloop *Enterprise* (12), the schooners *Royal Savage* (12), *Liberty* (8), *Revenge* (8), eight gondolas and five galleys. His speedy ingenuity forced the British to build a fleet of their own. It was significantly more powerful but its assembly took up most of the remaining campaign season. In a brilliant tactical battle near Valcour Island, Arnold was able to confound and delay the British fleet although ultimately losing most of his ships. Carleton was forced, however, to retire back to Canada for the winter, postponing the offensive. It was precisely this action which set up the subsequent decisive victory over General Burgoyne at Saratoga when the British resumed the campaign in 1777.

There was another, even more critical effect. With Arnold's victory, the French, still smarting from their humiliating defeat in the Seven Years' War, began to smell blood. The naval vacuum created by shifting the bulk of the Royal Navy to the American station made it clear to the French that the British were not having an easy time. In one of the worst lapses in British diplomacy in the 18th century, the government of Lord North had grossly mismanaged its traditional maintenance of the Continental balance of power. By 1778 Britain had no friends in Europe.

The French held back only because they doubted that the Americans could last long enough for French intervention to swing the balance. After news reached them of the dramatic American victory at Saratoga, they could resist Franklin's blandishments no longer. And thus a tactical feat by the greatest American traitor of the war was in fact America's greatest naval success.

On February 6, 1778, a Franco-American Treaty of Alliance was ratified, and France and England declared war shortly thereafter. French sea power would prove decisive. It meant a reliable flow of supply, ammunition, funding and direct military support. Above all it held out the promise of the deployment of a French fleet to bring the Royal Navy to a decisive battle. In July of that year France deployed its first fleet to assist the Americans under the timid Vice Admiral D'Estaing, although it had little effect other than boosting morale. The following year the French fleet returned for summer operations with little more success. But in July 1780, the French deployed a squadron, bringing with it thirty transports with 6,000 troops under the Lieutenant General Comte de Rochambeau. And finally in the fourth year of French participation in the war, a fighting admiral was deployed to North America commanding a strong French fleet.

AMIRAL COMTE FRANCOIS JOSEPH PAUL DE GRASSE: THE RIGHT MAN IN THE RIGHT PLACE AT THE RIGHT TIME

Unlike Jones and Barry, Amiral de Grasse did not come from humble origins. Indeed, the comte's illustrious family from Provence was one of ancient nobility, well known throughout France. Trained in the Jesuit tradition, he also attended a naval school in Malta that prepared boys for sea. At 16, he was commissioned a midshipman in the French Navy, serving aboard various vessels until he was captured at age 24 in 1747. Taken to England for two years of imprisonment, he made friends with his lenient jailers and undertook a study of the Royal Navy.

Returning to France in 1749, he received a lieutenant's commission, fought in the Seven Years' War and served in the East Indies. Earning his captaincy in 1762, he was brevetted a Knight of Saint Louis in 1764 at age 41. In his handsome maturity, he stood 6 feet 2 inches tall, and "6 feet 6 on days of battle."

One of those days came soon after the United States and France signed an alliance. On July 27, 1778, French and English fleets came to blows on the high seas off the tip of Brittany, near the island of Ushant. The battle was a standoff, but Captain de Grasse, in command of *Robuste* (74), was hotly engaged throughout.

By 1779, de Grasse was a rear admiral: grim, corpulent and intimidating. His professional reputation as flag officer made subordinates tremble. He was said to be self-important, to have a hair-trigger temper and to yank around his captains in a haughty manner.

Promotion did not lessen de Grasse's pride. Returning to France in 1781, he became vice admiral, and with an armada of twenty-three ships of the line set sail back to the West Indies on March 24, 1781. His flagship was *Ville de Paris*, a triple-decked goliath mounting 110 guns, one of the largest warships in the world at that time. A month later, he engaged Admiral Samuel Hood's fleet off Martinique and drove him into retreat. Cruising in the Caribbean, he captured Tobago and then headed for Santo Domingo, where he found a French frigate awaiting him with dispatches from both Rochambeau and Washington. Upon reading the dispatches, Amiral de Grasse saw that his hour of destiny was at hand.

Moving swiftly, the admiral ordered the messenger frigate back to Newport with hasty dispatches for Rochambeau and Washington. "He wrote that he was sailing from the West Indies to the Chesapeake and urged Washington to be prepared to employ him immediately, for he would have to return to the West Indies by the middle of October."

De Grasse's timetable now drove the forthcoming campaign's strategy. By August 15, Rochambeau and Washington were informed of the admiral's intentions and his window of availability, and a war-ending reality began to evolve. Washington "had never conducted a siege nor directed an amphibious campaign, but his grasp of the role of sea power was firm if only intuitive." Consulting with Rochambeau he brilliantly revised his original plan to attack New York into a feint designed to conceal his true intent—a forced march all the way to Virginia with Rochambeau to capitalize upon de Grasse's strategic positioning of his fleet.

In the last week of August, a French squadron in Newport commanded by Comte de Barras got underway to reinforce de Grasse. With eighteen supply vessels escorted by four frigates, the comte took a wide berth around New York to avoid the British fleet stationed there. Nevertheless, the British became aware of the French convoy's departure, and Rear Admiral Thomas Graves set out from New York to intercept it on September 1, 1781, with nineteen ships of the line, among other vessels. Because of adverse winds, it took Graves three days to get past the bar at Sandy Hook.

Meanwhile, de Grasse marshaled his assets. He gathered a treasure chest of hard money for the perennially bankrupt Continental Congress to pay the army, embarked 3,500 soldiers and some cavalry, and set sail on August 5, 1781, with twenty-eight ships of the line, "snapping up every British vessel in his path as he sailed up from Santo Domingo."

It must be noted that de Grasse had "decided to bring virtually his entire force, leaving behind only *Actionnaire* . . . to protect homeward-bound trade" from the West Indies. In making this decision on his own, he took an enormous professional risk, but luck is with the bold, and French commerce was uninterrupted during his absence. On August 30, he dropped anchor in Lynn Haven Bay, securely inside the Chesapeake's capes.

The stage was set for the greatest naval battle of the Revolutionary War.

THE BATTLE OF THE VIRGINIA CAPES

At dawn on September 5, Admiral Graves finally showed up off the Chesapeake. At first de Grasse thought he was Comte de Barras, but when the sail count rose to more than twenty, he knew his enemy had arrived in force. De Grasse immediately ordered anchor cables cut and sailed forth to challenge him. Graves, who also at first mistook his enemy for the weaker de Barras, came on equally strong.

De Grasse outmaneuvered a hesitant Graves who, despite his twenty-seven ships and 1,500 guns, was taken aback by the French strength of twenty-eight ships and 2,000 guns. Rattled, indecisive and soft stepping, Graves gave conflicting signals to his fleet and did not get all his ships into action. Historian Ernest Eller points out that "de Grasse also fought cautiously. Had he overwhelmed Graves, he would have easily achieved his other goals. However, had he lost, and the British were known as deadly fighters, all his effort to aid the American cause would have shipwrecked."

The Royal Navy's ships were faster, because of their copper-sheathed hulls, but owing to their superior seamanship and tactics, de Grasse's captains inflicted heavy casualties on the British during the course of the prolonged battle. After five days of thrust and parry in ever-changing and unpredictable winds, de Grasse was concerned that the British might tack past him and gain access to Yorktown. Prudently, he sailed back into the Chesapeake with two captured British frigates, ending the Battle of the Virginia Capes on his own terms. The French lost 209, the British 336 killed and wounded. The fate of America's future had been decided in a sea battle in which no American ships participated and no American lives were lost.

De Grasse was delighted to find that Comte de Barras and his supply convoy had slipped past both fleets and had arrived safe and sound in the bay. De Grasse now had thirty-five line-of-battle ships at his command. His transports immediately delivered their guns and supplies to Washington. The tide-turning power of this sealift cannot be overstated. The artillery delivered by de Grasse was, according to historian Marcel Villanueva, "the heaviest of the world's siege artillery. Cornwallis was unaware of these new weapons."

Graves headed for New York, taking with him any hope of breaking the blockade around his doomed comrade Lord Cornwallis. King George, not yet of a "desponding disposition," said when he learned what happened in the Virginia Capes, "I nearly think the empire ruined . . . this cruel event is too recent for me to be as yet able to say more."

Reinforced by de Grasse's troops, Lafayette tightened the noose around Yorktown on September 8, and the Franco-American trap was set to bag the British lion.

On September 14, Washington and Rochambeau arrived on the scene. De Grasse invited them and their generals to dine aboard his flagship. The French armada was the largest display of seapower Washington would ever see in his lifetime. Ushered aboard with a booming

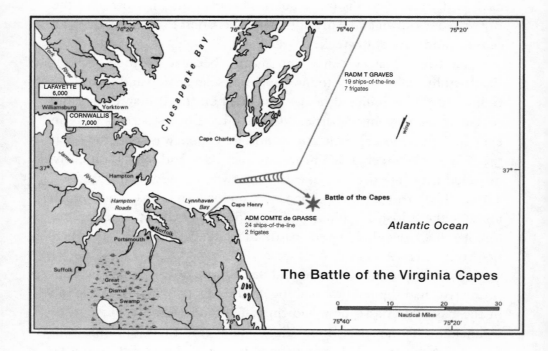

The Battle of the Virginia Capes

fleet salute, the first meeting between the domineering Washington and the delighted de Grasse soon became a Continental Army legend, because the "towering de Grasse embraced the taller, legendarily austere Washington, kissed him on both cheeks and cried, 'My dear little general!'"

In the end, of course, sea control dictated the outcome of the siege. The dilatory Admiral Graves finally set out from New York in a futile attempt to break the siege on the day of surrender, October 17, but he was too late. Cornwallis, outgunned, outnumbered and running low on ammunition and supplies including food, capitulated with about 7,500 troops to the combined Franco-American ground force of 16,000. Historian Samuel Eliot Morison described the significance of the battle succinctly: "Without the naval victory of de Grasse, it would not have been the capitulation of Cornwallis, but that of Washington that history would have registered."

· · ·

SOME WRITERS HAVE DERIDED the Continental Navy's contribution to American Independence. In all a total of fifty-three ships served during the course of the war, including the excellent newly constructed frigates and the more numerous merchant ships converted into combatants. By the end of the war only two were left—all the others had been captured, destroyed to avoid capture or lost at sea.

Because the Continental Navy was extinguished before the United States Navy was established, we know little about the building and the design of the thirteen new construction frigates. The only official plans in existence are for *Randolph*, built in Philadelphia by Joshua Humphreys. We also have drawings and specifications taken by the Royal Navy for each of the six frigates captured and put into British service. All of these indicate that the thirteen Continental frigates were definitely precursors of the great superfrigates of the next generation. All were larger and finer than their British counterparts and clearly reflect a design philosophy brought to perfection by Humphreys in *Constitution* and her sister ships. All six were considered superb combatants in the Royal Navy. *Hancock* (32) for example was captured in July of 1777, renamed *Iris* and remained active for the rest of the war. She was later captured by the French Navy, where she served with equal distinction.

Of the remaining six, two were never completed, but were burned to prevent capture on the Hudson River, two were scuttled at Philadelphia before completion as the British forces approached, *Delaware* was surrendered by her crew, and *Randolph* blew up in battle.

Of the thirteen, only *Alliance* (36) survived the war in American hands. She was sold into commercial service, ending her days in the late 19th century as a Delaware River barge. Her hulk was abandoned in the river near what is now Philadelphia's airport and was visible above water as late as 1907.

While certainly the Continental Navy did not have the impact on the outcome of the war that the privateers had, it did make a significant contribution. Benedict's Arnold's fleet on Lake Champlain (though not technically part of the Continental Navy) made possible the decisive victory at Saratoga the following year. In turn, de Grasse's brilliant victory (which, again, cannot be credited to the Continental Navy) made possible the more famous victory at Yorktown. Most important—and an accomplishment to which the Continental Navy *can* lay full claim— the real threat throughout the war of armed combatants forced severe operating restrictions on the Royal Navy and drew disproportionate numbers of combatants to the North American station, setting the stage for France's entry into the war. The Navy did invaluable service in carrying correspondence, diplomats, munitions and money, without which the American effort could not have continued, nor could privateers have done any of these tasks reliably.

These accomplishments would never have been plausible without the courageous action of men like Jones, Barry and Biddle. So different in temperament and manner, they were alike in their great personal courage and imagination. Rarely since have we seen their equals.

II

THE
PRIVATEERS

FROM THE BEGINNING of the American Revolution until the end of
the War of 1812, America's real naval advantage lay in its privateers. It
has been said that the battles of the American Revolution were fought
on land, and independence was won at sea. For this we have the enormous success of American privateers to thank even more than the
courageous actions and valuable diplomatic service of the small Continental Navy. Even in the War of 1812, when the American Navy was
far better organized, there were never more than twenty-five ships at
sea at a time. By contrast, there were always several hundred privateers
attacking British commerce worldwide, although in neither war could
privateers have been sufficient for victory regardless of their numbers
and success. Armed ships under national command are required to
wage war. But without the privateers, the outcome of both wars would
have been far less favorable to America.

Privateering is older than navies themselves. Professional navies as
we know them today did not emerge in Europe until the 17th century.
(Even in the great battles of the Spanish Armada of 1588 most of the
ships in both Spanish and English fleets were privately owned.) Sover-
eigns had long depended on issuing written commissions to shipowners giving them authority (not command) to attack, sink and seize
enemy vessels in time of war including private merchant ships and
neutral ships trading contraband or running a blockade. Such commissions came to be called "Letters of Marque and Reprisal," and by the
17th century were well recognized in international law. The incentive

for merchants to invest in privateers was based on their right to keep the enemy ships and cargoes that they were able to seize as "prizes." By the 18th century there was a well-ordered legal system for the processing of such prizes in all the maritime nations of the world.

The judge (or in some cases the prize agent) of the local government under which the trial took place was entitled to a variable percentage of the proceeds from the sale of the prizes. If the captor was a government-owned ship, the prize money was normally split between the government and the crew. If the captor was a privateer all prize money belonged to the ship's owners and crew. It should be no surprise that it was far easier to obtain crews for privateers than for the Navy.

By the late 18th century two distinct kinds of privateering had emerged. Some nations issued privateers' commissions as well as Letters of Marque and Reprisal. The former were given to ships often outfitted and designed for the specific purpose of capturing enemy prizes. On the other hand, Letters of Marque (the name for ships sailing under Letters of Marque and Reprisal) were cargo vessels whose primary mission was commerce but were armed and on the lookout to take prizes if they presented themselves. The American colonies issued both commissions and Letters of Marque and Reprisal. By the end of the war the distinction had become almost meaningless, and Letters of Marque were issued for both purposes.

The traveler will look in vain in for statues of privateersmen. The official canon of naval history in both Britain and the United States virtually ignores them. Theodore Roosevelt, for example, complained in *The Naval War of 1812* that although "the Privateers were of incalculable benefit to us . . . neither side ever chronicles a defeat . . . (and) there is very little hope of getting at the truth of such meetings . . ." John Paul Jones dismissed privateers as no more than "licensed robbers . . . actuated by no nobler principle than that of self-interest." These are not valid criticisms. Privateersmen weren't fighting for the history books but, as John Paul Jones said, to make money. While doing it they won wars for America.

Modern historians like Nathan Miller and Robert Love have at last given appropriate credit to privateers in the Revolution and the War of

1812 but give little space to the exploits of individual privateersmen. Still, buried in personal memoirs, diaries and logs scattered around the world, the stories can still be found of these courageous men. For investing in and sailing privateers was neither safe nor sure. Many investors lost everything, and many privateersmen were lost at sea, killed in action or died as prisoners.

PRIVATEERING DURING THE REVOLUTION

When the Revolution broke out in 1775, the colonies had no warships and no navy. When the British blockaded the New England ports, mariners, shipowners and fishermen found themselves in dire financial straits. Privateering sprang up instantly and by early 1775 British merchantmen were being seized regularly along the New England coast. Seizures of arms and munitions usually went directly to Washington's struggling Army and were its principal source of armament in its first year of existence.

Privateering was a good business to be in. The privateers were faster and smaller than the British blockaders and could usually outrun them or escape inshore. The building of privateers and blockade runners became a booming industry on the eastern seaboard. By 1776 in the port of Salem alone some 160 privateers had been outfitted, and the foundations of the great fortunes of the eastern establishment were being laid down. The Darby family of Salem, for instance, owned and operated a fishing fleet before the war and outfitted a total of eighty-five privateers during the course of the war. These ships successfully brought to port 144 prizes, making the Darbys the first millionaires in New England.

For the sailors, too, privateering held the promise of wealth. A typical recruiting broadside read:

AN INVITATION TO ALL BRAVE SEAMEN AND MARINES, WHO HAVE AN INCLINATION TO SERVE THEIR COUNTRY AND MAKE THEIR FORTUNES.

The grand Privateer ship DEANE, commanded by ELISHA HINMAN, Esq; and prov'd to be a very capital Sailer, will Sail on a Cruise against the Enemies of the United States of America, by the 20th instant. The DEANE mounts thirty Carriage Guns, and is excellently well calculated for Attacks, Defense and Pursuit—This therefore is to invite all those Jolly Fellows, who love their country, and want to make their fortunes at one Stroke, to repair immediately to the Rendezvous at the Head of His Excellency Governor Hancock's Wharf, where they will be received with a hearty Welcome by a Number of Brave Fellows there assembled, and treated with that excellent Liquor call'd GROG which is allow'd by all true Seamen, to be the LIQUOR OF LIFE.

Deane, alas, fell into the hands of the Royal Navy, and Hinman into Old Mill Prison.

In March 1776 Congress authorized privateering against any ship "belonging to any inhabitant or inhabitants of Great Britain." As the war progressed and these privateers took their toll, the British were forced to shift their merchantmen into convoying. Privateers then began to operate much as the German submarines did in World War II, waiting for and following the convoys to pick off the stragglers. The richest hunting was in the Caribbean, for it was there that the most lucrative volume of trade was to be found. There also the convoys had to disperse to go to the many different islands. The British fleets, Admiral Arbuthnot reported from Halifax, were hard pressed to defend "our trade, which they have really cut up almost without molestation."

According to the records of the Continental Congress 1,697 vessels were issued Letters of Marque or privateers' commissions. At least another 400 Letters of Marque or privateers' commissions were issued by the states of Massachusetts, New Hampshire, Rhode Island, Connecticut, Pennsylvania, Maryland and South Carolina. Benjamin Franklin and Silas Deane, Continental agents in France, also issued American Letters of Marque to French-financed privateers operating from France before that country's entry into the war. The ships ranged from small sloops armed with a single gun to sizable ships of twenty-four guns. On them, a total of 58,400 men shipped out to steal legally from the British.

At the beginning of the war all of the privateers were converted merchantmen, but investors soon commissioned new ships for the lucrative business. The preferred designs were brig, schooner or hybrid rigs that were essentially fore- and aft-rigged vessels built for speed and ability to sail close to the wind, but having at least one square-rigged sail for fighting. A square-rigged sail could be "backed" against the wind, which greatly aided maneuvering. It enabled a ship to come to an almost immediate stop in the course of a battle and reverse direction.

The archives of Lloyds Insurance Exchange in London contain the records of 3,087 British ships insured by Lloyds syndicates and captured by American ships—only about 400 were captured by the Continental Navy. It was 15 percent of the entire British merchant fleet during the war years and resulted in an almost immediate substantial increase in insurance rates, some 30 percent for ships in convoys and at least 50 percent increase for ships sailing alone.

Not all of these captures were condemned as prizes, however. The practice became very common in the latter years of the war for captains of British merchantmen to carry bonds for the value of ship and cargo which would be handed over to the privateers, allowing the merchantman to go on his way and saving a lot of hassle for both sides. The sometimes strange nature of such gentlemanly practice is well illustrated by the story of HMS *Savage* and *Congress*, a legendary privateer.

THE PRIVATEER *CONGRESS:*
AVENGER OF THE MOUNT VERNON SHAKEDOWN

In April and May of 1781, a British sloop-of-war, HMS *Savage*, (16) commanded by Captain Thomas Graves, sailed up and down the Potomac River, "destroying and looting plantations and tobacco warehouses." But when Graves got in the neighborhood of George Washington's plantation, Mount Vernon (named for a famous admiral of the Royal Navy), he instead simply sent ashore for provisions. Washington's cousin, Lund Washington, caretaker of the estate in the general's absence, informed Graves that he was under instructions from his cousin not to compromise in any way with the enemy. Graves assured him that he would in no way provide any offense to one so illustrious as General Washington. In gratitude Lund sent "sheep, hogs and an abundant supply of other articles" to *Savage*. Thus resupplied, Graves went on to burn all of Washington's neighbors' plantations while leaving Mount Vernon untouched. Needless to say this engendered a good deal of resentment against General George Washington. Upon hearing about it Lafayette wrote to Washington, "You cannot conceive of how unhappy I am to hear that Mr. Lund Washington went on board the enemy's vessels and consented to give them provisions . . . [this] will certainly have a bad effect, and contrasts with spirited answers from some neighbors that had their homes burnt accordingly." George wrote to his cousin to express his outrage: "to commune with a parcel of plundering scoundrels," he explained, "was exceedingly ill judged."

Revenge would come. Three months later *Savage* was cruising off the coast of Georgia on blockade duty. In the early morning of September 6, 1781, a large ship which she at first took to be a merchantman hove into view. It was in fact the largest privateer ever outfitted in Philadelphia, the 24-gun *Congress*. Heavily outgunned, *Savage* spread canvas and attempted to run. But *Congress* was purpose-built for privateering and very fast. She soon overtook *Savage* and began firing at her with her bow chasers. Drawing even with *Savage*, *Congress* pounded away with her broadsides. *Savage* aimed her fire at the ship's rigging realizing that her only hope was slowing down *Congress* enough to enable escape. At first it worked. *Congress*'s rigging was cut up and she was forced to break off to make repairs.

This done, however, she once again closed with *Savage* for an hour of close combat. It was all *Savage* wanted. As *Congress* prepared pistols, pikes and cutlasses for boarding, *Savage* struck her colors. Casualties were about even on both sides, with thirty killed and wounded aboard *Congress* and thirty-two aboard *Savage*, one of them her mortally wounded commander. Mount Vernon's humiliation was avenged.

CONGRESS WAS NOT the average privateer. Most of these ships went to lengths to avoid blows with the Royal Navy—that was the whole point. They instead sought unarmed merchant prizes. But they took many, and the economic impact of British losses to privateering was enormous and a significant factor in the appeals made to George III from Parliament to find a solution for the war. It was the privateers who tipped the scales towards the Americans after Yorktown.

One of the great ones was *Fair American*.

FAIR AMERICAN: MAKER OF FORTUNES

In the great collection of historic ship models at the Naval Academy Museum at Annapolis is the model of a privateer brig with the name *Fair American*, with particularly beautiful lines. The model itself dates from the late 18th century and was probably commissioned in London by Captain C. Chamberlayne, commander of HMS *Garland*, which captured *Fair American* on January 2, 1782.

Fair American makes her first appearance in the record books as a 14-gun privateer brig in the service of the South Carolina state Navy. It was sailing as part of the squadron under the command of Captain Nicholas Biddle in the frigate *Randolph* (32) when it fought the British two-decker *Yarmouth* (64) with the loss of Biddle and all hands save

Fair American, one of the most successful American privateers in the Revolution. This model in the Naval Academy museum is believed to have been commissioned by Captain Chamberlayne of HMS *Garland*, who captured her in 1782 and sent her officers, including George Lehman, to prison in England. *Courtesy Rogers Collection, U.S. Naval Academy Museum*

four. But *Fair American* escaped. When Charleston fell to the British in May 1780, *Fair American* had moved to Philadelphia.

The ship reappeared in April 1780 when a privateer's commission was issued to Stephen Decatur Sr. (the father of Stephen Decatur Jr. of the War of 1812 fame). It read:

> Philadelphia June 5, 1780
> I do hereby certify that a commission hath issued to Captain Stephen Decatur for the privateer brig *Fair American*, mounting sixteen carriage guns, navigated by 130 men, of the burthen of 150 tons, belonging to Charles Miller and Company, and bearing date the 20th day of April last. Signed, W. Matlack, Secretary.

Examining the model reveals a beautiful and obviously fast purpose-built combatant, fast enough to run away from anything she could not defeat while heavily enough armed to take virtually any merchant vessel or defend itself against Royal Navy ships smaller than a frigate.

For the next year and one half, *Fair American* operated out of Philadelphia "preying on British merchantmen like a bluefish running through menhaden." A list of the ships brought into just Philadelphia by *Fair American* includes the following: Tory privateer *Elphinstone* (12), Tory privateer *Arbuthnot* (14), brig *Sally*, ship *Eleanora*, brig *Three Sisters*, schooner *Secretary*, privateer ship *Queen*, schooner *Porcupine*, sloop *Polly*, brig *King George*, brig *Ann*, brig *Nancy* and the brig *York*.

On January 2, 1782, with Decatur no longer skipper, *Fair American*'s luck ran out while escorting a convoy of ships down to the West Indies. In a letter written to a New York newspaper by British Captain Chamberlayne he recounts the capture. "On Wednesday last January 2nd, we took *Fair American* rebel privateer, so remarkable for the depredations she has committed on the British trade for these two years past, and always escaping our cruizers by her swiftness of sailing. This I believe will incontrovertibly ascertain a fact which some people affect not to believe, but which nevertheless is true, *that the Garland sails superior to all the cruizers on this coast*. The *Fair American* had on board when taken, upwards of 550 barrels of flour, which she was to un-load at Havana, and afterwards cruize to windward of Jamaica; the pris-oners inform us, that seven vessels loaded in the same manner sailed from Philadelphia on the 31 of December along with her, that fourteen others had sailed two days before, and that vessels from Europe and the West Indies were every day arriving the Delaware."

Fair American was taken back into New York and her crew sent as prisoners to the infamous prison hulk HMS *Jersey*. Her officers were sent to Old Mill Prison in Plymouth, England.

Fair American herself was condemned as prize and bought by a group of Tory investors. She was sent out once again as a privateer—this time in service of the British. She began taking American prizes in April 1782. On April 8, 1782, she participated in the famous action at Cape May when cruising in company with the British brig *General Monk* (18)—a former American privateer named *Washington*—they en-countered a convoy of merchantmen being escorted by Joshua Barney in the sloop *Hyder Ali* (16). *Fair American* ran aground and took no part in the fight during which Barney captured *General Monk* and took her back to Philadelphia. *Fair American* was able to get off with the tide and continued to take prizes until her last recorded action in March 1783. Thereafter, she passes from history.

ON A TYPICAL CRUISE a privateersman like *Fair American* left port with as many men as could be accommodated aboard, many more than needed to sail and fight the ship. As each prize was captured a crew was put aboard it to bring it into a friendly port. A privateer might be forced to return to port because it ran out of crew rather than out of supplies. It was often when they were in that condition that the privateers fell prey to the blockading Royal Navy.

After 1780 things were made easier on the privateers when Dutch ports became available. Privateers were able to range around the British Isles and the Channel as well as throughout the lucrative Sugar Islands in the Caribbean. Their damage to Britain increased with each year, but their efforts were not appreciated by the Continental Navy, nor indeed by some members of Congress.

As William Whipple of the Continental Congress wrote in 1778, "besides all this, you may depend no public ship will ever be manned while a privateer is fitting out. The reason is plain: those people who have the most influence with seamen think it in their interest to discourage the public service, because by that they promote their own, viz. privateering." He was only partially right. The Continental Navy never was able to fully man its ships and they often lay in port for long periods with insufficient crews to go to sea. But the reason was not because of the scheming of privateer owners but because of the nature of duty in the Continental Navy. The purpose of the Navy was to go into harm's way and to fight to protect convoys and harass the Royal Navy. The risk of death or injury was high. While discipline was not as harsh as in the Royal Navy it was still far more strict than aboard privateersmen. And seaman's pay in the Navy was half that in privateers, the food worse and the voyages far longer. Finally, and most important of all, the chances of making a great deal of money were far higher in privateers. For these reasons, Congress made efforts to stipulate that one-third of every privateer's crew must be landsmen, in order to stop the privateers from taking all trained seamen away from the Navy. These efforts were completely without effect. This was not surprising; many of the members of Congress and indeed the Continental agents themselves were owners and operators of privateers. One wonders just how sincere the efforts were.

One must nevertheless conclude that the interests of the Revolution were far better served by the use of the manpower in privateering than in the Continental Navy. The captains and officers of the Continental Navy were for the most part extremely experienced mariners but, aside from Biddle, had virtually no experience in naval discipline, tactics and combat, where their talents did not always translate into success. Virtually every one of the Continental captains at one time or another during the Revolution took up privateering and in fact the distinction between the Navy and privateering during the Revolution is not as great as academic historians have made it. At least sixty of the most successful privateers during the Revolution were commanded by men who were captains in the Continental Navy or later became captains in the U.S. Navy. There were many others from both army and Navy who shipped out for one or more privateer cruises.

One such man was George Lehman.

George Lehman:
Doctor of Privateering

One of the men who had joined Stephen Decatur in Philadelphia when he took *Fair American* on its first cruise in 1780—and who was aboard its last sad cruise back to New York—was young George Lehman.

Lehman was born in 1753 to one of Philadelphia's founding families. His great uncle, Philip Lehman, was William Penn's secretary. He had accompanied Penn to his new colony in 1682 and stayed on to help manage Penn's affairs. Philip's younger brother, Godfryd, and Godfryd's son, Christian, joined Philip in Philadelphia in 1731. The family settled in the Germantown section of Philadelphia and at one time owned much of what is now Roxborough and Manayunk. Christian also worked for the Penn family and was appointed by Governor John Penn as tabellion, an authoritative magistrate. Christian's son George was born in 1753 and soon demonstrated extraordinary learning in science and languages, becoming fluent in English, German, French, Latin and more. But he made medicine his profession.

In 1776 George Lehman joined the Continental Army as a physician and was assigned to the newly constructed hospital at Yellow Springs serving Washington's army at Valley Forge. It was a well-designed and -operated facility for the time, quickly acquiring a reputation for being neat, and comfortably providing for the sick. General Washington himself visited the hospital in May, speaking "to every person in their bunks, which exceedingly pleased the sick," and was favorably impressed by the facility.

By 1780 Lehman had served four years with Washington. There

was now no more fighting in Pennsylvania and very little in the Northeast, the focus of the war having moved south. So when Stephen Decatur sought to raise a crew for *Fair American* he sought out the young doctor for both his medical skills and his talents as a linguist. Lehman readily accepted.

Fair American, as already recounted, was fabulously successful. George Lehman accumulated sufficient money for the future to set up a handsome medical practice and a pharmacy with plenty of money left over. But such a life was not without its risks. His income ended with his capture by *Garland*. His name appears on the list of 8,000 prisoners who suffered the horror of imprisonment in HMS *Jersey* in Brooklyn. His stay, fortunately, was brief and he was soon transported with the other officers to Old Mill Prison in Plymouth, England.

GEORGE WASHINGTON HAD MADE IT CLEAR from the very first days of the war that he expected American prisoners to be given full protection and treated as legitimate prisoners of war, and that he would treat British prisoners exactly as American prisoners were treated. The legal position of the prisoners was clarified by Acts of Parliament in 1776 and 1777, but some confusion continued. The status of privateersmen further complicated matters, but since they soon made up the great majority of naval prisoners they were simply treated as prisoners of war.

The treatment of common seamen, whether held in the *Jersey* or Old Mill Prison, was entirely different from that of officers and gentlemen. But for the most part the disposition of naval prisoners was dependent far more on the circumstances and location of their capture than anything else. If they were brought into New York, seamen were consigned to the hulks like *Jersey* in Wallabout Bay. There their prospect of exchange was bleak.

Officers, whether privateer or Navy, were given far better treatment and were eventually either paroled or exchanged. Here again if they were brought in as captives to New York they generally went straight to the hulks for processing but eventually were sent onboard Royal

Navy ships to England for imprisonment. If the returning ships were homeported in Portsmouth the prisoners went to the Forton Prison, and if they were homeported in Plymouth they went to the Old Mill Prison. Officers and seamen alike captured in European waters were sent directly to these prisons. American prisoners were also held at prisons in Edinborough, Scotland; Cork, Ireland; Shrewsbury, Bristol and Pembroke, England. In all cases these prisoners were far better treated than those that remained in the prison hulks. Old Mill Prison was well established, with a paid staff and medical treatment. Of course, the best of prisons in the 18th century were hardly resorts. Conditions varied greatly. The practice of the admiralty at the time was essentially to contract out the job of jailor, and corruption and abuse were rampant.

By the time George Lehman arrived in Old Mill Prison in 1782, however, there was a great deal of public sympathy towards the Americans and conditions were quite relaxed. Publicized figures like Captain John Manley and Joshua Barney were treated almost as celebrities. According to prison records the rations for each prisoner were specified to be "a quart of beer and one pound of bread, three quarters pound of beef for six days with four ounces of butter and six ounces cheese on Saturdays and a half pint of pease every other day." It is doubtful that many prisoners got such rich rations but what they did receive was supplemented by local sympathizers. At Old Mill Prison there was a "Committee for American Prisoners" which greatly improved the Americans' lot. According to one local account, it was possible for prisoners who had money to purchase whatever additional food and clothing they desired. Since George Lehman had made considerable money in *Fair American* before his capture he did not suffer. In fact, it was relatively easy to escape with the cooperation of jailors and locals suitably compensated. Many prisoners did so, although quite a few were grabbed by press gangs while attempting to find passage back to the United States.

"The prisoners disappeared singly and in large bands, breaking through walls, digging tunnels and even opening the main gates with abstracted keys and walking out; they were located in such places as

Belwharf, Ratcliffe Highway and Deale where they could negotiate for boats, and the country without an official police force could not hope to recapture many." A friend of Captain Elisha Hinman of the privateer *Deane* described his method of escape: "One Richard Coffin who formerly lived at a place called Nantucket in America, but now residing at number 118 in the Minories had advanced him money and procured him a suit of black cloathes to appear in the character of a clergyman . . . he would never mind being a prisoner in England for there were friends enough always to assist him to escape."

The last of the Old Mill prison buildings was demolished in 1911. The site is now a park, with a plaque at the location of the old main gate.

George Lehman needed to make no great exertions to gain his freedom. He walked through that gate before the end of the war, "liberated through the efforts of his aunt in Germany . . . whose husband was largely engaged in mercantile transactions with England." He returned to Philadelphia at war's end and with his privateering wealth set up his handsome medical practice. He married and produced five children, one of whom was William. William had a son George and George had a son James who became a collector of customs in Philadelphia. James had a son Joseph who became a physician and professor of medicine. Joseph had a son named John, and that John Lehman was my father.

THE VOYAGE OF DR. DROWNE

There is an amazing parallel to George Lehman's experience in the career of Dr. Solomon Drowne. Like Lehman he was born in 1753 but in Providence, Rhode Island. Drowne also completed his medical studies in Philadelphia and joined the Continental Army as a surgeon. Again like Lehman, Drowne signed on to a privateering voyage in 1780. But unlike Lehman, Drowne hated the sea and did not repeat his voyage— thus missing out on an opportunity to experience Old Mill Prison. Dr. Drowne's voyage lasted only seventeen days but he kept a journal. Because it shows so well the daily life of the privateer, it is worth quoting at length.

Tuesday, 3 October 1780

Sailed from Providence on board the Sloop *Hope*, mounting seven guns. Wind at N.E. drizzly, dirty weather. Outsailed Mr. John Brown in his famous boat. Put about for Capt. Munro, and take Mr. Brown and Capt. S. Smith on board, who dine with us . . .

11 October 1780

Whilst at Dinner, a Sail cried. Immediately give chase, and discover another. One, a sloop which bears down upon us; the other a brig. Make every preparation for an engagement; but, on approaching and hailing the Sloop, she proved to be the *Randolph*, Capt. Fosdick from New London,—mounting 18 four pounders, 140 tons. The Brig, with only two guns, her prixe from England, taken at 8 o'clock this morning.—Capt. Fosdick says her Cargo amounted to £20,000 Sterling. What good and ill fortune were consequent on that capture!—Hard for those poor fellows, their tedious Voyage being just accomplished, thus to have their brightening prospect clouded in a moment. If Virtue is the doing good to others, privateering cannot be justified upon the principles of Virtue;—though I know it is not repugnant to The Laws of Nations, but rather deemed policy amongst warring powers thus to distress each other, regardless of the suffering individual. But however agreeable to, and supportable by the rights of war; yet, when individuals come thus to despoil individuals of their property, 'tis hard:— the cruelty then appears, however, political.

12 October 1780

Early this morning two sail in sight, a Ship and Brig. Chase them chief of the day to no purpose. We conclude they sail well, and may be bound to Philadelphia.—Lat. 39º.6'. Soundings 19 fathoms. Lost sight of the *Randolph* by the chase . . .

14 October 1780

A sail seen from Mast-head; proves a Ship. We chase. Catch a Herring-Hog, which makes us a fine Breakfast, and dinner for the whole crew. Another sail heaves in sight. Upon a nearer approach the Ship appears to be of the line. Several in sight. Towards evening signal guns heard. We take them to be men of War, standing in, N.W. by W. Longitude by reckoning 73°.30". Lat 39°.34". 26 fathoms. A pleasant moon-light Evening. Spend it in walking the Quarter Deck.

15 October 1780

A pleasant day. See a Sail to windward; as she rather approaches us we lie a hull for her. I think it is more agreeable waiting for them, than rowing after them. Get a fishing line under way: catch a Hake and a few Dog-fish. It being Sunday, try the efficacy of a clean shirt, in order to be something like folks ashore. Give chase, as the vessel comes down rather slow. On approaching discover her to be a Snow. She hauls her wind and stands from us;—sails very heavy, and Capt. Munro is sanguine in the belief we shall make a prize of her. Get everything in readiness to board her. There seems something awful in the preparation for an attack, and the immediate prospect of an action. She hauls up her courses and hoists English Colours. I take my station in the Cabin; where, remain not long before I hear the Huzza on deck in consequence of her striking. Send our boat for the Captain & his papers. She sailed from Kingston, Jamaica, upwards of 40 days since, in a fleet, and was bound to New York: Capt. William Small, Commander. She has ten men on board and four excellent four pounders. Her Cargo consists of 149 Puncheons, 23 Hogsheads, 3 Quarter Casks and 9 Barrels of Rum, and 20 Hogsheads Muscovado Sugar. Send two prize Masters and ten men on board, get the prisoners on board our Vessel, and taking the prize in tow, stand towards Egg Harbour. We hardly know what to do with the prize: the wind shifting a little we stand to the eastward . . .

23 October 1780
Early, after breakfast, we set off again in the boat, with the Compass, being still surrounded with an excessive fog. Run ashore to the Eastward of Nayat Point, and mistake it for Connimicut: however, arrive at Providence about 11 o'clock, it having cleared off very pleasant. Thus ends our short, but tedious cruise . . .

Solomon Drowne made enough money from his share of the prize money from the two captures on this short cruise to clear all of his debts. The lure of wealth, however, was not sufficient to overcome his seasickness and his remorse at inflicting harm on the victims of his privateering. He never went to sea again.

THE LEHMANS MADE THEIR HOME in Philadelphia; Drowne had studied there. At the time of the Revolution it was this city, not Boston, that vied with Dublin as the second city of the British Empire. In furniture-making, silver smithing, painting and, above all, finance, Philadelphia was premier. No other single city financed and sent forth as many privateers as did Philadelphia. It became the principal industry of the port. Even during the few months of British occupation the Philadelphia privateers grew and flourished, operating out of other ports while many of their owners socialized happily with the British occupiers. As historian Nathan Miller described it, "the people of the seaport towns gambled in privateering as later generations gambled in stocks. They used their shares as collateral and bought and sold futures." Many a Philadelphia family fortune was founded on privateering. One of the greatest of the first years of the republic was that of the financier Stephen Girard.

STEPHEN GIRARD:
GLOBALIST AND NAVALIST

Stephen Girard is largely unknown today. His great philanthropy, Girard College in Philadelphia, put the name back in the news when in 1968 the U.S. Supreme Court modified his will providing for the education of "poor male white orphan children" to include nonwhites. In 1984, girls were also admitted by court order. Yet long before the college came into existence in 1848, Girard had given the United States of America a great gift.

Girard believed strongly that America could prosper only if open to the rest of the world's trade, qualifying him as an early "globalist," to use today's trendy word. And a policy of globalism in commerce, he argued, could only be sustained by a strong Navy capable of protecting that commerce. Girard was not alone in these positions, but he was called upon uniquely to put his money where his mouth had taken him. Fortunately for the American people, he did so.

Girard was born in Bordeaux, France, on May 20, 1750. Solidly built, of medium height at 5 feet 6 1/2 inches, his face was disfigured by a sightless left eye. His family were shipowners, and at the age of 14 he too went to sea as a *pilotes*, a sort of business agent who accompanied family-owned cargoes and ships, making sure that accounts were kept, risks minimized and profitable opportunities exploited.

After earning a captain's license in October 1773, Girard borrowed money to finance a cargo on a ship named *Julie;* he acted as supercargo and first-mate. Trading in furs, sugar, firearms and tools, primarily with Haiti, Girard had by 1776 made enough to buy half-ownership in a schooner, *Jeune Babe.* On May 14, in command of the ship he stood out from Cap-Francais (later Cap-Hatien), bound for New York. With the American colonies in rebellion and the Royal Navy beginning a blockade, he could not list that destination. On June 1, after taking on much-needed water at Lewes, Delaware, Girard made the fateful decision not to try to run the British blockade up the New Jersey coast. Instead, he hired a pilot to take him up the Delaware and landed in Philadelphia on June 6, 1776.

It was the beginning of a great career. Revolutionary Philadelphia did not daunt Girard. His optimistic nature and gift for business made him a superb contrarian: he always did well in a complex, adverse market. He was able to sell his cargo at a handsome profit and decided to stay.

Already Girard was a full-blown expert at the tricks of international trade. The British sanctions against the colonists were piled atop the great risks of doing business without banks, limited supplies of specie and widespread piracy and privateering. He reinvested his profits in privateers, but thereafter he stayed ashore. He soon became a vigorous patriot, and when the British occupied Philadelphia in 1777, he had to flee to Mt. Holly, New Jersey, where he hid out until they evacuated in June 1778.

Girard was to acquire a vast knowledge of international commerce and with it an extensive de facto intelligence network around the world. He almost always bought low and sold higher, never risked all in one stroke and accepted losses of ships and men as inevitable and part of the price.

He was an eccentric, but sensible in that the mere accumulation of wealth was never his goal. The richest man in America preferred plain, Quaker-style clothes, a solid but unostentatious house next to the wharf and counting house, a one-horse two-wheel gig (with neither carriage nor footman), the company of singing canaries and powerful watchdogs. His routine was resolutely 18th century in style and 20th-century workaholic in practice: A modest breakfast early; a large midafternoon meal, usually followed, as his employee and first biographer Stephen Simpson put it, by "the free indulgence of lubricity" with his wife or, later, a mistress; a late, light supper. Before, after and in-between these fixed points, with perhaps a visit to his model farm a few miles away in between, came work, work, work. He trained his own captains and apprentices, giving amazingly precise instructions and thought nothing of sending out talented 18-year-old boys with a quarter-million-dollar ship cargo and orders to return in two years with a profit. And usually they did.

This is the classic description of an immigrant making good. But

Girard did more than make good. He became one of the first American millionaires and a major influence on American and international trade. Girard knew all of the Founders but he played no real part in civil affairs until the terrible yellow-fever epidemic of 1793, when he set a standard of courage, freely risking his life to care for the sick.

By that time, Girard was already deeply interested in public health. His first wife, the beautiful and beloved (if impoverished) Mary Lump, had gone insane two years into the marriage. She was to spend much of the rest of her life in Pennsylvania Hospital, an institution largely supported by Girard himself (and which because of his largesse acquired a reputation for humane care of the mentally impaired). He never remarried, taking instead several mistresses who served him for long periods as the de facto head of his household.

His civil interest awakened, Girard became an advocate of an American Navy to protect oceangoing trade, including his own. The U.S. Congress sat in Philadelphia, for a decade the young nation's capital, and Girard organized more than one public demonstration to demand action against pirates and the hated British. (At one point in 1794 they held all five of Girard's ships.) He was instrumental in moving Congress to establish a Navy for the new republic in that year.

From 1801–1805, Girard was also active in advocating that the new U.S. Navy attack the Barbary pirates rather than pay the customary ransom. The Napoleonic wars were also once again making U.S. commerce vulnerable to the hated British practice of impounding cargoes, requisitioning ships and impressing U.S. sailors. A wealthy man like Girard could mount cannon on his merchant ships which would frighten off the pirates and privateers but were hardly a match for a British man-of-war.

In the run-up to the War of 1812, Girard's actions bespoke a man who wanted a war against British oppression on the high seas, feared the U.S. was unprepared and acted to protect his own assets. This produced one of the more incredible episodes in American history, when arguably Stephen Girard alone saved the independence of the United States while the United States simultaneously sued him.

The legal trouble preceded the War of 1812. Girard, foreseeing war with Britain, spent the better part of 1811 liquidating assets around the world. He brought back his Baltic trading ships through the British blockade of the continent. As he agitated for U.S. entry into the war against Britain, he knew that his ships would be the Royal Navy's first target.

From 1806 onwards the U.S. sought to pressure Britain to change its high-handed ways through economic sanctions. These laws forbade the import into the U.S. of British goods. But Girard and other traders still purchased such goods, either selling them for other commodities before importation or storing them in expectation of a change in the laws, which had become highly unpopular as they badly damaged the American economy, especially in New England. One of his ships, *Good Friends*, containing just such a British cargo, had been moored at Amelia Island, near the Georgia coast. The island belonged to Spain, then still in control of Florida, but in mid-March 1812, it was seized in a bloodless coup by U.S. forces.

Girard's ship's cargo was now contraband. But the Philadelphian got General Mathews, who captured the island, to issue a letter exempting the vessel from such a status. *Good Friends* sailed for Philadelphia, but on April 20, 1812, it was impounded at Wilmington, Delaware. The collector of customs, supplier of most of the federal government's revenue, sought triple value of the cargo, amounting to nearly a million dollars. Girard was able to secure the release of the cargo in May on court appeal, only to be sued by the Treasury Department on June 11, 1812, the day before the War of 1812 began.

In the face of the war, Girard, like other Philadelphians, outfitted a number of his fast merchantmen as privateers and, with Letters of Marque, sent them out to build his fortune further, at the expense of the British.

At first the war went well, but by February 1813, the U.S. government was without funds to support the struggle. Treasury Secretary Albert Gallatin developed a scheme to raise $16 million by public subscription. Extended twice, the subscription remained $10 million short in early April. Another month would find the U.S. bankrupt and the war lost, with catastrophic consequences.

Desperate last-minute fundraising still left the young nation's treasury $7 million in need, and on April 5 Gallatin went to Stephen Girard. Girard was greatly annoyed, not only by the lawsuit over *Good Friends*, but also by the obstacles that had been placed before his new bank, begun the year before as a buyout of the expired First National Bank of the United States. Beset by state-chartered competitors whose political influence denied him a charter, Girard had not been able to attract federal deposits.

Seven million dollars was more than Girard's net worth. Yet he knew that his future and America's were inseparable. He had agitated for years for the Navy to back up international trade. Now that America was doing it, he would not hesitate to put his money behind his vision. He agreed to provide the $7 million, insisting only that part of the money be deposited in his bank

With the money in the treasury, America's fortunes began to improve. By 1815 it was clear that American strength on land and sea was increasing. A peace was achieved that avoided any loss to American interests, and Napoleon's defeat had largely ended the need for impressment of American sailors by the British, a major cause of the war. As Girard was quoted by a contemporary, Stephen Simpson, "There could be no victory, no war, without money. Soldiers and generals he considered of secondary importance, observing that they could be created by money, and by money only."

Girard may very well have bought a victory, but his travail with *Good Friends* was not over. He never mentioned *Good Friends* in his negotiation with Gallatin, no doubt because he did not want to be accused of tampering with the law. It took until 1819 and an act of Congress to settle the lawsuit, largely on Girard's terms. Meanwhile, *Good Friends* had been captured by the British, who imprisoned the sailors and sold the vessel in 1812 to Baring Brothers, Girard's London agents, for only $8,500. Offered the chance to reclaim the ship, Girard refused. *Good Friends* was bad luck.

Girard lived until 1831, becoming an early financier of railroads and coalmines, and never losing either French accent or his well-developed eccentricities. He died at age 81, the richest man in America, with a net worth of over $7 million in a day when presidents of banks were paid $2,000 a year. (Today, the fortune, despite the huge costs for Girard College, exceeds $300 million.) His will, an epistle of 10,000 words, made him America's greatest philanthropist, much to the disappointment of his relatives. His nieces and nephews hired Daniel Webster to argue that Girard's will was invalid, which Webster did before the Supreme Court in 1844. Fortunately for the alumni of Girard, the relatives lost.

PRIVATEERING AND THE WAR OF 1812

Backed by Stephen Girard and men like him, American privateers in the War of 1812 made an enormous contribution to the war effort. But this time Philadelphia was not the leading city. The port of Baltimore provided more privateers than any other. Most of Baltimore's ships were purpose-built schooners or brigs which became known all over the world as "Baltimore Clippers."

The Baltimore Clippers did not, however, have as decisive an effect as their equivalents had had in the Revolution because circumstances had changed. In 1805 the Royal Navy had established unchallenged maritime supremacy with its victory at Trafalgar. While Napoleon fought on, the Royal Navy was able to impose a total blockade on French ports and maintain complete dominance on European and British waters. By mid-1813, the Royal Navy was able to shift sufficient ships to the American station to impose a similar tight blockade of all American ports. It was thus more difficult and riskier for American privateers to slip through the blockade and far more difficult to bring captures into port for condemnation as prizes, on both sides of the Atlantic. This difficulty was somewhat alleviated when Congress on May 13, 1813, wisely passed an act providing for the payment of half of the value of any armed British vessel that a privateer would "burn, sink or destroy" and then later that year offered privateers a bounty of $25.00 per prisoner. Congress also then provided for the payment by the Navy of pensions to wounded privateers.

GENERAL ARMSTRONG AND GENERAL JACKSON

One privateer had an interesting effect on Andrew Jackson's victory in the Battle of New Orleans. In the first week of September, the schooner *General Armstrong* sailed from New York with a Letter of Marque. It was armed with one long 24-pounder and eight long 9s and sailed with a complement of ninety men under Captain Samuel C. Reid. Reid was an interesting example of a privateersman. He had started as a ship's boy in the U.S. Navy, serving as a midshipman under Commodore Truxton. He was the son of a Royal Navy lieutenant captured at New London during the Revolution. His father had married the daughter of a Judge Chester of Norwich, Connecticut, into whose custody he had been paroled.

Shortly after clearing Sandy Hook, Reid was pursued by the blockading British squadron. He was able to escape during very light winds by pumping water on his sails and towing his ship with his boats. On September 26, he reached the harbor of Fayal in the Azores. Shortly after *Armstrong* arrived in Fayal, so did a squadron of British ships, including *Plantagenet* (74), *Rota* (38) and *Carnation* (18). The squadron was on its way with troops to support the British attack on New Orleans. Ignoring Portugese neutrality, the British squadron sent a number of boats to attempt to surprise *Armstrong*, but were repelled. At midnight, the British attacked again with 14 boats and 600 men. A furious battle of grape and musketry ensued, during which the British succeeded in boarding *Armstrong*, despite heavy losses. In hand-to-hand combat, the British were finally driven off with many casualties, including the British commander, killed by Reid in a cutlass duel.

Expecting a full-scale attack in the morning, Reid moved his ship closer to shore and cut new gunports, enabling him to move all of his guns to the seaward side of the ship. At dawn the shallow-draft *Carnation* came in to attack, but received such a brutal fire from *Armstrong* that she was forced to withdraw. The determined British now began to bring in the 74-gun *Plantagenet* to settle accounts. Reid, having suffered two killed and seven wounded, set fire to *Armstrong* and scuttled her, retiring ashore with all hands. The British had suffered thirty-four killed and eighty-six wounded.

The next day, Captain Reid was invited to tea with the surviving British officers at the British Consulate, where he was given three cheers by the British officers as a brave and resourceful foe.

Reid had delayed the British expedition against New Orleans for ten days. Andrew Jackson thus was able to arrive and prepare his defenses before the attack. Upon meeting Captain Reid after the war, Jackson told him, "If there had been no Battle of Fayal there would have been no Battle of New Orleans."

IF MOST PRIVATEERS IN THE WAR of 1812 were not quite as successful as Reid, their activities were nonetheless impressive: During the War there were 513 registered privateers and they took about 2,300 British merchant ships compared to 165 taken by the Navy.

As in the Revolution, many a fortune was made. The brig *Yankee* out of Bristol, Rhode Island, for instance made six cruises under three captains. It captured nine large ships, twenty-five brigs, five schooners and a sloop totaling about $5 million of enemy shipping and supplies destroyed while taking home over $1 million worth of prize money. On its fifth cruise, *Yankee* took the ship *San Jose Indiano*, an English merchantman, and sold ship and cargo for about $600,000. The owners received about $250,000, the captain $16,000, and even the first and second cabin boys got $1,129.89 and $738.19, respectively, which in 1812 was a great deal of money. As in the Revolution, a secondary market in privateer shares emerged almost immediately in all of the major seaports.

PRIVATEERING IN THE CIVIL WAR

As the nation and its Navy developed, privateering, always viewed with suspicion as only a small step away from pirating, became less common.

There were no Letters of Marque issued by the United States during the Civil War. In March 1863 Congress passed the Union Privateering Act, authorizing the President to commission Union privateers, an authority which he already inherently had. The measure was the result of lobbying by wealthy New Yorkers including the Vanderbilts who hoped to share in the huge sums of prize money that were being won by the Union Navy. Secretary of the Navy Gideon Welles was able to persuade President Lincoln not to exercise this authority. Welles made the case for the simple reason that all of his officers wanted to keep the prize money monopoly for themselves. The congressional act did have an unintended benefit: it was interpreted by the British as a new threat of reprisal against them if they continued to support the South.

By contrast the Confederacy had high hopes for privateering when the war started. In 1861 Confederate president Jefferson Davis began issuing Letters of Marque and Reprisal hoping to emulate the success of privateering in the Revolution and the War of 1812: "All those who may desire, by service in private armed vessels on the high seas, to aid this government in resisting so wantonly wicked an aggression, to make application for commissions or Letters of Marque and Reprisal to be issued under the seal of the Confederate States."

This bold move was initially met with enthusiasm by Southern merchants and shipowners, but Davis's high hopes for privateering were to be disappointed for several reasons. First, in June 1861, London proclaimed its neutrality and prohibited both belligerents' armed vessels from using the country's ports, making the possibility of bringing prizes in for condemnation difficult. Another deterrent was the threat by the United States to try all Confederate privateers as pirates, actually carried out in the case of the privateer *Enchantress*. Only forty prizes were taken by Southern privateers in 1861—and that was the highwater mark. After all, why take the risk? The opportunity of running the Northern blockade offered much greater profits at far lower risks.

Privateering in the South was not encouraged by the experience of *Jefferson Davis*. On July 6, 1861, *S.J. Waring*, a large schooner out of the South Street piers in New York City bound for South America, was seized by the Confederate privateer *Jefferson Davis* off the Virginia Capes. A prize crew was put aboard to take her into Charleston. While en route a black crew member of *Waring* named William Tillman, fearing that he would be sold into slavery, personally killed most of the Confederate prize crew with a hatchet. Tillman was able to bring the ship back to New York, where he became a hero and was awarded $17,000 in salvage money.

Confederate commerce raiding increased from mid-1862 on, but was done almost entirely by purpose-built or modified raiders of the Confederate Navy like *Savannah* and *Florida*. By the mid-19th century, then, privateering in America was already almost dead.

WHILE THERE ARE THOSE who would argue today that privateering no longer is countenanced by customary international law, it is by no means settled. The President still has the authority to issue Letters of Marque and Reprisal and a 300,000-ton Iraqi tanker loaded with $34/barrel crude would make a very nice prize.

With the disappearance of privateering, America lost an important dimension of its naval power. The need for great battle fleets to command the seas, so well articulated by Alfred Thayer Mahan, was thoroughly vindicated in the world wars. But harnessing private enterprise to raid enemy commerce served America well in its early wars and could have made a contribution in the Civil War, the Spanish-American War and arguably the First World War.

Successful privateer captains had all the personal courage, ingenuity and self-reliance prerequisite to those who make their living on great waters and found conspicuously in the great naval heroes. But very often they were of a temperament incompatible with the politics and hierarchy of career naval service. Without Letters of Marque, hundreds of men like Stephen Decatur Sr. and Samuel Reid would have had no opportunity to help the war effort. In no war has the American Navy ever had enough ships for the qualified captains available.

In today's much-reduced peacetime Navy there are only ships for a tiny fraction of even the number of qualified career naval officers. In times of future crises it is not inconceivable that a modernized version of privateering could play a useful role.

III

WAR WITH THE
BERBER PASHAS AND
REVOLUTIONARY FRANCE

THE PERFORMANCE OF the American Navy in the Revolution "was
enough to cause tears" among even its most ardent supporters like
John Adams and Robert Morris. As an eminent historian commented,
"Despite a few glittering moments with captains like John Paul Jones,
Lambert Wickes and John Barry, if the American Navy had never existed it is hard to see how the outcome of the Revolution would have
been any different." That is an unfair exaggeration. The Continental
Navy was extremely important to the Revolution. It forced the British
into convoying and other operations that spread them too thin to fully
enforce this blockade. The Continental Navy protected the essential
arms shipments to Washington's Army, and money shipments to keep
it in the field. It also provided the only safe means of communication
and movement of diplomats to Europe and the Caribbean.

Nevertheless, after the fighting there were few willing to speak up
for maintaining any navy at all. By the end of the war only two vessels
had not been captured or destroyed, a small packet and the excellent
frigate *Alliance* (32). Both were sold off by 1785. But even as the Navy
was being terminated, the realities of the perilous world were intruding
on the maritime traders of the newly independent nation.

The Berber states along the northwest coast of Africa were ruled by
pashas nominally under allegiance to the Ottoman sultan. They had long
financed their treasuries by extracting tribute for commerce passing

through the Straits of Gibraltar and the littoral of North Africa. The great powers—Britain, France, Holland and Spain—had Navies strong enough to protect their flag commerce. Other nations found it more convenient to pay the pashas tribute than to mount naval protection. After the Revolution the Royal Navy no longer provided protection to American merchantmen, and in October 1784, *Betsey* from Philadelphia was the first of many Yankee merchantmen seized by the "Barbary pirates."

It could easily be argued that these pashas—on-and-off enemies of the United States from the seizure of *Betsey* through war with revolutionary France until after the War of 1812—did more than any American to build the American Navy. Thanks to them one of the longest running policy divides in American government had by now taken shape: the navalists versus the anti-navalists. John Adams and the Federalists believed in a strong Navy for the new federal government. "Our great seaports and most exposed frontier places ought not to be neglected in their fortifications," he wrote, "but I cannot see for what purpose a hundred thousand militia are called out, nor why we should have so large an army at present. The revenue applied to these uses would be better appropriated to building frigates."

Jefferson and the Republicans, on the other hand, opposed maintaining a large Navy for important reasons. Their vision of America was an agrarian country spreading westward. The new government was having a hard enough time even coping with the Indians and was well aware that the British, French and Spanish had no interest in allowing the Americans to spread any farther west. To the Jeffersonians, the Navy represented a distraction and a likely involvement in global and European affairs that America could ill afford.

Seizures by Morocco were ended with a treaty in 1787 that among other things provided for the payment of tribute, but seizures by Algiers, Tunis and Tripoli continued. When the new American constitution was completed in Philadelphia that year it included a stipulation in Article II, with which no one now disagreed; Congress would "provide and maintain a Navy." Even Thomas Jefferson thought our maritime trade " . . . will require a protecting force on the sea. Otherwise the smallest power in Europe, everyone which possesses a single ship of the line may dictate to us, and enforce their demands by captures on our commerce. Some naval force then is necessary if we mean to be commercial." Nevertheless, more than a decade would pass before a new Navy would get underway.

It was not until 1794 that Congress approved a resolution calling for the establishment of a Navy. The resolution was unsuccessfully but bitterly opposed by the Jeffersonians, who, despite Jefferson's earlier comments, feared that "a Navy will be ruinously expensive, aristocratic institution, subversive of democratic ideals, whose glory-hungry officers will drag the country into unwanted adventures overseas."

The U.S. Navy was being midwifed by the Barbary pirates. As seizures and enslavement of Americans continued to increase, especially by the Algerians, President George Washington formally recommended the construction of six frigates to protect American commerce from the "corsairs," on April 22, 1793. The following year Congress authorized the construction or purchase of six frigates, three of 44 guns and three of 36. On March 27, 1794, the first officers of the United States Navy were appointed. George Washington picked the six captains and decided their seniority—in order, John Barry, Samuel Nicholson, Silas Talbot, Joshua Barney, Richard Dale and Thomas Truxton. Barney protested at being given such a low priority after his brilliant service in the Revolution, but Secretary of War Knox refused to reopen the matter. Barney then refused to serve and went off to France to fight in the French Navy. He was replaced by James Sever.

It would not be one of the six who was most crucial to the development of the young Navy but an individual with a wide array of talents who is today all but forgotten.

JOSHUA HUMPHREYS
AND THE SUPERFRIGATES

For a man as important as he was to the young Navy, in a field that is subject to the finest of pedantic combs, there is a surprising dearth of scholarship on Joshua Humphreys. No full-length or authoritative biography survives nor any portrait or drawing as I found to my frustration when I named a ship for him in 1986.

By the time Congress authorized construction of the six frigates, Joshua Humphreys had become the premier shipbuilder in the new nation's capital. He was a good friend of capitalist extraordinaire Robert Morris, and well-known by most of the members of Congress and George Washington himself. It was no surprise when he was picked to design the six frigates, but it was a turn of very good fortune. Humphreys was in fact the most innovative and revolutionary designer of the age of sail.

He was born in Haverford, Pennsylvania, now a "mainline" suburb of Philadelphia, on June 17, 1751, the descendant of Welsh Quakers who arrived with William Penn in 1682. He was early apprenticed to James Penrose, a prominent Philadelphia shipbuilder, after whose family the current bridge over the Schuylkill River is named. When Penrose died Humphreys took over as the master shipwright in his yard in 1771. He joined with cousin John Wharton and built the frigate *Randolph* (32 guns) for the Continental Navy in 1776. *Randolph* was a conventional design but significantly larger and of finer lines than European counterparts and, what was to become typical in American shipbuilding, built with a greater emphasis on speed.

By 1794 Humphreys had evolved a truly revolutionary concept for designing an American frigate. He won the commission by selling Knox on the concept embodied in a letter dated January 6, 1793:

As our Navy must for a considerable time be inferior in numbers, we are to consider what sized ships will be most formidable and be an overmatch for those of an enemy; such frigates as in blowing weather would be an overmatch for double-decked ships, and in light winds to evade coming to action, or double-decked ships as would be an overmatch for common double-decked ships and in blowing weather superior to ships of three decks, or in calm weather or light winds to outsail. Ships built on these principles will render those of an enemy in a degree useless, or require a greater number before they dare attack our

ship. Frigates, I suppose, will be the first object and none ought
to be built less than 150 feet keel to carry twenty-eight 32-
pounders or 24-pounders on the gun deck and 12-pounders on
the quarterdeck. These ships should have scantlings equal to
74s . . . They should be built of the best materials that could
possibly be procured.

It was simple and brilliant.

Reportedly Humphreys had been heavily influenced by a number
of French 74s that had been razeed or cut down to single-deckers and
made into frigates. The purpose of a frigate was to be able to range
ahead of the battle fleet and to sail faster than the ships of the line.
They were more lightly built than a two-decker and could not carry
more than 18-pounders in normal circumstances because the weight of
the heavier guns caused the hulls of the lighter ships to "hog," or bend
and distort, and because heavier guns were much more difficult to
manage on the smaller deck space of a single-deck ship. Thus a frigate
ranged against a two-decker carrying 24- or 32-pound guns built of
much heavier scantlings would normally fare very badly. The British
had also experimented with 44-gun frigates but they had been abandoned as a bad compromise. Humphreys's solution to this problem was
to take advantage of the far superior American materials, particularly
the live oak that enabled far greater strength for a given weight, and to
build the structure of the frigate to the robustness of a 74-gun ship-of-
the-line while maintaining the fast lines and length-to-beam ratio of
the faster frigates.

In order to carry the heavy topside weight of 24-pounder main
guns and to prevent penetration by 24-pound enemy cannonballs,
Humphreys introduced some real innovations. His design for the 44s
was 175 feet between stem and stern with a beam of 44 feet 2 inches,
making his ships 3 feet wider and 20 feet longer than their largest
British counterparts. He strengthened and widened the gangways con-
necting the forecastle and quarterdeck, creating a "spar deck" which
could mount great guns along its entire length. This gave it the firepower of a two-decker without the disadvantage suffered by two-

deckers of having to close their lower gun ports in rough weather. To achieve the strength of a 74 without excessive weight, Humphreys first placed his hull framing so close together that the interval between pairs was less than two inches compared to eight inches on a typical British frigate of the day. Second, to prevent hogging from the weight of the larger great guns, Humphreys seems to have borrowed a design from barns that were being built by the Pennsylvania Dutch in Lancaster County. This was an inverted cantilever system built into the hull. As described by Tyrone Martin, "His design called for three parallel pairs of prestressed diagonal riders rising forward from the sides of the keel to be joined to the opposite ends of berthdeck beams four, six and eight from the bow, and another three pairs rising aft to join with the fourth, sixth and eighth berthdeck beams from the sternpost." The result was an integrated system that distributed the weight of the gundeck and its armament evenly throughout the ship through the diagonals to the keel. This eliminated keel distortion and hogging while actually reducing structural weight. It was truly genius, as could be seen later in the life of *Constitution*.

In one of the overhauls in the 19th century, these difficult and expensive diagonals were removed from *Constitution* and a more conventional structure put in place. By the time that I had my first opportunity to inspect her in 1981 she had developed significant hogging. When the ship was put back for a full overhaul in 1992, Humphreys's diagonals were restored with great skill and some new materials. The virtues of the design were proved when the fully rigged *Constitution* sailed once again solely powered by the wind in 1998.

The great American advantage that Humphreys exploited was that of wood. The flooring of my own Bucks County, Pennsylvania, home built in 1738 is made of beautiful planking of yellow "pumpkin" pine. The boards on the third floor are fifteen to eighteen inches broad, whereas the equally attractive boards of the first and second floors are all less than twelve inches broad. The reason for the difference is that, until the Revolution, all fir trees greater than twelve inches diameter belonged to the king because of their great value in making masts for the Royal Navy. It was illegal to cut down and use a pine tree greater

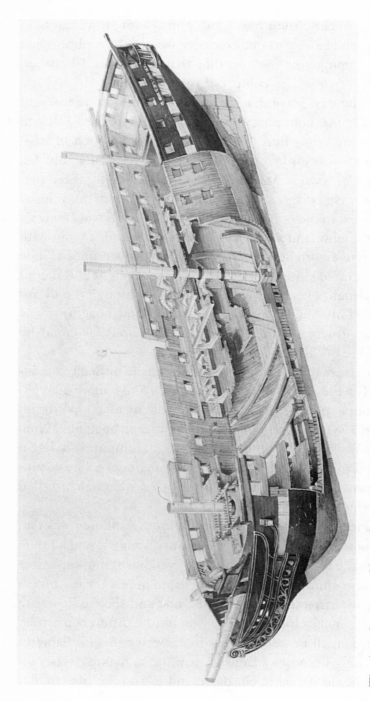

The American superfrigate *Constitution*, the pinnacle of warship design in the age of sail, showing the ingenious innovations of designer Joshua Humphreys. *National Geographic Society*

than twelve inches in thickness. There were bounties paid for viola-
tions, and so when colonists illegally used such great trees (as they very
frequently did), they used the wider planking in what was then the at-
tic, where nosy informers would not be likely to venture. After the
Revolution the Royal Navy no longer had cheap access to these great
trees and was forced to rely on weaker composite masts made by joining three or four smaller European trees together for their main and
foremasts.

Despite the builders of Bucks County, Joshua Humphreys had no
trouble finding abundant trees for the best masts in the world. There
were ample supplies also available to Humphreys and his shipwrights
of white oak, longleaf pine and cedar of a superior quality for planking
and specialized fittings. But far and away his greatest advantage was
the availability of live oak.

A species of beech, the live oak tree grows in the southeastern
United States. It is a magnificent semi-evergreen tree and the best possible material for constructing wooden warships. First, it is a very dense
and strong wood, weighing seventy-five pounds per cubic foot compared to fifty-six pounds for white oak and forty-one pounds for red
cedar. Second, it grew in elaborate shapes that made the junctions of its
huge branches with the trunks perfect for the massive structural
frames of elbows and the like. Third, it was extremely resistant to dry
rot, which was and is the curse of all wooden ships. Fourth, unlike
white oak, pine or cedar, it did not splinter under impact, a huge advantage in a battle between wooden ships. Most casualties in man-of-
war battles were caused by the spalling effect of cannonballs striking
the sides of the ships—this caused the showering of sharp splinters on
the other side of the impact, which acted like shrapnel with devastating effect on flesh and bone. Live oak could absorb the impact and
would not spall.

Live oak was known to 18th-century shipbuilders other than
Humphreys. The British shipbuilders largely ignored it because of an
unfounded prejudice against anything but English oak. The French
had used it whenever they could obtain it for most of the 18th century,
and it was in part responsible for the superiority recognized by the

Royal Navy of captured French ships. It was nevertheless a bold move
by Humphreys to demand the use of live oak for the construction of
the superfrigates because the wood was hard to obtain from the malar-
ial swamps of the South and difficult to work in the shipyards. Cutting
tools had to be sharpened about every half hour when working on live
oak compared to once a day for normal oak. Thus it was used only at
great added expense, difficulty and delay. Whole teams were dispatched to St. Simons and other islands off Georgia to cut the live oak
necessary to meet Humphreys's requirements. It is estimated that each
of his six superfrigates took between 360 and 460 live oak trees for
their construction.

The results of his insistence were well worth the cost and effort.
One is struck in reading the accounts of the battles of all of the superfrigates with the huge disparity in casualties on both sides. Those
sailors aboard the adversaries of the superfrigates typically suffered
three, four or even ten times the casualties of those aboard ships like
"Old Ironsides." Indeed that nickname came directly from the battle
between *Constitution* and *Guerriere*. When exchanging broadsides, no
cannonballs from *Guerriere* penetrated *Constitution*. *Guerriere*, typically
of British frigates, had sides between wind and water fourteen inches
thick, with eight inches spacing between frames made of Baltic oak.
When hit with 24-pound cannonballs from *Constitution* her sides were
shattered and splintered with dire consequences for the men working
the guns. *Constitution* by contrast had a hull twenty-two inches thick
with frames of live oak spaced an average of one and one-half inches
apart. Humphreys's ships were in effect the first armored battleships.

A testimony to the robustness of Humphreys's designs and the
quality of the materials was the long lives of all six of the frigates. A
normal life of a Royal Navy frigate of the period was only about ten
years. All six far exceeded that lifetime.

The longest serving, of course, was *Constitution* (44), which remains
in commission and fully able to sail to the present day. After service in
the war with France and the Barbary wars, she became a legend during
the War of 1812, capturing three British frigates, *Guerriere* (38), *Java*
(44), *Cyane* (34), and one ship-sloop *Levant* (18), as well as many smaller

craft. She remained on active service around the world until the Civil War, when she served as a training ship for the Naval Academy. Thereafter she has been kept in service ever since, being used for various utilitarian purposes and eventually as a fully rigged sailing museum.

United States (44) was built by Humphreys himself at Philadelphia in 1797 and had nearly as distinguished a career as *Constitution*. Adorned with a figurehead carved by Benjamin Rush, she saw active service in the French war and the Barbary wars, and under Stephen Decatur captured the second British frigate in the War of 1812, *Macedonian* (38).

When *United States* was on patrol in the Pacific thirty years later, she signed on a seaman who had jumped ship from a Massachusetts whaler. His name was Herman Melville, and he sailed for fourteen months as a maintopman on *United States* and wrote *White Jacket* based on those experiences. *United States* served actively until the Civil War. When the war started in 1861 the Confederates seized the Norfolk Navy Yard on April 20 and *United States* had the misfortune of being in the yard at the time. She was set afire by the withdrawing Union Navy, along with eight other vessels. She was not completely destroyed, but at the end of the war was judged beyond repair and sold to the breakers.

The remaining four ships also had impressive lives. *President* (44) was launched in 1800 in New York and achieved world fame when under the command of Captain John Rogers she chased and attacked the British sloop of war *Little Belt* (20), inflicting thirty-two killed and wounded while suffering one boy wounded on May 16, 1811. Commanded by Stephen Decatur toward the end of the War of 1812, she was the only 44 captured by the British when overwhelmed by four men of war after running aground on Sandy Hook bar. Taken back to England with severe damage, she was proven unusable. Instead, an exact copy was made. The doppelgänger assumed the name *President* and served for decades in the Royal Navy, while the original was sold to the breakers in 1818.

Congress, launched in Portsmouth, New Hampshire, in August 1799, served during the War of 1812, and in 1820 became the first American

naval ship to visit China. In 1834 she was sold to the breakers at the
Norfolk Navy Yard. *Chesapeake* (36) was also launched December 1799
and served in the war with France 1800–01 and in the Tripolitan war
1802–03. She was captured by the British in 1813 and served in the
Royal Navy until 1820 before being broken up and used in the construction of a pub called the "Chesapeake." Her timbers can now be
seen in that building near Portsmouth, England, currently converted to
a warehouse.

Finally, *Constellation* (36) was launched on September 7, 1797, and
served with distinction in the French war. She stayed active in the fleet
until 1853, when she entered the Norfolk Navy Yard for what was to
become a very controversial refit. She emerged as a rebuilt corvette
and continued in commission until 1955, when she was stricken from
the Navy list and turned over to the City of Baltimore. Purists insist
that this in fact was not the same ship as the original. After extensive
and often passionate debate and research the most accurate view is that
a new corvette hull was built with much of the hardware fittings and
many of the timbers from the original. Regardless, it has recently been
restored and is once again on display in Baltimore's inner harbor.

HUMPHREYS'S FRIGATES HAD BEEN BORN thanks to the Barbary pirates. But in 1795 peace was negotiated with Algiers and the following
year with Tripoli. The pirates had been bought off; for the time being
the enemy for which the frigates were initiated had disappeared. Nevertheless President Washington urged Congress to continue construction and Congress funded the completion of *Constitution* (44), *United
States* (44) and *Constellation* (36), with the other three unfinished ships
put in mothballs.

In the meantime, relations with revolutionary France were deteri-
orating rapidly because of the French refusal to respect the neutrality
of American merchant shipping. In 1798 Congress directed that the
three completed frigates be prepared for combat operations and approved President Adams's request to begin construction of twelve

more ships. In April of that year Congress created the cabinet-level Department of the Navy and approved the nomination of my fellow Penn alum Benjamin Stoddert as the first secretary of the Navy.

On May 28, 1798, an undeclared naval war with revolutionary France began when Congress instructed American warships "to capture any French vessel found near the coast preying upon American commerce." The new secretary of the Navy issued some 365 Letters of Marque and Reprisal for privateering, and Humphreys's last three frigates, *Congress* (36), *Chesapeake* (36) and *President* (44) were soon launched.

On February 9, 1799, the first of Humphreys's superfrigates drew blood when *Constellation*, under Captain Thomas Truxton, engaged the larger French frigate *L'Insurgente* (40). Truxton's skillful sailing enabled *Constellation* twice to cross *L'Insurgente*'s bow to deliver murderous raking fire. When *L'Insurgente* struck her colors her casualties were eighty killed and wounded to the Americans' two killed and three wounded. *L'Insurgente* joined the U.S. Navy as *Insurgent*.

A year later in those same waters *Constellation* engaged the still larger French frigate *Vengeance* (56) in a brutal five-hour battle. With devastating casualties—more than 160 killed and wounded—the French skipper twice tried to surrender, but in the smoke his colors were not seen. When *Constellation* lost her main mast, *Vengeance* was able to limp into Curacao. American casualties were fourteen killed and twenty-five wounded.

VICE ADMIRAL HORATIO VISCOUNT NELSON: THE IMMORTAL MEMORY

One notable observer of these actions and others in America's war with revolutionary France was that country's most implacable enemy, Horatio Viscount Nelson. He commented admiringly of the big American 44s and the courage of their sailors.

The Royal Navy and the U.S. Navy have a long intimacy, most recently demonstrated in the instant and enormous support given to the

Royal Navy by the U.S. Navy during the Falklands War. This special relationship has deep roots. Naval culture, usages, language and traditions are heavily derived from the British (with a strong French admixture from our Revolutionary War alliance: i.e., American sailors serve "on" ships, like the French, not "in" ships like the Brits). George Washington's first military appointment was as a 16-year old midshipman in the Royal Navy (although he never actually served).

Reading the chronicles and letters of the American naval officers of the 19th century, a most formative period of the culture of the U.S. Navy, one is particularly struck by the frequent references to Horatio Nelson. By mid-century Nelson had become a living legend not only in the Royal Navy but the American Navy as well. His heroism, audacity, practical innovation, aggressiveness and compassion for his sailors and brother officers have contributed as much to the values and standards of the U.S. Navy as to the Royal Navy, and he deserves to be mentioned here.

As a personality he was captivating: vain and humble, fearless and vulnerable, pompous and lovable. We know all this because he was a great letter writer. "I was born September 29, 1758, in the parsonage house, was sent to high school at Norwich . . . from whence, on the disturbance with Spain relative to the Falkland Islands, I went to sea with my uncle, Captain Maurice Suckling, in *Raisonable* of sixty-four guns." One reason there are so many dozens of biographies of him are that troves of letters keep emerging from estates and attics. From the day he joined *Raisonable* at age 12 in 1771, until the day he died in the most dramatic possible circumstances on board HMS *Victory* (100) on October 21, 1805, at the height of the Battle of Trafalgar, Nelson wrote letters daily to family and friends. By the time he made rear admiral, he was writing as many as a hundred a day. They are elegantly written, full of chatty information and still a pleasure to read. Many were plainly written for the historical record. To insure the survival, for instance, of his last diary and his famous prayer before Trafalgar, he handwrote two separate copies of each. The prayer illustrates his style: "May the great God I worship, grant to my country, and for the benefit of Europe in general, a great and glorious victory; and may no misconduct in anyone tarnish it; and may humanity after victory be the predominant feature in the British fleet. For myself individually I commit my life to him who made me, and may his blessing light on my endeavors for serving my country faithfully. To him I resign myself and the just cause which is entrusted me to defend. Amen Amen Amen."

One of Nelson's most striking virtues was his pure bravery—not the bravado of Hollywood movies, but the much more admirable intellectual and emotional acceptance of horrifying dangers as a necessary part of his duty. He was not reckless or foolhardy, but from his earliest days he wanted to lead and win. "I wish to be an Admiral in command of the English fleet," he wrote, "I should very soon either do much or be ruined."

Nelson himself spent much time "on the American station" during the Revolution, commanding a brig and a frigate between 1777 and 1783. Luckily for the U.S., in 1781 Nelson was "the merest boy of a captain" in the Caribbean and not present when the British fleet was defeated by de Grasse off the Virginia Capes. Nelson had led an amphibious assault in Nicaragua in 1780, contracting a fever that nearly killed him. He was almost religiously loyal to his sovereign and held no sympathy whatsoever with the American rebels, actively supporting the impressment of Americans into the Royal Navy. For years after the American Revolution Nelson was plagued by legal claims against him by American shipowners.

During an attack on Calvi, Corsica, in August 1794, he lost the sight of one eye. In another attack at Tenerife in July 1797, he lost his right arm. Earlier that year in February in a major battle off Cape St. Vincent, in violation of standing orders, Nelson veered his flagship into the enemy line and rammed the stern of a Spanish opponent. He crawled out the bowsprit, kicked in a stern gallery window and led his sailors to capture the ship, then used it as a bridge to board and capture the Spanish flagship lying alongside.

During the attack on Copenhagen in April 1801, he once again disobeyed his commander (who was safely out of range) when he was ordered to break off and retreat in the middle of the battle. Upon being told of the order, with characteristic humor he replied, "Why, to leave off action! Now damn me if I do!" Then, turning to his flag captain, he said "You know, Foley, I have only one eye. I have a right to be blind sometimes." Putting his spyglass to the blind eye, he exclaimed "I really do not see the signal!" This begat the phrase "to turn a blind eye." During that battle with cannonballs "howling and snapping" over his head, he turned to his aide with a smile and said, "It is warm work, and this day may be the last to us at any moment, but mark you, I would not be anywhere else for thousands."

During the Battle of the Nile in Aboukir Bay in 1798, he was badly wounded in the forehead by a shot fragment, suffering among other things a severe concussion. When carried below for treatment he refused to be treated ahead of his wounded sailors: "No, I will take my turn with my brave fellows." His behavior for some years after was consistent with frontal lobe damage. While based in Naples during that period he was scandalous, pompous, vain and cruel. He lived in a *ménage a trois* with Emma Hamilton, the wife of the British ambassador to the King of Naples and his indiscretion was used in London as an excuse to keep from promoting him. From the beginning to the end of his career, Nelson found himself junior to admirals who never heard a shot fired in anger, another Royal Navy tradition that is not entirely unknown in the U.S. Navy.

What has made him truly immortal, however, was his brave and brilliant leadership at Trafalgar, the smashing victory over the combined French and Spanish fleets off Cadiz that gave Britannia unchallenged rule of the waves for the next one hundred years. As he always did, knowing his presence inspired the fleet, Nelson remained on the quarterdeck throughout the battle, in full dress, highly visible and highly vulnerable. As men dropped around him, he remained, pacing and unperturbed. A French cannonball hit the deck and bounced howling between him and his flag captain, Thomas Hardy. He again smiled and said "This is too warm work, Hardy, to last too long." He was mortally wounded soon after by a sharpshooter and died hours later in the knowledge that he had won a total victory.

The "Nelson touch" (his own term) was made of several elements: a genius for bold strategy based on giving his trusted subordinates both

a simple plan and great autonomy to carry it out; an inspiring and calculated bravery; and a charming capacity for kindness, concern and affection that inspired genuine love throughout the fleet. In an age of
Draconian discipline, he rarely allowed flogging and saved several condemned sailors from hanging. Once while pursued by a superior Spanish force, he risked capture to search for a sailor who fell overboard. As
the Trafalgar battle was about to begin, he saw a downcast sailor whose
letter home had just missed the mail packet. "Hoist a signal and bring
her back," said Lord Nelson. "Who knows that he may not fall in action tomorrow."

At the end of Trafalgar, when word of his death was passed through
the fleet, the expression of grief from sailors and admirals alike was un-
matched. A young sailor named Sam wrote to his father, "Our dear Admiral Nelson is killed so we have paid pretty sharp for licking 'em. I
never set eyes on him, for which I am both sorry and glad; for to be
sure, I should like to have seen him—but then all the men in our ship
are such soft toads, they have done nothing but blast their eyes and cry
ever since he was killed. God bless you!! Chaps that fought like the
devil sit down and cry like a wench."

On reflecting upon "the immortal memory" it is interesting to note
that just as in our own times when men like Ernest King were called in
to replace the peacetime admirals, Nelson was not at all effective in
peacetime—out of favor, without command and ridiculed as vain, disruptive and faintly ridiculous. War fighters do not prosper in peacetime
service in any age.

ALWAYS A KEEN OBSERVER despite his blind eye, Horatio Nelson
would have had little trouble seeing which way the tide was turning in
America's war against revolutionary France.

A peace agreement was signed in Paris ending the war on September 30, 1800. The final tally was enough to make any American navalist proud: the new Navy lost one warship, the schooner *Retaliation* (14),
and captured eighty-five French ships, including two frigates. As Jef-

ferson had predicted, the new U.S. Navy had quickly become an elite fighting force, but without the extreme aristocratic vanities he had feared.

THE SUBSCRIPTION SHIPS

In the years before a reluctant federal government was forced to act against the French, their seizures of American merchantmen were having a severe impact on some Yankee traders. Before the government acted, the merchant communities along the East Coast decided to take matters into their own hands. The result was the unique phenomenon of the subscription warships of 1798. That year the shipowners and merchants of Newburyport, Massachusetts, opened a subscription to build a 20-gun warship for the United States Navy, a Navy that had only been founded on April 30 of that year. In June, Congress authorized the president to accept ships on loan from private citizens, to be paid with interest-bearing government bonds. As word of the Newburyport effort spread, merchants in nine other cities began subscriptions for warships. With a combination of patriotism and self-interest the merchants and shipowners of Salem, Boston, Providence, New York, Philadelphia, Baltimore, Charleston, and Norfolk and Richmond together began to build ships to be contributed to the common defense.

Overlooked in most Navy histories, these non-naval Navy ships had colorful careers. Newburyport's *Merrimac* (20), for example, had distinguished service against the French but then fell victim to Thomas Jefferson, who ordered it sold a month after his inauguration.

The merchants of Baltimore built two fast 18-gun sloops of war, *Patapsco* and *Maryland*. After active service in the French War they were sold out of the Navy in 1801 by Jefferson.

The Boston subscription produced a small but fine 24-gun frigate named *Boston*. After active service in the French war and against the Tripoli pirates, she too fell victim to Jefferson in 1802, but lingered in ordinary at the Washington Navy Yard until having the distinction of being burned in 1814 to keep her from the invading British.

Captain Nicholas Biddle, the first American naval hero. *U.S. Naval Institute*

The American frigate *Randolph* explodes during battle with *HMS Yarmouth* east of Barbados, killing Captain Nicholas Biddle and all hands but four. *Courtesy Mariners Museum, Newport News, Virginia*

The infamous British prison hulk *Jersey* anchored in Brooklyn. More than twice as many Yankee soldiers and sailors died in her and her sister hulks than were killed in battle. *U.S. Naval Historical Center*

Captain John Barry, one of the greatest naval leaders of the Revolution, and the first and senior captain of the U.S. Navy. *U.S. Naval Historical Center*

Admiral Compte Francois de Grasse. The French Admiral's children all emigrated to America ahead of the Terror. *U.S. Naval Institute*

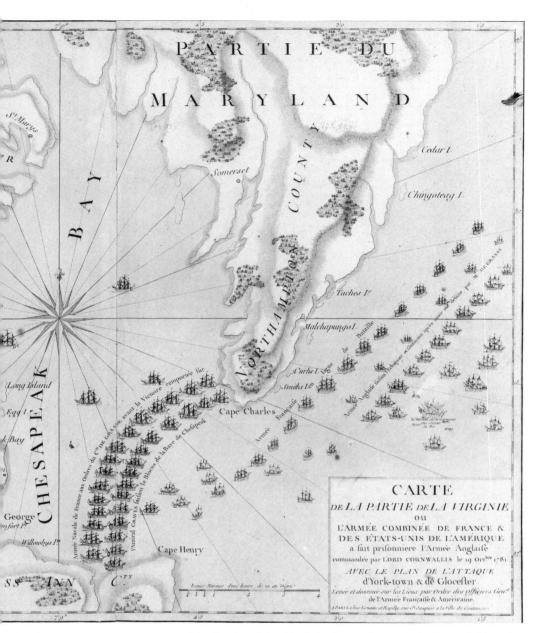

An elegant contemporary map of the Battle of the Virginia Capes, Francois de Grasse's blow for American independence and the naval battle that made victory at Yorktown possible. *Courtesy Beverly R. Robinson Collection, U.S. Naval Academy Museum*

John Paul Jones' greatest hour in the brutal battle between his converted merchantman *Bon Homme Richard* and the stronger HMS *Serapis. Courtesy Beverly R. Robinson Collection, U.S. Naval Academy Museum*

The privateer *Congress*, Captain Geddes commanding, engaged the sloop HMS *Savage*, Captain Sterling commanding, in a day-long battle some 10 leagues east of Charleston, South Carolina. *Congress* forced *Savage* to strike her colors. *Savage*, now a prize, was recaptured by HMS *Solebay* before her crew could bring her to a safe American port. *Courtesy Mariners Museum, Newport News, Virginia*

Stephen Girard, sea dog, patriot, financier of the War of 1812, and the founder of Girard Bank and Girard College. *Culver Pictures*

The privateer *General Armstrong*, under Captain Samuel Reid at the battle of Fayal, as depicted by Edward Moran. But for *Armstrong*, the British would have taken New Orleans. *U.S. Naval Institute*

U.S.S. Constitution smashing HMS *Guerriere*, confirming Nelson's prediction that there would be "trouble from those big American frigates across the sea." *U.S. Naval Historical Center*

Vice-Admiral Horatio Viscount Nelson, the greatest naval leader of the age of sail. *Courtesy Beverly R. Robinson Collection, U.S. Naval Academy Museum*

Edward Moran depicts the burning of the frigate *Philadelphia* in the harbor of Tripoli by Stephen Decatur, Jr., declared by Nelson to be "the most daring act of the age." *Courtesy of the United States Naval Academy Museum*

Captain David Porter, Midshipman Farragut, and USS *Essex* succumb to HMS *Phoebe* and HMS *Cherub* at Valparaiso, Chile. *Courtesy Beverly R. Robinson Collection, U.S. Naval Academy Museum*

The superfrigate *United States* under Captain Stephen Decatur, Jr., captures the British frigate *Macedonian*, beginning the latter's long career in the U.S. Navy. *Courtesy Beverly R. Robinson Collection, U.S. Naval Academy Museum*

Commodore Stephen Decatur, Jr., audacious hero of the Barbary coast and the War of 1812 was killed by Captain James Barron in a duel outside Washington, D.C. *U.S. Naval Institute*

Commodore Uriah Philips Levy, courageous, handsome, and rich. He commanded *Macedonian* and saved Monticello. *Courtesy of Mrs. Charles Mayhoff*

Joshua Barney, a naval hero of both the Revolution and the War of 1812. He would be a naval legend today if he had not fought on the wrong side during the quasi-war with Revolutionary France. *Author's Collection*

Commodore Oliver Hazard Perry, victor in the largest fleet battle in the War of 1812, on Lake Erie. *Courtesy Beverly R. Robinson Collection, U.S. Naval Academy Museum*

Commodore Thomas Macdonough, hero of the fleet victory in the Battle of Lake Champlain. *U.S. Naval Institute*

Rear Admiral David Glasgow Farragut, the very picture of a naval hero. He led in combat in two wars a half century apart. *National Archives*

Preparing to run the gauntlet at New Orleans. Note the anti-boarding nets and hammock bins characteristic of the age of sail. *National Archives*

The initiative in Providence had a murkier outcome. Rather than building a new ship, a merchant ship owned by John Brown called *George Washington* was bought by the subscription stock and converted to a warship. The ship turned out to be a dog and after very undistinguished service was sold in 1800.

The Virginia ship was *Richmond*. It was already under construction in Norfolk as a merchant vessel when the subscription was begun, and it was completed as a 16-gun brig. Going immediately into active service against the French it turned out to be a "very fine sailer" in Secretary of the Navy Stoddert's words and one of "the most useful vessels in our service." After strenuous service in the conflict with France, along with most of the Navy she was sold off by the new administration in 1801.

Joshua Humphreys's son Samuel designed the New York subscription ship. It was a 36-gun frigate named *New York*. Unfortunately her construction was repeatedly delayed and she was not completed until the conflict with France was nearly over. The ship had one uneventful cruise and then was laid up in ordinary. She was reactivated in 1802 and spent a year cruising in the Mediterranean before returning to ordinary at the Washington Navy Yard. She gradually sank into the mud of the Anacostia, where she is said still to be at the present day.

The Charleston ship was a 28-gun light frigate designed by Josiah Fox. Named *John Adams* she was destined to have the longest service of any of the subscription warships. Commissioned in 1799 she was almost continuously at sea throughout the conflict with France, with considerable success taking privateers and rescuing seized American vessels. Laid up for a year after the close of the conflict, she resumed cruising in the Tripolitan war in 1802, where she saw much successful action. In 1805 she was back in mothballs for two years after which she was converted to a flush-deck corvette and put back on active service. At the beginning of the War of 1812 she was converted at Boston to what was called a "jackass" frigate and joined the squadron in New York, where she was promptly blockaded. Her only service in the war was to take the peace commissioners to Europe in 1814. After the war she spent several years chasing pirates in the Caribbean and then catching slave ships off the coast of west Africa. *John Adams* was once again converted in 1830 into a sloop of war and thereafter saw continuous service in the Mediterranean, South Atlantic and a cruise around the world. She saw action in the Mexican War blockading Veracruz and Tampico. At the outbreak of the Civil War she became a sail training ship for the U.S. Naval Academy. Then in 1863 she was assigned to join the blockading squadron at her old birthplace, Charleston. At the end of the war, after 68 years of service, she returned to the Boston Navy Yard, where she was sadly sold to the breakers.

THE CRUISE OF *ESSEX*

The most successful of all of the subscription warships was the last to come into existence. The merchants of Salem, Massachusetts, did not immediately spring to the patriotic campaign as did their neighbors in Newburyport. It was not until the Newburyport's *Merrimac* was well launched that work on *Essex* began. But once built, she was soon in harm's way. *Essex* would serve under many captains and fight the Barbary pirates, the French and the British before ending in the Royal Navy.

Merrimac's designer William Hackett was also the designer of *Essex*. Hackett had been the designer of the best of the revolutionary war frigates, *Alliance*, built in 1778, and from all evidence, *Essex* of thirty-two guns was a close copy of that ship. *Essex* was launched in September 1799, and when her new captain Edward Preble first took her to sea she proved to be a very fast and stiff sailer.

Her first cruise under Preble was a strategic move by Secretary of the Navy Stoddert. He sent her all the way to the East Indies to protect the newly emerging East India trade of American vessels from the active French privateers. Her passage across the Atlantic was stormy and difficult, and revealed to Preble that some of the materials and workmanship of the Salem shipbuilders was "infamously bad," requiring extensive repairs when she arrived at Capetown.

Reaching Batavia (present-day Jakarta) on the Sunda Straits in May

1800, Preble wrote to Stoddert: "I cruised in entrance of Straits for a fortnight, in which time I boarded thirteen sail of American merchant ships richly loaded, whole of which would have been captured had a single French privateer been cruising in my stead."

In July, Preble was ordered to convoy fourteen U.S. merchantmen back to America. A long and stormy passage of five months brought them all safely home, and *Essex* returned to the Washington Navy Yard and was placed in ordinary (mothballs) to undergo extensive repairs. Once again the workmanship of the shipbuilders of Salem was heavily criticized. While *Essex* was in the yard, a treaty with Napoleon was signed early in 1801, ending the quasi-war with France. Naval attention could be turned once again to the predations of the Barbary pashas.

In May 1801, Jefferson sent a squadron to the Mediterranean to deal with Tripoli, including *Essex*, but she returned to the U.S. for repairs the following year. Refurbished, she was ordered once again to join the Mediterranean squadron arriving in August 1804 now under the command of Captain James Barron. For the next ten months she participated with the American squadron operating against Tripoli. *Essex*'s former skipper, now Commodore Preble, described his mission as "we . . . must endeavor to beat and distress his savage highness into a disposition more favorable to our views than what at present he possesses."

In May *Essex* carried the U.S. consul general to Tripoli to begin negotiations with the pasha and a week later a peace treaty was signed. *Essex* remained on duty in the Mediterranean until May 1806 under two different captains, before returning to ordinary at the Washington Navy Yard to undergo extensive repairs for the second time.

By 1809 the Napoleonic Wars were increasingly impinging on American neutrality and trade, and tensions with both England and France were becoming severe. The president decided to reactivate eleven warships, including *Essex*. Under Captain John Smith, *Essex* was ordered to bring home U.S. Ambassador William Pinckney when relations with Britain were severed in February 1811. War was declared a little over a year later.

When that happened *Essex* was in the Boston Navy Yard getting yet another extensive makeover. This time it was a huge mistake that proved fatal to the ship. The decision was made by the yard superintendent against the strong wishes of *Essex's* new captain, David Porter, to replace most of the ship's 12-pounder long guns with 32-pound carronades, which had much shorter range. Carronades were effective at close ranges, having a higher rate of fire and throwing a larger shot, but had such a short range that they were useless against a ship that could stand off with long guns. To add to Porter's problems other changes had been made during previous refits, including repositioning the foremast, that slowed the ship. She was no longer one of the fastest sailing frigates. Porter's objections were prophetic:

> Considering as I do that carronades are merely an experiment in modern warfare and that their character is by no means established I do not conceive it proper to entrust the honor of the flag entirely to them. Was this ship to be disabled in her rigging in an early part of an engagement, a ship much inferior to her in sailing and in force, armed with long guns, could take a position beyond reach of our carronades, and cut us to pieces without our being able to do her any injury.

Porter's father, David, had fought in the American Revolution and young David was bred to the sea. He had seen a great deal of combat during the French war and then in the conflict with Tripoli and had been a lieutenant on *Philadelphia* when it was captured in Tripoli harbor, spending nineteen months in prison in Tripoli. In the summer of 1811, Porter was given command of *Essex*, along with a commission as midshipman for his young ward David Glasgow Farragut. Farragut also had naval roots: he was the son of George Farragut, a fellow naval veteran of the Revolution and close friend of Porter's father.

Essex's first cruise of the war began in July 1812 and was spectacularly successful. Within a month she had captured nine British merchantmen and recaptured a number of Americans taken by British privateers. On August 13, she had the honor of capturing the first

British warship in the War of 1812 in a battle that took only ten minutes.

After the action Porter continued to complain about the ship's armament: "Insuperable dislike to carronades and the bad sailing of *Essex* render her in my opinion the worst frigate in the service."

On October 28, *Essex* set out on its second cruise of the war, intending to rendezvous with *Constitution* and the sloop *Hornet* (18) in the south Atlantic. The meeting never happened because *Constitution* had encountered and defeated the British frigate *Java* (44) thirty miles off the coast of Brazil and returned to the U.S. Improvising, Porter decided to go round Cape Horn and cruise against British shipping in the Pacific in what was to become one of the most successful operations of the war.

Essex rounded the Horn on February 14, 1813, and immediately began to take prizes, eventually making twelve significant captures in all. One of these, the British whaler *Atlantic*, he renamed *Essex Junior* and converted into a 20-gun brig. More important, however, Porter was so successful in destroying and capturing British whalers that the Pacific whaling industry came to be completely dominated by American whalers for the remainder of the century as a direct result. Since the British whalers carried supplies for as much as three years' worth of cruises, Porter was able to provision himself in an area without any friendly ports largely through these captures (supplemented by tortoises from the Galapagos).

By the end of the summer the British had become quite alarmed by the successes of *Essex* and resolved to take action. A letter was sent by Commodore William Bowles to the Admiralty stating in part, "letters are just received here from Chile giving accounts of the continued success of the American frigate *Essex* on that coast. It appears that on the 11th ultimo the 8 English whalers, *Catherine, Hector, Policy, Montezuma, Atlantic, Greenwich, George* and *Anne* had arrived at Valparaiso and the Americans were fitting out one of them (*Atlantic*) with 20 guns and 90 men to cruise in company with *Essex*."

A small squadron including the frigate *Phoebe* (36) and sloops *Raccoon* (26) and *Cherub* (18) were already on their way round the Horn to support the British effort to evict the Americans from the coasts of Oregon and Washington. They were diverted to cruise after *Essex*. By late October 1813, with *Phoebe* under Captain James Hillyar in the vicinity of the Galapagos, Porter had gone to the Marquesas Island of Nukuhiva to rehabilitate his scurvy-ridden crew and repair his ship. There he stayed, busying himself with local politics and island warfare while his men were busy among the women. The repairs to the ship were made and the crew's health restored by the end of December, and Porter set sail for Valparaiso, where word reached him of the British squadron. He now had every hope of attacking *Phoebe* and achieving the renown garnered by the captains of *Constitution* and *United States* after their captures of *Guerriere, Java* and *Macedonian*.

Essex arrived back in Valparaiso on February 3, 1814, and *Phoebe*, who was about to give up the chase and head for Oregon, took one last look into Valparaiso on February 7. Porter and Hillyar were old friends from the Mediterranean service and each inquired after the other's health. They exchanged letters for several weeks with Porter requesting a single ship duel and Hillyar understandably having no intention of giving up his advantage in numbers. *Phoebe* was almost an exact match in size for *Essex* and had a distinguished combat record including the Battle of Trafalgar. Unfortunately for Porter, she was armed principally with long guns, which gave her a huge advantage if well-handled because she could stand off out of the range of *Essex*'s carronades. This is exactly what she did when on March 27, upon hearing news that three more British men-of-war were headed to Valparaiso, Porter made a run for it.

Since *Essex* was the faster sailer and on that day had the weather gauge, she may very well have escaped except that as she was coming out of the harbor under full press of sail, a squall fell upon her without warning, and as *Cherub*'s captain later wrote, "at 3:10 observed her main topmast go over the side." She now could not possibly outrun her pursuers. She entered a nearby bay and anchored on the chance that Hillyar would not violate Chile's neutrality. Such faint hope was of course soon dashed and Porter now found himself in exactly the position he had warned against, with his maneuvering severely restricted by dam-

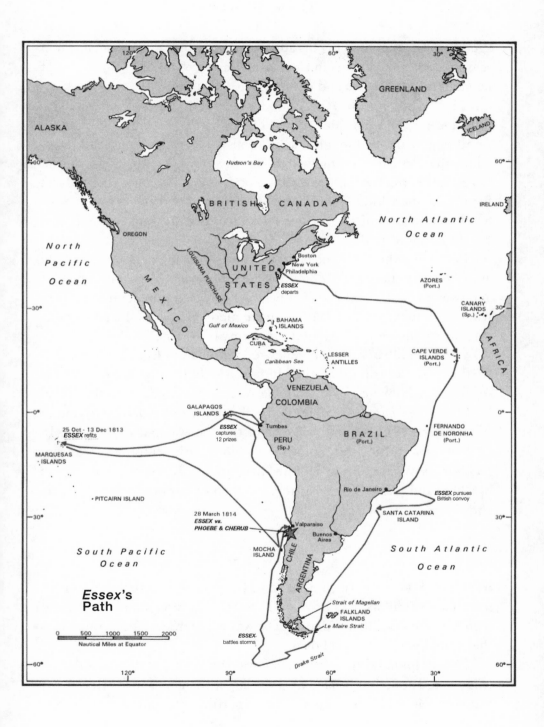

GREENLAND

ICELAND

ALASKA

Hudson's Bay

BRITISH   CANADA

IRELAND

North Atlantic
Ocean

OREGON

*North
Pacific
Ocean*

LOUISIANA PURCHASE

UNITED
STATES

Boston
New York
Philadelphia

ESSEX
departs

AZORES
(Port.)

CANARY
ISLANDS
(Sp.)

M E X I C O

Gulf of Mexico

BAHAMA
ISLANDS

CUBA

Caribbean Sea

LESSER
ANTILLES

CAPE VERDE
ISLANDS
(Port.)

A F R I C A

VENEZUELA

COLOMBIA

GALAPAGOS
ISLANDS

25 Oct - 13 Dec 1813
ESSEX refits

ESSEX
captures
12 prizes

Tumbes

PERU
(Sp.)

B R A Z I L
(Port.)

FERNANDO
DE NORONHA
(Port.)

MARQUESAS
ISLANDS

• PITCAIRN ISLAND

Rio de Janeiro

ESSEX pursues
British convoy

28 March 1814
ESSEX vs.
PHOEBE & ***CHERUB***

Valparaiso

SANTA CATARINA
ISLAND

MOCHA
ISLAND

Buenos
Aires

*South Pacific
Ocean*

CHILE

ARGENTINA

*South Atlantic
Ocean*

***Essex*'s
Path**

Strait of Magellan

FALKLAND
ISLANDS

Le Maire Strait

0   500   1000   1500   2000
Nautical Miles at Equator

ESSEX
battles storms

Drake Strait

aged rigging, thus allowing his adversary—one of the most capable and seasoned frigate captains in the Royal Navy—to maneuver just out of range of his carronades and pound *Essex* to splinters.

The eighty guns of *Phoebe* and *Cherub* fired broadside after broadside. Despite the onesidededness of the battle the crew of *Essex* refused to give up, and fought back furiously for two and one-half hours while the British fire "mowed down my brave companions by the dozen," as Porter recounted. Finally Porter struck his colors. He had lost fifty-eight men killed, thirty-one missing and sixty-five wounded—nearly 60 percent of *Essex*'s crew. The two British ships lost only five dead and ten wounded.

Porter and the surviving crew members were given letters of parole and allowed to take *Essex Junior* for the return voyage around the Horn and back to the United States. The practice was common on both sides when on remote station. Parolees were pledged not to take part in further hostilities until exchanged for enemy prisoners.

Captain Hillyar had emergency repairs made to *Essex* and then proceeded with her trip round the Horn to Rio de Janeiro. Here more extensive repairs were made, and she was then bought in to the Royal Navy as HMS *Essex* (36). She then sailed back to England, arriving in November 1814, and with the end of the war was put in ordinary. In 1824, she was turned into a prison hulk along with her former adversary *Phoebe* and was tied up in Dublin. In March 1837 she was sold to the breakers and passed out of history. Sixteen of her original subscribers and David Porter were still alive.

STEPHEN DECATUR JR., destined to become one of the U.S. Navy's most famous sailors, had been on *Essex* when she was under the command of William Bainbridge. But it was a different subscription ship that would win him his renown.

Philadelphia's ship, *Philadelphia*, was the largest of the subscription ships, rated at 36 but in fact 400 tons larger than a standard British 36. Moreover it was designed to the superfrigate standards of Joshua

Humphreys by Josiah Fox, one of Humphreys's protégés. *Philadelphia* was active throughout the war against France and then after in the Mediterranean. During one of the recurrent conflicts with the Barbary pashas, on October 31, 1803, while on patrol off Tripoli under the command of William Bainbridge it ran aground on an uncharted reef just outside the harbor. After token resistance, Bainbridge surrendered to the attacking gunboats of the Dey of Tripoli. The ship was soon refloated and taken into the Navy of Tripoli.

A few months later, in February 1804, the remarkable Stephen Decatur became a national hero after conducting a daring raid into Tripoli harbor—the object of his purpose, *Philadelphia*.

STEPHEN DECATUR JR. AND THE MOST DARING ACT OF THE AGE

Stephen Decatur Jr. was born in Sinepuxent, Maryland, in 1779, the son of the famous privateer captain. His commission as a naval officer was signed by President John Adams on April 30, 1798, the same day that Congress passed legislation separating the Navy from the War Department and granting it cabinet status. The United States and its Navy were still small enough for the young man to know and be known to such men as the commanding officer of the new Navy, John Barry, and Joshua Humphreys.

John Barry, a friend of Decatur's father, had observed Stephen's spiritedness as a youth—the lad often engaged in competitions and fistfights—and offered the young man a commission as midshipman in his command, the newly launched *United States*. Decatur left a clerkship with Humphreys and embarked on his first cruise in the summer of 1798.

United States sailed, escorted only by the refitted merchantman *Delaware*, commanded by Decatur's father. Barry used training time, both in port and at sea, to drill the crew in the speed and accurate use of its 24-pounders. Young Decatur's later exploits show he too learned well.

On *United States*, Stephen already demonstrated the poise in personal dealings and the bravery that drew other men to his leadership. Early in 1799, while on station among the Windward Islands, *United States* engaged and crippled a French privateer, *L'Amour de la Patrie*, off the coast of Martinique. Sent by his commanding officer to save the crew from the badly damaged French ship, Decatur fished its commanding officer out of the sea. He claimed astonishment at the encounter with *United States*. "I did not know that the U.S. was at war with the French Republic," he declared. The 20-year-old Decatur answered without missing a beat, "No, sir, but you knew that the French Republic was at war with the United States, that you were taking our merchant vessels daily, and crowding our countrymen in prison at Basseterre [in nearby Guadeloupe] to die like sheep."

On the same cruise, Decatur showed the bravery and dedication to the men under his care that defined him. As trade winds rose one morning in the Caribbean, the cry of "man overboard" went up, along with orders to man the cutters. Decatur saw an outreached hand in the seas and dove over the side, immediately pulling the failing sailor to air and supporting him until the cutters pulled them aboard and returned to the ship. The young midshipman was thereafter a hero to the crew.

At the end of this cruise, Captain Barry recommended Decatur for promotion to lieutenant. Decatur quickly proved that he deserved the nomination. Following the cruise, as was often the case, some of the sailors had "run," and Decatur was sent to find them. He located some of them aboard a merchantman, went aboard and—following the advice of his father—challenged the ringleader to a duel. Having devoted extensive practice to personal weapons, Decatur declared his intention of merely wounding the offending party and proceeded to do so, returning with all the deserters in tow. None of this harmed his professional prospects.

At the age of 22 Decatur was appointed first lieutenant on *Essex*, sailing in 1801 for the Barbary coast under the command of William Bainbridge. *Essex* provided armed protection from pirates for American shipping and got into a scrape with the commanding officer of a Spanish guardship in Barcelona. To force the American captain to come aboard for recognition, the Spanish officer fired shots over Bainbridge's gig one evening. Seeking to avoid an incident, Bainbridge ignored it. The following night, Decatur was in the gig and the firing was repeated. Decatur came aboard the Spanish guardship at daylight but was refused his request to see the offending officer. Decatur, referring to the prizes awarded matadors in bullfights, said, "Very well, tell him that Lieutenant Decatur of the frigate *Essex* pronounces him a cowardly scoundrel and that when they meet on shore, he will cut his ears off." There was no more firing.

Lieutenant Decatur was soon thereafter given command of the schooner *Enterprise* (12) and sent along with the brig *Argus* (18) to join *Constitution* in the western Mediterranean in November 1803. Under the command of Edward Preble, the squadron's first mission was to destroy *Philadelphia*, now in the hands of the Tripolitans.

In February of the next year, with seventy-four men from his own command, a Sicilian pilot, Salvatore Catalano, for navigation and deception, and five midshipmen from *Constitution*, Decatur embarked in *Intrepid*, a captured lateen-rigged ketch, to escape detection. He glided swiftly alongside *Philadelphia* in the harbor of Tripoli. Overcoming surprised opposition, Decatur's men set fire to the captured ship. With flames blowing over their only means of escape, guns from the shore batteries and other Tripolitan ships began to speak. *Intrepid* made good its escape just ahead of a colossal explosion that disintegrated *Philadelphia*. Horatio Nelson called the feat "the most bold and daring act of the age."

The squadron's campaign against Tripoli concluded in August with a bombardment of shore targets in Tripoli in which Decatur rammed, boarded and overpowered a far more heavily manned enemy vessel. Stephen was joined in the engagement by his brother, Lieutenant James Decatur, who forced the surrender of a Tripolitan vessel and was then shot fatally in the head by the enemy captain *after* he had struck his colors. Stephen learned his brother's fate while towing out the enemy ship he had just taken. Enraged, he turned back, plowed into the side of the treacherous Barbary ship, boarded her and personally killed his brother's murderer.

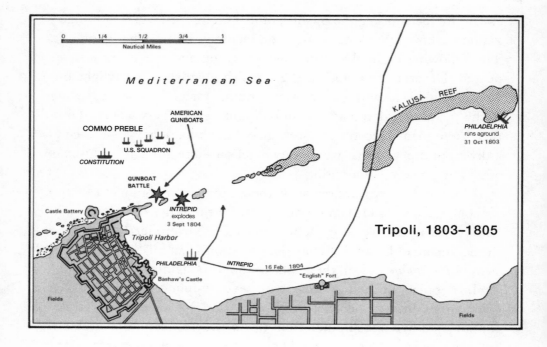

When the relieving squadron arrived, Decatur was promoted to the rank of captain.

In the War of 1812, Decatur was given his own command, the first ship on which he had served, *United States,* and he proved he also had a natural instinct for public relations. After defeating the British frigate *Macedonian* (38), he spent two weeks lying to and repairing his shattered prize so that he could bring it back to New London in triumph. In a move worthy of Douglas MacArthur or George Patton, Decatur sent one of his lieutenants, Archibald Hamilton, son of the Navy secretary, to the naval ball that had been planned to honor Isaac Hull following *Constitution*'s brilliant capture of *Guerriere*—uninvited, of course. Lieutenant Hamilton rode hard for four days, appeared at the ball immediately after dismounting, greeted his parents and delivered *Macedonian*'s flag to an astonished President Madison along with an account of the successful action.

Unfortunately this triumphal return to American shores took place as British naval strength reached its peak in the Western Atlantic. Decatur, along with other Navy skippers, found themselves effectively blockaded in their own ports. Decatur, now commodore, moved his pennant from *United States* at New London to *President*, based in New York, where he thought he would have a better chance of breaking out. On January 14, 1815, as a northeaster scattered British ships, Decatur made his run for the open seas. Despite precautions that included marker boats in the channel with covered lights, the pilots ran the heavily provisioned ship hard aground, breaking her keel and providing time for the British squadron to come up.

Badly injured by the grounding, *President* engaged *Endymion* (44), a large frigate armed with 24-pounders that had been one of four enemy ships in the area specifically sent to America to try to deal with the superfrigates. Decatur managed to turn to deliver broadsides into *Endymion* and seriously damage her masts and sails. But he could not make good his escape before the arrival of *Pomone* (38), *Tenedos* (38) and the much more powerful *Majestic* (54). Decatur surrendered.

He returned from a short captivity in Bermuda, after being exchanged for British prisoners, and found himself as much in demand as ever and admired for his courage and skill. From the shipwrights of New York who pledged 1,600 hours of labor on a replacement frigate for the one he had lost, to the musical tributes of New London, to the Navy's offer of another command, Decatur received a hero's welcome.

By this time the early treaties with the Berber pashas had proved to be worthless. Seizures by their corsairs had begun again almost as soon as the ink was dry and continued steadily through the punitive expeditions launched by the American Navy against them from 1798 through the War of 1812. With the War of 1812 over and the United States at last possessed of a Navy full of combat experience and great self-confidence, Commodore Stephen Decatur was sent to settle these pirates "once and for all."

A week and a day after the peace treaty with England was ratified in 1815, President Madison asked Congress for a declaration of war on Algiers, which had declared war on the United States, captured two

American merchant ships, enslaved their crews and ordered her Navy to prey upon American shipping in the area. In May 1815, Decatur embarked to do battle in *Guerriere* (44), a new frigate named for the British frigate sunk by *Constitution*. Anxious to make up for the loss of *President* to the British, he led a squadron including *Constellation, Macedonian,* a new sloop, three brigs and two schooners to the Mediterranean.

The squadron located and engaged the large Algerian flagship *Mashouda* (46), forcing her to strike, but only after slicing the enemy admiral, Rais Hammida, into halves by cannon shot. Continuing northeast, Decatur encountered, defeated and made a prize of the heavy brig *Estedio* (22). He headed for Algiers with his victories, transmitting word of his presence in the region, whereupon he secured release of all prisoners and dictated a peace treaty "at the mouths of our cannons."

Before sailing home from Gibraltar, Decatur performed one more task—one of his own initiative. Contrary to accepted international practice at the time, the British prizes captured by the Boston privateer *Abaellino*, which had been sent to the neutral ports of Tunis and Tripoli, were confiscated by local authorities and then handed back to the British. Decatur sailed into Tunis and demanded compensation in the amount of $46,000. The commodore's reputation did the trick and the Dey turned over the money rather than risk bloodshed.

Decatur, alone now, then sailed *Guerriere* into Tripoli to demand compensation for the prizes wrongfully turned over to the British from that port. There he encountered the entire Algerian fleet—seven ships. When asked where he was bound, Decatur answered in words that Admiral "Bull" Halsey used again 132 years later: "American ships sail where they please." Thus ended "once and for all" the Barbary wars.

It was also the end of Stephen Decatur's life as a seagoing naval officer and the beginning of his short career as a staff officer. Appointed to the Board of Naval Commissioners, Decatur chose and argued persuasively for the selection of Norfolk as the Navy's major Atlantic base. Sailing a desk, however, did not please him. Unhappy with the frustrations of bureaucracy and dealing with the Navy's contractors, Decatur in 1818 wrote to a friend: "What shall I do? We have no war, nor sign of a war, and I shall feel ashamed to die in my bed." Unfortunately—for the Navy and the nation although not for Decatur's renown—he escaped the death he was ashamed to contemplate.

As commissioner he had opposed the application of Captain James Barron to command of the new ship of the line *Columbus* (74). Barron had been skipper of *Chesapeake* during Jefferson's administration when the British *Leopard* (56) had approached him and demanded to be allowed to search Barron's frigate for British seamen. Barron was overwhelmed without a fight when *Leopard* fired as many as seven broadsides into *Chesapeake* at point-blank range. The townspeople of Norfolk were sufficiently angry at the outcome of this one-sided engagement that they nearly lynched the Royal Navy lieutenant who came ashore with dispatches for the British consul. Decatur cited the incident in declining Barron's request to command *Columbus*.

Believing that he had been dishonored, Barron challenged Decatur to a duel in a series of letters. Decatur tried to prevent the affair, but eventually agreed. They met on a field in Bladensburg, Maryland, on March 22, 1820. Both men were injured in the exchange, Decatur fatally. He was returned to his home across from the White House at Lafayette Square, where he died several hours later. His widow lived in the house for a few years before the house was sold to a succession of prominent owners, eventually passing into the Beall family. In 1958 the house was to be bequeathed to the Navy as the official residence of the Navy secretary. President Eisenhower, however, was planning on dropping the office of Navy secretary from the cabinet and had no desire to see it dignified by such a beautiful residence—and so close to his. He arranged to have the house given to the National Trust for Historic Preservation. The secretary of the Navy today has only the right to use it for official entertaining. I did so often.

THE WARS WITH THE BERBER PASHAS and with Revolutionary France had established the U.S. Navy not only as an elite fighting force, but as a permanent American institution. Its successes and its heroes ensured continuing public support and congressional funding. Extensive action had created a corps of experienced leaders and a glamorous career to which adventurous youth could aspire.

Nearly as important, the battle-testing of the dramatic design innovations of Humphreys and others provided the U.S. Navy with individual ships superior to any equivalent in the world.

As America soon found itself snarled in Britain's war against Napoleon, it would soon need every one of these naval assets.

IV

THE WAR OF 1812

THE AMERICAN NAVY has had several "golden ages" according to its chroniclers. Most recently the Reagan era of the "600-ship Navy" is now so described by many Navy veterans. My father's generation, with undisputed justification, looked on the years of their naval service in the great Pacific war of 1941–1945 as the greatest of all golden ages. But until that war the golden age of the U.S. Navy was always viewed as the era of the War of 1812, and with good reason. Certainly no era better demonstrates that the course of history has often been affected by great naval individuals and great and unusual ships.

Before the War of 1812 the young republic did not have an organized naval service in the truest sense. Gradually, the need to defend the commerce of the fragile new nation against warring European powers, Barbary pashas and pirates created the foundations of the U.S. Navy in fits and starts. It also produced battle-experienced naval commanders of a very high quality.

But with the possible exception of Herbert Hoover, no American president had more antipathy to navalism than Thomas Jefferson, and by 1808 he had succeeded in reducing the Navy to almost nothing. He believed that small, defensive gunboats should be the extent of the Navy: "gunboats are the only water defense which can be useful to us and protect us from the ruinous folly of a Navy. . . ." Most of the officers who were to fight the War of 1812 were either ashore on half-pay or at sea on American merchantmen during the Jefferson administration. Yet the very hostility of their government bound them together in an astonishingly high *esprit de corps*. Jefferson himself worried about them as "a seagoing aristocracy." One hundred and forty years later,

Harry Truman echoed the same sentiments when he described the Navy as "a bunch of fancy Dans."

The War of 1812—or as it was often then referred to, "the second war of Independence"—was a direct result of the Napoleonic Wars between Britain and France from 1793 to 1814. Many historians have taken the position that the war was unnecessary and almost inexplicable. It was neither. The United States was still very much a maritime nation with most of its internal commerce traveling by coastal shipping, and much of its wealth created by international trade with Europe and the Caribbean sugar islands, and in whaling and fisheries. Because of American neutrality in the Napoleonic Wars, a huge opportunity was opened up for American merchantmen. They could carry Continental trade goods where they were allowed access to European continental ports as neutrals so long as they stopped in an American port along the way. This trade circumvented the British blockade of the Continent and increased American trade some thirtyfold from the blockade's start to 1807. Because American agricultural goods were carried on the east-bound leg, the growth of American trade came at the expense of the British sugar islands, cutting their exports almost in half. The impact on the British economy was so severe that in 1806 the British unilaterally revoked the rights of neutrals, especially Americans, to trade. A severe decline hit American traders, shipowners and the entire agricultural economy of the United States.

Closely related was the issue of impressment. During the height of the Napoleonic Wars, the Royal Navy maintained nearly 1,000 ships in commission requiring more than 150,000 officers and men to sail them. A frigate, for instance, of which the Royal Navy had more than 110 in commission, required more than 300 seamen, and a first-rate line-of-battle ship like HMS *Victory* required nearly 1,000. After decades of warfare, the Royal Navy had long been scraping the bottom of the barrel and was short of manpower throughout its fleet. Impressment, the involuntary seizure of merchant seamen and able-bodied landsmen for service aboard men-of-war, had long been legal and normal practice in time of war by the British, and occasionally other Continental powers.

After 1806 the Royal Navy aggressively asserted the right to stop and search American merchantmen and even American warships for British deserters.

The issue was complicated by the fact that at the time the accents and speech of most Americans and most British were little different. Issues of citizenship were also complex. The Crown maintained that anyone born in Britain was always a subject of the king. Every American born in the colonies before Independence was claimed as a British subject.

American merchant and warship captains of course welcomed the appearance aboard their ships of highly experienced British deserters. Naturalization and citizenship papers could be had by simply swearing allegiance. There were indeed many British-born deserters aboard American ships, and the Royal Navy (quite apart from the morality of impressment), had a legitimate reason to search. But the Royal Navy undoubtedly took extreme advantage of the situation. The memoirs of all participants leave no doubt that when an American ship was searched, many native-born Americans had their credentials torn up and were pressed into the Royal Navy simply because they were needed. Some estimates count 300 Americans in the 1,000-man crew of Nelson's flagship, HMS *Victory*, at Trafalgar.

In addition to these very real maritime issues, there were many Americans who were looking for an excuse to invade and annex Canada; Thomas Jefferson himself was tempted.

A final cause of war-fever was the humiliating attack by the British man-of-war *Leopard* (56 guns) upon the American frigate *Chesapeake* (36) at Hampton Roads in Chesapeake Bay in 1807, at the very spot that Admiral de Grasse had anchored his fleet prior to the battle of the Capes in 1781. *Leopard* suddenly opened fire on an unsuspecting *Chesapeake*, killing and wounding nineteen American sailors, boarded her and took off four alleged deserters, all of whom had indeed deserted from the Royal Navy but three of whom were native-born Americans who had been impressed to begin with. One was hanged as an example.

The Americans were blessed with a robust maritime industry and a shipbuilding tradition that had produced a class of super-frigate that was the best all-around ship of war in the era of sail. But the policies of Jefferson and his successor, Madison, ensured that there were insufficient frigates to mount any decisive challenge to the superiority of the Royal Navy in American waters.

When the War of 1812 began, there were only seventeen ships available for operations. Because of the lack of numbers, and a fear that concentrating them in squadron-size operations would risk losing all in a single engagement, a wise decision was made in the first months of the war by Secretary of the Navy Paul Hamilton to deploy the Navy's scarce warships in single-ship operations to attack British commerce and seek out individual British warships for attack.

The Navy of 1812 included a few veterans of the War of the Revolution who had served under John Barry, John Paul Jones and other legends. The officers were veterans of the undeclared war with France and the numerous forays against the Barbary pashas. Their seamen were for the most part well-fed, well-paid volunteers bred to the sea in the merchantmen, whalers and fishermen of this maritime nation. Many of them were also professionals, having served in the privateersmen and Navy of the Revolution and the undeclared wars of the turn of the century. Thus, while small, the American naval service of June 1812 was a superb, elite fighting force. It was a universe apart from the ragtag crew of 1776.

Because of Jefferson's ideological preference for small gunboats (reminiscent of anti-carrier reformers of the 1970s), the U.S. Navy was in no material condition to fight Britannia's rule of the waves. By 1808 there were but one frigate and two sloops in commission. The Royal Navy had three well-equipped naval shipyards in North America.

Even by 1812, there still had not been a significant warship put on order or under construction. When war was finally declared by a reluctant President Madison on June 18, 1812, he gave Congress a list of four grievances: illegal impressment, illegal blockades, refusal to recognize the American rights of neutrality, and support of Indian attacks on American settlements in the west. At that time the U.S. fleet consisted of seventeen ships: nine frigates and eight smaller vessels, plus Jefferson's gunboats. The Royal Navy had more than 1,000 ships, including 120 line-of-battle ships plus 110 frigates deployed around the world.

Yet, because of Secretary of the Navy Hamilton's canny single-ship operations, the first year of the war proved an unsettling shock to the British and a huge boost to the new republic.

The first shot of the war was fired by Commodore John Rogers in the frigate *President* (44) against the British frigate *Belvidere* (36). The battle was something of a draw. The first naval success came with the cruise of the small frigate *Essex* (32) in which Master Commandant David Porter captured the British sloop-of-war *Alert* (20) on August 13. The next success came not in a victory but in an escape, when the frigate *Constitution* (44), commanded by Captain Isaac Hull, succeeded in escaping a British squadron of seven ships through brilliant seamanship, within sight of what is now the Trump Casino in Atlantic City, New Jersey.

But the first *real* jolt to the complacency, if not arrogance, of the Royal Navy came on August 19 with the first engagement of ships of the same class, the frigate *Constitution* and the British frigate *Guerriere* (38). Because of the excellence of the design and construction of *Constitution* and the marked superiority of her gunnery crews, the battle was over in less than an hour with the British ship so badly damaged that she was burned and sunk. *Guerriere* lost seventy-nine men killed and wounded whereas *Constitution* was only slightly damaged and suffered fourteen killed and wounded. The news was like a thunderclap around the world and filled the United States with celebrations.

On October 25 came the second severe jolt to the Royal Navy with another duel, between the brand-new British frigate *Macedonian* (38) and *United States* (44). In a hard-fought action lasting less than two hours, *United States* proved that *Constitution*'s victory over *Guerriere* in August was not a fluke.

MACEDONIAN AND SOME OF HER PEOPLE

Among the joys of deerstalking and hiking in the Scottish highlands are the dramatic vistas of treeless moors and mountains covered in heather and bracken. It is hard walking, however, because there are constant lumps, tussocks and unseen holes. If the walker troubles to dig through the layer of turf and lays a patch bare, he will find the cause: ancient tree stumps, and pits from rotted stumps. It is hard to envision today, but only a few hundred years ago these hills were thickly forested. They disappeared, along with most forests in England and Wales, to build the thousands of ships for the East India and other trading companies that created the British Empire and the men-of-war that protected it.

It took the clearcutting of about forty acres to build one line-of-battle ship. Once cut, sheep in the lowlands, and red deer in the highlands, grazed away any chance of regrowing the forests. The last known deer predator—a lone wolf—was shot in the mid-18th century and the deer population exploded.

By the time of the American Revolution, the Royal Navy was almost entirely dependent on the new world for its oak skantlings (the ship's framework), planking and tall pine masts. After that war commercial prices for American timber drove British shipbuilders to the Baltic, where the wood was cheap but inferior.

The problem was increased by a deeply rooted corruption in the British naval shipyards. As early as 1668, the great diarist Samuel Pepys wrote matter-of-factly about it. He had become the *de facto* secretary of the Navy for Charles II, a post, he confided to his diary, that was coveted "not for what one is paid, but what one has the opportunity of getting while in the job." A century later, the first lord of the admiralty, Lord Sandwich (who invented the sandwich) allowed that already-entrenched corruption to grow to such an extreme that it was estimated only about half of the monies appropriated to the Royal Navy actually produced any goods or services. Rotten food and defective materiel delivered with handsome kickbacks were the norm.

It was from such dubious provenance that His Britannic Majesty's frigate *Macedonian* was born at the Woolwich naval dockyard on June 2, 1810. She was the third frigate built from the original drawings, and the first two, *Lively* and *Undaunted*, had established reputations as "well found" and very fast. She was the largest-size frigate, at 38 guns, then being built by the Royal Navy. They had experimented with designs almost as big as the American superfrigates, armed like the Americans with 24-pound guns rather than the 18-pounders then standard, but had abandoned them because their ships were not strong or stable enough to handle such big guns.

The commissioning skipper of *Macedonian* was Captain Lord William FitzRoy, the 29-year-old third son of the Duke of Grafton. FitzRoy illustrated the unique social mix that was the Royal Navy. Unlike the army, in which commissions were purchased and wherein it was extremely difficult to rise from the ranks, the Royal Navy had long been a source of upward mobility for ambitious and talented young men without privilege. It also was an honorable profession for the non-inheriting sons of the aristocracy like FitzRoy, not least because the service offered the opportunity of making substantial fortunes through prize money.

FitzRoy would have to seek his fortune elsewhere, as his contribution to *Macedonian*'s history was minor and brief. Unlike commissioning skippers in the United States, FitzRoy did not see his ship until it was afloat. The ship that was to defeat *Macedonian*, *United States*, in the continuing practice of the U.S. Navy, had its captain on site from the time its keel was laid to see that the little details born of experience would be incorporated in the ship. The sole contribution made by FitzRoy to *Macedonian*'s construction was to improve the luxury of the appointments of the captain's cabin. As it turned out that effort helped to keep *Macedonian* a prominent ship in its later service in the U.S. Navy, as famous naval persons chose the ship above others because of the comforts of the captain's cabin.

FitzRoy did not last beyond his first shakedown cruise, carrying troops to Wellington's army in Lisbon. When he arrived he was court-martialed and dismissed from the service following a bitter feud with his sailing master.

After two interim skippers, Captain John Carden took command of *Macedonian*. Carden had the typical career of the era, serving mostly at sea during the Napoleonic Wars, including duty in India, Africa and Ireland. Like many upper-class British of the time, he was decidedly anti-American. His father had been killed fighting in the Revolution, and his family had lost their fortune by investing in the colonies. He was not happy when his first orders dictated he sail *Macedonian* from Lisbon to Norfolk, Virginia, with official dispatches, including a large shipment of secret money drafts.

Carden's fears were confirmed. The dispatches that he had sent on to Washington were revealed as a scheme by perfidious Albion, and he was humiliated. But while he was in Norfolk awaiting the return of his mission, he was entertained several times by Stephen Decatur, whose ship *United States* was then based in Norfolk. As was his wont, Decatur apparently boasted to Carden of the great superiority of his frigate and of the effectiveness of its large 24-pound cannons. Carden responded that the Royal Navy liked 18-pounders better on frigates and was dismissive of the big American 44s. *Macedonian* was anchored almost alongside *United States* during the entire stay. Alas, so biased was Carden that he didn't once bother to inspect her. It is said that on their last meeting the two men wagered a beaver hat on the outcome of the battle between them if it ever came to pass, and there seemed little doubt that there would soon be war between their nations. ("I see trouble for Britain in those big frigates across the sea," Lord Nelson had observed when he first heard of them ten years before Carden's visit to Norfolk.)

Carden returned from Norfolk to Lisbon and then to England, where he used his influence to get assigned to the western ocean where he would have the opportunity to take on the Americans, war having just been declared. *The Times* expressed the general British view of the new enemy, "a few fir-built frigates with strips of bunting, manned by sons-of-bitches and outlaws." Carden surely agreed. On October 25, 1812, he got the opportunity to win a beaver hat when, on the edge of the Sargasso Sea, Carden encountered his old friend from Norfolk, Stephen Decatur in *United States*.

Decatur had originally sailed as part of a squadron with Com-

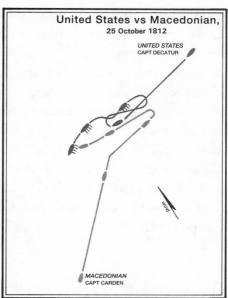

modore Rogers, but he had no desire to share credit for the actions that he sought, and like Rogers he had been raised to commodore rank. While *United States* was one of the superfrigates, she had the reputation of being the slowest of all of them, and had been nicknamed "the wagon" (the source of reference ever after in the U.S. Navy to battleships as "battlewagons"). *Macedonian* was in fact a distinctly faster ship and better sailer, as her long experience in the U.S. Navy would prove.

The crew of *United States* was more than fully manned at 478. *Macedonian*'s crew was slightly undermanned at 301. This numerical advantage could be important in the number and rapidity of guns firing, the numbers of sharpshooters aloft in the rigging and potentially decisive in the event of boarding. Equally important was the difference in the amount of firepower. The American superfrigate fired a broadside amounting to 786 pounds of iron compared to *Macedonian*'s 547.

Decatur was well aware that his fellow captain Isaac Hull in command of *Constitution* had drawn first blood with his capture of *Guerriere*. But in Decatur's eyes Hull had made a blunder by burning and sinking *Guerriere* rather than risk bringing her back to the U.S. as a prize. Decatur was determined to make no such mistake, and even to minimize damage to his adversary so that she could be sailed back with a prize crew. He adopted tactics to take advantage of the extra range of his 24-pounders and to keep his distance and dismantle his opponent's rigging. Despite repeated attempts by Carden to close, Decatur was able through brilliant seamanship to keep the distance that retained his advantage and to pound away with his long guns. *Macedonian* lost her mizzen and much of her upper rigging but continued to fight on, while *United States'* long guns picked her to pieces. With *Macedonian* uncontrollable, Decatur took his time and twice crossed his helpless opponent's bows in a devastating raking position, but held his fire while he waited for Carden to come to his senses and surrender.

SAMUEL LEECH:
A VOICE FROM THE MAIN DECK.

When Lord Fitzroy departed *Macedonian*, he left behind a ship's boy, Samuel Leech, age 14, whom he had brought aboard at commissioning. His account of the battle is vivid.

Leech's mother and father were servants to various members of the Spencer and Churchill families of the Duke of Marlborough and Leech started life as a child working in the gardens in Blenheim palace, the family seat. Through his mother's influence with Lady Spencer, at the age of 12 Leech was signed on as a ship's boy under Lord William Fitzroy, Lady Spencer's brother, who was taking command of *Macedonian*. This was a great opportunity, since it was the normal first step to becoming a midshipman and officer in the Royal Navy. Boys were normally employed first as servants to the officers, and Leech began as a servant to the ship's surgeon. At battle stations the boys (normally aged 10–14) were assigned as a member of the nine-man crew serving each of the big guns. They were known as "powder monkeys," their job to run back and forth delivering the gunpowder cartridges from the magazine to the gun.

While *Macedonian* was in Lisbon preparing to sail to the American station, Leech recounted the traditional method of recruitment: "Being in want of men, we resorted to the press gang, which was made up of our most loyal men, armed to the teeth; by their aid we obtained our full numbers. Among them were a few Americans; they were taken without respect to their protections (proof of American citizenship) which were often taken from them and destroyed."

With a nearly full complement *Macedonian* sailed for the American station. Then, on the morning of October 25, 1812, "We had scarcely finished breakfast, before the man at the masthead shouted, 'sail ho!' The captain rushed upon deck exclaiming 'mast-head there!' 'Sir!' 'Where away is the sail?' . . . 'What does she look like?' 'A square rigged vessel sir' was the reply of the lookout. 'A large ship sir, standing toward us!' 'A large frigate, bearing down upon us, sir!' A whisper ran along the crew that the stranger ship was a Yankee frigate. The thought was confirmed by the commander 'All hands clear the ship for action, awhay!'"

The rest of Leech's account is as follows:

My station was at the fifth gun on the main deck. It was my duty to supply my gun with powder . . . a woolen screen was placed before the entrance to the magazine, with a hole in it, through which the cartridges were passed to the boys; we received them there, and covering them with our jackets, hurried to our respective guns.

Then came the order to 'wear ship' and prepare to attack the enemy with our starboard guns. Soon after this I heard a firing from some other quarter, which I at first supposed to be a discharge from our quarterdeck guns; though it proved to be the roar of the enemy's cannon.

A strange noise such I had never heard before, next arrested my attention; it sounded like the tearing of sails, just over our heads. This I soon ascertained to be the wind of the enemy's shot. The firing, after a few minutes cessation, we commenced. The roaring of the cannon could now be heard from all parts of our trembling ship, and, mingling as it did with that of our foes it made a most hideous noise. By-and-by I heard the shots strike the side of our ship; the whole scene grew indescribably confused and horrible; it was like some awfully tremendous thunderstorm, whose deafening roar is attended by incessant streaks of lightening, carrying death in every flash, and strewing the ground with the victims of its wraths: only, in our case, the scene was rendered more horrible than that, by the presence of torrents of blood which dyed our decks . . .

The cries of the wounded now rang through all parts of the ship. These were carried to the cockpit as fast as they fell, while those more fortunate men, who were killed outright, were immediately thrown overboard. As I was stationed but a short distance from the main hatchway, I could catch a glance at all who were carried below. A glance was all I could indulge in, for the boys belonging to the guns next to mine were wounded in the early part of the action, and I had to spring with all my might to keep three or four guns supplied with cartridges. I saw two of these lads fall nearly together. One of them was struck in the leg by a large shot; he had to suffer amputation above the wound. The other had a grape or canister shot sent through his ankle. A stout Yorkshireman lifted him in his arms, and carried him to the cockpit. He had his foot cut off, and was thus made lame for life. Two of the boys stationed on the quarterdeck were killed. They were both Portuguese. A man who saw one of them killed, afterwards told me that his powder caught fire and burnt the flesh almost off his face. In this pitiable situation, the agonized boy lifted up both his hands, as if imploring relief, when a passing shot instantly cut him in two.

I was an eye-witness to a sight equally revolting. A man named Aldrich had one of his hands cut off by a shot, and almost at the same moment he received another shot which tore open his bowels in a terrible manner. As he fell two or three men caught him in their arms and as he could not live, threw him overboard. . . .

I have often been asked what were my feelings during this fight. I felt pretty much as I suppose everyone does at such a time. That men are without thought when they stand amid the dying and the dead, as too absurd to be entertained a moment. We all appeared cheerful, but I know that many a serious thought ran through my mind: still, what could we do but keep up a semblance, at least, of animation? To run from our quarters would have been certain death from the hands of our own officers; to give way to gloom, or to show fear, would be no good, and might brand us with the name of cowards and insure certain defeat. Our only true philosophy, therefore, was to make the best of our situation, by fighting bravely and cheerfully. I thought a great deal however of the other world; every groan, every falling man, told me that the next instant I might be before the judge of all the earth . . .

Suddenly, the rattling of the iron hail ceased. We were ordered to cease firing. A profound silence ensued, broken only by the stifled groans of the brave sufferers below . . . we were in the state of a complete wreck . . . any further resistance was therefore folly. So . . . it was determined to strike our bunting. This was done by the hands of a brave fellow named Watson, whose saddened brow told how severely it pained his lionheart to do it. To me it was a pleasing sight, for I had seen fighting enough for one Sabbath; more than I wished to see again on a weekday. His Britannic Majesty's frigate *Macedonian* was now the prize of the American frigate *United States*.

After Carden struck his colors he was rowed across to his adversary to present his sword. Decatur, on the quarterdeck in his usual eccentric garb, this time a large straw hat against the sun, gallantly refused Carden's sword and complimented him on his courageous defense. He then joked to his captain of Marines, "You call yourselves riflemen, and have allowed this very tall and erect officer, on an open quarterdeck to escape your aim. How was it that you let such a figure of a man survive unscathed?" In fact the Marine sharpshooters had shot all but nine of the fifty-two officers and men who had manned *Macedonian*'s quarter-deck.

The damage to *Macedonian*, despite Decatur's efforts, was severe. In addition to being dismasted she had seven feet of water in her hold and many shotholes below the water line. Her decks were full of carnage with thirty-six dead and sixty-eight wounded. The *United States* by contrast had only one penetration of the hull and only seven killed and five wounded. Determined to bring in his prize, Decatur spent two full weeks standing to, repairing the damage and jury-rigging the sails. *Macedonian* was then sailed back with the *United States*, setting off national celebrations and further igniting Decatur's fame when she arrived in Newport. Even in her jury-rigged condition, *Macedonian* outsailed the *United States* on the return voyage.

Back in New York, a prisoner, Leech escaped and became an American. He shipped out on the brig *Syren* (16) which was captured by the British off of Africa. After prison in England, he returned to America and shipped out again on the brig *Boxer* for two years. He then came ashore married, prospered and lived happily even after in Boston.

Macedonian was bought into the U.S. Navy for the sum of $200,000. She was swiftly overhauled and made ready to join the war effort under the command of Captain Jacob Jones, who had recently achieved fame in *Wasp* (18) with his capture of the British *Frolic* (18). Unfortunately the British blockade was now steadily closing upon *Macedonian*, and when she made sail in 1813, in the company of Decatur and *United States*, they got only as far as Montauk Point on Long Island before being chased into New London by a large British squadron. There both ships remained, unable to escape until the end of the war.

It was not the end of *Macedonian*'s career. As already recounted, she went on to give exemplary service against the Barbary pirates, was mothballed for years, and was finally rebuilt in 1837 and relaunched as flagship of the West Indies squadron based in Pensacola under Commodore William Shubrick. In August 1840 she returned north and while visiting the Brooklyn Navy Yard was opened to the public for tours. One of the first to come on board was none other than Samuel Leech, now an American.

MACEDONIAN WAS KEPT ON active duty through the 1840s, including three years on the coast of West Africa in the antislavery patrol. In 1847 she was used in a unique disaster-relief mission when George DeKay (the great grandfather of James DeKay, author of an excellent book on the ship), a wealthy former sea captain living in New York, organized a private relief mission to the starving people of Ireland in the grip of the great famine. *Macedonian* carried the donated food to Cork amid great publicity.

That might have been the end of *Macedonian* but for her splendid cabin. Commodore Matthew Perry had served on *Macedonian* on the African station and knew firsthand that she had the most comfortable accommodations of any American warship. *Macedonian* was therefore included in his mission to open the strictly closed ports of Japan to American commerce. The result of Perry's mission was the Treaty of Kanagawa, entered into on March 30, 1854. *Macedonian* then became flagship of the new Asiatic squadron, and remained in Hong Kong. She returned from the China station to Boston Navy Yard in 1856 and was refitted for deployment to the Mediterranean. When she was completed a new captain was assigned. His name was Uriah Philips Levy, and he promptly directed the ship's carpenter to install a mezuzah on the frame of Lord Fitzroy's great cabin door.

COMMODORE URIAH PHILIPS LEVY: PRIDE AND PREJUDICE

Levy's love of country—and adventure—led him to the U.S. Navy, and he served with distinction if not complete success during the War of 1812 on *Argus* during its famous raid on Channel shipping. He was entrusted with a prize-ship, thereby avoiding the capture of *Argus* in August 1813. He was, however, captured soon after and survived sixteen months in the notorious Dartmoor prison. There, too, his luck held. He was released days before the massacre of American prisoners in the riot of April 6, 1815.

While the big American frigates remained blockaded in port during most of that period, Levy's imprisonment kept him from the most active naval period of the war on the Great Lakes, the British raiding in the Chesapeake and the height of American raiding of British commerce.

But it is not his service in the War of 1812 for which Levy is remembered today. In 1783, the Constitution of the United States forbade the establishment of an official religion and prescribed equal rights for all citizens. These truly revolutionary acts were imposed upon a society European in origin and full of the prejudices of the era.

Uriah Philips Levy, a practicing Jew from Philadelphia who eventually became commodore of the Mediterranean squadron, was the personality that put the Revolution to test by launching a celebrated Naval Board of Inquiry that exposed anti-Semitism in the service. Levy's career illustrated not only his pride and the Navy's prejudice in America's first century, but also the great potential of the American experiment.

Levy was born of a distinguished lineage. His maternal great-grandfather had been one Dr. Samuel Nunez, physician-in-waiting to the king of Portugal who had secretly maintained his Judaism while publicly professing Christianity. In 1732, Nunez, whose family had evaded the Inquisition for a hundred and thirty years, fled Portugal steps ahead of arrest. He landed in Charlestown, where he openly practiced Judaism and resumed the family name of Machado. His daughter, Rebecca, married Jonas Philips, a poor emigrant from Prussia. (Among the wedding guests on November 10, 1762, was George Washington, described in the guest list as a planter from Virginia.) Later, the family moved to Philadelphia, where Jonas became a prominent merchant who served as a foot soldier in the Revolution. He was also elected the first *parnas*, or president, of the newly organized

Mikve Israel of Philadelphia, known as the Portuguese synagogue, which still exists today.

Among Philips's twenty-one children was Rachel Philips, who followed her mother's example and married another poor German immigrant, Michael Levy, also destined to become a successful merchant. Rachel bore Michael fourteen children, the third of whom, Uriah, came into the world on April 22, 1792.

The small Jewish community in colonial America (about 3,500 all told, perhaps 500 in Philadelphia) was extraordinarily close-knit. But unlike the heavily restricted European countries from which many of colonial America's Jews had come, they were also equal in law. Uriah Levy was to take the American promise very seriously, describing himself as "an American, a sailor, and a Jew."

At age 10, bewitched by the seafaring life he could see every day along the Philadelphia docks, Uriah Levy ran away for a two-year apprenticeship. Paid $4 a month, he stipulated a two-year contract so he could return in time for his bar mitzvah. He also declined the standard seafaring rations of shellfish and pork, observing the Jewish dietary laws as best he could.

True to his word, after two adventurous years at sea, he returned to his joyful parents. Shortly after the bar mitzvah, he announced his intention of becoming a professional sailor. Old Jonas Philips and his father arranged for him to serve in the fleet of a prominent Philadelphia shipowner, John Coulter.

Uriah Levy was a lucky man. He went to sea carrying on his person a certificate of American citizenship. Still, in 1809 he was impressed—that is, kidnapped—by the British Navy while on shore leave. In turn, he so impressed his captors that they offered him British citizenship, but he refused. Levy returned to America to sail again, only to be sunk by a French pirate and left with a few others adrift in an open boat for five days. Soon after, he earned the title of sailing master at age 20.

It was soon after his adventures in the War of 1812 that Levy encountered the two obstacles of his naval life: anti-Semitism and professional resentment. While there were a surprising number of Jews serving in the early American Navy during the Revolutionary War and

later the War of 1812, few made it a peacetime career. Worse, Levy had
never served as a midshipman, transferring laterally from his civilian
station as sailing master. Then as now, the Navy's officer cadre, having
come up through the ranks together, did not welcome outsiders. In
1817, Levy was granted a lieutenant's rank by the Board of Navy Commissioners, among them Stephen Decatur and David Porter, for his excellence in seamanship. As Levy himself put it, in addition to "the
prejudice generated by the promotion itself, there was also mingled
another of earlier date and greater intensity. . . ."

It was a combustible mix and Levy, a proud man, usually gave
better than he got in the then-customary fashion. Hard words were
followed by fisticuffs and sometimes more. In 1816 the socially prominent Levy (he was painted by Thomas Sully in 1817) attended the
Philadelphia Patriots Ball when he encountered Lieutenant William
Potter, an old enemy and open anti-Semite. Insults were exchanged
and Potter challenged Levy to a duel, although dueling was strictly for-
bidden by naval regulations and the laws of Pennsylvania. The two,
joined by their seconds, went across the river to Camden, New Jersey,
where on June 21, they exchanged shots. Potter missed. Levy then
fired in the air and announced his readiness to be satisfied with a written apology. Potter, who may not have been sober and was certainly a
poor shot, fired and reloaded three more times, finally grazing Levy's
ear, whereupon Levy shot him dead. We know all this because of the
subsequent court-martial, the first of six that Levy was to endure, only
one of which had anything to do with seamanship.

Levy was not a conventional sailor either. He grossly offended the
service through his increasing agitation against the practice of flogging.
Ordinary seamen, unlike officers, were considered a lower order of human to be kept in check by brutal methods. A drunken sailor, for example, could be chained in irons and then flogged, according to regulations
of 1799, no more than twelve lashes but very often given several times
that number. Levy proposed an alternative: that the man be put to bed,
admonished when sober, then put back to work. If a habitual drunk, he
would wear a bottle around his neck—a kind of shunning symbol that
might be very effective in the closed society of a warship.

Levy had plenty of time to perfect his ideas because like many officers, he was "on the beach" with half-pay for long periods of time. Levy used this time to enter the financial world of New York, where he prospered, cutting a wide swath. Finally appointed captain, then the highest rank, on February 9, 1837, at the age of 45, he won command of *Vandalia* a year later. This cruise ended in scandal: it was the first voyage of a U.S. warship where no flogging was permitted. Instead, to cite the case that led to his court-martial, he punished a cabin boy by having him strapped to a gun with trousers down. A bit of tar the size of a half-dollar plus a few feathers were then applied. The shocked court-martial ordered Levy's dismissal, but was overridden by President Tyler himself, who recommended that flogging not be used if an alternative existed. The Navy was not amused.

Despite frequent requests, Levy was given no further sea duty, even during the Mexican War. The reasons emerged during the celebrated Court of Inquiry touched off by Levy's protest when on September 13, 1855, he and 200 other officers were abruptly dismissed from service. Among those called to testify was my predecessor, George Bancroft (Secretary of the Navy, 1845–46), who among other things founded the Naval Academy. Bancroft offered three reasons for not giving Levy command: (1) too many officers, (2) younger men needed the experience, and (3) "strong prejudice . . . in a considerable part attributable to his being of the Jewish persuasion. . . ." Both Bancroft and the Navy's advocate general professed their shock that this prejudice might be widespread, but both saw "harmony at sea" as key to naval effectiveness.

Levy indignantly repudiated these excuses, producing witnesses that testified he had rigorously enforced the Christian Sabbath on his commands. He warned that prejudice against Jews would soon become prejudice against Catholics and Nonconformists and insisted that only "inflexible support" for the "impartial guarantees of the Constitution" was worthy of true Americans.

As a result of this sensational inquiry, Congress reinstated a third of the officers, including Levy. He was also rewarded in 1858—at the advanced age of 66—with the command of *Macedonian*. This was followed a year later with the rank of commodore in command of the Mediterranean fleet. He performed his duties under unusual circumstances. Levy had married his niece, Virginia Lopez, forty-three years his junior, and the Navy allowed her to accompany him on the voyage. Among other things, Levy took home a wagonload of earth from Palestine for the use of Congregation Shearith Israel in New York, where he had moved some years before.

Levy was a patriot who hated partisanship. On July 4, 1833, at a Paris dinner attended by the Marquis de Lafayette, he offered a toast to President Andrew Jackson. There followed hisses and boos whereupon Levy challenged the loudest of the protestors to a duel; the offender wisely chose a formal written apology instead. In 1837, appalled at the ruin of Monticello, Jefferson's estate (he had died a virtual bankrupt), Levy bought and restored it, often spending summers there. He buried his mother near the path to the house.

Uriah Philips Levy died in 1862 a rich man, without children, leaving an estate worth over $250,000. In his will he left Monticello to the people of the United States, or failing that, the state of Virginia. But he had reckoned without the Civil War and the skill of lawyers. After six years of litigation, the will was modified on grounds of vagueness and impracticality. Neither the federal government nor the state of Virginia wanted Jefferson's estate. Levy's wife, nieces and nephews quarreled, and Monticello fell into ruin until a nephew—Jefferson Levy—bought out the rest of the family and restored it. Finally in 1923, the current Monticello Foundation purchased it from him.

Levy wanted to be known as the man who abolished flogging in the Navy, but there were many who advocated this measure. Perhaps Levy's greatest contribution was his insistence on establishing an apprenticeship program that, by making the trade a profession, began to attract a better class of seaman, the sort who did not need to be flogged. He also proved that anti-Semitism would not stand in America against a determination to excel. Levy's words in the historic 1857 inquiry echo down to our own day: "It is important that I overcame the religious difficulty; not for my sake only, but for the sake of the Navy and the nation."

To Levy's story and that of his last ship, *Macedonian*, a final note must be appended. When the Civil War broke out in 1861 steam-powered warships had become the Navy's front line. Nevertheless, *Macedonian* was immediately put on blockade duty in the Gulf of Mexico. The following year she was ordered to the Naval Academy as a training ship, her final assignment. For eight years she made midshipmen cruises annually to destinations around the Atlantic. In 1871 she was put back into mothballs at the Norfolk Navy Yard, and then on December 31, 1875, the 65-year-old dowager was sold to the breakers for $14,071. In 1887 her timbers were used to build a hotel and tavern on City Island in New York City, in which Lord FitzRoy's great cabin was preserved intact. The resulting Macedonian Hotel was a popular watering spot on City Island until June 9, 1922, when it burned to the ground. *Macedonian*, after 112 years, passed from history.

ONE-HUNDRED AND TEN YEARS earlier, in the opening year of the War of 1812, a third decisive frigate action left no doubt as to the superiority of the American ships and their crews. In what was the most evenly matched of all the frigate battles *Constitution* (44) captured and destroyed *Java* (44) thirty miles off the coast of Brazil.

On December 26, 1812, Britain declared a blockade of both the Delaware and Chesapeake Bays, but allowed New England and New York to continue to trade. The reasons were that Baltimore and Philadelphia were the main sources of the privateers, and there was considerable antiwar sentiment in New England that the British hoped to exploit.

With the British so far in the war able only to capture a few small sloops and brigs, American naval momentum continued with the successful cruising of *Essex* and the sloop *Hornet* (18), which on February 24, 1813, captured the British brig *Peacock* (18) off British Guiana.

But in 1813 the British began to remind the Americans what command of the seas really meant. In March, Commodore, and later Rear Admiral Sir George Cockburn, aboard *Marlborough* (74), with several frigates and smaller vessels raided up and down the navigable rivers of Maryland and Virginia, destroying shipping and burning supplies and warehouses. It is easy to find local historians in Chestertown and Georgetown, Maryland, who will enthusiastically recount the depredations of Cockburn upon their towns.

It would take a great hero to stand up to Admiral Cockburn, and the hero who did it had to walk a strange and tortuous path. Much of the trouble was of Joshua Barney's own making. The American veteran of three wars was at one time an enemy of the United States.

JOSHUA BARNEY:
HERO OF THREE WARS

Joshua Barney is one of the most adventurous and colorful figures in American naval history yet also one of the least known.

Born in 1759 to a prosperous farming family not far from Baltimore, Barney went to sea at the age of 11. By the age of 15, thanks to the death at sea of his captain, Barney found himself in command of his first ship, *Sidney*, a merchantman out of Alexandria, Virginia. After a series of adventures, Barney returned home to discover that the colonies were now in rebellion. Returning his ship and a profit to its astonished owner, he immediately signed on as master's mate aboard the Continental sloop *Hornet* (10).

Barney went on to serve on several ships, including *Andrew Doria*, which received the first salute of the American flag on November 16, 1776, and *Saratoga*, which took many prizes. He was captured five different times by the British and once escaped from Old Mill Prison in Portsmouth, England, in 1782, returning to Philadelphia to meet his newborn son, William, for the first time. After the Revolutionary War, Barney was ranked fourth of the six captains in the new United States Navy, but refused to take the commission because it was below Silas Talbot's. He instead outfitted his own small fleet of privateers (having become rich by now off prize money) and took a commission in the French Navy in March 1796.

Barney later claimed, and all evidence supports, that he sedulously avoided combat with Americans while in the French Navy, but the fact that he served for France while she was at war with the United States was forever held against him. Barney seems to have been quite naive in this regard. He was surprised when, upon arrival in Baltimore in 1798 in command of a French squadron, he was greeted with derision. He was also blockaded in by the British. After several months he was able to get his two frigates out of the Chesapeake Bay in the dark of night.

His service to the French did much to damage Barney's reputation in the United States, but it made him a fortune in prize money. In 1798 he returned to Paris and became a favorite of Napoleon's. In 1800 he was awarded a pension and returned to Baltimore, where he lived as a gentleman farmer while continuing to invest in maritime trade.

When war finally came with Britain in 1812, Barney, still shunned by the U.S. Navy, outfitted a Baltimore schooner, *Rossie*, mounting 13 guns and with a Letter of Marque took to the sea again. He had not lost his touch. He captured four ships, eight brigs, three schooners and three sloops, totaling more than $1.5 million in value. By December 1812, however, the British under Cockburn had effectively blockaded the Chesapeake and Delaware Bays and were burning and pillaging towns and farms along the Chesapeake. Cockburn had become increasingly vexed at the guerilla tactics practiced by the Americans. He wrote that they "took every opportunity of firing with their rifles from behind trees or haystacks, or from windows of their houses upon our boats . . . in short whenever they thought they could get a mischievous shot at any of our people." He steadily increased his retribution, aiming to teach them "what they were liable to bring upon themselves by building batteries and acting towards us with so much useless rancour."

Barney was then living in Elk Ridge, Maryland, and he approached his friend President Madison with a plan to defend the Chesapeake with small gunboats equipped with oars, sails and one large gun each. Madison agreed and by April 1814 Barney was once again in the U.S. Navy in command of a flotilla, this time with seven 75-foot barges, six

50-foot barges, two gunboats, one galley, one lookout boat and Barney's flagship, the schooner *Scorpion*. This motley crew succeeded in fighting the British fleet to a standstill at the first battle of St. Leonard's Creek but eventually the British forced the flotilla up into the shallower waters of the Patuxent River, near where the current Naval Air Station is located. Admiral Sir Alexander Cochrane and Major General Sir Robert Ross joined Cockburn and were bent on a punitive expedition to the nation's capital at Washington. With his flotilla no longer able to fight, Barney took off their guns and burned the boats. He organized his sailors, including many freed African-Americans, into artillery batteries, marching and hauling their guns overland to Bladensburg, where U.S. defense forces, primarily militia, intended to make their stand.

CHARLES BALL:
ONE OF BARNEY'S BLACK JACKS

President Madison, while reviewing the men just before the fight, asked Commodore Barney if his "Negroes would not run on the approach of the British?" "No, sir," Barney replied. "They don't know how to run; they die by their guns first."

Charles Ball, a runaway slave who had been one of the men reviewed, left a remarkable account of the battle at Bladensburg:

> When we reached Bladensburg, and the flotilla men were drawn up in line, to work at their cannon, armed with their cutlasses, I volunteered to assist in working the cannon, that occupied the first place, on the left of the Commodore. We had a full and perfect view of the British Army, as it advanced along the road, leading to the bridge over the east branch; and I could not but admire the handsome manner in which the British officers led on their fatigued and worn out soldiers. I thought then, and think yet, that General Ross was one of the finest-looking men I ever saw on horseback.

I stood at my gun, until the Commodore was shot down, when he ordered us to retreat, as I was told by the officer who commanded our gun. If the militia regiments, that lay upon our right and left, could have been brought to charge the British, in close fight, as they crossed the bridge, we should have killed or taken the whole of them in a short time. . . .

THIS WAS NOT CHARLES BALL'S first naval service. He had served in the United States Navy on the frigate *Congress* in the Washington Navy Yard as a slave for two years. "One Saturday evening when I came home from the cornfield, my master told me that he had hired me out for a year at the City of Washington, and that I would have to live at the Navy Yard. . . . It was night when we arrived at the Navy Yard and everything appeared very strange to me. I was told by a gentleman who had epaulettes on his shoulders that I must go on board a large ship which lay in the river. . . . This ship proved to be the frigate *Congress* and I was told that I had been brought there to cook for the people belonging to her."

Ball's service on *Congress* started when he was about 20 years old. He had been born about 1780 in Leonardtown, Maryland. When he was 4, his owner died and his mother was sold, along with Charles, to an owner in Georgia. When he was 12, this master died, and be became the property of his dead master's father. It was this man who hired him out to the Navy.

While at the Navy yard, Ball married a slave from a neighboring plantation and had a number of children. He was then sold to a slave trader who took him to South Carolina and sold him to an owner from Georgia. His new owner in Georgia was extremely abusive—in 1808 Charles ran. He followed the main roads heading north, steering primarily by the stars, traveling by night and living off the land. It took him nearly a year to get back to Calvert County, Maryland, to his wife and family. His wife's master was kindly disposed and encouraged him to work for wages as a free man in the local area. He obtained work in a fishery until, "in the spring of the year 1813, the British Fleet came into the Bay . . . a British vessel of war came off the mouth of the river and sent her boats up to drive us away from our fishing ground. There was but little property at the fishery that could be destroyed; but the enemy cut the seines to pieces and burned the sheds belonging to the place. They then marched up two miles into the country, burned the house of a planter, and brought away with them several cattle that were found in his fields."

Throughout the spring and summer of 1813, Admiral Cockburn ranged up and down both shores of the Chesapeake, setting free slaves and burning crops, plantations and canneries. After nearly one hundred slaves from one plantation were taken aboard the British squadron, consisting of *Dragon* (74) and two frigates and two sloops. Ball was hired by the plantation owner to try to arrange to get the slaves returned. He went aboard the flagship where, "I was invited and even urged to go with the others who, I was told, were bound to the island of Trinidad, in the West Indies, where they would have lands given to them, and where they were to be free. I returned many thanks for their kind offers, but respectfully declined them."

When the war was over Ball stayed in Baltimore and went to work. "And by constant economy I found myself in possession, in the year 1820 of $350 in money, the proceeds of my labor."

Ball's adventures, however, were far from over. One day while he was working in the fields, he was seized by slave catchers who had tracked him down from Georgia, whence he was returned to the brother-in-law of his previous owner.

After suffering severe abuse from this new owner, who in fact had no legal title to him, Ball again managed to escape to Savannah, where he was able to stow away aboard a merchant ship sailing to Philadelphia. In Philadelphia he was able to seek out the Quakers, who helped him get settled in a job. Traveling to Baltimore he found that his second wife (the first having died) and children had been taken shortly after he had been grabbed and were now in Georgia. The narrative which contains this story, circulated by abolitionist Quakers, ends with Ball living again in Philadelphia and planning to recover his family.

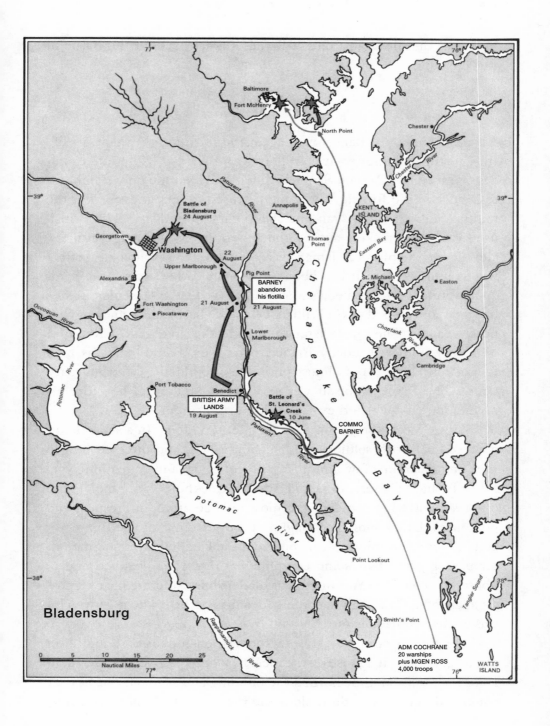

Baltimore
Fort McHenry

North Point

Chester

Patuxent River

Battle of
Bladensburg
24 August

Annapolis

KENT
ISLAND

Georgetown

Washington

22
August

Thomas
Point

Chester River

Eastern Bay

Upper Marlborough

Pig Point

BARNEY
abandons
his flotilla
21 August

St. Michaels

Easton

Alexandria

21 August

Fort Washington
Piscataway

Lower
Marlborough

Choptank River

Cambridge

Occoquan River

Port Tobacco

Benedict

BRITISH ARMY
LANDS
19 August

Battle of
St. Leonard's
Creek
10 June

COMMO
BARNEY

Potomac River

Potomac River

Point Lookout

Bladensburg

Smith's Point

Tangier Sound

Rappahannock River

ADM COCHRANE
20 warships
plus MGEN ROSS
4,000 troops

WATTS
ISLAND

0   5   10   15   20   25
Nautical Miles

Such was the life of just one of Barney's Black Jacks at the Battle of Bladensburg.

A T B L A D E N S B U R G, Ball proved again the fortitude to which his life story testifies. Barney's naval artillery with Ball, and U.S. Marines under command of Captain Samuel Miller, provided the only significant resistance to the British. These men refused to retreat even after the militias on both flanks "ran like sheep chased by dogs." The British used Congreve rockets against the Americans as direct fire artillery, and though the physical damage was minimal, the psychological effect was as impressive as it had been a few years earlier against the hardened veterans of Napoleon's army in Spain. The spectacular rockets had been developed by Sir William Congreve based on an ancient Chinese weapon. They were later to provide the "red glare" over Fort McHenry immortalized by Francis Scott Key. Barney and his men fought until they were almost entirely surrounded by the redcoats. Only when Barney himself was severely wounded did he order his men to retreat—which they did in skirmishing order.

Barney was taken prisoner. As he later reported: "In a short time I observed a British soldier, and had him called, and directed him to seek an officer; in a few minutes an officer came, and on learning who I was, brought General Ross and Admiral Cockburn to see me. Those officers behaved to me with the most marked attention, respect and politeness, had a surgeon brought, and my wound dressed immediately. After a few minutes conversation, the General informed me (after paying me a handsome compliment) that I was paroled and at liberty to proceed to Washington or Bladensburg; offering me every assistance in his power, giving orders for a litter to be brought, in which I was carried to Bladensburg."

The British occupied Washington without opposition, and after dining at the White House on the meal hastily abandoned by President and Mrs. Madison, they burned the building and as much else as they could and quickly withdrew along the route by which they had come.

Though Barney was no longer with them, the remainder of his flotilla force marched to Baltimore, where they took an active part in its defense. Having had more time to prepare, sink ships in the channel and ready Fort McHenry, the Americans there put up a staunch defense. After twenty-four hours of fighting by land and by sea, during which General Ross was killed by an American sniper and more than 1,500 shells and Congreve rockets were fired, Admiral Cochrane reluctantly concluded that the city could not be taken. As the British withdrew, Francis Scott Key, who had been sent by President Madison to negotiate the release of a prisoner and seen the battle from a British ship, now back on his own ship sailed into Baltimore harbor, checked into the Indian Queen Hotel and finished the poem that became the *Star-Spangled Banner*. Barney was brought into Baltimore four weeks later as a great hero, his reputation fully restored (at least in Maryland). He died in 1818 with the British musketball still in his thigh.

WHILE COCKBURN WAS MARAUDING on his first raid into the Chesapeake Bay the seeming invincibility of the American frigates came to an end when the bay's namesake, *Chesapeake* (36), commanded by Captain James Lawrence, was captured by the British frigate *Shannon* (38), commanded by Captain Philip Broke. *Shannon* under Broke was a highly seasoned ship. Lawrence was equally experienced but had not had a chance to drill his entirely new crew on *Chesapeake*. Broke sent a challenge in to Lawrence that he apparently never received. With perhaps too finely honed a sense of honor he was already planning to attack *Shannon* despite his new crew. On June 1, 1813, *Chesapeake* sailed out of Boston and the fight began. Lawrence was mortally wounded in the first broadside and bequeathed to the Navy one of its legendary rallying cries as he was carried below to die, shouting "Don't give up the ship!"

The engagement lasted only another fifteen minutes before his overmatched crew did exactly that. Captain Broke led a boarding party to capture *Chesapeake*. American casualties were extremely high, 148

men killed and wounded to 83 for the British, including Captain
Broke, severely wounded in the head with a cutlass. He was knighted
as a baronet for reversing the humiliation of the Royal Navy.

Chesapeake illustrates an odd phenomenon in the U.S. and other
navies, an unfortunate ship from birth to decommissioning. It was humiliated in 1807 in the *Leopard* affair before being captured by *Shannon*. *Chesapeake* had an equally undistinguished service in the Royal
Navy and ended up being sold to the breakers. There have been many
such jinxed ships over the years: the destroyer *William D. Porter* in
World War II and the super-carrier *Saratoga*, for example, both plagued
by ill fortune, groundings and humiliations throughout their careers.

The American superfrigates spent most of the remainder of the war
bottled up in port by the British blockade, made increasingly effective
as Napoleon's defeat freed up the Royal Navy. The smaller American
combatants continued to slip through the blockade, however, and their
depredations against British commerce and superiority in single-ship
engagements continued throughout the war. The brig *Argus* (18) captured twenty British merchant ships in the summer of 1813 and the
British brig *Pelican* (18) on August 14. In 1814 and early 1815, the brig
Enterprise (16) captured the British brig *Boxer* (14); the ship sloop *Peacock* (18) captured the British brig *Epervier* (18); the ship sloop *Wasp*
(18) captured the British brig *Reindeer* (18); *Wasp* sank the British brig
Avon (18); and the sloop *Hornet* (18) captured the British sloop *Penguin*
(19).

An exception to the inactivity of the big frigates in the latter part of
the war was the final cruise of *Constitution* when she was able to elude
the blockade in the last days of 1814 and cross the Atlantic. Off
Madeira, in February 1815 under the command of Captain Charles
Stewart, one of its ablest skippers, *Constitution* captured two British
cruisers, the frigate *Cyane* (34) and the ship sloop *Levant* (20) at the
same time, a brilliant feat of seamanship and tactics.

Of the many successful commerce-raiding cruises of the American
brigs and sloops of war, those of *Hornet* and *Peacock* in 1814 and 1815
were perhaps the most significant. These ships ranged throughout the
British Isles and along the coasts of Europe and Africa, taking many

prizes. In its final cruise *Peacock* ranged as far as the East Indies and Indian Ocean and was the first American ship ever to visit the Persian Gulf, proving to the world that the U.S. Navy could indeed operate globally. The final naval action of the War of 1812 took place in the Sunda Strait in the Indies, when *Peacock* took the British East India company brig *Nautilus* (14).

The most important fleet actions of the war, however, took place not on the high seas but in the Great Lakes. Here, in two set-piece battles, the Battle of Lake Erie on September 10, 1813, and the Battle of Lake Champlain on September 11, 1814, the United States got the best of the British in a way that made the world take notice.

THE BATTLE OF LAKE ERIE

American strategists, with Jefferson retired at Monticello chief among them, thought the easiest way to twist the British lion's tail was to threaten, if not conquer, Canada. The British had only 500,000 citizens in that vast domain to the Americans' 7 million. Moreover, many Canadians who lived on the border had expressed an interest in breaking away from the Crown and joining the United States.

What was lost to strategic thinkers of the time was the de facto sea frontier presented by the Great Lakes. In order to conquer Canada, the lakes had to be controlled just as the high seas must be controlled in a land campaign. If the United States could not control the lakes, the major avenues of advance into Canada would be blocked.

Master Commandant Oliver Hazard Perry was the commodore in command of all American naval forces on Lake Erie. Perry's adversary was Commander Robert Barclay, who had been with Nelson at Trafalgar. It was Perry's assignment to establish naval supremacy on the lake and support General William Henry Harrison in crossing the lake and invading Canada.

The opposing fleets had been built in shipyards around the lake largely from unseasoned timber because of the lack of planning time. The British ships had a slight advantage in that the most difficult

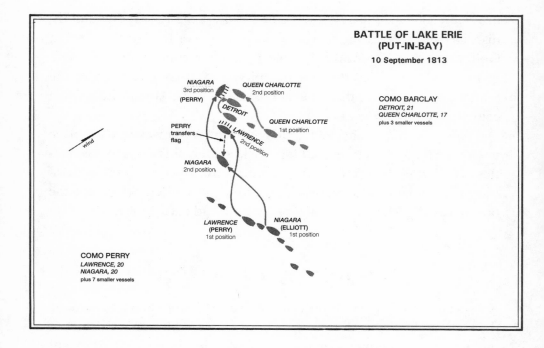

BATTLE OF LAKE ERIE
(PUT-IN-BAY)
10 September 1813

COMO BARCLAY
DETROIT, 21
QUEEN CHARLOTTE, 17
plus 3 smaller vessels

NIAGARA
3rd position
(PERRY)

QUEEN CHARLOTTE
2nd position

DETROIT

PERRY
transfers
flag

LAWRENCE
2nd position

QUEEN CHARLOTTE
1st position

NIAGARA
2nd position

wind

LAWRENCE
(PERRY)
1st position

NIAGARA
(ELLIOTT)
1st position

COMO PERRY
LAWRENCE, 20
NIAGARA, 20
plus 7 smaller vessels

skantlings and fittings had been shipped over from England and transported to the lake, but the opposing fleets were roughly equal in firepower and manning. Perry had a squadron of nine ships mounting 54 guns while Barclay had six ships mounting 64 guns.

On September 10, 1813, the opposing fleets met off South Bass Island, not far from Detroit. After a brutal slugfest lasting the better part of the day in which Perry's flagship, the brig *Lawrence* (20), was destroyed, forcing him to shift to the brig *Niagara* (20), Perry eventually managed to vanquish and capture all six of the enemy ships. He then provided the U.S. Navy with yet another of its timeless epigrams when he wrote to General Harrison that "we have met the enemy and they are ours." (Not ". . . and he is us," as Walt Kelly and Pogo would have it.) With that dramatic news, Harrison was able to attack Detroit, previously captured by the British, and to recapture it on September 29, and to defeat 1,800 British regulars six days later at the Battle of the Thames. The British had lost the Northwest theater for good.

THE BATTLE OF LAKE CHAMPLAIN AND MASTER COMMANDANT THOMAS MACDONOUGH

The British had their own territorial ambitions. Critical to their plan was the control of the Lake Champlain corridor that thrust down the Hudson River Valley to New York. If the Canadians could seize control of this corridor and capture the port of New York, they could sever New England, where there were still many powerful British sympathizers, from the rest of the states and possibly help the Crown recover the richest of its former colonies.

This aggressive plan was conceived after Wellington defeated Napoleon and a large number of crack regiments were freed up to come to North America. Sir George Prevost was chosen to command a powerful invasion force of some 11,000 seasoned veterans of the victorious Peninsular Campaign against Napoleon.

On September 3, 1814, Sir George led his army across the New York state border and struck southward. A much smaller American force of about 1,500 under Brigadier General Alexander Macomb had no choice but to withdraw toward the village of Plattsburgh, New York, on the western shore of Lake Champlain, where Macomb planned to make a stand. Macomb's force—it cannot be called an army—had no organized battalions and was made up mostly of recruits and convalescents, but did have a cadre of four companies of regulars from the U.S. Army's 6th Infantry Regiment, which included some Revolutionary War veterans. As Macomb retreated, he gathered men and boy volunteers from the New York countryside, and his troop began to grow.

Macomb skillfully employed delaying tactics against Sir George until he reached Plattsburgh, where Master Commandant Thomas MacDonough awaited him. (Master commandant was a naval rank between lieutenant and captain. It was replaced by commander in 1838.) MacDonough had positioned his little squadron in the shallow waters adjacent to Cumberland Bay, protected by Cumberland Head to the east, all in accordance with a secret army-Navy battle plan.

In house-to-house fighting in Plattsburgh, Macomb continued to extract a heavy toll from the British. He crossed the Saranac River immediately south of the village and destroyed its bridges behind him. There he took his stand, using bridge planks to build breastworks on the Saranac's high south bank, where he could count on powerful naval gunfire support from MacDonough's squadron to his east in Cumberland Bay. In effect, Macomb and MacDonough had cleverly combined forces in the face of Sir George's potentially overwhelming invasion force.

MacDonough, a deeply religious Delaware native, was a 31-year old career officer who had served with Decatur in the Tripolitan campaign. His flagship was the frigate *Saratoga* (26), and his command was comprised of the brig *Eagle* (20) under Lieutenant Robert Henley, the schooner *Ticonderoga* (17) under Lieutenant Stephen Cassin, and the sloop *Preble* (7) under Lieutenant Charles Budd. To round out his squadron, MacDonough also had ten oar-powered galleys, each mounting one gun. These galleys had been specifically designed to operate in the shallow coves and inlets of Lake Champlain. In all, MacDonough had 820 men and 86 guns under his command.

Meanwhile, Macomb's thin ranks continued to swell with more armed volunteers from the Hudson River Valley. The British attempted a European-style crossing of the Saranac with pontoons, scaling ladders and battering rams, only to be picked off by Macomb's sharpshooters. Lacking heavy guns to blow the Americans out of their emplacements, Sir George ordered his naval component to put on full sail and join him at Plattsburgh. Under tremendous pressure from Prevost to get moving, Captain George Downie led his squadron incautiously around Cumberland Head about nine o'clock on Sunday morning, September 11, 1814—right into a well-laid trap.

Downie's flag was in the large frigate *Confiance* (38), and under him were the brig *Linnet* (16) and the sloops *Chubb* (11) and *Finch* (11). He also had twelve galleys, each mounting more than one gun. Downie had the advantage in men, 1,050 vs. 820, and more and longer-range guns, 95 to the Americans' 86.

Knowing his adversaries' advantages, MacDonough had taken some bold but risky steps. He anchored his squadron in the deep recesses of Cumberland Bay in water as shallow as he dared. On a line extending from southwest to northeast were *Preble, Ticonderoga,* the flagship *Saratoga* and then *Eagle.* Interspersed among the bigger four were the ten galleys, with one anchoring the southern end of the line at Crab Island. The postage-stamp island, and a well-placed battery upon it, effectively served as a fifth ship in the line of battle.

Seeing the enemy MacDonough knelt on the deck of *Saratoga* and, surrounded by his officers, said a prayer. Meanwhile, hundreds of spectators gathered on the Vermont shore to watch the upcoming battle. They heard the trill of boatswain pipes, and the rattle of drums, as the crews beat to general quarters. On the New York shore, Sir George and his staff officers broke out their long glasses in anticipation of seeing the stupidly anchored American ships blown out of the water like so many tethered ducks.

He would be disappointed. Sailing into the wind, Downie ran into trouble within minutes after entering the narrow confines of the bay. He ordered *Confiance* to come about hard, and in the desperate maneuver a huge cannon broke loose from its carriage, killing Downie on the spot. (Other accounts have the gun dismounted by shot, killing Downie a bit later.) Unable to tack and maneuver to bring their superior long-range firepower to bear on the anchored Americans, Downie's disheartened subordinates lay their four ships in close and parallel to the American battle line, dropped anchors and opened fire, breaking the Sabbath calm. In doing this, they forfeited their range advantage at the outset of the battle, but they really had no other option. They were now trapped in MacDonough's watery briar patch.

The horrendous battle was fought with a continuous roar that lasted some two hours and twenty minutes. The ground shook under the Vermont spectators, and the two squadrons were soon covered in boiling clouds of smoke. On the northern end of the battle line, HMS *Linnet* battered *Eagle* and temporarily took her out of action. However, *Linnet*'s sister, *Chubb,* further north, took a horrific pounding from low-lying American galleys and had to surrender. On the southern end of the line, HMS *Finch* ran aground near Crab Island—as MacDonough had hoped at least one of his assailants might do—and was out of the fight for good. This left *Confiance* to carry on alone. With her 38 guns and 300 tars, she went after *Saratoga* and her 26 guns and 200 blue-jackets. In the flagship vs. flagship duel that ensued, shell explosions twice knocked MacDonough off his feet. Later in the cable-length fighting, a gun captain's severed head slammed into MacDonough like a cannonball and sent him flying off his quarterdeck.

In the meantime, Macomb had his hands full with Sir George's gunners, who pounded his line with an incessant cannonade of rockets, mortars, bombs and shot. During a lull in the bombardment, Macomb's troops heard the offshore shelling abate and thought MacDonough had struck his colors. He had not. MacDonough had instead pulled a neat tactical trick that he had trained his men to perform in anticipation of the battle. After anchoring, his fleet had carefully rigged spring lines to bower anchors. On his command, they swung the ships around on their spring lines, exposing their heretofore-unused guns, and opened afresh. It was too much for the British. After several smashing broad-sides, they struck their colors. The Americans had lost 100 killed and wounded, the British 200.

With his landlines of supply overextended, and any hope of resupply and bombardment support from the Royal Navy gone, Sir George now found himself in an untenable position. He ordered an immediate and full retreat to Canada, in the middle of the night, leaving behind mountains of baggage; the British dead, sick and wounded were left to the Americans.

As at Yorktown and the Battle of the Capes, the victory at Platts-burgh was decided by the Battle of Lake Champlain.

In several ways the battle was one of the most decisive of the War of 1812. It dashed British ambitions to seize American territory once and for all. More importantly, it broke loose the stalled peace talks at Ghent. Upon learning of the victory, the British delegates gave up all hope of negotiating a treaty favorable to the Crown.

A grateful nation saw MacDonough's victory on Lake Champlain in the same light as Commodore Perry's on Lake Erie a year before. The much-heralded hero of Lake Champlain was advanced to the rank of captain and bestowed the honorary title of commodore. Macomb

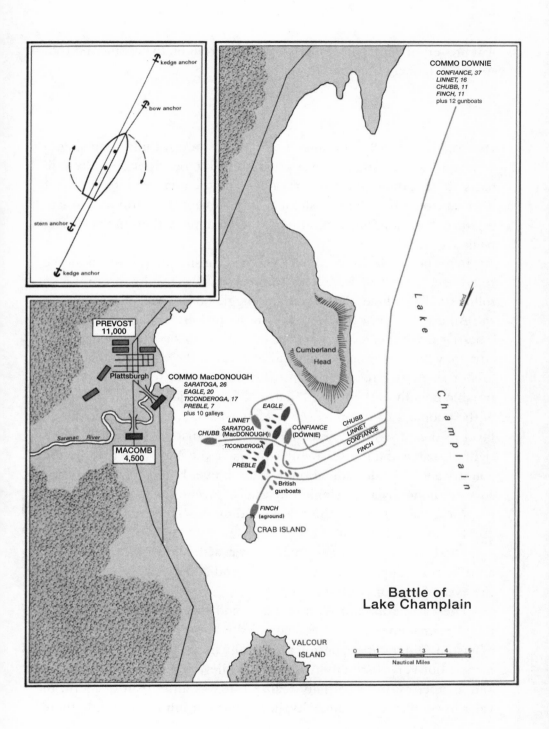

kedge anchor

bow anchor

stern anchor

kedge anchor

COMMO DOWNIE
CONFIANCE, 37
LINNET, 16
CHUBB, 11
FINCH, 11
plus 12 gunboats

Lake

Wind

Champlain

Cumberland
Head

PREVOST
11,000

Plattsburgh

COMMO MacDONOUGH
SARATOGA, 26
EAGLE, 20
TICONDEROGA, 17
PREBLE, 7
plus 10 galleys

EAGLE

LINNET

CONFIANCE
(DOWNIE)

CHUBB
LINNET
CONFIANCE
FINCH

CHUBB

SARATOGA
(MacDONOUGH)

Saranac   River

TICONDEROGA

MACOMB
4,500

PREBLE

British
gunboats

FINCH
(aground)

CRAB ISLAND

VALCOUR
ISLAND

Battle of
Lake Champlain

0   1   2   3   4   5
Nautical Miles

was brevetted with major-general stars and went on to become the U.S. Army's senior commander.

IN THE WAR OF 1812 in pursuit of a naval strategy built upon single-ship actions, the American Navy had proved to be superior in the skill of its officers, the training of its seamen and the quality of its ships. Yet it was unable to lift the British blockade, prevent the burning of Washington or halt Admiral Cockburn's repeated depredations in the Chesapeake.

In his book *The Naval War of 1812*, still considered the authoritative reference, Theodore Roosevelt summarized the results of the war as follows: "The whole history of the struggle on the ocean is, as regards the Americans, only the record of individual cruises and fights. The material results were not very great, at least in their effect on Great Britain, whose enormous Navy did not feel in the slightest degree the loss of a few frigates and sloops. But morally the result was of inestimable benefit to the United States. The victories kept up the spirits of the people, cast down by the defeats on land; practically decided in favor of the Americans the chief question in dispute—Great Britain's right of search and impressment—and gave the Navy and thereby the country a worldwide reputation. I doubt if ever before a nation gained so much honor by a few single ship duels." According to TR the Americans lost 9,718 tons on the sea, including 431 guns, and the British 13,512 tons and 605 guns.

The U.S. Navy emerged from the war with many new heroes, with a pride in its ships as the best in the world and a glamorous image in the eyes of the American public.

The early efforts of Adams, Jones and Barry to establish institutional permanence were now accomplished, complete with a rich store of custom and tradition, borrowed liberally from the British and French navies, but very distinctly American. While Jefferson's fear of elitism and aristocracy were partially realized, it was an elitism of merit, of valor in combat and of audacity, not of birth or influence. While there were successive generations of naval Biddles, Decaturs and Porters, their rank for the most part came from their own achievements, not those of their forebears.

The new republic now had a formidable instrument to build a global commerce, enforce a Monroe Doctrine and, when the test came, to preserve the Union from rebellion.

V

THE
CIVIL WAR

THERE ARE MANY TIMES more books written about land battles in warfare than about sea battles. The reasons are understandable. With the exception of the great sea battle between the Persians and the Ionian League around the Island of Lade in 494 B.C.—a battle site in western Turkey that you can now walk around, since the bay has silted in—it is difficult to see the arenas in which these contests took place without a boat. And if you do have a boat, there is nothing to see but sea. Another reason is that throughout history casualties in naval battles have been far, far lower than land battles of comparable importance. This was certainly true in the American Civil War, in which the Union Army lost 110,000 killed, and the Union Navy 2,100.

An unfortunate result of this literary disparity is a general lack of appreciation of the contributions made to victory of the naval forces in each of our wars. This is certainly true of the Civil War. But here, as in other great wars, the importance of naval action was disproportionate to the number of casualties suffered at sea.

All that the average person can tell you about the naval Civil War is that in the world's first battle between ironclad ships the USS *Monitor* fought the CSS *Virginia* (on March 9, 1862) to what was basically a draw. (Alas for the Union, this happened after *Virginia* had wreaked havoc on the wooden ships of the Union fleet.)

The battle was indeed an important one: it was recognized around the world as the end of the age of wooden warships. Thereafter ironclads were the cutting edge of naval war, and no wooden warship could survive against one. But the prominence of these two ironclads has largely obscured the story of the ships that won (and lost) the naval Civil War. The war on the water was fought by vessels of three distinct types: gunboats, which prosecuted the war on America's rivers; blockaders; and commerce raiders.

The actions of these vessels were not only crucial in the war but contributed to a permanent strategic debate in American military circles. Ever since the Union victory was achieved through Ulysses Grant's bloody war of attrition, Army orthodoxy has tended to be grounded in positional warfare in the "heartland," while U.S. Navy orthodoxy has been built upon maneuver, sea-control, blockade and control of the "rimland." There have of course been army advocates of "hit 'em where they ain't" maneuver, usually cavalrymen like Philip Sheridan and George Patton, and there have been naval advocates, like Alfred Thayer Mahan, of direct, massed attack, but the different strategic philosophies continue to rule the services today.

The United States Navy entered the Civil War well prepared relative to earlier wars. There were still a few veterans like David Farragut of the glorious victories (and occasional defeats) of the War of 1812. Secretary of the Navy George Bancroft had institutionalized the warfighting traditions, disciplines and training of the Navy with the establishment of the Naval Academy at Annapolis in 1845, so there was a truly professional core around which to build. Contrary to popular myth many naval leaders were at the forefront of new technology. John Dahlgren had led the world in developing more powerful and safer naval guns. John Ericsson, the designer of *Monitor* and a former Swedish cavalry officer, was one of the most innovative naval architects in the antebellum period; and the U.S. Navy had pioneered the introduction of steam power to naval warships. The success and glamour of the Navy in the War of 1812 had established its permanence and funding, although not at a level satisfactory to the service. For the half-century prior to Fort Sumter, American warships cruised the world's oceans. It had become a truly world-class service.

The Navy thus entered the war with a cadre of seasoned professional sea officers and was blessed with two first-class leaders in

Gideon Welles, the twenty-fourth secretary of the Navy, and Gustavus V. Fox, his assistant secretary. The Union, moreover, was in the full bloom of the industrial revolution, with six times as many iron and steel mills and foundries, steam-engine plants and armories, and three times the railroad infrastructure as the South. The economy in the North was still dominated by the merchant trading ports of the East Coast, and shipbuilding and its supporting industries were thriving.

The Navy of the Confederacy was born on February 20, 1861, with the very competent Stephen R. Mallory, former chairman of the U.S. Senate Naval Affairs Committee, as secretary. Many of the professional officers of the American Navy were from the South. Of the 1,554 naval officers on active duty at the beginning of 1861, 373, or 24 percent, "went South," a percentage not very different than the Army.

The South had a good maritime infrastructure and a great many excellent ports and harbors on the Atlantic and Gulf coasts, but it did not have the industrial infrastructure to outfit and support the building of naval combatants in large numbers. The South's sensible strategy was instead to concentrate on attacking the Union's commerce on the one hand and seeking rapid recognition by the European powers on the other. The former goal sought to bring rapid and intense pressure on the North to settle through blows to its economic interests; the latter if achieved would effectively neutralize the blockade imposed by the North and gain access to the war materials that could not be manufactured or obtained in the Confederacy.

The Union's strategy was also sound and simple. General Winfield Scott, the Union's senior commander at the beginning of the war, outlined what came to be called the "Anaconda Plan," based on a "complete blockade" of the Confederate coast and a "powerful movement down the Mississippi . . . so as to envelop the insurgent states." While few people accepted the plan initially or ever gave credit to Scott, this was in fact the strategy pursued successfully throughout the war by the Union Navy. The objective was to seal off Southern ports from exporting agricultural products and importing war supplies, while splitting the Confederacy with a two-pronged offensive, down the Mississippi from the north and up the Mississippi from New Orleans.

DAVID FARRAGUT: ANACONDA'S EXECUTOR

If—following Plutarch's biographical method—Stephen Decatur's life could be paired with the life of the dashing Civil War cavalry hero Jeb Stuart, then David Glasgow Farragut's parallel life would surely be Horatio Nelson's. Where Decatur and Stuart were hot-tempered and romantic, Nelson and Farragut were deliberate and calculating. Where the former pair had tactical brilliance, the latter possessed this as well as the uncommon strategic insight capable of changing the course of great events.

Farragut was born one day after the twenty-fifth anniversary of the Declaration of Independence's signing. His father, George, had fought on both sea and land in the Revolutionary War and accepted an appointment as sailing master in the U.S. Navy in March 1807, along with orders to New Orleans. There he befriended David Porter, the father of the naval officer of the same name who would later distinguish himself, in many instances alongside Farragut, in the Civil War.

A strong connection grew between the Farragut and Porter families. When Mrs. Farragut died of yellow fever in 1808, David Porter Sr. offered to take care of the 7-year-old David Farragut and one of his sisters. "Thus commenced my acquaintance with the celebrated Commodore David Porter, late of the United States Navy," wrote Farragut four decades later. "And I am happy to have it in my power to say, with feelings of the warmest gratitude, that he was ever to me all that he promised, 'friend and guardian.' "

When Porter completed his tour at New Orleans and sailed for Washington, he introduced the now 9-year-old David Farragut to Secretary of the Navy Paul Hamilton. Porter explained that the boy very much wanted to go to sea, and Hamilton arranged an appointment as midshipman before Farragut's tenth birthday.

Farragut joined his surrogate father when in August 1811 Porter took command of the frigate that had been built with $75,000 contributed by the citizens of Essex County in Massachusetts. *Essex* sailed from Norfolk in October.

With his skipper also his adoptive father, poor Farragut was able to get away with very little. For instance, when Captain Porter caught his charge chewing tobacco, the C.O. placed his hand over the boy's mouth, forcing him to swallow the wad, a measure that ended David's tobacco days. Sharing the labors and perils of a man-o'-warsman at so early an age would horrify children's-rights advocates today but seems to have turned out to Farragut's and the nation's satisfaction.

Farragut was with *Essex* for her successes, and also for her capture by the British frigate *Phoebe* (36) and her smaller escort *Cherub* (28). In the battle he acted as captain's aide, quarter-gunner and powder boy, and had an excellent view of the increasing casualties that eventually forced *Essex*'s commander to surrender. "I will remark here the horrid impression made upon me," Farragut later wrote, "by the death of the seamen. It was a boatswain's mate, his abdomen was taken entirely out, and he expired in a few moments ... I well remember, while standing near the captain just abaft the mainmast, a shot came through the waterways which glanced upwards, killing four men who stood by the side of the gun, taking the last man in the head, and his brains flew over us both."

With well over half the crew severely wounded, missing or killed in action, the most grievously injured went ashore: Farragut offered the attending surgeon to help care for them. His later account of this service will ring true with anyone who has ever had the unhappy experience of visiting men wounded in combat: "I never earned Uncle Sam's money so faithfully as I did during that hospital service." He was soon after paroled with Porter and sailed home with him.

Farragut grew to manhood in the Navy, serving in the Mediterranean and studying language, literature and mathematics ashore under the tutelage of a Navy chaplain who had become the American consul at Tunis. He sailed in the Gulf of Mexico, hunted pirates in the Caribbean and saw service again off the South American coast—in all the places to which the Navy was dispatched to protect the nation's expanding commerce. During these years, time passed slowly for many naval officers who suffered experiences like Farragut's: He waited for orders at home, in Norfolk, for nearly four years.

Even when the Mexican War began in 1846, his extensive service in Spanish-speaking theaters of operations failed to bring forth from the Navy the orders to command that Farragut had hoped and lobbied for. Finally the next year he received orders into the sloop-of-war *Saratoga* (20) as commanding officer. Little distinguished the deployment that followed except the crew's yellow fever and the necessity of relieving five of the ship's junior officers. Farragut went back to the Norfolk Navy Yard and gunnery lectures. His career, like the Navy, drifted in still air.

But, as the rumblings of the Civil War brewing began to make themselves heard, there were signs of a breeze. Promotion to the highest pre-Civil War rank of captain came in 1855 and with it command—for the first time in a decade—of *Brooklyn,* one of six new steam sloops that also carried a full complement of sails. But Farragut was relieved after an uneventful command in late 1860 and again returned home to Norfolk.

Like most men, Farragut hoped to be spared the choice between loyalty to the state, Virginia, that had been his home for most of his life, and the nation. However, unlike Robert E. Lee, when the decisive moment came—and perhaps influenced by the operating Navy's distance from the land it defended as opposed to the Army's identification with the soil on which it is based—Farragut never wavered in his allegiance to the United States. "God forbid that I should have to raise my hand against the South," he had said. But the expression showed that the hand was willing if it were required.

In April 1861, after Virginia passed the ordinance of secession, Farragut attended an informal town meeting and spoke in support of the national government's seizure of forts and arsenals in rebellious states. In the passion of the moment, a secessionist answered that someone with such opinions could not live in Norfolk, and was seconded by others in the crowd. "Very well, I can live somewhere else," said Farragut. He, his wife, his sister-in-law and son left that evening by steamer for Baltimore.

Under suspicion for his Southern origins, Farragut was initially assigned as a member of a board to recommend officers for retirement from active duty. In the end—or more properly, at the beginning—Far-

ragut was redeemed by recognition of the promptness and decisive-
ness of his departure from Norfolk. At the council of war attended by
the president that decided to force the southern end of the Mississippi
as a step towards joining with the invading force heading southwards
from the north, Farragut's faithfulness to the United States and the
dramatic way he had proved it weighed in the balance. In the first days
of 1862 he was appointed to command the West Gulf Blockading
Squadron. The peacetime doldrums of his adult career disappeared.

THE BATTLE OF NEW ORLEANS

The Mississippi River divided the Confederacy. Commerce across it
was vital to the rebellious states' shaky economies. The Texas beef
that fed Southern forces in the field could never reach them without it.

If the Mississippi could be seized and held, it would allow the
North to break the South into fissures such as the one that Sherman
later opened with his march to the sea. If New Orleans could be blockaded and taken, the Confederacy would be denied a critical port with
immediate access to seaborne supplies that were conveyed upriver.
The North could then turn its descending advance southwards upon
the river into a pincer movement in accordance with the Anaconda
plan. Another prominent virtue of attacking the river at its mouth as
well as from the direction of its headwaters was the implausibility of
such an attack to the high command of both sides. Twice did the Confederate Navy turn down pleas from a subordinate officer not to transfer several rams from New Orleans upriver to Memphis.

The problem in taking New Orleans was its seaward defenses, the
strong forts Jackson and St. Philip that guarded both sides of the Mississippi below the city and above the river's junction with the Gulf of
Mexico. The vulnerability of this fixed defensive system was its dependence for supply. If cut off from the city above or the ocean below,
the fortifications must eventually wither and surrender. David Farragut's mission was to insure just that.

It was materially complicated by the orders he held "to reduce the defenses which guard the approaches to New Orleans, when you will appear off that city and take possession of it under the guns of your squadron." Farragut believed that he could force the forts' surrender by going past them and preventing their resupply, rendering them militarily useless. But his orders reflected McClellan's and the army's concern that the failure to subdue them would neither starve the forts nor stop them from interdicting Union communications between the city and the ocean. He was supposed to reduce the forts with artillery before trying to sail around them.

Farragut embraced the assignment joyously along with the mortar flotilla that—notwithstanding his opinion of its dubious utility—had been added to bombard Jackson and St. Philip. He hastened south, arriving at Ship Island off the coast of Biloxi on February 20, 1862. Much of the next few weeks would be spent assembling the fleet and moving its larger ships over the shallows that restricted their entrance to the Mississippi.

On April 18 at 10:00 a.m. the mortar flotilla under Commander David Dixon Porter, son of the famed commander of *Essex*, commenced operations primarily against Ft. Jackson. The bombardment continued during daylight for six days, during which one shell a minute was fired. Throughout the period, fleet gunboats worked to reduce the floating defensive barriers of hulks chained together completely across the river. It was finally breached on April 20 by the gunboat *Itasca* commanded by Captain Henry Ball.

Meanwhile, Farragut instructed his captains to trim their ships so that if they ran aground they would not swing around to point downriver. He ordered an augmentation of weapons on deck that could lay down fire fore and aft, and he had the hulls painted with mud to lessen the chances of detection at night.

Preparations made, the awful truth now had to be confronted: the bombardment of the forts had not significantly injured them. Farragut faced a decision: should he wait for something that the previous week's shelling had failed to bring to pass? Or should he, sweeping aside the tactical direction of his orders, complete the strategic objective that they sought to accomplish?

The uselessness of the bombardment had been established. Farragut decided that there was greater danger in procrastination than in separating his command from its ocean source of supply; the forts were more likely to suffer the consequences of being cut off from their supply base in New Orleans than he was to be cut off from his own logistics to the south. Years later, Alfred Thayer Mahan rightly noted, "A fleet is not so much an army as a collection of floating fortresses, garrisoned, provisioned and mobile. It carries its communications in its hulls, and is not in such daily dependence upon external sources as its sister service."

Farragut gave the signal on April 23 that the attempt to bypass the forts would take place that evening an hour and a half before moonrise at 3:30 a.m. The battle itself is a record of individual ship captains' daring and fortitude. Farragut's virtue lay in the pains he took in advance to guarantee that each of his subordinate commanders knew exactly what was expected, in his own personal exposure to fire and in the gallantry this inspired in his commanders. But above all it lay in the methodical plans he drew up for the engagement and in his willingness to fight when he could have found refuge in the letter of his orders.

Farragut's seventeen ships were all wooden, but all nonetheless made it past the forts despite the pounding they received. *Itasca* was disabled with shot through her boilers as she ran the gauntlet upstream through the forts' fire, but made it through. Upriver the fleet soon engaged a powerful Confederate flotilla. In the furious melee that followed, the Confederates were defeated utterly, with the loss of only one Union steam sloop, *Varuna*, and 210 sailors killed or wounded.

The fleet reached New Orleans on the 25th where it beheld a scene of civil unrest bordering on anarchy. An eyewitness recorded that into the chaos that had been spurred by the mayor's decision to raise the state flag over city hall Farragut sent an emissary to demand the city's surrender. "Two officers of the United States Navy were walking abreast, unguarded and alone, not looking to the right or left, never frowning, never flinching, while the mob screamed in their faces,

The Battle of New Orleans

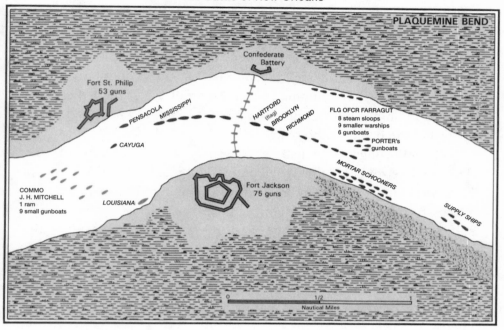

cursed, crowded and gnashed upon them. So through these gates of death those two men walked to the City Hall to demand the town's surrender. It was one of the bravest deeds I ever saw done."

Three days later the forts surrendered, in large measure because of mutinous ringleaders who, in holding further resistance useless, demonstrated a greater appreciation of the strategic facts than did General McClellan, who had blindly insisted upon eliminating the forts before proceeding to capture the city. On the same day, the American flag was hoisted again over New Orleans.

With the capture of New Orleans, the Mississippi was opened up to the United States and denied to the Confederacy. It was one of the most significant Union victories of the war and a much-needed boost to Northern morale at a time when the Union Army had little to brag about.

. . .

FARRAGUT QUICKLY USED the tactical advantage gained with New Orleans to pursue new objectives, proceeding upstream against Vicksburg while Ulysses S. Grant attacked the city by land. The siege of
Vicksburg was at first inconclusive because the water depth was falling
with the rising heat of summer, preventing full use of the Union's advantage in ships, and because the Union Army had not established
control of the banks of the river.

The following year Vicksburg was separated from the Confederacy.
The crucial stronghold finally fell on July 4, 1863. With the Mississippi
held firmly now in the Union's grip the campaign in the West could
successfully be concluded. Identifying the Union cause with nature itself, Lincoln noted "the father of waters again goes unvexed to the
sea."

THE BATTLE OF MOBILE BAY

As commander of the West Gulf Blockading Squadron, there remained
one task before Farragut: the capture of Mobile Bay. After New Orleans, the Alabama port was the next most important Gulf port, a center for ocean-borne trade and traffic along the Mobile River that
stretched thirty miles upstream before dividing into the Alabama and
Tombigbee rivers that provide extensive interior lines of communication into the South. In the first days of 1864, Farragut departed for the
Gulf.

The Confederate states' longest rail line stretched north from
Mobile to Columbus, Kentucky, and uncharacteristic of the South in
general, Mobile possessed important manufacturing capacity that contributed to the construction of the South's most powerful ironclad, *Tennessee*. As the use of New Orleans and other lesser harbors was denied
to the rebellious states, Mobile grew in strategic importance.

The effectiveness of blockading Mobile would be greatly multi-
plied by capturing Fort Morgan's shore batteries at the mouth of Mobile Bay, which covered the quarter-mile of navigable channel used by

ocean-going vessels. Denying the port to the enemy would be accomplished by seizure of the other position, Fort Gaines, on the western side of the approach to the harbor and within effective range of channel shipping. Farragut, who had learned of Major General William T. Sherman's plan to move through Georgia toward the sea, also expected that joint operations against Mobile would include a feint at the city itself to draw Southern forces away from the line of Sherman's advance.

Unlike at New Orleans, Mobile's fortifications could be resupplied by land. Running past the forts and placing his vessels across the enemy's line of water communications would constrict but not silence the fortifications' ability to live and shoot; they would still be able to threaten the resupply of combatants that had run the gauntlet. The naval movement thus had to be complemented by land forces' capture of the forts, while ground forces' possession of the fort must be covered by the Navy or risk Confederate naval assault—it would require a truly joint force operation. Withal, Farragut's plan entailed a considerably smaller level of military effort than was required imperfectly to enforce Mobile's blockade at sea.

Two significant obstacles remained before the attack could begin. The large Confederate ironclad ram, *Tennessee*, completed in haste and hindered by its draft, was working its way downriver to join the small clutch of river steamers that had been converted to gunboats in defense of the bay. Farragut, despite an early stated mistrust of these new ships, had realized the damage that *Tennessee* could inflict and asked the Navy Department repeatedly for support in the form of ironclads. When *Tennessee* arrived on scene, Navy headquarters finally sent the admiral the ships he had requested.

By an even more fortuitous stroke of luck, General Grant in March became the senior commander of U.S. forces in the field. Grant, since the fall of Vicksburg, had sought to take Mobile. As he notes in his autobiography, "Halleck disapproved of my proposition to go against Mobile, so that I was obliged to settle down and see myself put again on the defensive. . . ." By early June, Grant had directed that an attack on Mobile be combined with naval operations.

Farragut's battle plans were characteristically detailed. The admiral wanted his flagship, *Hartford*, to lead with the gunboat *Metacomet* lashed to her side. But in the event, and as a result of Farragut's yielding to his captains' wish that their commander take a less exposed place in line, the ironclad *Tecumseh* paired with *Brooklyn* had the honor of going first. Succeeding pairs of combatants would pass in strict formation but at sufficient distance to prevent the aft guns of the forward vessels and the forward guns of the following ones from endangering one another.

The four ironclads would proceed in line, screening the wooden ships from the Fort Morgan batteries. *Tecumseh*, with its two 15-inch guns, would lead. Once past the batteries, the fourteen-ship detachment would attack and destroy the Confederate gunboat flotilla inside the bay while other Union ships concentrated their fire on the forts from their sea side and stood guard to prevent any possible rebel combatants from entering the harbor and distracting the main engagement from the rear.

On August 1, General Granger's Federal troops arrived by ship. They began their march on Fort Gaines on the 4th. At a few minutes before 7:00 a.m. on Friday, August 5, *Tecumseh*'s guns opened on Fort Morgan. Granger's artillery barrage against Ft. Gaines began almost simultaneously, and quickly incapacitated the fort.

As the ships moved north slowly, suffering casualties, the area of most intense combat filled with smoke. Farragut found his view increasingly obscured. The 63-year-old started climbing and kept going until the flagship C.O., Captain Drayton, could barely see his superior through the smoke. Fearing for Farragut's safety and no doubt aware of the futility of persuading him to descend to where a violent motion of the ship would have less chance of throwing the admiral off his perch, Drayton sent a quartermaster above with a line to lash Farragut to the rigging.

Farragut demurred, but the quartermaster obeyed his captain's orders. So on sailed *Hartford* into the face of intense enemy fire with her admiral woven to the ship's shrouds just below the maintop. The picture of the flag officer so fixed to his ship captured the popular imagination when reported later in the press, but Farragut was only amused:

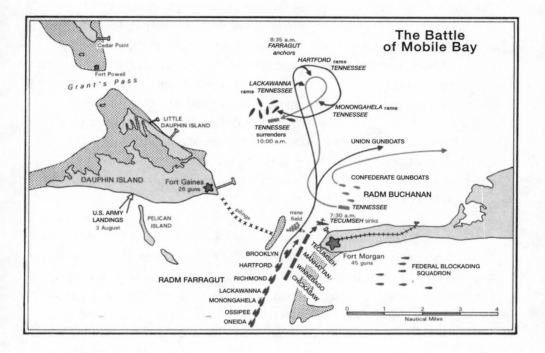

The Battle of Mobile Bay

he had simply been doing his duty, he said, when the quartermaster appeared with a rope.

Shortly afterwards the line of Union ships began to bunch. The slower wooden ships were catching up to the faster ironclads as they slowed, looking for mines. But Farragut's plan required them to go full speed ahead and ram *Tennessee* before the Confederate commander could form his ships into the crossbar of a "T" and rake the oncoming line of Union ships. Then, as Farragut urged his captains on, an explosion shook the entire harbor. *Tecumseh* had hit a mine—or torpedo as they were then called—and with propeller biting only the air, it slid below the surface in less than thirty seconds with ninety-three officers and men aboard. Farragut sent a boat that picked up ten survivors and the battle suspended for minutes on both sides as more rescue attempts eventually saved others. In the flowery Victorian language of 1882, the captain's fate was described in a *Harper's* magazine article:

No nobler instance of heroism adorns the page of history than that exhibited by the chivalrous Craven, her commander, who, having given orders for the abandonment of the ship, and finding himself and his pilot at the foot of the ladder leading to top of the turret and to safety, gallantly stepped to one side, saying, with a polite wave of the hand, "After you, sir" thus (so short was the time) going down with his ill fated craft, while the pilot, the water following close upon his heels, reached the roof of the turret, and was saved—saved to tell the story how the gallant Craven gave to his subordinate the one chance for life which remained between the two.

The moral effect of the loss was no less immediate for Craven's gallantry. Fearing a similar fate, *Brooklyn*'s C.O. slowed and then reversed her engines. Sitting there, she blocked the channel and lay open all the ships to Ft. Morgan's fire. The line of ships now bunched even more tightly, threatening to dissolve into chaos.

Under fire from Fort Morgan and the Confederate fleet, surrounded by the deadly torpedoes, Farragut now faced a split-second decision even more dramatic than the one he had faced at New Orleans: Should he risk more ships to the same danger that had sunk *Tecumseh*, or call off the attack? Pulling the foot of his pilot, Freeman, who was perched just above him, Farragut cried, "I shall lead." The pilot passed the order through a specially rigged speaking tube, and *Hartford* moved ahead, the rest of the line following.

As she came alongside the stopped *Brooklyn*, Farragut raised his voice to ask what the trouble was. Up came the answer, "Torpedoes." Down went the immortal response, "Damn the torpedoes. Four bells, Captain Drayton," thus telling his flagship C.O. to go full speed ahead.

The line passed Ft. Morgan's fire quickly. Farragut's guess that the length of their submersion would incapacitate other mines was proven correct. The Confederate ram *Tennessee* attacked several ships of the Union fleet and fled to the cover of Ft. Morgan's guns. She emerged not to flee to safety but—gallantly reminiscent of Pickett's doomed charge at Gettysburg—to attack the numerically superior Federal fleet.

During the endgame of the Battle of Mobile Bay, the Federal ship *Lackawanna*, in maneuvering to ram the Confederate ironclad, hit *Hartford* near where Farragut stood. Fearing the worst, the cry went up to "Save the admiral. Get the admiral aboard the *Lackawanna*." Mahan notes that the crew's reaction "by its ignoring of their own danger, testified how Farragut's martial and personal qualities had won a way into the affections of his subordinates." But the admiral was unhurt. Forced by ramming, pointblank fire and mounting casualties, *Tennessee* surrendered at 10:00 A.M., nearly three hours after the battle began.

When the battle's dead were placed on the deck Farragut wept. The quartermaster reported, "It was the only time I ever saw the old gentleman cry, but the tears came in his eyes, like a little child."

DAVID GLASGOW FARRAGUT was distinguished by several outstanding characteristics. As there are natural athletes or composers, he was a natural at war. His longer biographies show that he constantly sought to improve his professional understanding. Mahan notes in his biography's remarkable concluding chapter, "The Character of Admiral Farragut," that even when he visited Europe after the Civil War, the old admiral would look over the harbors of the cities he visited with a careful, critical eye. Mahan also argues that his habit of study and reading propelled him beyond the technical grasp of the ship that the Navy rewarded, to an understanding of naval warfare that the Navy placed less stock in. Not much has changed since.

His mind was as flexible and open to looking at things anew as his eye was watchful. Farragut wrote to Assistant Secretary of the Navy Fox after the capture of the ironclad *Indianola* on the lower Mississippi in 1863 that, "I never thought much of ironclads, but my opinion of them is declining daily. At any rate, I am willing to do the little fighting left to me . . . in the wooden ships." But a year later at Mobile he saw the value of the ironclads and reversed himself.

Finally, Farragut knew both how to weigh risks and how to take them. Both the decision to proceed against New Orleans without reducing the intervening forts as directed by orders and the decision to continue the advance into Mobile Bay despite the shocking loss of *Tecumseh* were big chances. But the dramatic situations and words belied the coolly calculated weighing of risk and reward that had in fact taken place before Farragut proceeded. Here was a man who was not afraid to die—"conquer or . . . be conquered," he had told his officers before New Orleans—who was also not willing to take needless risks. His strength was neither blind courage nor absolute calculation. In this, he will remain a fine example for all who would lead.

THE *COMMODORE*-CLASS GUNBOATS AND SOME OF THEIR PEOPLE

In addition to the coastal blockade and the drive to control the Mississippi, a third and equally important dimension of naval strategy emerged as the war proceeded: support of land operations by naval gunboats in the inland waterways. The importance of the gunboats in the Battle of Mobile Bay has already been discussed, but historians have often overlooked the courageous efforts of the gunboats and the men who sailed them. Much of the South that is east of the Mississippi is interlaced with navigable waterways; Union logistics there were entirely dependent on these waterways and a few railroads. Union armies were rarely far from navigable waterways and came to depend on naval amphibious operations, flanking maneuvers, direct gunfire support and, of course, logistics supply. On the Atlantic coast particularly, the missions of blockade and of riverine warfare in support of the Army were simultaneous and intertwined.

When the war started, the Navy had no craft suitable for such mission, but under Welles's forceful leadership the Union Navy was soon transformed. After 1861 every vessel constructed was steam-powered. New classes of fast, blue-water steam sloops to catch blockade-runners, steam-powered shallow draft gunboats, and thirty-six coastal monitors were immediately commissioned, with larger classes to follow. Captain Benjamin Isherwood, the chief of the Bureau of Steam Engineering, made it happen. Two huge 5,000-ton blue-water ironclads were built, *New Ironsides* and *Dunderberg*. A new class of thirty-seven double-ended ironclads designed for the inland waterways was also built. By the end of the war, 170 new steam warships had been built, most of entirely new designs.

None of the newly constructed monitors and ironclads, however, could enter the fleet until 1862. The ability of the Navy to take the offensive before that was made possible by a massive effort directed by Welles to obtain ships from the merchant marine. He issued commissions to George D. Morgan and John M. Forbes as Navy agents to buy vessels for the Union fleet. By the end of 1861, Morgan had purchased ninety vessels from New York alone. By the end of the war the Navy had acquired, principally from the merchant marine, a total of 479 vessels of different types.

The most successful of all of these acquisitions was an early purchase of double-end steam ferryboats, abundant in New York harbor in the era before a single bridge or tunnel existed. Ultimately more than eighty were bought or built. They turned out to be almost perfect for the riverine warfare that ensued and were procured by the Navy throughout the war. They were fast and shallow draft, but had very large deck area and carrying capacity, and being double-ended could quickly reverse out of difficult and confined waterways. The first of these boats were named after famous commodores of the Navy, but they became so valuable and popular that heroes' names were soon exhausted and they were thereafter named at the whim of the Bureau of Steam Engineering.

Commodore Jones was an excellent example of the class. It was 154 feet in length with a displacement of 542 tons, it had a beam of 32 feet 6 inches but drew less than 9 feet. A normal crew consisted of eighty-eight men, and when commissioned she was armed with four 9-inch smoothbore cannon, one 50-pounder rifled cannon, two 30-pounder rifled cannon, and four 24-pounder cannon. She could carry, in addition to her regular crew, several hundred troops for amphibious operations. The *Commodore Jones* was purchased by Morgan in New York in early 1863 and was commissioned on May 1, after being modified and armed at the Brooklyn Navy Yard with Lieutenant Commander J.G. Mitchell commanding. One of her "plank owners" (the naval term proudly claimed by sailors who are part of a vessel's crew when the vessel is commissioned) was 18-year-old Joseph V. Kelly, a combat veteran who a month earlier had joined the ship after passing the examination for Surgeon's Steward.

JOSEPH V. KELLY:
RIVERINE DOCTOR

Joseph Kelly was born in Philadelphia on July 19, 1844. He was an aspiring medical student when three days after his birthday in 1862, flushed with patriotism, he enlisted in the colorful and dashing regiment being raised in Philadelphia by an Irish-American, Colonel Charles Collis. His men were known as Collis's Zouaves because of their peacock uniform of red trousers, short blue jacket and white turban, copied from Napoleon III's elite Zouaves, which he had copied from the soldiers of the Ottoman Mamalukes of Egypt. Several such Zouave units were raised in the war but the 114th was the only such regiment to remain in Zouave uniform throughout the entire war.

Kelly got his first taste of infantry combat when he took part in what became a famous feat of gallantry by the 114th at the Battle of Fredericksburg on December 15, 1862. But after more infantry combat and General Ambrose Burnside's infamous "mud march," Kelly became extremely ill, and there being virtually no medical facilities for any but the most gravely wounded, he made his way back home to Philadelphia to recover.

Nursed back to health, he did not return to the Army. He had enjoyed about as much infantry experience as he cared to, and traveled to the Brooklyn Navy Yard, known to be far and away more advanced in medicine and medical care than the Army. During the Civil War one out of every twelve soldiers died from disease, while the Navy lost only one in every fifty. The Army Medical Corps was disorganized and ill supported by the War Department while the Navy Department had an early established Navy hospital system. From 1799 until 1830 it was based on paying civilian doctors to treat sailors ashore, and enlisting medically trained civilians to serve aboard ships as ships' surgeons. In 1830 the Navy established its first hospital in Portsmouth, Virginia, and by the end of the Civil War was operating eight main hospitals and many branches. The center of this system was the Brooklyn Naval Hospital, where in 1853 the Navy opened its own medical laboratory. During the Civil War the lab provided a reliable supply of high-quality medicines based on the latest worldwide research and was the center of recruiting, training and commissioning ship's surgeons. It was there that Kelly presented himself for examination, and upon passing was assigned to the pre-commissioning crew of *Commodore Jones*, assigned to the fleet off Virginia, arriving on May 11.

If avoiding combat had been Kelly's motivation for switching services, he had made a big mistake. *Commodore Jones* was in combat almost immediately, and continued in close action for Kelly's entire tour.

Several days after joining the squadron, *Jones* was sent up the James River to assist an evacuation of the army from West Point, Virginia. Soon thereafter she took part in the offensive expedition up the Mattapony River from June 3 to 7. Three days later, the *Commodore Jones* was assigned to a similar mission up the Chickahominy River. In the middle of the expedition, on June 13, *Commodore Jones* was recalled to sea in chase of the Confederate raider CSS *Tacony*, called by U.S. sailors *Florida II* after the notoriously successful CSS *Florida*. Between June 12 and June 24, with *Commodore Jones* among others in hot pursuit, *Tacony*, under Lieutenant C. W. Read, captured fifteen vessels. With the Union Navy closing in on Read he captured his last prize, a fishing schooner, and burned *Tacony* on the 25th, escaping in the schooner to Portland, Maine.

The action was a mere prelude to what lay ahead for *Commodore Jones* and Kelly. On September 12, while *Commodore Jones* was patrolling in the York River, the ship's surgeon W.C. Drennan was shot. Joseph Kelly was appointed surgeon's steward-in-charge on October 7.

Commodore Jones continued in myriad small actions and skirmishes in the rivers and waterways of Virginia in support of Grant's campaign

Dr. Joseph V. Kelly. His early medical training was hazardous to his health.
Lehman Family Collection

against Richmond. On May 5, 1864, 40,000 troops of Benjamin Butler's ill-fated army were loaded on an armada of transports of every description at Newport News and proceeded up the James for a landing at Bermuda Hundred. *Jones* and five other gunboats led the vanguard. By sunset they had landed the first brigade without interference. "But on the morning of the sixth," recalled Kelly, "the picture changed. A runaway slave came on board one of the gunboats and reported that numerous mines were up ahead, especially in the vicinity of Deep Bottom. He had seen the Confederates working at them, and he knew they were there."

He was right. The following is a report by the commanding officer of USS *Mackinaw*, which was accompanying the *Commodore Jones* along with *Commodore Morris:*

> In obedience to orders from Fleet Captain Barnes, I proceeded up the river with the *Commodore Morris* and *Commodore Jones*, following at a safe distance boats from the different vessels, which were dragging for torpedoes. When within about 500 yards of the position of some torpedoes, as informed by the contrabands, I anchored, ordering the *Morris* and *Jones* not to approach nearer than the boats, explaining to them both the danger to be anticipated by so doing. While endeavoring to get a more convenient berth farther down the river, and occupied by the movements of my own vessel, the *Jones* disregarding repeated orders she had been given, ran over a torpedo, which exploded instantly and totally destroyed her. I am unable at this time to furnish the names or number of those who were lost in this disastrous occurrence.

"It seemed as if the bottom of the river was torn up and blown through the vessel itself," wrote one eyewitness. "*Jones* was lifted almost entirely clear of the water, and she burst in the air like an exploding firecracker. She was in small pieces when she struck the water again."

While debris was still settling down on the ruffled surface of the water, three men were seen to run out of the bushes along the bank of the river. A coxswain in a cutter, dragging for mines, shot one of them dead. The other two, P.W. Smith and Jarvis Johnson, were captured and revealed that *Jones* had been destroyed by 2,000 pounds of powder in a sealed barrel placed in the river the previous fall.

A majority of the ship's company were killed or wounded, including the skipper, Thomas F. Wade, who was severely wounded. When he was able to write he made the following report:

> It becomes my painful duty to inform you of the total loss of the U.S. gunboat *Commodore Jones* on the 6th instant, off deep bottom James River, Virginia.
>
> While dragging for torpedoes and covering the boats, which were also searching for them, a torpedo was exploded directly under the ship with terrible effect, causing her destruction instantly, absolutely blowing the vessel to splinters. Of the loss of crew I am unable to inform you, as the rescued were distributed among the fleet and sent to the naval hospital, being seriously wounded myself and unable to attend to duty.

Only nine years later was it learned that the mine was in fact command-detonated by the three operatives—members of the Confederate Torpedo Service—who were waiting in their riverbank bunker. Waterproof wires were connected to an early galvanic battery located in a hidden spot on the riverbank. The wires were in turn connected to the torpedo. The position of the torpedoes in the water was indicated to the men on the shore by two inconspicuous sticks planted about ten feet apart on the bluff, and in line with each other and the torpedoes. As *Commodore Jones* proceeded up the channel and lined up with the two sticks the two wires were connected by the hidden rebel and the 2,000 pounds of gunpowder at the bottom of the river detonated.

Joseph Kelly was one of the lucky ones. He was blown high in the air and fell unconscious into the water. One of his shipmates grabbed him and dragged him to shore, where he was soon taken back aboard one of the Union vessels.

After recovering in Portsmouth Naval hospital, Kelly was reassigned to the steamer *Britannia*, then on blockade off Wilmington, North Carolina. Because of its geography, Wilmington was one of the most active blockade-running ports of the Confederacy and was not wholly shut down until the very end of the war. The *Britannia* was itself a captured blockade-runner, and while aboard Kelly took part in several hot pursuits of blockade-runners off Fort Fisher, but failed to earn any prize money.

On March 25, Kelly was detached from *Britannia* and ordered for duty aboard *Shokoken*, another commodore-class converted ferry. At this time he received his promotion to acting assistant surgeon. *Shokoken*, like *Commodore Jones*, saw continuous action ferrying and supporting troops, but further south in the rivers and sounds of North Carolina.

By the war's end, although it had not been a particularly religious lad who had enlisted in the Zouaves in 1862, the young man who returned to medical studies in 1865 had been changed by his many brushes with the grim reaper. Kelly created a fuss in Philadelphia society when, upon proposing marriage to Emma Jane Ferguson, the daughter of a prominent Presbyterian divine, he insisted that she convert to the Catholic faith, which she did. They were married in 1866, and he graduated from Jefferson Medical College in 1868. Years later when a young doctor from one of Philadelphia's oldest families, Doctor Joseph Davis Lehman, asked Dr. Kelly for the hand of his daughter Frances my grandmother, in marriage, Kelly again demanded that the Episcopalian Lehman first become a Catholic. Dr. Kelly practiced medicine in Philadelphia for fifty years and died in December 1918. One of his obituaries noted that he was "a daily attendant at holy mass." Given what he had survived it is not surprising.

William B. Cushing:
Academy Washout

Another sailor on *Shokoken* and other commodore-class gunboats was William Cushing. It has often been noted that success in the peacetime Navy and in the closed world of the Naval Academy has little correlation with wartime leadership. Senator John McCain was always on the verge of being thrown out of the Naval Academy; Admiral Harold Stark, a great success in Washington, had to be removed as chief of naval operations shortly after the fighting started in World War II. Fighting ships in war requires attributes that are not necessarily appreciated in peacetime.

Such a man was William Cushing. Born in 1842 in Delafield, Wisconsin, he was the fifth of seven children of a country doctor who died when he was four. He entered the Naval Academy in 1857 and quickly made an impression. He earned 99 demerits his first year and 188 the second. He was a fun-loving boy who had a "casual approach to discipline and academics." Despite excelling at such skills as gunnery, in which he finished third in his class, finishing last in languages precipitated his expulsion from the academy. The superintendent, Captain George S. Blake, found him "Deficient at February semi-annual examination, 1861 . . . Deficient in Spanish. Aptitude for study: good. Habits of study: irregular. General conduct: bad. Aptitude for Naval Service: not good. Not recommended for continuance at the Academy." He was ordered to leave the academy just months before his class was expected to graduate in 1861.

But then as now, political influence was never far from the Navy. Cushing's mother's cousin was a commodore, and a close family friend was a congressman. An appeal was made directly to the secretary of the Navy, Gideon Welles, at the very time that South Carolina began the Civil War by firing on Fort Sumter. The secretary appointed Cushing acting masters mate in the U.S. Volunteer Navy, and he was assigned to the steam frigate *Minnesota* (47), where he quickly distinguished himself in action, first by successfully commanding two prize vessels and later in charge of the eight-gun quarterdeck division of the frigate.

After conspicuous coolness under fire and leadership exhibited during the assault against the forts around the Hatteras Inlet, Cushing was reinstated as midshipman. Shortly thereafter he was assigned as executive officer of one of the commodore-class gunboats, *Commodore Perry*. Almost continually in action, Cushing was promoted to lieutenant nine months later.

In October 1862, Cushing was cited for gallantry during a six-hour battle with Confederate infantry along the Blackwater River near Franklin, Virginia. As the war proceeded in the South, the Navy developed tactics to enable its shallow-draft but heavily armed gunboats to go far inland in the tidal rivers and creeks. In cases where the creek bend was too sharp for a ship's turning radius, men were put ashore and ropes tied to trees, and the bow of the ship swung round the bend. It was during one of these maneuvers during the battle that Cushing's ship came hard aground on the left bank of the river.

Confederate infantry, which had tried to block the river, seized the opportunity and attacked *Perry* and two other gunboats, *Hunchback* and *Whitehead*. In a photograph of *Hunchback* taken during the war, a small artillery fieldpiece is in evidence on the upper deck housing of the ship. Such small, easily movable guns were helpful in defending these boats against land-based forces by supplementing the main battery. They were 12-pound howitzers, designed to be moved about on the larger river gunboats or put aboard smaller boats, or taken ashore by naval landing parties. Cushing and seven volunteers wheeled one of these movable howitzers out on deck as a horde of Confederate infantry stormed *Perry*. Under withering fire from the charging infantry, Cushing calmly aimed and fired a round of canister into the rebel line with devastating effect. The Confederates were driven off and the mission succeeded. In the report to the Navy Department, Cushing was singled out for gallantry, with the senior officer, Commander Davenport, adding "while I cannot praise too highly the gallantry and heroism displayed by the officers and men on the occasion, I think it extremely hazardous for our gun boats unprotected as the men are by bulwarks or any other defenses, to go up these narrow and tortuous channels."

Following that action Cushing was given command of his own gunboat, *Ellis*. In November 1862, *Ellis* sailed boldly through New River Inlet to capture Jacksonville, North Carolina. Cushing captured two schooners, some arms and mail. On her way downriver, *Ellis* ran aground on November 24 and could not be refloated. After dark her commanding officer, with great coolness, moved all the crew except six and all her equipment and supplies except for a swivel gun, some ammunition, two tons of coal and a few small arms, to one of the captured schooners. While the schooner slipped down the river to wait, Cushing and five of his men remained. Early on the morning of the 25th, the Confederates opened fire on *Ellis*, and in a short time Cushing was about to be overwhelmed. Before leaving, he set fire to her in five places, leaving the gun trained on the enemy so that the ship herself would carry on the fight as the flames fired the cannon. Cushing and his men reached the schooner and made for the sea, getting the vessel over the bar just in time to escape several companies of cavalry trying to cut them off at the mouth of the inlet. *Ellis* was blown to pieces by the explosion of her magazine shortly thereafter.

Cushing was immediately given command of another of the commodore-class gunboats, choosing this more dangerous and less potentially lucrative work over the offer of command of a faster vessel intended to go after blockade-runners. While in *Commodore Barney* in April 1863 Cushing commanded a squadron of four other ships, *Mount Washington, Stepping Stones, Cohasset* and *Alert,* in support of the Army defending Suffolk from General Longstreet. During the three weeks of the campaign, he saw action nearly every day against Confederate artillery and infantry. When the rebels finally retired, *Barney* had received so much shot and shell that she had to be sent to Baltimore for refit and repair. Cushing was once again cited for gallantry and meritorious service, this time by Gideon Welles himself.

In August of 1863, he received command of Kelly's *Shokoken* and was sent against blockade-runners in the shoal waters and sand bars off Wilmington, North Carolina. Cushing immediately had doubts about the seaworthiness of his ship in this role but pursued the challenge with his usual aggressiveness, making numerous raids and expeditions around the sounds of coastal North Carolina. His fears soon proved to be well founded when he nearly lost the ship during a northeaster near Frying Pan Shoals, at one point taking on water at the rate of 450 gallons per minute. Cushing officially reported that the ship was not fit for blockade duty, and she was assigned to more sheltered waters in the sounds and rivers of North Carolina.

Cushing was given command of *Monticello*, a swift seagoing vessel then undergoing repairs in Philadelphia. She was a 180-foot schooner-rigged steamship armed with a large Dahlgren gun, several large smoothbores and assorted other arms. But Cushing was destined for a run-in with a far more formidable vessel.

The Confederates had developed a plan for five armored rams early in the war with which they felt they could clear their coastal waters of the Union Navy. The first of these, *Albemarle*, was built in a cornfield, at Edward's Ferry on the Roanoke River in North Carolina. When completed she was 158 feet long, with a shallow draft and a beam of 35 feet. She had an eighteen-foot ram, two layers of two-inch armored plating over four-foot yellow-pine timbers and six gunports. She was more than a match for the unarmored commodore-class gunboats of the Union river force. Had the Confederates built all five of these ships, the Union would indeed have had a difficult time maintaining control of the coastal waterways. Fortunately for the Union, only *Albemarle* was finished.

In April 1864, *Albemarle* steamed down the Roanoke River to assist the Confederate Army's attack on Plymouth, North Carolina. She encountered one of the converted ferryboats, *Southfield*, and sank her, with *Southfield*'s companions *Miami* and *Whitehead* beating a hasty retreat. As a result of this success, the Confederates were able to take Plymouth, and the Confederate Congress gave a vote of thanks to *Albemarle*'s commander.

Early the next month, *Albemarle*, with two smaller steamers, the CSS *Cotton Plant*, and the CSS *Bombshell* (eighty-five and ninety feet respectively) proceeded into Albemarle Sound and attacked Union Navy forces, including four heavily armed gunboats, at the mouth of the Roanoke River. *Bombshell* was captured early in the action, and *Cot-*

ton Plant escaped back into the Roanoke River, but the *Albemarle* continued to fight against the four U.S. ships, severely damaging *Sassacus*. *Sassacus*, during the battle, had turned the tables on *Albemarle* and "rammed the ram"—at great risk to her own unreinforced bow. For thirteen minutes the ships remained attached, the *Sassacus*'s shattered bow clinging to *Albemarle*'s iron casement. Then a shot from one of *Albemarle*'s guns pierced a boiler on *Sassacus*, scalding many of the engineering gang (the chief engineer stayed at his post though blinded and scalded by the steam, throughout the action). The rebels attempted to board, but were repelled by musketry and grenades from men in *Sassacus*'s rigging, and by the ship's gun crews. The ships were both enveloped in clouds of steam and gun smoke, with the *Sassacus*'s guns battering away to little or no effect at the armored casement of *Albemarle*. Fighting continued until darkness fell, when *Albemarle* withdrew back up the river, leaving *Sassacus* to limp to safety and *Commodore Hull* on picket duty, nervously awaiting her return.

The engagement had really spooked the Union commanders, one of whom wrote, "The ram is certainly very formidable. She is fast for that class of vessel, making from 6 to 7 knots, turns quickly, and is armed with heavy guns. . . ." The commander of *Sassacus* agreed: "I'm forced to think that *Albemarle* is more formidable than *Merrimack* or *Atlanta* for our solid 100-pounder rifle shot flew into splinters upon her iron plates." Her own commander, however, Commander Cooke, complained to the Confederate Navy Secretary Mallory that the ram "draws too much water to navigate the sounds well, and has not sufficient buoyancy. In consequence she is very slow and not easily managed. Her decks are so near the water as to render it an easy task for the enemies vessel to run on her, and any great weight soon submerges the deck. . . ."

Destroying *Albemarle* became the top priority for the U.S. Navy for the next five months. One of a number of attempts to sink her is described in *Dictionary of American Naval Fighting Ships:*

The first of those missions was concocted and attempted by five sailors from USS *Wayalusing* on 26 May. They rowed up Middle River that afternoon carrying two 100-pound torpedoes

and then carried them by stretcher across the swampland separating the Middle and Roanoke Rivers to a point just above and
opposite *Albemarle*'s mooring place at Plymouth. Two of the
sailors swam across the River with a towline attached to the ex-
plosive devices and then hauled them across . . . Unfortunately,
the Confederates caught sight of both swimmer and torpedoes
when they were just a few yards short of their goal. A hail of
musketry from the shore followed soon after the sentry's
hail . . . The five union sailors scattered. Three returned to
Wayalusing on the evening of 28 May. The remaining two re-
joined their ship the following night after rescue by USS *Commodore Hull*. All five ultimately received the Medal of Honor
for their daring attempt.

Welles sought to have one of the new Union ironclad monitors pursue *Albemarle*, but that was determined to be infeasible. It was decided
instead that a small-boat mission was the only option.

William Cushing was chosen for the daring—almost suicidal—mission. A plan developed using thirty-two-foot open steam launches with
spar torpedoes. A spar torpedo was a warhead on the end of a twenty-
foot pole, which was to be extended out in front of the boat that carried
it, to be detonated next to the hull of the target ship by pulling a lan-
yard. Cushing chose the two vessels at the Brooklyn Navy Yard, and
they traveled down the Delaware and Raritan Canal through Trenton
and Philadelphia, then through the Delaware and Chesapeake Canal
and on down the Chesapeake Bay. On the way down, one of the boats
sought refuge in a creek on the Virginia shore because of heavy
weather and was promptly captured.

Albemarle was moored on the waterfront of Plymouth, North Carolina, seven miles up the Roanoke River. In order to increase manpower and to make up for the loss of the captured launch, a cutter with
fifteen volunteers was towed behind the remaining launch to attack
pickets expected downriver from *Albemarle*. After traveling up the river
without discovery, a dog bark alerted a sentry, and Cushing's hope to
board *Albemarle* by stealth was dashed. Nevertheless, Cushing contin-

ued with the plan to destroy the ship with the spar torpedo. The cutter
was released, and Cushing ordered "ahead fast," as the Confederate
sentries sounded the alert. By the light of a bonfire the Confederates
had prepared for situations just like this, Cushing noticed a log boom
deployed in the water around *Albemarle* to protect against a torpedo attack. Cushing gave the order for full speed ahead, and the launch
struck and rode partway over the log while under continuing fire from
the sentries. Now only ten feet from *Albemarle*, with its guns staring
him in the face, Cushing extended the torpedo and pulled the trigger
as bullets tore holes in his clothing. With *Albemarle*'s guns firing at the
same time as the thunderous torpedo explosion, Cushing ended up in
the water. Ten of his sailors were captured and two drowned, but Cushing and one seaman were able to swim back down the river to Union
forces. *Albemarle* promptly sank at her mooring.

With no ironclad threat, the Union Army and Navy retook Plymouth by the first of November. *Albemarle* was raised and brought to
Washington, where she was condemned as a prize and sold to the U.S.
Navy. In 1865 Cushing received $18,000 prize money, and eight years
later, with the cases reopened, another $38,000. Cushing was now a na-
tional hero. The dropout was promoted to lieutenant commander, and
Congress voted him a resolution of thanks.

While there is still no Cushing on the rolls of the Naval Academy,
class of 1861, there have been five ships on the rolls of the U.S. fleet
that bear his name.

IT IS HARD TO OVERSTATE the importance of the *commodore*-class and
other side-wheeler gunboats. They were ideally suited to the geography and tactics of the war in the South where the Union Navy most
needed augmentation. They were easily maintained with steam plants
long in common use. They provided the Army with mobility and fire
support while substantially denying the Confederacy the use of the inland waterways so valuable for transportation. That such a pragmatic

solution was embraced so enthusiastically is a tribute to Welles and his captains.

RAPHAEL SEMMES AND CONFEDERATE COMMERCE RAIDERS

At first the South had little difficulty in penetrating the Union blockade, but as the size of the blockading fleet grew rapidly and tightened its coverage, blockade running became more challenging and more expensive in the quality of ships demanded, and competed directly with the Confederate commerce raiding strategy.

In May 1861, Theodore Roosevelt's uncle, James D. Bulloch (the source of his naval inspiration), was sent to England by Confederate Navy Secretary Stephen Mallory to commission the building of commerce raiders and to purchase and arm merchant vessels suitable for the purpose. He procured and outfitted *Alabama, Florida* and *Shenandoah*, and together these three excellent ships and a variety of lesser craft effectively destroyed the American-flagged Merchant Marine. By the end of the war three-quarters of the Union merchant vessels, which before the war had dominated both the Atlantic and China trades, had been reflagged to foreign jurisdiction. The American Merchant Marine has never recovered from that Confederate success.

Commanded by the South's most famous naval officer, the Confederate commerce raider *Alabama* displaced 940 tons and was powered by sail and steam-driven propeller. Since the South lacked the requisite shipbuilding capability, she was constructed at Liverpool and launched in May 1862, the best efforts of U.S. Ambassador Charles Francis Adams notwithstanding. On the copper rim of the *Alabama*'s wheel was inscribed her motto: *Aide toi et Dieu t'aidera*, "Help yourself and God will help you." Was God really on the Confederate side? Lincoln in his second inaugural said that it is "strange that any men should dare to ask a just God's assistance in wringing their bread from the sweat of other men's faces."

Alabama's commanding officer, Captain Raphael Semmes, had no such doubt. In a letter to his brother Samuel, he wrote:

> Although I cared very little about the institution of slavery, I thought that the subordinate position of the inferior race was its proper position. I believed that the doctrine of States' Rights was the only doctrine that would save our Republic from the fate of all other Republics that had gone before us.

Other distinguished officers, such as Lee and Longstreet, felt the pull of their home states in deciding to transfer allegiance from the Union to the Confederacy. Few who became famous in the war were as passionate in their embrace of slavery or distaste for the egalitarian, commercial North as Semmes. It is perhaps appropriate that Semmes would earn his reputation by attacking this commerce as it was carried on the high seas.

Semmes was born in Charles County, Maryland in 1809. Orphaned at 10, he grew up in Georgetown. In 1826, his uncle, Benedict, who had recently been elected to the Maryland House of Delegates, secured a presidential appointment for Raphael as a midshipman in the Navy.

For the next five years of his probationary period as a midshipman, he sailed aboard *Lexington, Erie* and *Brandywine* on cruises to the West Indies and Mediterranean before being ordered to the Washington Navy Yard. There Semmes studied for and completed, at the head of his class, the written tests required of a "passed midshipman." He stayed ashore for the next three years superintending the care of the Navy's chronometers and beginning his study of the law, before returning again to the sea to serve aboard a number of vessels.

When the Mexican War broke out in 1846, Semmes was first lieutenant on *Porpoise,* a member of the squadron that blockaded Vera Cruz, Mexico's deepest water port. While embarked on this unexciting mission, Semmes found time to extend a practice he had begun earlier in his career, keeping a journal. The notes he composed during the war were published in 1851 under the title *Service Afloat and Ashore during the Mexican War.* The book was popular. It is a social, political and geographical account of Mexico's history leading up to the war and of the causes of the conflict. Although still used as a reference work the book is also a straightforward account of Semmes' political passions. Commenting on the cause of the war, he says:

> An all-wise providence has placed us in juxtaposition with an inferior people, in order, without doubt, that we may sweep over them, and remove them (as a people) and their worn out institutions from the face of the world. We are the northern hordes of the Alani, spreading over fairer and sunnier fields . . .

His political commentary aside, the war gave Semmes, as it did other officers who would achieve distinction in the Civil War, his first combat command. He became skipper of the brig *Somers* in October 1846. It was an unlucky ship. Accusations of a planned mutiny by the previous captain had resulted in the hanging of three sailors. Under Semmes, the ship capsized with loss of half his seventy-six-man crew. His later career would prove that there was nothing wrong with his seamanship, and a court of inquiry exonerated Semmes of all blame.

Semmes served out most of the years between the end of the Mexican and the beginning of the Civil war "on the beach" as an author and lawyer. Upon recall in 1856 he became a senior official in the bureaucracy that cared for lighthouses, a critically important aid to commercial shipping in the days before radio, radar and global-positioning satellites. When the war began in 1861, Semmes was almost 52, a highly responsible naval officer who had served in combat and possessed deep experience in blockade operations, with long familiarity with the winds and currents of the Gulf and Caribbean, a practical background in land maritime law and a keen grasp of commercial shipping's importance.

Unlike Robert E. Lee, who was torn between the loyalty he felt to his Virginia birthplace and the oath he had sworn "to bear true allegiance to the United States of America," there was little doubt about whose side Semmes should take. In a letter written after Lincoln's election and before his March inauguration, Semmes told the Georgia politician and later vice president of the Confederacy Alexander H. Stephens that "my judgment, my inclinations, and my affections all incline me to link myself with the first movement of the South."

But Semmes was troubled. "Maryland is my native State," he wrote. "Suppose she lags . . . and in the meantime the more remote Southern States form themselves into a confederacy, and organize their government including their Army and Navy, would the door be open for officers circumstanced like myself?"

Not wanting to wait, Semmes joined the war effort at once. He drafted a long memorandum that assessed the South's Navy yards and argued that rather than relying on the North's merchant shipping or the more costly option of foreign bottoms, the Confederacy would have to step in and conduct its own coastal trade. An effective coastal defense would also be needed. And commercial profit, in the form of privateers, should be harnessed to prey upon the Union's vulnerable seagoing trade.

Despite Semmes's enthusiasm, the South was not well prepared for naval war. While the United States at the beginning of the conflict possessed the world's second-largest merchant fleet, the seceded states' portion of this tonnage amounted to one-tenth. This crippling shortage could not be overcome by the South's own means. As Semmes noted in his autobiography, "we had not the means in the entire Confederacy of turning out a complete steam engine of any size, and many of our naval disasters are attributable to this deficiency."

In strategic terms, the naval understanding of the Confederacy's president, Jefferson Davis, reflected his states' meager naval equipage. A graduate of West Point, and secretary of war in Franklin Pierce's administration, he had little knowledge of, or interest in, things naval.

Early in the war, the British East India Company—following the disastrous Indian Mutiny of 1857—transferred its powers to the crown and sold ten of its first-class East Indiamen. At half-price, the steam-powered vessels were a steal. As configured, they could already carry cargo, naval guns and troops. Conversion into naval combatants capable of operations against the Union blockade would be swift and simple. The South could then hope to keep its economic lifeline—the sea-lanes over which cotton was conveyed to foreign ports and essential war materiel brought back—from being throttled. Foolishly the Confederate government rejected the purchase.

In his carefully researched account of the raider CSS *Alabama*, Charles M. Robinson III argues persuasively that Jefferson Davis is the most likely culprit. The only other possibility—Secretary of the Confederate Navy Stephen Mallory—would have understood the immense advantage of purchasing the ships and is unlikely to have made such a strategic blunder.

Davis also seems to have lacked imagination in other professional dealings. Raphael Semmes met the future president of the Confederacy in Montgomery in February when Davis was president of the provisional government. Instead of assigning this most experienced naval officer to desperately needed naval planning, he sent Semmes north on a shopping trip "to make contracts for machinery and munitions for the manufacture of arms and munitions of war." He went, and found Northern merchants who would for the right price sell a potential enemy such militarily critical tools as those used for rifling cannon (only confirming his views of greedy, unprincipled New Englanders). But he could have been better used elsewhere.

The Confederate economy depended on trade by sea and river almost entirely. The Confederacy should have copied the successful American strategy in the Revolution and War of 1812, and concentrated a massive effort against the Union's huge and defenseless commerce on the seven seas. In the end, Jefferson Davis's failure to understand this allowed the execution of only a partial effort. But that was where Semmes made his mark.

Within days of the outbreak of war, Mallory was meeting with Semmes in Montgomery and going over the list of available, capable ships that could conduct effective operations against Union commercial traffic. Semmes noticed a 184-foot-long, approximately 500-ton steamer, *Havana*, and asked Mallory to "give me that ship. I think that I can make her answer the purpose." The vessel was renamed *Sumter*, to honor the war's first action.

Semmes left for New Orleans almost immediately and upon arriving there got his command ready for sea. *Sumter* carried four 32-pound howitzers and an 8-inch pivot gun aft of her foremast. She was ready to sail within two weeks. On June 18, at night, *Sumter* cast off and sailed downriver toward the Union blockade.

Four steam-propelled U.S. Navy ships—one for each of the channels that lead to the Gulf—maintained the blockade of New Orleans. The smallest was four, the largest eight, times *Sumter*'s displacement. Semmes told the pilot to proceed and that "if he ran us ashore or put us in the hands of the enemy, we would swing him to the yardarm as traitor." *Sumter* made it to the mouth of the channel—just as the 2070-ton *Brooklyn* hove into sight at a range of about 6,800 yards and closing. Semmes pressed on sail, lightened the ship and, increasing steam pressure by almost 40 percent, made a run for it. *Sumter*'s sailing points were her salvation, allowing her under Semmes's skilled con to squeak through.

Sumter made for the Caribbean and the waters around Cuba, with which much U.S. trade was conducted. Since Semmes was the first Confederate commerce raider to break the blockade, there were no Union combatants in those waters, but there remained the challenge of keeping repaired and supplied without rerunning the blockade.

Britain was the answer. Having declared itself neutral in the war, she recognized the Confederacy as a belligerent just short of full diplomatic recognition. Under international law, this allowed Semmes to provision his command with everything except munitions—and they could be had elsewhere.

Sumter's other means of feeding and provisioning itself would be to live off the sea. On July 3, Semmes captured his first prize, the 600-ton bark *Golden Rocket*, out of Brewster, Maine, and bound for Cuba. *Golden Rocket* carried ballast, as well as a normal supply of cordage, paint and sails. Semmes took these as well as the ship's chronometer. He moved her crew aboard *Sumter* and burned her.

For the rest of his career as a commerce raider, this was Semmes's standard procedure: grab the valuables and fire the hapless freighter. His exception was when he bonded a captured ship. Upon seizing a British or other foreign ship that carried an American cargo, Semmes would release the ship in exchange for the captain's promise to pay a specified bond to the Confederate government at the conclusion of hostilities—a promise eventually made worthless by the war's outcome.

There was one other possible exception to a fiery end: if the hull was American and the cargo foreign-owned. Such was the case with the two victims that followed *Golden Rocket*, *Machias* and *Cuba*, both American-owned vessels carrying British-owned cargoes of sugar.

Some countries—for example, Britain and France—would not accept captured prizes sent in by belligerents. But Spain would. Semmes put prize crews aboard both vessels, and the *Machias* and *Cuba* headed together for the port of Cienfuegos on Cuba's south coast. As he escorted them, he captured two more American-owned ships, *Albert Adams* and *Ben Dunning*, both with Spanish-owned cargoes.

The prizes kept piling up. Inbound to the Cienfuegos channel, *Sumter* encountered a steam tug pulling three American vessels in the opposite direction—out to sea. Semmes and the ships in his growing convoy broke out Spanish flags and, to allay any suspicion, raised signal flags asking for the tug's services. As soon as it was clear that the American ships had passed the legal five-mile limit, Semmes replaced the Spanish colors with the Stars and Bars, and took chase—notwithstanding that neutral territory was prohibited from being used as a launching site for a belligerent's combat operations.

Semmes's disciplined mind and legal training were excellent preparation and served him well in his work. Landing at Cienfuegos, Semmes sent an emissary ashore to replenish the ship with coal and to deliver a letter to the Spanish authorities, who he hoped would allow *Sumter*'s prizes into their ports for ultimate adjudication by Confederate admiralty courts. The argument having been duly presented, Semmes left his prizes in the safekeeping of a hired agent and put to sea before news of his exploits, telegraphed by the local U.S. consul to Havana, could summon a Union warship from Key West. But days before Semmes broke the U.S. blockade at New Orleans, Spain had declared its neutrality. Queen Isabella's representatives subsequently applied their bureaucratic skills to avoid offense to the *Yanqui* traders who were critical to the economy of the crown's Caribbean possessions. Semmes's prizes were released because the local authorities, winking, decided that they had been seized inside territorial waters.

Diplomatic and legal winking was easier than usual, not only for Spain, but for all foreign authorities. To the Union, Semmes was a pirate, to everyone else, a man at war. Northern hatred of Semmes grew in part because some foreign states still refused to accept Semmes's prizes, leaving him with no other option except to burn the American ships he seized. He burned three-quarters of the eighty-two ships he captured.

As targets became scarce—the result of his successes—and with *Sumter*'s boilers corroding under heavy usage as well as a problem developing with a crack in the propeller sleeve, the ship headed for Europe in late November. By this time Semmes had forced Gideon Welles to weaken the blockade by sending six combatants to find and destroy *Sumter*. This was a daunting task, given the Confederate raider's abundant supply of foreign flags, her ability to lower her funnel and no paddle wheel to identify the vessel as a steamer.

Sumter headed east toward Gibraltar and, following a late-season hurricane, arrived at the Straits in mid-January.

Confederate Navy officials were evidently satisfied enough with Semmes's performance—the cruise had resulted in the capture of eighteen ships since breaking the blockade at New Orleans. While in the Mediterranean, *Sumter*'s boilers finally gave out and Semmes was ordered to England to take on a new command.

The little raider and a handful of Confederate privateers could claim tangible success in less than a year of operations. By the end of 1861, insurance rates for American-flagged vessels had doubled, and they continued to climb throughout the war. American shipowners began shifting to British Registry.

ALABAMA, BEAUTIFUL SHARK
OF THE CONFEDERACY

The Confederacy's problem in shopping for an English-made combatant was the Foreign Enlistment Act, which forbade the preparation for war of a belligerent vessel. James Bulloch overcame this obstacle by arranging for the William C. Miller Company of Liverpool to build what was referred to as *Enrica*, and then to complete its arming beyond Britain's territorial waters. Whisking *Enrica* off to sail under the Confederate flag was complicated because the Confederate commerce raider *Florida* had followed the same course not four months earlier and the local U.S. consul was now on the alert. But Bulloch had his own well-placed agents.

Keeping his personal distance from the almost completed ship and a weather eye on Prime Minister Palmerston's office to raise an alarm if a move was detected to seize *Enrica*, Bulloch quietly moved the plot forward. When he learned that legal impoundment was imminent, the Confederate agent told the shipbuilders that a short but immediate trial was required. With all the appearances of a celebration, including refreshments and liquor to entice a crew, as well as a month's salary up front, *Enrica* weighed anchor in late July just hours ahead of what would have amounted to the British government's restraining order. Semmes caught up with her in the Azores and pronounced her "a beautiful thing to look upon."

Within days, the ship was armed and ready. Before sailing, however, Semmes needed to find a personal steward. While sailing to Liverpool, Semmes noticed a young man who was acting as steward on board.

> He was an obedient, respectful, and attentive major-domo, but unfortunately . . . too much addicted to wine. . . . Bartelli did not seem to have the power of self-restraint, especially under the treatment he received, which was not gentle. The captain was very rough with him, and the poor fellow seemed very much cowed . . . trembling when spoken to harshly. His very

forlornness drew me toward him. He was an Italian, evidently of gentle blood, and as with the Italians, drinking to intoxication is not an ineradicable vice.

Semmes "felt confident that he could be reformed under proper treatment" and offered the young man a position as personal steward aboard *Alabama* so long as Bartelli promised never "to touch a drop of liquor on board the ship on duty." I cite Semmes's short description of Bartelli not because it captures the steward so well but because it is Semmes in a nutshell: observant, decent, given to unwieldy characterizations based on race or ethnicity, and effective in his discipline. Semmes notes that Bartelli kept his promise.

On August 24, Semmes read his commission as captain in the Confederate Navy, and his orders to take command. The now properly named CSS *Alabama*—a fast ship because of her retractable propeller—got underway and headed straight for Yankee whalers as they harvested the leviathans at the height of the season.

Alabama's first prize was *Okmulgee*, which, besides her flammable cargo, carried an abundant supply of food, which was promptly brought aboard. The whaler's crew were put in boats to make their way back on a calm sea to one of the nearby Azores, and the ship was torched. The schooner *Starlight* was *Alabama*'s next victim. Having learned that Federal authorities had imprisoned one of *Sumter*'s crew, Semmes put the *Starlight* crew in the brig—before freeing them ashore in the Azores. His legal sense of proportionate justice matched his revulsion at being called a pirate. Putting Union sailors in irons, he hoped, would underscore the injustice and thus end the practice of imprisoning Confederate sailors. It did.

In September 1862, the first full month of her cruise, *Alabama* captured and destroyed ten ships. The next month, after the whaling season peaked, Semmes changed his operating area to the Canadian Maritime Provinces' and New England littoral. His monthly tally increased to eleven.

Semmes then headed to the Caribbean, meeting and burning *Levi Starbuck*, another whaler, on the way. He met up with his coal tender,

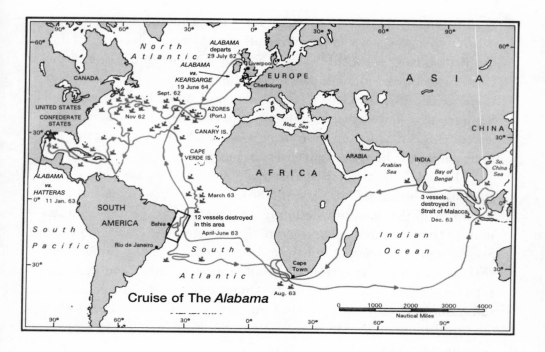

Cruise of The *Alabama*

Agrippina, in Venezuelan waters, and replenished. While there he hosted the master of a passing American whaling schooner. The master came credulously aboard and told *Alabama*'s C.O. that this was "the very ship 'to give the pirate Semmes fits.'" Semmes unmasked himself to the terrified whaler and told him that because they were in Venezuelan waters, the American ship was safe. The whaler should not worry: there was no danger to "the various little ventures which he had on board with which to trade with the natives along the coast and turn that 'honest penny' which has so many charms in the eyes of his countrymen."

   Alabama's success was unchanging but the times were not. In the Boston newspapers of one of his victims Semmes read of a Union expedition against Texas. He wanted to play a role. In doing so, Semmes disregarded his orders to avoid engaging enemy ships. In his memoir Semmes makes it clear that *Alabama*'s crew wanted to fight.

On January 11, Semmes enticed a single Union combatant, *Hatteras*, from a group of five patrolling off the coast of Galveston. Flying the British flag, *Alabama* closed to within one hundred yards of the Union warship and identified herself as the Royal Navy ship *Petrel*. Satisfied by the response that his opponent was indeed a U.S. warship, Semmes revealed the deception and opened fire. The engagement lasted less than a quarter-hour: *Hatteras* surrendered after suffering serious damage at her waterline and to her engine.

This would be the last combat action Semmes and his crew would see until July the following year, 1864, when *Alabama* engaged USS *Kearsarge* off the coast of Cherbourg. During the intervening eighteen months they captured and burned their way across the equator into the South Atlantic, through the U.S.-to-Cape Horn sea-lanes, to the Horn of Africa, as far east as what is now Indonesia, and back to northern Europe by way of India. All the while, Union shipowners accelerated the reflagging of their vessels. In 1863 the number of U.S. merchant ships sold to Britain alone, 348, represented a fourfold increase in tonnage over the previous year's hemorrhage.

Insurance rates also continued to skyrocket, and Semmes and *Alabama* achieved international reputation. Before arriving at Cherbourg, the Confederate raider had logged 75,000 miles, burned fifty-two ships, bonded another ten, sold one, commissioned another into the Confederate Navy and sunk one Union combatant.

Semmes went ashore at Cherbourg on Sunday June 12 to arrange for port services and repairs to the ship's boilers and copper sheathing. His health had deteriorated and he wanted to be relieved. The possibility of a speedy departure from service disappeared two days later when *Kearsarge* steamed into Cherbourg. Semmes could not walk away from a fight, nor would he content himself with pinning down for an indefinite period the several other Union combatants that would predictably arrive shortly to keep *Alabama* from emerging to destroy more commerce.

Semmes sent a message to *Kearsarge*'s commanding officer, Captain John A. Winslow: "If you will give me time to recoal, I will come out and give you battle." The Navies of the 1860s were completing the transition to steam propulsion, breech-loading guns, and had introduced ironclad ships. At the same time Semmes was challenging his opponent to fight, as did the heroic warriors of the *Iliad*. The Civil War, it has often been observed, was fought with the technology of the era to come and the customs of the era that had passed.

Winslow prepared his ship for combat and word of the contest began to draw sightseers, including the press and artist Edward Manet (whose painting of the battle was recently acquired by the Philadelphia Museum of Art). The two combatants possessed roughly similar armament: *Alabama* had one more gun than *Kearsarge*, but the larger bore of the latter's weapons allowed her to throw more metal in a broadside. (In his biography, Semmes angrily denounced his opponent for a tactic he took to tip the scales: anchor chains were strung along the sides of *Kearsage* to increase its protection against Confederate shells.)

On a clear Sunday morning, June 19, 1864, Semmes sallied forth to meet his foe. He addressed all hands as the gap closed, reminding them of their triumph over the Union warship *Hatteras* and of their long string of successes in destroying the enemy's commerce. When he asked whether *Alabama*'s name should be "tarnished by defeat," the crew roared, "Never, never!" Finally, Semmes called on his shipmates to "remember that you are in the English Channel, the theatre of so much of the naval glory of our race, and the eyes of all Europe are at this moment, upon you."

Similar crowds had gathered at Plymouth, on the opposite shore, in 1588 to watch the opening battle with the Spanish Armada. Now crowds arrived from as far away as Paris and formed along quays, hills and breakwater. The venturesome had piled into boats and bobbed about as the two ships closed the seven miles that separated them.

They were not disappointed. According to Semmes's account, *Alabama* opened fire about a mile from *Kearsarge*, which turned to present her starboard guns and replied. The two vessels began a series of clockwise circles, maintaining a range of between three-quarters to one-half a mile while firing constantly. When *Alabama*'s shells found their target, they caused little damage. A well-placed shot buried itself in *Kearsarge*'s sternpost and failed to explode. Captain Winslow's firing, however, found its mark *and* did damage. Shells exploded in *Alabama*'s side and below the waterline. The sea poured in. Semmes tried to sail back to shore, but the cold water snuffed his furnaces, and *Alabama* started to settle. She struck her colors and the crew abandoned ship. Within twenty minutes, the Channel's waters closed over her bow. Semmes, his trusted lieutenant, John Kell, and others were plucked from the water by the British yacht *Deerhound* and reached Southampton that evening. *Alabama* had lost thirty killed and wounded, *Kearsarge* three.

As much controversy subsequently surrounded *Alabama*'s final engagement as swirled about her commerce raiding exploits. Semmes accused the Union commanding officer of deceit by cladding his ship with the anchor chain. Captain Winslow countered that by escaping to England in the British pleasure craft that fished him from the water, Semmes had violated the terms of the surrender implicit in striking *Alabama*'s colors.

Semmes recovered his strength at a friend's home in London. He returned to the Confederacy, sailing by way of Havana and Mexico, and traveling by carriage and skiff across the Rio Grande. Escorted by enthusiastic admirers, Semmes waded through the Union-held Mississippi's swampy approaches and crossed undetected at night. He arrived home in Mobile and was reunited with his wife, Anne Elizabeth, and children after an absence of almost four years. Two weeks later Semmes traveled to Richmond with his 12-year-old son, Raphael Jr. The man who had taken eighty-two enemy vessels for the Confederacy was promoted to rear admiral and served out the remaining months of the war in a variety of inevitably unhappy positions.

Still accompanied by his son, Rear Admiral Semmes surrendered on May 1, 1865. In exchange for swearing not to take up arms against the United States, he received written permission to return home and "not to be disturbed by U.S. authorities, so long as he obeys this obligation. . . ."

Semmes bent his efforts to caring for his now-impoverished family, a return to the legal profession having been proscribed after the Confederacy surrendered. But in December 1865, in the sort of action that Lincoln's survival would likely have prevented, Semmes was arrested for having broken the terms of his surrender to *Kearsarge*. His parole notwithstanding, Semmes was taken to New York to stand trial.

It is clear from all accounts that the U.S. Navy's judge advocate general John A. Bolles worked overtime to find a charge that would hold up in court against Semmes. Cruelty to prisoners, fraudulently obtaining a cease-fire in the engagement with *Kearsarge* and then continuing to fire, violating the terms of *Alabama*'s surrender—nothing stuck. Neither law nor evidence supported the accusations. Bolles ordered Semmes released.

Semmes returned home to a succession of positions as newspaper editor, college and then seminary professor, paid speaker and, eventually, author of his interesting and readable if tendentious autobiography. He was eventually permitted to practice law again and opened a practice with his son Oliver, living out his remaining years as a respected member of the Mobile community. He died on August 30, 1877, at the age of 67.

The U.S. Post Office issued a first-class stamp of Semmes in 1994. This seagoing lawyer is pictured standing on the quarterdeck, the decks of *Alabama* holystoned and clean, rigging taut and crew standing to their polished guns. They are watching a distant ship sinking in flames. I am told that the American Trial Lawyers Association bought up the entire issue.

JAMES BULLOCH'S ACCOMPLISHMENTS in England had been made possible because British government and merchant interests were sympathetic to the South. Since the Royal Navy still ruled the waves at the time and maintained a large squadron on the North American coast, based in Halifax, Nova Scotia, recognition of the South by England or France would have been catastrophic to the Union cause.

Britain's prime minister, Lord Palmerston, and his foreign minister Lord John Russell were long known to be anti-American and especially anti-Union. They saw the Civil War as an opportunity to weaken the United States and revise the North American balance of power more favorably to their interests. The early military successes of the Confederate Army encouraged them toward recognition. Only the firmness of President Lincoln and the very skillful diplomatic brinkmanship of John Adams's grandson, Ambassador Charles Francis Adams, the American Minister in England, averted full diplomatic recognition in late 1861. As it was, Palmerston issued a neutrality proclamation recognizing the South as a belligerent, which allowed the Confederacy to buy arms and exercise many of the rights of a legitimate nation, thus protecting Bulloch and his procurement of Confederate raiders.

It was only after Union victories at Antietam and Gettysburg, and the growing effectiveness of the Union blockade that the tide began to turn in London. Adams and Lincoln made full use of their successes, skillfully hinting that recognition of the Confederacy would result in war and the seizure of Canada.

But an overlooked factor in swinging the critical balance in 1862 against British recognition of the Confederacy was the special relationship between the Royal Navy and the American Navy. As noted earlier, there were strong bonds of friendship and common usage in the two Navies going back before the Revolution and continuing. Fresh in the minds of both Navies was an event in 1859 in China when Commodore Josiah Tattnall, commander of the U.S. East India Squadron, went to the aid of the embattled British flagship during the Second Opium War, remarking, "Blood is thicker than water." The admiral in charge of the North American station from 1860–1864 was Vice Admiral Sir Alexander Milne. Milne's quiet pro-American bias, his friendship with many American naval officers, and his skillful handling of numerous incidents growing out of the blockade, may well have been the decisive influence in preventing London from recognizing the Confederacy.

A massive ironclad shipbuilding program in the North had rapidly followed *Monitor,* and Milne had watched with alarm and reported these developments fully to London. Russell warned the British cabinet to "think of our position if . . . the Yankees (begin) turning on us by means of iron ships and renew the triumphs they achieved in 1812–13!" Thereafter realpolitik required Britain to be more accommodating to the Union position despite the desires to regain empire lost.

In 1862 Congress added the threat of the Privateering Act, pushed by Commodore Vanderbilt and other New York shipowners hoping to get a share of the huge prize settlements being collected by the Union Navy's blockade. London and Paris saw this as a direct threat, and the impression was skillfully magnified by Adams. The tide turned in mid-1863 when the British authorities, under pressure from Adams, impounded the steam sloop *Alexandra,* about to be transferred to the Confederate Navy. At the same time Bulloch had commissioned the building of two heavily armed ironclad rams, another *Alabama*-class raider and an armored frigate in British yards. Adams warned Russell that this was equivalent to an act of war. Russell reluctantly impounded them. With this setback, Bulloch secretly arranged to have the recently purchased *Shenandoah* raider slip out of Britain, and he decamped to France. *Shenandoah* went on to virtually destroy the American whaling fleet in the Pacific, operating against them for four full months after Appomattox. Already under pressure from kerosene, a much cheaper alternative to whale oil, the whalers never recovered.

In France, Bulloch set about commissioning new rams and four more *Alabama*-class raiders, but Secretary of State William Seward and Secretary of the Navy Gideon Welles were hot on his trail. Seward immediately "fired off the first of a barrage of menacing protests to Napoleon III." With Union arms now ascendant in the war, and possessed of the largest Army and Navy on the Atlantic, France backed off and shut down Bulloch.

Confederate commerce-raiding operations were very successful against Union shipping at very little cost, ultimately sinking about 5 percent of the Union merchant fleet. *Alabama* and its cousin raiders built in foreign yards, as well as converted vessels that served the same purpose, amounted to a dozen or so ships but these few drove shipping and insurance rates up and forced a large-scale reflagging of American bottoms—ultimately more than half of the U.S. merchant fleet.

Equally important, they drew many Union ships from blockade and river offensives to protect merchantmen and hunt raiders. So vast and accelerating, however, was the Union's industrial base that it had little real effect on the material balance of the war.

After the war, the U.S. government aggressively pursued claims for damages against Britain for enabling the raiders. In a landmark case before an international arbitration tribunal in 1872, the U.S. won an award of $14.5 million. But these millions of dollars' worth of damage had not been nearly enough to win the Confederates victory. For in fact the Confederacy was strangled to death by Winfield Scott's Anaconda. The monitors and gunboats on the Mississippi, the Gulf and the waterways of the Southeast; and the blockading squadrons on the Atlantic Coast choked the life out of the South, and there was nothing the heroics of men like Raphael Semmes and Robert E. Lee could do about it.

The Civil War on land is known for its horrendous casualties. That cannot be said of the naval war. More powerful Dahlgren guns, rifled and breech-loading cannon had greatly increased offensive firepower, but iron armor and steam power had utterly changed naval tactics. The classic line-ahead exchange of broadsides disappeared, with a new premium placed on speed and maneuver. Galvanic mines, or "torpedoes," came into wide and effective use. The war saw the beginning of an entirely new naval technology with the sinking of USS *Housatonic* by CSS *H. L. Hunley*, the first true submarine.

Naval war, much more than land war, had become a contest of machines and technology. The human "butcher's bill" in battle actually went down, in sharp contrast to the war as fought on land.

The impact of these new technologies launched a period of creative thinking in naval strategy after the Civil War, which completely transformed fleets, tactics and weapons by the end of the century. This was again in contrast to European and American Army strategists, who remained in the straitjacket of the Clausewitzian ideology of attrition warfare that led logically to the carnage of World War I.

VI

MANIFEST DESTINY: THE "NEW NAVY"

WHEN LEE SURRENDERED, the United States had a Navy of nearly 900 ships, the most innovative, progressive and powerful Navy in the world. But with a whole continent west of the Mississippi to settle and develop, fractious Indian tribes to subdue and 3,000 miles of ocean to insulate America from Europe's turmoils, the nation once again disarmed. Budgets were slashed and bureaucracy and conservatism took charge of the Navy. The familiar pattern of peacetime disarmament took hold.

A general order issued in 1869 stipulated that all naval vessels must have full-sailing capability. (Coal was expensive, and without colonies the Navy had virtually no coaling stations.) The cutting-edge steam-powered Navy of the Civil War reverted to sail power. Although there were brief periods of excitement—punitive expeditions to Korea in 1871, Honolulu in 1874 and 1893, Egypt in 1882 and Panama in 1885—the Navy was bored. It was not a recipe for making strong, successful leaders. Richard W. Thompson upon taking office as Navy secretary in March 1877 expressed surprise upon visiting the fleet to find that Navy ships were in fact hollow.

From not long after the end of the Civil War to the eve of the last day before World War II, the U.S. Navy was essentially expansionist in mindset, its doctrine forged by a handful of strong naval men. The period was an incredibly important one in the development of the Navy. Were it not for the absence of even minimal funding for modernization, it would have been more important still.

By 1880, the U.S. Navy ranked twelfth in size, inferior to Chile's. It had only forty-eight obsolete ships in commission, manned by fewer than 6,000 sailors, most of whom were foreigners. With the size of the Navy so much reduced, the opportunities for promotion disappeared. It was not uncommon for lieutenants to remain in that rank into their fifties, with promotion to flag based on seniority only. As a result, talented and ambitious men sought their fortunes elsewhere. The Navy was becoming a backwater.

By 1882 new Secretary of the Navy William E. Chandler found the Navy to be "a subject of ridicule." He set about implementing reforms begun by his predecessor, William H. Hunt, and nurtured support in Congress for rebuilding the Navy. In 1883 the so-called ABC cruisers were authorized, *Atlanta, Boston* and *Chicago*. They were the first modern ships to enter the fleet since the Civil War. Far more important to the future of the Navy was Chandler's establishment in Newport of the Naval War College and his appointment of Commodore Steven B. Luce as its first president. Luce was an intelligent and innovative reformer with good ideas, the best of which was to bring an obscure captain from the Asiatic fleet named Alfred Thayer Mahan to be the War College's first lecturer in naval history.

ALFRED THAYER MAHAN: STRATEGY AND HISTORY

For its first eighty years, the United States had the luxury of needing no overarching military strategy. Absorbed by its own western frontier, it was protected by the two great seas.

By the 1880s, there remained a vestigial Army largely employed in small-unit warfare against the Indian tribes and incapable, as proved by the Spanish-American War, of fielding even a minimum professional force. The brilliant tactics of the Civil War generals, although widely studied abroad, were confined to obscure textbooks at home. As for the Navy, the dead hand of the coastal defense doctrinaires kept it even from exploiting the startling breakthroughs of technology in guns and armor produced by Ericsson, Dahlgren and the Civil War Navy. America was out-producing in steel and coal its major European rivals, the military superpowers of Great Britain and Germany, but could not build a first-class battleship.

Yet somehow, from this most stony ground, there flowered in the last decades of the 19th century a world-class naval strategist, a man who excelled at history and literature and who educated a generation of American leaders. He was Alfred Thayer Mahan. Before Mahan, there were no American naval thinkers taken seriously abroad. After him, there was no naval thinker anywhere who could ignore his thought.

Mahan, born in 1840, came from military stock and was well-educated. His father lectured in engineering at West Point, then the singular focus of the school, but was enlightened enough to introduce a course on history and strategy. The young Alfred took two years at Columbia University before deciding on a naval career, graduating from the Naval Academy in 1859.

Young Lieutenant Mahan spent most of the Civil War on tedious blockade duty. In fact, Mahan later confessed that he may not have been cut out for his profession: it was boring and the technological revolutions of the steam age so exciting to his contemporaries left him cold. In the 1870s he began agitating, like his father, for a broader naval education including history and literature. This was all very bookish, and Mahan's contemporaries, aspiring sea dogs with lots of use for machinery and none for ideas, were not enthusiastic.

Mahan's future looked as bleak as the South American coast he was condemned to monitor in the barely seaworthy steam-sloop, *Wachusett*—a kind of sentry duty to protect American businessmen from Latin revolutionaries. But he had impressed a fellow officer, Stephen Luce, first president of the Naval War College, and Luce invited him to join the faculty. This proved difficult: the college had its enemies, but Mahan (and the world) benefited from the very decrepitude of the Navy; in 1885, Mahan was released from sea duty because *Wachusett* could no longer be repaired. Too late for the new semester at the War College, Mahan got leave from Luce to do some studying. In New York's Astor

Library, the very collection Theodore Roosevelt had used some years earlier to write *The Naval War of 1812*, Mahan commenced what was to become *The Influence of Sea Power Upon History, 1660–1783*.

True to his intellectual calling, Captain Mahan's ideas germinated not from his own naval experience, but rather from a decidedly un-naval book, Theodor Mommsen's *History of Rome*. (Mahan had gotten his copy from the library of the English Club in Lima, Peru, and read it during his South American patrol duties.) "It suddenly struck me," he wrote, "how different things might have been could Hannibal have invaded Italy by sea, as the Romans often had Africa. . . ."

While contemporary critics of Mahan were quick to dismiss him as an impractical historian, his impact on practical men was immediate. On the weekend of May 10–11, 1890, Theodore Roosevelt, who often read a few books in a weekend, plowed through the thick volume. Himself a recognized naval historian with his political future still ahead of him, TR, at 32, was the very picture of the man of action. He had lectured at the War College on his own work and knew Mahan. Upon finishing the book, he wrote Mahan high praise: "That I found it interesting is shown by the fact that . . . I have gone straight through and finished it . . . It was a very good book—admirable; and I am greatly in error if it does not become a naval classic." Roosevelt followed up this letter with a hugely enthusiastic review in the October issue of *Atlantic Monthly*, writing, *inter alia*, that Mahan "neither loses sight of nor exaggerates the bearing which the history of past struggles has upon our present problems."

Roosevelt had caught the classic and timeless proportions of the work that make it profitable reading even today. Nor was this praise mere rhetoric. When TR was assistant secretary of the Navy, he consulted Mahan often. When I was a new member of the Metropolitan Club in Washington, I was proudly taken by an ancient steward and shown the corner in what was then the first-floor dining room, where he had served lunch regularly to TR and Mahan, both members.

The strength of *Sea Power* was its author's ability to synthesize and distill. He brought together the history of sea power with general history to show how, at critical junctures, naval strength or weakness had modified the course of events. Mahan had the knowledge of the specialist with the vision of the generalist and in relating one to the other, he offered insights for both professional seamen and their political masters. While he by necessity took the age of the sailing ship—now obsolete, he noted—for his case studies, he drew careful lessons which he called principles—as distinct from mere tactics—not bound in time or technology. It would be folly to handle a modern Navy using Nelson's precise tactics, yet the questions Nelson and the British government had asked and answered before setting sail remain crucial: questions about the Navy's function, its points of concentration, its means of communication and supply, and primary and secondary uses of a fleet (e.g., main engagements vs. commerce raiding or blockade).

Mahan ranges through all of the elements of sea power, commenting on the United States, where he carefully demonstrates that the old doctrine of coastal defense was quite obsolete: "The enemy must be kept not only out of our ports, but far away from our coasts." A discrete footnote explodes the argument that engagement of the enemy on the high seas is "offensive"—that depends on the purpose of the operation. And there is a phrase that gladdens every naval heart: "Passive defenses belong to the army; everything that moves in the water to the Navy, which has the prerogative of the offensive defense."

This, of course, was the very argument convulsing the Congress as it weighed the building of a modern Navy. Mahan's work, including twenty-eight maps and plans, was a masterpiece of timely scholarship that influenced the debate. There were enough principles in the book to show that a great American commercial power needed the "offensive defense" of a first-class battle fleet if its prosperity and interests abroad were to be safeguarded. And this fleet had to be handled with the strategic lessons of history as a guide. From Mahan's work came concrete tenets that even politicians could understand: concentration of force (do not divide the fleet); centrality of purpose (defeat or confine the enemy's Navy); and focus on result (destruction of the enemy's military power, not the indirect pains of commerce raiding).

Mahan spent much time relating resources to strategy. There could be great land powers and great naval powers, he argued, but not one country dominant in both, for such was the nature of geography and politics. That meant colonies, if need be, for the sea powers, and huge conscription armies for the others.

Mahan's book had a dramatic effect on more than Theodore Roosevelt. Mahan became an instant celebrity in Britain and Germany. A few months after publication, Congress authorized the first American battleships, the symbol and substance of the new sea power he had advocated. Two years later, Mahan followed up with a sequel to *Sea Power—The Influence of Sea Power upon the French Revolution and Empire, 1793–1812*—which saved the War College itself. Secretary of the Navy Hilary Herbert was about to close it down as an extravagance until he read the book.

Mahan's sudden fame, however, put his career at the War College in jeopardy. The head of the Bureau of Navigation—the Navy's personnel office—was one Francis M. Ramsey. "It is not the business of a naval officer to write books," he wrote Mahan, turning down his request for permission to stay at Newport rather than command a ship. Mahan appealed to TR, who in cabal with Henry Cabot Lodge and Stephen Luce, tried to override Ramsey but failed, provoking a Rooseveltian rage: "Oh, what idiots we have to deal with!" Mahan did not help his case when he penned a popular article advocating annexation of Hawaii, not the prerogative of a serving officer.

In summer of 1893, Mahan's enemies rejoiced as he was finally compelled to go to sea. As a senior officer, his "punishment" consisted of command of *Chicago*, one of the first modern American capital ships. To the consternation of his opponents, Mahan received a hero's welcome in Europe. He was greeted by Queen Victoria and the Kaiser and was feted by the great men of England and the Continent. This infuriated his superior, Rear Admiral Henry Erben, whose revenge took the form of an Admiral's Inspection, followed by a devastating fitness report. The next year saw the same sequence: high honors, including honorary degrees from Oxford and Cambridge; a low rating from Admiral Erben, with whom he communicated only in writing.

Upon his return to the United States in 1895, there could be no doubt that Mahan would never have a distinguished career at sea. Erben's reports had seen to that. But Mahan's fame abroad now translated into equal fame at home, including honorary degrees from Harvard, Yale and Columbia. His opponents may have hurt his pride briefly but they never understood him, stopped him only where it mattered little and ironically boosted him where it mattered most.

Mahan finally attained seniority on the naval list and made rear admiral before retiring in 1896. A tall, thin man, with an elegant beard and bearing, he was happily married and the father of two daughters and one son. Already 50 when he became famous, he kept an illustrious correspondence with all the leading lights of the day and was regarded on par with the great scientists of his time.

Not all the results were perfect, however. The Kaiser loved Mahan's book, but did not accept that great land powers could not also be great sea powers. Mahan also quarreled with Theodore Roosevelt when, as president, TR had to decide the debate over the all-big-gun battleship.

Roosevelt had been attracted by the designs that were later to be seen in HMS *Dreadnought,* and he was greatly influenced by Commander William S. Sims, one of the Navy's most dogged reformers and gunnery experts who advocated heavy guns. Mahan argued against a fleet of hyper-expensive capital ships; larger numbers of adequately sized ships, derived from naval consensus, such as the frigates of the age of sail, were more important than the fewer numbers of more powerful vessels that might become too precious to risk in battle. Their greater speed would matter little when they were with slower ships in a mixed fleet.

These arguments dragged on as the British built *Dreadnought,* until in the summer of 1905, the Japanese fleet under Admiral Togo destroyed the Imperial Russian armada at the battle of Tsu-shima. The superior speed and firepower of the Japanese clinched the argument for Roosevelt; America needed fast, big-gun, turbine-driven battleships, not the 18.5-knot, smaller *Michigan* and *South Carolina,* with their reciprocating steam engines similar to those Mahan called for. Mahan opposed Roosevelt: in June 1906, he published his own analysis in the Naval Institute's *Proceedings* arguing that position, not speed, and intermediate-sized guns, not the biggest ones, had been decisive for the Japanese. Long-range guns, Mahan said, would inhibit command-ers from "closing," sinking the opponent in a climactic encounter at short range.

Roosevelt talked it over with Mahan. The two men had agreed on so much. Now they could not. TR, always more savvy than his rhetoric led critics to believe, recognized that Mahan, unlike his political oppo-nents, offered a more formidable obstacle and asked Admiral Sims to rebut Mahan.

Mahan, steeped in sailing-ship tactics and never strong on techno-logical change, was vulnerable, and Sims found his mark. In a letter to Roosevelt on September 24, 1906, later published in the December is-sue of *Proceedings*, Sims showed that superior long-range gunnery could "close" an opponent more efficiently than the old close-order broad-side. Speed explained the superior Japanese positions at Tsu-shima (Ernest J. King would later advocate the separation of the fast aircraft carriers from the slower battleships of the 1930s, neatly disposing of Mahan's other speed issue). Also, Sims said, many inferior ships would not necessarily offset fewer superior ones, because the smaller could not deal with the longer range, greater caliber and heavy armor of the larger.

Mahan had already lost this battle. On June 29, 1906, Congress approved Roosevelt's request for "a single battleship a year" program not limited—for the first time—in maximum displacement. The *Delaware*—20,000 tons, 21 knots speed, carrying ten 12-inch guns—was the *Dreadnought*-like result.

Much honored and still influential, Alfred Thayer Mahan lived un-til December 1, 1914. Theodore Roosevelt was among his eulogists. He did not live to see the great naval battle of Jutland, which con-firmed at least one of his fears, that captains of dreadnoughts might be reluctant to risk their ships in a duel to the death. But Mahan's place as a key shaper of modern sea power remains intact. More important, his way of thinking remains valid.

Naval power does not function well in a vacuum, but must be re-lated to overall strategy, resources and national purpose. Maritime strategy means the offensive defense. Naval officers should be more than glorified engineers, and the Naval War College exists to make them so—the life of Alfred Thayer Mahan proves it. It also helped prove that the United States, as the world's only Atlantic and Pacific nation, is especially fitted for the exercise of naval power.

NEXT TO *The Influence of Sea Power in History,* Mahan's greatest deed had been a gesture: an invitation to Theodore Roosevelt to visit the Naval War College. Mahan had been impressed by the publication of Roosevelt's book on the War of 1812; Roosevelt's visit rekindled his interest in the Navy and began the lifelong collaboration between the two men that changed the Navy and the nation forever.

THEODORE ROOSEVELT: A NAVY SECOND TO NONE

Theodore Roosevelt played many parts in his life but his role as navalist was his most forceful. His great epigram—"Speak softly and carry a big stick"—was most assuredly not a naval expression. Sailors don't carry sticks and, in the era of hissing steam and clanking iron, they all spoke loudly. But this landlubber metaphor became a declaration of naval supremacy.

TR was an indefatigable champion of both the power and flexibility of sea-going forces. He served as assistant secretary of the Navy during the greatest warship-building program to that point in U.S. history. His statecraft can only be understood in the context of the naval theories of the time. Finally, TR's greatest international triumphs—his Nobel Prize-winning mediation between Japan and Russia, the Panama Canal, the world tour of the Great White Fleet, even the semi-comic Pedicaris kidnapping, his little-known face-down of the Kaiser—all these episodes were framed and shaped by sea power.

The biographical details are too well-known to rehash here. He impressed his contemporaries with an impetuous manner and a pugnacious temperament. So well-established was the latter that when he died peacefully in his sleep, one editorialist remarked that had he been awake "there would have been a fight." Roosevelt was tempered not only by the hard exercise of building his defective lungs, but by tragedy. He lost his beloved mother and wife on the same awful day. He was to lose one son in World War I, a war he would have entered earlier and fought differently. Another son suffered grievous wounds. Roosevelt's was also a life marked by accident. From an early age there were a sufficient number of life-threatening mishaps to convince him that he was destined for great deeds. Why otherwise was he spared? These accidents continued throughout his life. Accounted too independent by New York state's leading politicians in the great Age of Machines, Roosevelt was foisted on McKinley and expected to wither away under the pressure of a do-nothing vice presidency. Made president by grace of a bullet, he was saved from his own assassination later only by a thick speech in a breast pocket.

Roosevelt's often-commented-upon physical vigor and sense of destiny did not preclude a life of the mind. Perhaps our most intellectually gifted president, he read huge amounts, enjoyed a prodigious memory and wrote and spoke in invigorating prose—no ghostwriters. In an age of great American writers and historians, he was nevertheless a substantial figure by virtue of his literary output. His history of the naval war of 1812 still stands as a landmark in the field.

What drew Roosevelt to the Navy was his realistic sense of national power and its projection. He was among the first American presidents to realize that the United States was a world power whether Americans liked it or not. TR was the midwife who delivered from the old isolated America the new international United States. And his instrument was the Navy.

We can hardly understand this today, accustomed as we are to a large standing army. But for most of our history, such a force was regarded as un-American. The Congresses and the presidents of the 19th century were not so far away from the Revolution that they felt comfortable with the expense or management of European-style armies.

There could be no Napoleons, it was thought, in the absence of large ground forces. Even half the Civil War had been fought without conscription. When TR and his famous Rough Riders shipped off to Cuba in 1898, trained troops were so few that the Buffalo Soldiers—the black cavalry otherwise consigned to the frontier—were used to fill out the ranks. (John J. Pershing, commander of the U.S. Expeditionary Force of World War I, acquired the nickname "Black Jack" because of his willingness to command such units.) The Founding Fathers and their successors had always regarded the Navy as the first line of defense, the real (and tolerable) "standing force." This could be seen even in the government's organization: there was a secretary of war and there was a secretary of the Navy, and the latter spent most of what we would call today the "defense budget."

Although initially unready, the Union Navy had played a decisive role in the Civil War, blockading the Confederacy and, through its gunboats, controlling its rivers. But the most important naval development to come out of that war was the end of the centuries-long reign of the wooden ships-of-the-line. The clash of *Monitor* and *Virginia* forecast the new era of steam-powered ships, steel armor and growing firepower that culminated in the *Dreadnought* battleships that fought World War I.

Monitor and *Virginia* may have started this new arms race, but the U.S. Navy soon fell far behind. Following the Civil War, the Navy's appropriations were reduced to prewar levels, hardly able to sustain the obsolete wooden warships, let alone the costly steam-powered ironclads. A slow rebuilding campaign began only in the 1880s and only after long delays and hard-fought arguments over propulsion and armor design.

It was upon this leisurely scene that the young Theodore Roosevelt burst forth with his first major literary work. He had grown up on tales of the derring-do of Southern commerce raiders; one maternal uncle had been a Confederate sailor and the other, James Bulloch, the Confederate agent in England who had procured and provisioned the devastating voyages of Confederate raiders like *Alabama*. TR's book, *The Naval War of 1812*, was completed in 1881 when he was only 23. It exhibits prodigious learning; the author, using original sources on both sides of the Atlantic, taught himself the art of war in the age of sail. But Roosevelt's lessons are strategic and political rather than confined to naval detail. He excoriated such American icons as Jefferson and Madison for negligence of the fleet—"criminal folly"—leading to weakness that invited war.

TR's book, like Mahan's, also influenced the national debate over building a new Navy. *The Naval War of 1812* was placed onboard every ship and studied at the recently organized Naval War College. A year after publication, the Congress succumbed to those who, like TR, argued that the United States could not afford naval weakness. They appropriated $1.3 million for the beginning of what was to be called the "New Navy."

For Roosevelt himself there followed a near decade-long diversion into New York state politics, including a highly colorful stint as New York City's police commissioner. By the end, however, Roosevelt had fallen afoul of the New York political bosses. But he worked hard for McKinley's election and he was politically popular; this, plus the New York machine's desire to get him out of New York, won him an appointment as assistant secretary of the Navy.

TR had landed in the right place. The Navy, under former Massachusetts governor John Long, was preparing its new warships for what appeared to be an inevitable clash with Spain over Cuba.

Long, apparently reluctant to take TR as his assistant secretary, has left us a curious description of his understudy. "His ardor," wrote Long archly, "sometimes went faster than the President or the department approved," notably in ordering a squadron to meet the Caribbean-bound Spanish battle fleet "without waiting for a more formal declaration of war. . . . His typewriter had no rest. He, like most of us, lacks the rare knack of brevity . . . His room in the Navy Department . . . bubbled over with enthusiasm filled with bright young fellows . . . guns, uniforms, all sorts of military trappings and piles of paper . . ." Among these artifacts was the desk used by the first assistant secretary of the Navy, Gustavus Fox, during the Civil War, a unique piece of furniture with the stars and stripes carved in the front, flanked by wooden cannon extending from the sides. Long did not credit Roosevelt with much impact on the Navy itself, leaving the impression that he had more enthusiasm than knowledge, though he grants that TR distinguished himself in the tricky business of procuring private vessels for the rapidly expanding fleet.

This portrait of picturesque but not very effective chaos is amusing but inaccurate. In fact, Roosevelt became a key figure in preparing the Navy for war with Spain. TR saw a powerful Navy as the symbol and substance of America's new rank among the nations. He found a ready ally—one is tempted to say co-conspirator—in Captain Mahan. TR wanted a dozen new battleships, a canal to connect the Atlantic and the Pacific, and the Spanish out of Cuba. He got them all and more.

Moreover, unlike Long, TR rapidly learned the details of the Navy, and soon became the man others sought when decisions were needed. He possessed a keen foresight for the impact of new inventions on warfare. He wanted to experiment with submarines, and he insisted upon a thorough examination of the prospects for flying machines. As secretary of the Navy, one of my more amusing discoveries was Roosevelt's request for an admiralty investigation on this subject. The admirals duly complied. I had their neatly typed conclusion that the machines had no foreseeable application to naval warfare framed on my wall as testimony to bureaucracy's lack of imagination.

When TR was writing, the U.S. fleet was grossly inferior to those of the major European powers. There were only a few American yards capable of building modern warships and, as late as 1891, only one was able to service battleships. American steel manufacturers could cast ingots only of the size for 6-inch guns. America's bigger ships were fitted with cannon and armor purchased abroad. Moreover, the Congress was full of armchair strategists who spoke assuredly of the Navy's old role of coastal defense and commerce raiding. (The first true American battleship, *Indiana*, launched in 1895, was authorized for coastal defense and indeed her slow sixteen-knot speed meant she was good for little else.)

Bringing his usual combativeness to the problem, TR made public speeches that roused public support while angering Long and the senior admirals. He stimulated "scenario" problems at the War College and in a widely reported speech there on June 2, 1897—his first great oration—asserted that "diplomacy is utterly useless when there is no force behind it; the diplomat is the servant, not the master, of the soldier." One can hear the echo of his high-pitched voice, oddly emanating from a powerfully built body as he perorated, "No triumph of peace is quite so great as the supreme triumphs of war. . . . As yet no nation can hold its place in the world, or can do any work really worth doing, unless it stands ready to guard its rights with an armed hand." After another, similarly aggressive speech insulting to Japan, Secretary Long felt constrained to give Roosevelt a reproach. But he then left for a month's vacation, putting TR in full charge of the Navy.

Roosevelt took advantage of this situation not only to make decisions, but also to lobby the affable McKinley on the subject of Cuba. He urged a strategic plan to deal with Spain that, among other things, would employ the small U.S. Asiatic squadron to take the Philippines. It was a plan for a six-week war. To head it, TR wanted a warrior and secured the appointment of the relatively junior George Dewey, another veteran of the gunboats of the James River, to command the Asiatic squadron over a more senior but less decisive officer.

After stirring up the public, "educating" the president and placing his own man in power, TR's final move was to put the fleet into offensive deployment. When USS *Maine* exploded in Havana harbor on February 15, 1898, war fever swept the United States. On February 25, even as his wife lay dangerously ill in a Baltimore hospital, Roosevelt had his chance. Long took the afternoon off, and TR mobilized the fleet. He cabled Dewey to concentrate at Hong Kong with a full load of coal and to look to possible offensive action against the Philippines. Long was furious, but did not cancel the orders. When the McKinley administration, bowing to popular fears, began to divide up the fleet to defend the East Coast from the imaginary Spanish naval threat, the future governor of New York wrote to Mahan, "Even if New York were bombarded, it would amount to absolutely nothing as affecting the course of the war or damaging permanently the prosperity of the country."

Almost entirely due to Roosevelt's persistence, the Navy was far better prepared for the war than was the Army. Ironically, when war began on April 19, 1898, Roosevelt decided to join the latter service. Forty years old, a father of six, nearly blind without his spectacles, a "veteran" of three years in the N.Y. National Guard, Roosevelt was propelled by a desire to fight after having preached the necessity of war. He recognized, as he wrote a friend, "that we are armchair and parlor jingoes who wish to see others do what we only advocate doing . . . my power for good, whatever it is, would be gone if I did not try to live up to the doctrines I have tried to preach." It was his destiny and, as Long later noted, it "led straight to the Presidency."

But there was one last act that destiny had preserved for Theodore Roosevelt before he left the position of the assistant secretary of the Navy. On May 7 he sent notice to the press that Commodore George Dewey had destroyed the Spanish fleet in Manila Bay before going to war against the Spanish himself.

THE SPANISH-AMERICAN WAR, *OLYMPIA* AND THE BATTLE OF MANILA BAY

Olympia, Commodore George Dewey's flagship, rests securely today at Penn's Landing in Philadelphia. She is the sole survivor of America's "New Navy," the steam and steel flotilla that inaugurated modern sea power. Those who visit her are bound to be impressed by the careful fittings that reflect industrial pride—the captain's beautifully appointed cabin, the scrolled inscriptions on the machinery, the relatively spacious passageways. So were her contemporaries, and European navalists in particular saw the accommodations, including the very first ice-cream maker on board a warship, as excessively solicitous of her crew of 400 sailors and 33 officers.

The ship owes her fame not to her ice-cream maker but to the battle of Manila Bay on May 1, 1898, when the small American Asiatic squadron successfully destroyed the Spanish squadron defending the Philippines, inflicting 400 casualties on the enemy and suffering but 6 wounded in the process. This astonishing—and unexpected—victory, the most important naval action of the Spanish-American War, seemed to announce to the world the superiority of America's naval forces and her ships. Yet America's technological lead, almost assumed to be our birthright now, was not at all the case then. There was nothing to be learned from *Olympia* as a warship except her obsolescence. This was not due to any profound defect. *Olympia* was a sound, well-designed warship, but she was also a compromised example of a rapidly changing naval technology that left naval architects, sailors, captains, admirals and their political bosses in a state of expensive confusion—not too different from our present time.

Consider the appearance and capabilities of warships over the twenty years that separated the beginnings of the "New Navy" in 1880 and the cruise of the Great White Fleet in 1907–8 at the end of Theodore Roosevelt's presidency. The design of American ships in 1880 made clear their primary purpose was coastal defense. Many lay close to the water, resembling the Civil War ironclads from which they descended. Sails predominated; steam was an auxiliary power source the sailors disliked because of dirty coal, heat and the mechanical complications of reciprocating engines. Training hardly differed from Nelson's day, the crew having available to it a full range of weapons and equipment for grappling and boarding enemy vessels and preferring to capture rather than sink. Once out of land's sight, these ships were incommunicado unless another vessel was sent as messenger.

Twenty years later, a sailor who had served on one of those ships could hardly understand its successors. Wind, the navigator's ally and adversary ever since man had put to sea, was no longer a tactical consideration. Warships of 26,000 tons displacement, dwarfing even the largest ships of 1880, were propelled at over twenty knots by smooth turbines humming far below decks and operating on either coal or oil.

Naval tactics changed, too. Ships of the 1880s and 1890s all sported reverse prows, at the end of which was a ram in expectation of close combat. But steam power and steel allowed for even more powerful guns of greater range. Once the muzzleloader had been replaced by a breechloader, and the steel industry could cast larger and larger cannon able to withstand great pressures, the range and hitting power of naval weapons increased exponentially. Bigger broadsides and greater velocity challenged the hull designers. A metallurgical race began, ultimately won by Krupp in Germany, to harden armor plating against the new weapons. This in turn put greater pressure on power plant engineering to accommodate the need for greater weight and speed. The day was not far off when something would happen unimaginable to the men of the 1880s: long-range naval duels in which the ships never saw each other. And by the end of the period, the naval profession had also changed. The new ships required more engineers and more technological skills, including the new one of telegraph operator.

All of this was terribly expensive. Opponents of the New Navy were generally silenced in the wave of pride ignited by the victories at Manila Bay and Santiago in 1898. But the critics recovered their voices over the rising costs of participating in the technological revolution. Between 1883 and 1905 the U.S. spent over $1 billion on the Navy, three times more than the entire budget of the federal government in 1883, twice that of 1905. Naval expenditures were running $118 million a year. TR's forty-ship Navy (twenty-eight battleships and twelve armored cruisers) put the U.S. second to France in numbers of capital ships and about on par with Germany, although following the revolutionary British *Dreadnought*, most of the U.S. ships were considered too slow and short of range and firepower.

Where did *Olympia* fit on this spectrum? She was an effective compromise between those who wanted a true blue-water navy like those of the major European powers and a Congress still insistent on coastal defense. *Olympia* also included a dose of rapidly changing military technology although she also exhibited some familiar and retrograde capabilities. She was designed for the Far East, where the great naval powers sent only cruisers and obsolete ironclads. When she joined the Asiatic squadron as flagship in 1895, she was the most formidable warship in the Pacific.

Authorized as part of the Navy buildup of 1888, *Olympia* was known as a "protected cruiser," which meant that she had a deck of 4 and 3/4 inches of steel plate protecting her magazine and engines. This odd designation reflected the problem of sizing American industrial capabilities to strategy. Cruisers normally escorted battleships; they were not powerful enough to take on such capital ships, but were prized for speed and agility. Given the engine and coal capabilities of the day, this forced the designers to choose speed or protection and firepower. In *Olympia*, America adopted a solid compromise position that favored speed.

Olympia was almost as fast as the two fastest cruisers in the world, USS *Columbia* and *Minneapolis* at 23 knots each, but her four 8-inch guns, ten 5-inchers, and twenty-four cannon of various calibers gave her a high-powered broadside. At 340 feet long with a beam of 53 feet and total displacement of 5,865 tons, *Olympia* was a narrow but well-proportioned ship. She had two masts schooner-rigged for auxiliary sailing, and fighting tops equipped with Gatling guns—a nice touch. Named for the capital of the new state of Washington, *Olympia* was a wholly American creation, constructed at Union Iron Works in San Francisco, with guns made at the Washington, D.C., Navy Yard and armor forged in Pennsylvania. Delays and shortages had developed, not least because steel armor was undergoing its own evolution, with the French "Harveyized process" winning out over the much more vulnerable British sandwich-board construction only to be superseded by the even harder Krupp steel. "By 1891," naval historian Kenneth Wimmel noted, "a large portion of key American industries and large numbers of American workers, among them some of the most highly skilled technicians in the country, were committed to manufacturing something only the government wanted or could buy: armored warships." *Olympia* was the product of the first American military-industrial complex.

Launched at last on November 5, 1892, *Olympia* began life under an omen. The sponsor, Miss Anna Bell Dickie, daughter of the general manager of the Union Iron Works, cut her hand on the champagne bottle as she smashed it against the hull. Admiral Belknap, the presiding officer, saved the day by observing that this meant *Olympia* would be the first ship of the New Navy to shed the blood of America's enemies. So it was to be at Manila Bay.

The ship's silhouette and some of its features said volumes about the uncertain and sometimes backward-looking designs of the day. Her elegant cabin woodwork was a fire hazard during battle, and Dewey ordered as much of it as possible to be removed before his encounter with the Spanish fleet. But she also showcased modern American industrial power. *Olympia*'s reciprocating steam engines, exhausting through two funnels, had a huge appetite for coal. They were also incredibly noisy and vibrated underfoot. Engine rooms were overheated, and fire was an ever-present hazard as the coal-storage areas lacked ventilation. (Hyman Rickover led a study in the 1970s which concluded that coal dust and an electric spark were the cause of the *Maine*'s explosion in Havana harbor.) But they were strong and *Olympia* was capable of 22 knots.

With ships that had similar advantages and flaws, the United States would fight the Spanish-American War. Luckily Spain had much less capable ships on station in the Caribbean and the Pacific. The relative superiority of American ships, and the professionalism of their officers and crews, resulted in swift victory over Spain, then still considered a major world power.

On May 1, 1898, Commodore Dewey aboard his flagship, *Olympia*, led a squadron of six ships into Manila Bay to attack the Spanish squadron of two obsolete unarmored cruisers and five gunboats. The Americans mounted fifty-three guns of 5 inches or larger. The Spanish had only thirty-one of 6 inches or smaller.

At 5:22 A.M., at a range of 5,500 yards, Dewey gave his legendary order to *Olympia*'s captain: "You may fire when you are ready, Gridley."

A stoker on *Olympia* left a graphic description of conditions at Manila Bay in the engine room. With portholes and latches secured, "it was so hot our hair was singed. There were several leaks in the steampipes, and the hissing hot steam made things worse. The clatter of the engines and the roaring of the furnaces made such a din it seemed one's head would burst. . . . when our guns opened fire . . . the ship shook so fearfully that the soot and cinders poured down on us in clouds." Lieutenant Ellicott, the intelligence officer on the cruiser *Baltimore*, described her gun crews at work: "naked to the waist and grimy with the soot of powder, their heads bound up in water-soaked towels,

sweat running in rivulets over their glistening bodies, these men who
had fasted for sixteen hours now slung shell after shell . . . each weighing one to two-hundred and fifty pounds into their huge guns . . . under a tropical sun which melted the pitch in the decks." The battle
began at 5:30 A.M. and the sailors did not pause for breakfast until 7:30,
when an erroneous report of a shell shortage led Dewey to cease fire
until the inventory was corrected.

How efficient was *Olympia* as a warship? She certainly passed the
test at Manila Bay: the Spanish fleet was devastated. But in the aftermath of the war, it was clear that America had been fortunate to face a
weak fleet and demoralized opponents. The enthusiasm of Dewey's
gunners had not matched their accuracy. At the outset of the battle, a
small boat thought to carry torpedoes—a greatly feared threat at the
time—sallied forth. *Olympia*'s big guns and secondary batteries fired at
it in vain. Finally, a shot from a Marine hit the boat's steam cylinder.
Lieutenant Calkins on board *Olympia* later revealed the embarrassing
truth: the mystery ship was "only a humble market boat." Later in the
battle, working in calm waters under conditions most favorable to continuous broadsiding, Dewey's ships fired nearly 6,000 shells, but only
142 found their mark. The battle of Santiago toted up a similar score:
9,400 firings with 122 hits.

Nonetheless, the latter battle, fought on July 3, was even more
one-sided than Manila Bay. The Spanish squadron of four cruisers and
two destroyers was entirely wrecked with the loss of only one American sailor killed and one wounded.

The shocking ratio of hits to misses could be explained in part by
the heavy pall of smoke that shrouded every battle fought with the
powder then used. But a larger role was played by the same factor that
so disconcerted naval planners: the technology had far outrun the experience and skills of those who ran and commanded the ships.
Dewey's gunners used Decatur's method: hold the target in open sight
and fire when the roll of the vessel brought the target momentarily in
line with the gun. The British, using an American invention, the tele-
scopic sight, markedly improved their aim around the turn of the century, but this escaped U.S. practice until then-Commander William

Sims, a great Anglophile, convinced President Theodore Roosevelt of the value of the change.

THE HUMILIATING NAVAL DEFEATS at Manila Bay and Santiago, not the Gilbert and Sullivan fighting on land, led Spain to sue for peace and give up the Philippines and Cuba.

The Navy was now immersed in Far Eastern politics, with sprawling colonies to defend. It was set upon its collision course with Japan.

For the turn-of-the-century Navy, however, the outlook was good. Three years after the war with Spain, Theodore Roosevelt was in the White House, determined to see America build a Navy to command the seas. If John Adams is the father of the Navy, Roosevelt is the father of the *modern* Navy. Within months of becoming president he presented Congress with a plan to build a Navy second to none: "The American people must either build and maintain an adequate navy or else make up their minds definitely to accept a secondary position in international affairs, not only in political but in commercial matters."

By 1903 he had begun construction of seven battleships and by 1907 he had a fleet of twenty. On December 16 of that year Roosevelt reviewed sixteen of them—the Great White Fleet—as he sent them off from Hampton Roads on a round-the-world trip to demonstrate the nation's new global naval power. The White Fleet steamed 46,000 miles in fourteen months and became the symbol of Roosevelt's "big stick" diplomacy.

As president, TR did far more than build ships. He identified bright young reformers like William S. Sims and Bradley A. Fiske. He reformed gunnery, training, recruiting, promotion and pay scales. He even gave the Navy its most famous recruiting slogan: "Join the Navy and see the world."

In 1906 the Royal Navy commissioned *Dreadnought*, the first true battleship: 18,000 tons powered by steam turbines and carrying ten 12-inch guns and armor plate eleven inches thick. *Dreadnought* rendered every other naval ship in existence obsolete, but not for long. TR's first two battleships, the 16,000-ton *Michigan* and *South Carolina*, were actually authorized before *Dreadnought* but delays caused them to follow her by three years. The Germans and the Japanese immediately followed suit, and the great battleship arms race was on.

With Roosevelt's hand-picked successor, William Howard Taft, as president, the Navy continued to advance. *Michigan*, the first American dreadnought, as all battleships were called in the years immediately following the British ship, was followed by larger and improved ships. Naval aviation began its fitful development with the first shipboard landing in 1911 and the first naval aviator commissioned that year on April 12. The Navy bought its first two aircraft from Glen Curtiss in May.

The election of a Democrat, Woodrow Wilson, in 1912 did nothing to slow the growth of the Navy. Wilson authorized the *New Mexico* class of battleship displacing 32,000 tons and mounting 14-inch guns. Wilson also chose for his secretary of the Navy one of the more colorful characters of the period, Josephus Daniels. Daniels knew nothing about the Navy and was a pacifist, teetotaler and sex-hygienist. One of his first acts was the "sinking of John Barleycorn"—he ordered the Navy dry. From that day until I rescinded the order in 1982, alcohol (except for medicinal alcohol) was prohibited at all times aboard Navy ships. The order was observed fairly closely on all ships except aircraft carriers, where among aviators it was observed in the breech. In 1982 I issued a naval secretary instruction permitting beer and wine for "representational purposes" only, when ships were tied up or at anchor.

To balance his eccentric secretary of the Navy, Wilson chose a young navalist cousin of Theodore Roosevelt and fellow disciple of Mahan to assist him: Franklin Delano Roosevelt.

FRANKLIN ROOSEVELT: NAVAL VICTOR

When attacked for avoiding military service, President Clinton frequently cited Franklin Roosevelt as a great commander in chief who never served. Clinton was wrong. FDR served in the Navy for seven years, including the First World War. He was a "naval person" through and through. He was "never more at home with himself than when on the water," Eleanor Roosevelt's biographer Joseph Lash noted. As a young swell, FDR had been proud to vote Republican for his famous relation. But by 1912, he had aligned himself firmly with the Democratic Party of Woodrow Wilson, no doubt to TR's dismay In 1913, his hard work on behalf of Wilson earned him the post he sought, assistant secretary of the Navy. He was 31 and a coming man.

Franklin Roosevelt was surely aware that TR had made himself a national name through his tour with the Navy. But Teddy had done it thanks to the Spanish-American War, and in 1913, a European war was not at all expected, much less a world war that might involve the United States. Worse yet, FDR's boss's unusual proclivities—pacifism and prohibitionism—did not easily lend glory to the office.

After but a year at the job, FDR was ready to leave. The post at that point had consisted of little more than endless tours of ships and lots of signatures on procurement papers that FDR freely confessed he hardly understood (FDR's formidable mother, Sara, had advised him to adopt a large signature, as a small one "gets a cramped look"). By August 1914, his wife had just given birth to another son, and FDR had sought the senate nomination in New York. But he lost the primary against a Tammany Hall candidate. As had been the case with Uncle Teddy, a political defeat in New York proved to be a lucky stroke.

The outbreak of the European war caught the Wilson administration without a policy. Woodrow Wilson's interests were domestic; his New Freedom sought social change and government reform. Moreover both Secretary of State William Jennings Bryan and Josephus Daniels were isolationists. FDR had been brought up on Alfred Mahan; he and the admirals saw eye to eye and they were increasingly angry at the way Daniels was managing the Navy.

FDR also thought the U.S. should get in early against Germany, unlike Wilson, who advocated a cautious neutral approach. So FDR soon found himself doing at the Navy in 1914 what TR had done in 1896. First there was the very tempo of the department: "everything asleep and apparently utterly oblivious to the fact that the most terrible drama in history was about to be enacted," as Franklin wrote to his wife, Eleanor. By 1915, he was in a state of near insubordination to Daniels. The Navy secretary habitually procrastinated on decisions in which he felt himself in opposition to the admirals—these were left for FDR to decide in his absence. But when Daniels returned, he never reversed Roosevelt—again, an uncanny repeat of TR's experience. Matters reached fever pitch with the sinking of *Lusitania* and U-boat warfare. When Wilson insisted on neutrality still—"there is such a thing as a man being too proud to fight"—TR denounced him for cowardice and weakness. Finally, the cabinet came apart. Bryan resigned on June 8, 1915, to lead the fight against war. But Daniels held on. Meanwhile, Wilson, freed of his nettlesome secretary of state, asked Congress for defense preparations on a huge scale, with the Navy to be the first beneficiary.

In a strange precursor for FDR's own 1940 campaign, Wilson won the 1916 election on the motto "he kept us out of war." Nonetheless Wilson slowly increased the U.S. diplomatic and military role; his agonizing hesitations were finally ended by the German resumption of unrestricted U-boat warfare and the infamous Zimmerman telegram proposing a German-Mexican alliance that would allow Mexico to reclaim its "lost territory in Texas, New Mexico and Arizona." On April 2, 1917, Congress declared war, Wilson announcing that "the world must be made safe for democracy."

FDR became the decisive man at the Navy. His easy ways led some to underestimate him, one of whom was Joseph P. Kennedy. In the spring of 1917, Kennedy represented Bethlehem Steel in a dispute over the price of warships then under construction for one of Germany's enemies, the Argentine Navy, in the shipyards at Quincy, Massachusetts. Supported by his powerful boss, Charles Schwab, Kennedy strode into Roosevelt's office for arbitration. When Roosevelt suggested that Kennedy turn over the ships—the State Department would collect the debt, he said; in wartime contracts had to be more flexible—Joe Kennedy refused. So FDR ended the session, stating af-

Battle of *Kearsage* and Raphael Semmes' ship, *Alabama*, painted in 1864
by Edouard Manet (1832–83). *Philadelphia Museum of Art*

Commodore class gunboat believed to be *Commodore Jones* at Newport News, Virginia. *U.S. Naval Institute*

The crew of *Commodore* class gunboat *Hunchback* somewhere on the James River, Virginia. *National Archives*

Naval officers of the *Commodore* class gunboat *Hunchback* and one of her bronze 9 pounder howitzers, in "undress" uniform. *National Archives*

Lieutenant Commander William B. Cushing, USN, whose exploits presaged the Navy SEALs, was a disruptive influence in the peacetime Navy. *U.S. Naval Historical Center*

Rear Admiral Raphael Semmes, CSN. This portrait by Maliby Sykes depicts Semmes wearing the belt buckle of a Confederate States Navy Admiral. *Courtesy the State of Alabama*

Surrender of *Tennessee*, Battle of Mobile Bay. *Official U.S. Navy Photograph*

C.S.S. Alabama (1862–1864). Purpose-built in England, beautiful, and devastating to the Union merchant fleet. *U.S. Naval Historical Center*

Admiral Porter's fleet running the rebel blockade of the Mississippi at Vicksburg, April 16, 1863. *Courtesy Beverly R. Robinson Collection, U.S. Naval Academy Museum*

Rear Admiral Alfred Thayer Mahan, a theorist among sea-dogs, made naval strategy into an intellectual discipline. *U.S. Naval Institute*

Assistant Secretary of the Navy Theodore Roosevelt in his office in what is now the Old Executive Office Building. I shared this office in 1969 while assistant to Richard Allen on the National Security Council staff. *Official U.S. Navy Photo*

U.S.S. *Olympia* (C-6), in New York Harbor following her arrival from Manila, circa late September 1899. *Courtesy Louis Smaus*

FDR on the bridge, a naval person through and through. Even as President he often referred to the Navy as "us," and the Army as "them." *Associated Press*

A German submarine diving to attack an Allied convoy during World War I. *U.S. Naval Institute*

Pearl Harbor, December 7, 1941. The bombs strike home on "battleship row" as seen from the submarine base. *Official U.S. Navy Photograph*

Depth-charging a German U-boat in the winter, North Atlantic, 1942. *U.S. Naval Institute*

Admiral Ernest J. King, Commander in Chief, Atlantic Fleet, one of the "sons-of-bitches" sent for when the shooting started, and Secretary of the Navy Frank Knox, who had been one of TR's Roughriders. *U.S. Naval Historical Center*

Countless coats of gray paint still defend the *Yorktown's* guns from corrosion more than a half century after it was swallowed by the Pacific. Some thirty crew members killed during the fighting went down with the vessel, but Bob Ballard discovered no sign of human remains when he visited her in 1998. *David Doubilet*

The USS *Yorktown* listing heavily and fighting for survival during Midway. *Official U.S. Navy Photograph*

The Japanese carrier *Hiryu* during the battle on June 4, 1942 at Midway easily evades a string of bombs from high-altitude B-17's from Midway. The heavy bombers, up too high, never got a single hit through the entire battle. *National Archives*

LCS-8 stands off Corregidor's shore on February 16, 1945, to provide fire support. *LCSs* had more firepower per ton than any ship in the war. The chutes of paratroops, dropped by USAAF C-47 planes, can be seen just over the ridge. *National Archives*

Admiral Chester W. Nimitz, USN, Commander in Chief Pacific Fleet and Pacific Ocean areas, puts on a battle helmet while visiting a U.S. Navy ship, circa 1944. *Courtesy of FADM Nimitz*

Andrew Jackson Higgins, who designed and built the amphibious boats that took the Pacific islands and liberated Europe. *Courtesy Higgins Family*

Troops disembark from a Higgins LCVP during an amphibious assault. *Courtesy Higgins Family*

LCS-18 under Kamikaze attack, painting by John Hamilton. *Author's Collection*

The destroyer *Franklin* provides close in fire to the GIs landing on Omaha Beach, June 6, 1944. *Courtesy Tom Freeman*

fably that Navy tugs would be dispatched to get the ships and that he hoped Kennedy would see him again soon.

Upon his return, Kennedy described FDR as "a smiling four-flusher," and Schwab held his ground. Both men were soon astonished to see four Navy tugboats steaming up the Fore River with armed Marines onboard. Word went out that the Hudson River dandy could play hardball.

Roosevelt was anxious to see war. With the German fleet inactive following the battle of Jutland, the U.S. Navy had only their U-boats to fight. FDR partially conceived and then carried forward, over British and U.S. Navy objections, an $80 million scheme to blockade the North Sea with a mine barrage that would bottle up the U-boats then wreaking havoc in the North Atlantic. Eventually six subs were sunk and the war ended before the scheme could be fully realized; a fortune then had to be spent to remove the mines. It was, as Daniels said, "a stupendous undertaking," and FDR proved himself a master at marshaling the military and political forces necessary to see it through. In later years, he convinced himself that the mines had fatally impaired German submarine morale, leading to mutinies that eventually convinced the German High Command to seek an armistice. This was an exaggeration: the mutinies actually began on the dreadnoughts and battle cruisers. But when FDR revived his claim in a letter to the "former naval person" Winston Churchill on February 14, 1944, Churchill thought it wise not to contradict him.

For FDR the highlight of World War I was his visit to the front in July 1918. Wined and dined in England, he had gotten on famously with the king and was persuaded by then-Foreign Secretary Arthur James Balfour to undertake a special mission to Italy to persuade the Italian fleet, idle through the whole war, to attack the Austrians, equally idle. Even FDR could not change the convenient logic of their situation, but in trying to do so he offended both the French and Wilson, who resented this unexpected foray into high diplomacy by an assistant secretary. Meanwhile, FDR toured all the battlefields, fired an artillery round, and smelled and saw the terrible scenes of carnage. He decided to volunteer upon his return, but these plans came to naught when he was overtaken by twin disasters.

The first of these was physical. Despite his robust appearance, FDR was constantly ailing and his correspondence from that period refers to colds, flus and erratic fevers. In September 1918, he came down with the infamous influenza that was to kill millions. As he struggled to recover, his wife Eleanor came to Washington to assist. There she discovered amidst his mail a packet of love letters from her social secretary, the well-born but needy Lucy Mercer. The crisis was immediate and devastating. Eleanor offered a divorce; Louis Howe pointed out to FDR that marriage to the Catholic Mercer would kill FDR's political chances. On top of this, Sara Delano Roosevelt threatened disinheritance. FDR promised never to see Lucy Mercer again, a promise he had little intention of keeping.

Rebounding from both illness and the crisis with Eleanor, FDR plunged himself into the massive task of unwinding the Navy after the war. The job was made more difficult by William S. Sims, now a rear admiral and an FDR favorite who, upon resuming his post as president of the Navy War College, blasted Josephus Daniels's decisions on the awarding of medals. He demanded an inquiry, and just before a subcommittee of the Senate Naval Affairs Committee met on the subject, he dispatched a sensational memo to Daniels, claiming that the Navy's failure (meaning Daniels's failure) to act promptly on the outbreak of war had cost 500,000 lives, $15 million and 2,500,000 tons of shipping. It leaked to the press.

FDR privately deplored this public washing of the linen. Then, on February 1, 1920, speaking to an audience of 1,500 at the Brooklyn Academy of Music, Roosevelt confirmed Sims's charges while depicting himself as the real hero of the department without whom nothing would have happened. He confessed proudly that he had broken the law and acted without congressional permission in the name of the national interest. FDR also charged Wilson with opposition to defense preparedness.

Roosevelt's act of disloyalty wounded and confused Daniels while earning Wilson's permanent enmity. He was compelled to make a public apology on February 3. Still, the impression was left that here was one prominent Democrat, regarded by all as an attractive and effective leader, who shared public anger at Wilson's conduct of the war. For a Democratic Party anxious to find new blood, the disloyalty was a trumpet note. Nonetheless, after another controversy on naval criminal policy, FDR left the Navy for good.

Throughout his seven years in the Navy, Franklin Roosevelt showed the characteristics that would later make him among our most famous presidents. Although a very young man (only 31 at his appointment in 1913), FDR took to Washington like a sailor to liberty ashore. His charming personality and lighthearted ways disguised ruthless ambition. Roosevelt proved time and again that he could get things done despite hidebound government bureaucracy. In fact, he often used official procedure to obscure his purposes and confound his enemies. He also showed a marked ability to find good men—among them Admiral Leahy, whom he first met as the lieutenant commanding his official yacht—regardless of background or affiliation and to inspire their loyalty.

The other, less attractive side of FDR could also be seen. He was a snob; neither he nor Eleanor manifested any of the social sympathies that later made them popular, but then there had not been any Great Depression either. If FDR sensed that the war spelled the end of the old order, he certainly did not alter any views to accommodate it.

But FDR was not yet the egalitarian man of the New Deal. In the Navy, he was simply a snob; he and Eleanor enjoyed a rarefied Washington social scene that featured clubs excluding Jews, blacks, even businessmen. More important, he was disloyal. Both Josephus Daniels and Woodrow Wilson had reason to fire him more than once but did not. FDR repaid their indulgence with convenient betrayal once their stars were in decline.

Yet for the large part, FDR had begun at the Navy hoping to duplicate Teddy Roosevelt's rise to power and had succeeded. The triumph had left him drained but, like his famous cousin, he was to draw supreme personal strength from adversity. TR had gone west to save his life by forcing his inadequate lungs to develop. FDR's frequent illnesses in

1916–18 were the forerunner of the crippling disease that threatened his life and career. His triumph over his own physical weakness was in turn a forerunner of his triumph over "fear itself" for the nation.

Roosevelt's formative experience in Washington and in foreign affairs was as a naval person. A review of the presidential memorabilia at Hyde Park makes abundantly clear that throughout his life this was an important dimension of his self-image. During a White House meeting with his military chiefs in 1944, Army Chief of Staff General George Marshall pleaded in exasperation, "Please, Mr. President, stop referring to the Army as 'them' and the Navy as 'us.'

FDR should remain in American memory a naval person: the jaunty uplift of the jaw, the invincible optimism, the confidence and pride of a mighty warship—all are elegantly draped in the official cape of the United States Navy.

THE FIRST WORLD WAR

The outbreak of World War I in August 1914 had little effect on the Navy, as the war was expected to be short and America to remain neutral. With the sinking of *Lusitania* in May 1915, however, that changed dramatically.

In 1916 Wilson asked Congress for a major new construction program of 156 ships, including 10 more battleships, 16 cruisers, 50 destroyers and 67 submarines. The first of these battleships were to be the most powerful in the world, displacing 33,000 tons and equipped with eight 16-inch guns. When the Germans resumed unrestricted submarine warfare in February 1917, Wilson opted for war, and on April 6, 1917, the United States entered the war on the side of the Allies.

The principal naval operations of the United States during World War I were in escorting troops and supplies across the Atlantic and in assisting the Royal Navy in hunting submarines. In the course of the war, eighty-five American destroyers were sent to Europe operating principally under the control of the Royal Navy from Queenstown, Ireland, and other ports on the Continent. The U.S. Navy proved to be very effective in this role, ultimately transporting more than two million men to France without the loss of a single ship. In addition to this, five battleships—*New York, Florida, Delaware, Texas* and *Wyoming*—were assigned to the British Grand Fleet of Admiral Jellicoe. Three additional battleships—*Nevada, Oklahoma* and *Utah*—were sent to Ireland to free up Royal Navy forces for the crucial anti-submarine warfare effort.

By the time the United States entered the war, the Allies were losing nearly a million tons of shipping a month, with one out of four ships leaving port being sunk by U-boats. Admiral Jellicoe informed the U.S. Navy that Germany would "win unless we can stop these losses—and stop them soon." In addition to the aggressive destroyer reinforcement, the United States began turning out large numbers of 110-foot subchasers that would provide a counter to the German submarine warfare. By the end of the war, 447 of these ships were built for the U.S. and the French navies.

It was not long after the arrival of the American Navy that the tide began to turn. By the end of 1917, Allied losses had sunk below 300,000 tons per month, no longer a threat to the Allied war effort.

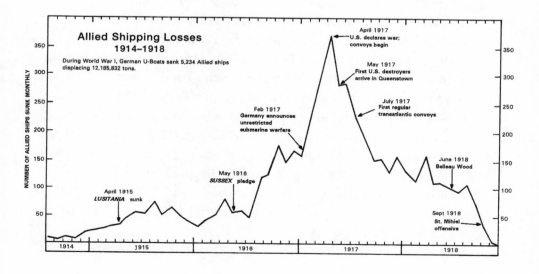

They remained at that level for the rest of the war. The hinge, as a former naval person would say about a later war, had turned.

THE END OF WORLD WAR I found the Navy not only with a huge and balanced fleet, having expanded from 67,000 men when war was declared to nearly 500,000 men and women at Armistice Day, but also with high prestige and support from President Wilson and Congress for further expansion in the postwar period. Wilson sent a major expansion plan to Congress and resumed active deployments in the Pacific, shifting battleships, cruisers and destroyers from the Atlantic and creating a powerful new Pacific Fleet. This fleet would operate under Japan's increasingly watchful eye.

After the United States annexed the Philippines and increased the activity of the Asiatic squadron, including playing an active role in suppression of the Boxer Rebellion in 1900, the Japanese became deeply concerned. After the Japanese victory over Russia in 1905 many in Japan began to view the United States as an unwarranted intruder in its sphere of influence.

During World War I, far from the fighting in Europe, Japan maximized its power. In 1915 Japan declared war on Germany, promptly seizing its area of influence in northern China and taking over all of Germany's island holdings in the central Pacific including the Carolines, the Marshalls and the Marianas. The British, concerned at the rapid growth of American naval power in the Pacific, secretly negotiated an agreement with Japan to support Japan's permanent possession of all German holdings north of the equator. In return Japan would support Britain's annexation of all of Germany's holdings south of the equator in the Pacific. Following the armistice, Japan embarked on a huge naval building program, which by 1921 represented almost a third of its entire national budget. Under the leadership of the victor of Tsushima, Admiral Togo, Japan built an elite all-volunteer naval force, highly trained, and superbly equipped.

It is often said that the seeds for World War II were planted in the soil of the infamously unsuccessful Versailles peace treaty ending World War I. Many historians view the two European conflicts as different phases of one war for mastery of the Continent. The German threat would indeed reappear within a generation of the 1918 armistice. But to the Navy between wars, the specter of conflict with the East loomed even more threateningly, and more obviously.

WAR PLAN ORANGE: MAP TO VICTORY IN THE PACIFIC

Napoleon once observed that no strategy survives the first volley of battle. He was proved wrong by the most successful strategic document in the history of warfare, War Plan Orange.

The genesis of War Plan Orange is well documented in secret files that have been opened to the public in the years since World War II and the surrender of the Japanese Empire aboard *Missouri* in Tokyo Bay in 1945. The files reveal forty years of dialogue among intellectuals and sea dogs over a uniquely American evolving document. There are no chosen few like a king and his ministers or an omnipotent German general staff who come up with a plan that the rank and file must follow like lemmings. American junior officers have a treasured propensity to question plans, offer alternatives and often come up with a better way to win. And so it was for over four decades of planning for war against Japan that started at the turn of the century.

On December 7, 1941, the U.S. Navy had a detailed plan—in reality a grand strategy—that would survive the opening Japanese attack and become the blueprint for victory in World War II. Like Caesar crossing the Rubicon, American naval leaders knew exactly what they were going to do from Pearl Harbor forward. They would cross the Pacific in a grueling but inexorable campaign that would ultimately lead them to Tokyo.

In looking back, it is clear that it all started when Dewey steamed into Manila Bay during the Spanish-American War. In its aftermath, the United States became a de facto colonial power with possessions stretching from the Caribbean to the far distant Western Pacific. Up until then, most Americans had never heard of the Philippines and would not have been surprised to learn they were a type of canned vegetables instead of an archipelago the size of Britain consisting of some 7,000 islands with a collective coastline longer than that of the United States.

How to protect these war prizes, especially the Philippines, became a major question in the War and Navy Departments after peace was restored with Spain. Theodore Roosevelt initiated the project, and his administration provided an infrastructure for the plan: a world-class fleet with bases on the Pacific coast, in Hawaii and by the Panama Canal.

On March 30, 1900, a small board of Army and Navy officers was convened in Washington to try to answer this question. Chaired by George Dewey himself, they set about trying to come up with a plan to defend not only the Philippines, but Guam and Hawaii as well, along with some other minor American possessions in the Pacific like Midway and Johnston Islands. With the U.S. designated Blue, Japan was identifed as Orange, the prime opponent in one of twenty-five "Rainbow Plans" assigned for development. (Other opponents were Red for Britain, Black for Germany, Purple for Russia, etc.) Plan Orange was the only plan developed seriously.

Concurrently, at Newport, Rhode Island, the faculty of the Naval War College, under the visionary leadership of Alfred Thayer Mahan, began to address the same question on a broader scale. They undertook an all-encompassing study of campaign planning, and developed war gaming into a necessary militaristic art form. Over the years, hundreds of promising young naval officers moved model ships across wooden ocean floors at Newport in mock engagements prescient in determining the outcome of future battles on the high seas. The games were drawn from the latest drafts of Orange and tested. Results were incorporated in revised drafts. Thus for nearly forty years naval officers assigned through Newport contributed to, and had impressed upon them, the logic of Plan Orange. After World War II, Admiral Nimitz often said that there was not a battle in the Pacific war that had not been war-gamed at Newport in the 1920s and 1930s.

Meanwhile, the aging Admiral Dewey, an authentic American hero whom everyone revered, realized his staff's limits in cerebral fire-power. He created a supporting staff of junior officers—the best and the brightest of that day—to do the scut work of research, assessment and planning, much as the talented and invaluable "action officers" of today do in the Pentagon's inner sanctums.

With all these people thinking, Japanese power began to loom large during the Russo-Japanese War of 1904–5. Not lost on anyone was the tired Russian fleet's Tsu-shima debacle. The Russians had steamed all the way from the Baltic Sea to the Japanese Sea, only to find themselves depleted and soon whipped by a fresh and tactically sound Japanese fleet lying in wait for them. Here for all to see was an obvious parallel: If the U.S. fleet steamed out of the Chesapeake Bay, it would be faced with a Hobson's choice of two much longer routes—either east across the Atlantic and Indian Oceans or south around the horn and west across the Pacific. Would America meet in the Philippines the same fate as the Russians in the Tsu-shima Straits? Even if the fleet sortied from the West Coast, it was still a marathon distance to travel before taking on a battle-tested Navy resting in its own backyard.

If the distances involved were not enough of a headache, when the Japanese mortared Port Arthur into submission from landward, naval planners envisioned Japanese heavy mortar shells fired from the Bataan Peninsula raining down on Corregidor, the army's cork in the bottle at the mouth of Manila Bay. To further complicate planning, the Japanese seized German possessions in the Central Pacific during World War I. This Micronesian group of a hundred or so islands and atolls fell astride the sea-lanes between Hawaii and the Philippines. After the war, the Japanese were mandated permanent possession of Micronesia, the best-known of the islands being Truk in the Carolines.

In the age of steam, there were other daunting issues: coaling stations and the number of colliers required to sustain the fleet on the other side of the world. Steam-powered ships consumed coal at a tremendous rate. Then, once in a fight, they could empty their ammo magazines in a couple of hours. Finally, individual ships were always in need of some type of in-port maintenance and repair. Where could they receive it? In sum, logistics became the essential bedrock needed by the Navy if its fleets were going to project offensive sea power into the Pacific during a war with Japan.

Against this challenging backdrop, planning began as the aggressive Japanese Empire continued to expand into China and, later on, into Korea and French Indochina. The rather basic tactical question of how to defend the Philippines evolved into a far larger strategic question of how to defeat the Japanese in the event of general war. War Plan Orange began to grow from a sketchy army trench line across Luzon into a full-fledged campaign planning document with a seemingly impossible objective given the size and capabilities of the Navy before World War I.

The geopolitical premise of the plan held that, in spite of historically friendly relations, a war would erupt between the United States and Japan in which neither could rely on the help of allies. The root cause would be Japan's quest for national greatness by attempting to dominate the land, people and resources of the Far East. Japan would mobilize its every sinew for a war of vital national interest. When ready, it would strike suddenly. It would easily seize its objectives in the Western Pacific but not be able or willing to carry the war to American shores. It would settle down to a grueling struggle in the mistaken belief that the American people would tire of fighting for a faraway region of no vital interest and demand a peace conceding most of Japan's gains.

This plan and the perceptions that lay behind it never varied after 1914. Despite the fact that the Jones Act had promised Philippine independence as early as 1916, both the War Department and Navy Department became more and more opposed to withdrawal as Plan Orange made the islands indispensable for fighting a successful war against Japanese aggression. The fundamental naval attitude underlying the next thirty years of planning the strategy against Japan's attack was well expressed by Admiral Dewey when he declared that the U.S. should make war "with all its power . . . with the single purpose of accomplishing the object of the war in the most complete and businesslike manner and the shortest period of time." The fundamental axiom of Plan Orange was the defeat of a land power by the use of sea power. The greatest departure from Plan Orange strategy was driven by the Army and its War Department. Plan Orange had proposed to bring about victory through blockade and strangulation. The War Department argued according to its orthodoxy, that massive land invasion of the Japanese homeland would be necessary to terminate the war before the patience of the American people ran out.

Specifically, the plan forecast potential Japanese attacks on Hawaii, the Panama Canal and the West Coast. It entertained the possibility of Japan invading Alaska and occupying the Aleutians as jumping-off points into the northwestern states of Washington and Oregon. In contrast, the plan had no contingency for an American expeditionary force to occupy the Japanese homeland. The Pacific's geography dictated that the war would be won on the high seas, far from American homeports and at the end of a long and tenuous supply line.

Primal assumptions were straight from Mahan: the U.S. Navy's main objective would always be the destruction of the Imperial Japanese Navy. To that end, the U.S. fleet was never to be divided because the concentration of combat power was needed to sink the Japanese fleet in a major, decisive engagement. Moreover, the plan assumed that sea power would never try to fight land power, although amphibious landings would be necessary to gain coaling stations, port facilities and, later on, airfields. Nelson's dictum that only a fool of a captain would fight a fort still applied. Bypass, isolate and let them die on the vine was the maneuver of choice in Plan Orange. Although MacArthur promoted the idea that he was the father of island-hopping, the go-around-them tactic was well embedded in the Orange plan long before the American Caesar ever promised to return to the Philippines.

At the outset of planning, the authors of Plan Orange were at first amazed and then confounded by the size of the Pacific Ocean. They were dealing with the largest theater of operations in military history.

How accurate was War Plan Orange? War with Japan, it held, would start in the Western Pacific with simultaneous Japanese surprise attacks on U.S. possessions aimed at gaining access to much-needed raw materials, especially oil. The majority of the U.S. Navy homeported in the U.S. would be of no help and the Philippines indefensible. But the nation would awaken, and support a painful, inexorable march across the Pacific. A mobilized United States would send major expeditionary forces westward, led by the fleet that would seize Japanese mandated islands in the Central Pacific, where advanced bases would be established to support the next phase. Distance would be on the Japanese side, but time would not. The weight of American sea power would prove unbearable in major battles of attrition. The Philippines would be retaken, and a blockade would start to be emplaced around Japan's home islands. The final phase anticipated Japan's defeat because of its geography. For all its martial power, it was still an island nation. With its fleet sunk, it could be isolated and choked off from resources by blockade, and then defeated by aerial bombardment of its industries and population centers. In effect, the Japanese could be bombed and starved into submission, while their Army looked hopelessly on from China.

In the end, with the exception of the invention and use of the atomic bomb, this is exactly what happened. At the heart of the Orange plan were a number of conditions and assumptions that did not change over the years despite new technological and political developments including radar, diesel power, aircraft carriers, underway replenishment and the opening of the Panama Canal. The naval planners who saw it all were not clairvoyants but conservative men who took nothing for granted and mapped it all out point by point. This does not mean they were without imagination. On the contrary, they watched carefully the development of the airplane, aircraft carrier and catapult. When these three elements combined to give the fleet a new offensive capability, they incorporated aircraft carriers into their plan.

It is notable that no Orange plan was ever enacted by Congress or signed by a president; even in mid-1941 Franklin Roosevelt gave only oral approval. The secretaries of war and Navy had signed formal Orange plans from 1924 onward; previously they were endorsed only by the senior military officers responsible for planning.

Had the Navy been provided the ships required to implement Plan Orange, it could well have deterred the predicted Japanese behavior. Unfortunately, the ambitious plans of the Navy following WWI failed to take into account the great war weariness of the Allies and the isolationism that became the dominant political factor in the United States. With the election of Warren Harding, naval disarmament soon became an overwhelming political force. The Washington Conference on Naval Disarmament got underway in November 1921 and swiftly resulted in a treaty which established the 5:5:3 ratio of capital ship tonnage for Britain, the United States and Japan respectively. Japan, with a one-ocean Navy, was given de facto superiority in the Pacific with three-fifths of the U.S. allowance for two oceans. In addition the Washington Conference produced a prohibition on the United States' fortification of Guam and the Philippines. The effective result of the naval disarmament treaties, extended and confirmed by the succeeding Coolidge and Hoover administrations, was to prevent the U.S. Navy from building up even to the treaty limits while allowing Japan effectively to exceed them. With the naval lessons and buildup of World War I now in the past, the path to the greatest naval war in history was set.

VII

WORLD WAR II

THERE IS NO PRECEDENT to the naval war that raged simultaneously in all the world's oceans from 1939 to 1945.

On the day of Japanese surrender in August 1945 the United States Navy had 105 aircraft carriers, 5,000 ships and submarines and 82,000 vessels and landing craft deployed around the world, manned by experienced citizen-sailors and led by aggressive and seasoned admirals. They and their allies had conquered Japan, liberated Europe and sunk the entire navies of Germany, Japan and Italy. Thirty-nine months before, they had been a small, mediocre force, repeatedly humiliated in battle, nearly driven from the Pacific by a superb Japanese Navy and unable to stop German submarine devastation in the Atlantic. America's naval turnaround in World War II is one of the greatest sagas in all military history.

The war itself was rooted in the gap between the bellicose diplomacy of the free nations and their equally steadfast refusal to maintain sufficient military preparedness to back up policies that confronted the despotism of Nazism, Fascism and Japanese imperialism. It was rather the reverse of Theodore Roosevelt's "speak softly but carry a big stick." In the Pacific, Japan knew perfectly well that the United States Navy had been planning for war with them for decades. Yet Coolidge, Hoover and the first Roosevelt administration pursued mindless policies of naval disarmament.

A series of international pacts known as the Washington Naval Agreements were seized on by opportunistic politicians in England and the United States to avoid the expense of maintaining an adequate naval capability. Through these agreements Japan was able to block the building of American fortifications west of Hawaii and British strengthening of Singapore. Japan, concerned only with the Pacific, was permitted a fleet three-fifths the size permitted the U.S., which had a two-ocean requirement. While democracies rigidly policed their admirals, the Germans and Japanese built their navies. The U.S. and British navies became in the words of one observer "hollow, unbalanced forces, lacking the numbers and variety of ships their global responsibilities demanded." Meanwhile, American policy towards Japan's expansion in the Pacific became ever more truculent.

The policies of President Roosevelt and his staff in the year leading up to Pearl Harbor can indeed be characterized as attempting to goad the Japanese into attack. In late 1940, Roosevelt had directed that a substantial part of the Pacific Fleet be shifted to the Atlantic, despite the protests of Secretary of the Navy Frank Knox and CINCPAC Admiral James Richardson. In July Roosevelt froze Japanese assets in the United States and halted the sale of oil to Japan. A courageous, technologically resourceful, incredibly warlike nation, Japan was cut off from the raw materials it needed to fulfill its imperialist goals. The infamous surprise attack should not have been very surprising.

Pearl Harbor: Who Knew?

If the blindness of America's prewar policy toward Japan seems absurd, no less absurd are the recurring claims that the American government knew specifically where and when the Japanese blow would fall, yet allowed them to decimate our fleet anyway.

Japan's onslaught, beginning December 7, 1941, was brilliantly planned and executed. Some weeks before the attack, Navy Secretary Knox had written: "If war eventuates with Japan, it is . . . easily possible that hostilities would be initiated by a surprise attack upon the fleet or the naval base at Pearl Harbor." On the morning of December 7, Knox met with his admirals. "Gentlemen," he asked, "Are they going to hit us?" "No, Mr. Secretary," replied Rear Admiral Richmond Kelly Turner, "They are going to hit the British. They are not ready for us yet."

They were not, but they were going to strike just the same. British and American naval intelligence knew that a huge Japanese strike force had put to sea but did not know that one arm of it was heading towards Oahu. Everyone in leadership in Washington knew that an attack was coming, and all of the commands in the Pacific had been alerted, but no one was prepared.

Anglo-American intelligence had cracked PURPLE, the high-level Japanese diplomatic machine cipher, but were not reading JN-25, the Imperial Japanese Navy's Fleet Code, which was the only code that contained information related to Pearl Harbor attack planning. From reading PURPLE, everyone expected a Japanese attack within days or weeks, but in Washington the translation of the most critical messages revealing the timing (but not the targets) was either delayed or not forwarded to higher authority because of urgent weekend golf games. The capital was still on a peacetime footing and did not work on Saturday or Sunday. There is no doubt that FDR expected and wanted a Japanese attack to get us in the war, but not at Pearl Harbor and not with the devastating effect that resulted.

The Japanese made no effort to hide the massive task forces heading to invade Thailand, Malaya and Singapore, but took extreme pains to maintain cover and deception over their Pearl Harbor force. They flooded the airways with many new transmission sources and traffic, both phony and real, overwhelming American and British intelligence-processing capacities. Recent declassification of documents and the steady production of new oral histories from participants, including Japanese sailors from the mini-subs that took part in the raids, pilots and intelligence officers from the Japanese carriers and planners in Tokyo, is creating a much clearer picture than was available only a few years ago. It brings into sharp focus the incompetence of the commanders at Pearl Harbor. An American destroyer had sighted and attacked a Japanese submarine at the harbor mouth hours before the Japanese attack. When the report was given to Admiral Kimmel, he refused to believe it and dressed for his golf game.

None of the Army's thirty-one antiaircraft batteries had ammunition, and all of the army aircraft at Hickam Field were parked wingtip-to-wingtip to make it easier on the guards. The Army's radar on Oahu detected the attackers 137 miles offshore, but the planes were dismissed as American aircraft overdue from California. The information was not shared with the Navy.

The brass at Pearl Harbor performed dismally, the ordinary soldiers and sailors heroically. At 7:55 A.M. the first of 191 bombers and fighters from the carriers *Akagi, Hiryu, Kaga, Shokaku, Soryu* and *Zuikaku* hit the anchored fleet. Thirty minutes later they were gone and a second wave of 170 aircraft attacked.

Luckily the carriers *Enterprise* and *Lexington* were at sea delivering Marine aircraft to Wake and Midway Islands, and *Saratoga* was on the West Coast. Battleships took the brunt of the attack. *Arizona* was destroyed by a bomb to her forward magazine, eventually killing 1,103 of her 1,400-man crew. *Oklahoma* capsized losing 415 of 1,354. *California* and *West Virginia* were sunk at their moorings and *Maryland, Pennsylvania* and *Tennessee* were all heavily damaged, as well as *Nevada*, the only battleship to get underway during the attack. Eighteen ships, eight of them battleships, were sunk or crippled. More than 300 aircraft were destroyed or badly damaged on the ground. There were 2,403 Americans killed and 1,178 wounded. The Japanese lost only 29 aircraft.

After Pearl Harbor the Japanese attacked the Philippines. Despite commanding officer General Douglas MacArthur's knowing of Pearl Harbor days before, virtually the entire American bomber force was destroyed on the ground. On December 10 the Japanese forces occupied Guam and landed in the Philippines and the next day attacked Wake Island. Within a few months after Pearl Harbor, Japan had taken Wake Island, Guam, Hong Kong, Malaya and the Dutch East Indies. The performance of American and British forces against these attacks was pathetic.

Admiral Kimmel and General Walter Short, the Army commander in Hawaii, deserved the axe and got it almost immediately. But other top officers—MacArthur and the Army and Navy chiefs General George Marshall and Admiral Harold "Betty" Stark—should at least have been reprimanded for negligence. They were not because quite simply they were each too politically powerful, MacArthur with the Republicans and Marshall and Stark with the Democrats.

It was doubtless little comfort to the Americans that the British commanders in Malaya and Singapore were even more incompetent. With far more direct warning than Pearl Harbor, the British General Robert Brooke-Popham lived up to his Gilbert and Sullivan name and refused to heed the urgent request of his subordinates to implement his defense plan, repeating only that "there should be no undue alarm" until the bombs were actually raining on Singapore. The Navy commander, Admiral Tom Phillips, frittered away two of Britain's most powerful warships, *Repulse* and *Prince of Wales*, by steaming around indecisively without any air cover. They were promptly sunk by Japanese dive-bombers.

Ironically, when they heard of the attack, Allied leaders rejoiced, thinking the lost battle signaled the won war. Churchill wrote: "So we had won after all! . . . I went to bed and slept the sleep of the saved and thankful." French General Charles de Gaulle exclaimed, "This war is over . . . nothing can resist the power of American industry." More surprisingly the reaction of many Japanese, including Admiral Yamamoto himself, and Nazi leaders, excepting Hitler, was much the same. Japanese journalist Soichi Kinoshita recalled, "Another feeling ran down my spine: We'll be beaten." On December 11, in a fit of irrationality, Hitler and Mussolini each declared war on the United States.

THE BATTLE FOR THE NORTH ATLANTIC: A NEAR RUN THING

Their war was primarily in the Atlantic, and for much of World War II, American attention was directed to Europe. The Allies had formally agreed on a "Europe First" strategy even before the war started at the March 19, 1941, Washington Conference, and reaffirmed it throughout the war. Until January 1943, the U.S. devoted 85 percent of its resources to the European theater and 15 percent to the Pacific. At the

Casablanca Conference the ratio was changed to 70 percent Europe and 30 percent Pacific.

The central naval battle in the European theater was the battle for control of the North Atlantic. It began for the U.S. Navy with the 1941 Washington Conference, where it was decided that the United States Navy would commence assisting the Royal Navy in Atlantic convoy escort immediately. "Roosevelt's Secret War" had begun.

The U.S. Navy suffered its first casualties in this secret war in October, when the destroyer *Kearny* was torpedoed south of Greenland with the loss of eleven sailors. The naval oiler *Salinas* was hit two weeks later, and the destroyer *Reuben James* was sunk soon after with the loss of 115 sailors. Something was already being done to make up for the loss. In September 1941, the first Liberty ship, *Patrick Henry*, was launched. By the beginning of 1943, the United States was turning out two Liberty ships a day, yet the German submarines were sinking them even faster. In one three-week period in March they sank eighty-five Allied ships. The battle to cut Europe off from the arsenal of democracy was being won by the German Navy.

A principal reason for the Royal Navy's inability to cope with the U-boats was the decision in 1918 to consolidate all aviation under the new Royal Air Force. After pioneering naval aviation and building the world's first aircraft carrier, the Royal Navy fell far behind Japan and the U.S. The British entered WW II with biplanes on their carrier decks and no effective anti-submarine aircraft.

The turning point came halfway through 1943, when the convoy system with full air cover all the way across the Atlantic was at last achieved. From that point onward, the ratio of shipping to submarine losses began to change steadily in favor of the Allies. The German Navy had almost won the battle for the North Atlantic (and with it likely the war itself), but failed because Hitler and the German General Staff refused to provide the Navy with naval aviation. The Germans fought the battle for the North Atlantic entirely without air cover. Once the Allies had it, Germany began to take horrendous losses in her U-boats, ultimately losing 821 submarines in the Atlantic and Caribbean, 47 percent to aircraft. Their submarine effort was also heav-

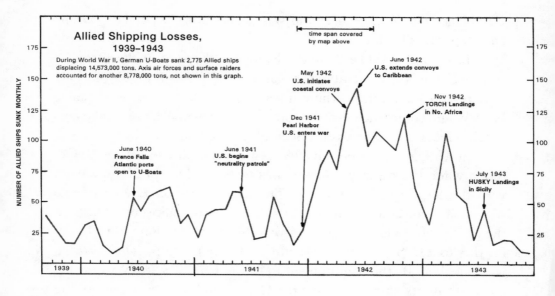

Allied Shipping Losses, 1939–1943

During World War II, German U-Boats sank 2,775 Allied ships displacing 14,573,000 tons. Axis air forces and surface raiders accounted for another 8,778,000 tons, not shown in this graph.

time span covered by map above

June 1942
U.S. extends convoys to Caribbean

May 1942
U.S. initiates coastal convoys

Nov 1942
TORCH Landings in No. Africa

Dec 1941
Pearl Harbor
U.S. enters war

June 1940
France Falls
Atlantic ports open to U-Boats

June 1941
U.S. begins "neutrality patrols"

July 1943
HUSKY Landings in Sicily

NUMBER OF ALLIED SHIPS SUNK MONTHLY

ily compromised by the Allied success in codebreaking—"Operation Enigma," it was called—because the German General Staff system of centralized control "required an astonishing number of radio transmissions."

LONG BEFORE THE BATTLE of the Atlantic was won, of course, was the stunning defeat at Pearl.

Pearl Harbor was the low point for America, but also the starting point. De Gaulle was quite right: once energetically mobilized, nothing could stop American industry. But what de Gaulle and others did not recognize was the ferocity and effectiveness with which Americans would wage this global war. The clock was ticking for Japan, and her top officers knew it. On the American side, the cadre of men who would deliver the war-winning blows was already in place.

ADMIRAL CHESTER W. NIMITZ: THE MAN FOR ALL SEASONS

Fleet Admiral Chester W. Nimitz holds an honored place on the Mt. Rushmore of America's World War II commanders. He had a hero's profile—he never took a bad picture—and his white-haired countenance radiated a calm authority. There is a photograph of him on October 5, 1945, riding through Washington in victory. Half a million citizens of all ages had been released from work for the day to cheer him. Nine ships in the Potomac, a thousand Navy aircraft overhead, and a grand parade of Navy units provided suitable backdrop. The focus of all this, Nimitz himself, having just finished an address before an adoring Congress, sits high on the back seat of an old touring car, as he receives the accolades of the crowd. The car itself, FDR's old favorite, the Lincoln twelve-cylinder "sunshine special," a mark of favor from the new president, Harry S Truman. Altogether, it was a very Roman scene.

Nimitz's story is an often-told American tale: a youth from Texas escapes small-town limits, rises through the Navy, and finds himself in the right place at the right time to run the greatest naval war ever known to mankind, which ends in total victory. A thankful nation rewards the modest hero with medals and honors. He returns to serve as chief of naval operations after the war, then a tour of somewhat less successful diplomatic service, a term as university president and a comfortable sunset. A whole class of American supercarriers, the Nimitz class, memorializes him.

Yet there is another side here, fairly full of nagging questions. When the war began, Nimitz was head of the Bureau of Navigation, then the personnel department of the Navy and usually the last stopping place for officers judged subpar before retirement. How did Nimitz rise from there to supreme command in the Pacific? He had none of the fighting qualities or martial skills of Ernest King above him or Spruance and Halsey below him. A similar question may be asked of the postwar Nimitz. In 1945–6, he advocated greater unification of the military, then opposed it. How did Nimitz manage to secure Truman's patronage even as he opposed the president's policy?

Nimitz was no simple old salt. He rose by dint of good contacts, the instincts of Macchiavelli and a fair amount of luck. Not lacking ambition, Nimitz could and did play political hardball. But this was not his normal way. He made himself very useful to those more powerful than he and never shrank from giving them the credit he might have deserved. Nimitz had principles and ideas to be sure, but these were conventional. What he really possessed was a personality gifted for dealing with the prima donnas and racehorses thrown up by war, a good grasp of administration and a solid, reliable character appealing to his masters. These were not necessarily war-winning characteristics, but they served Nimitz well.

Before 1939, he had had a distinguished but not outstanding career. In 1907, only an ensign, Nimitz commanded a destroyer, *Decatur,* during the sudden mobilization that preceded the cruise of the Great White Fleet. Among his duties, he had carried TR's secretary of war, William Howard Taft, on part of his goodwill tour in the Philippines. But on July 7, 1908, he carelessly ran the ship aground, normally a career-ending event; a court-martial and reprimand follow. Despite his desire to join the battleship admiralty, Nimitz was sent to the submarines. This turned out to be a stroke of luck, and he made a name in application of new diesel technology. Later, he helped to introduce the new tactic of circular formation derived from his studies of the World War I naval battle at Jutland. But, as Nimitz's son related, his gifts were in the "people" area, not ordnance or sea command.

At age 54, the appointment of Nimitz to the Bureau of Navigation, the Navy's quaint term for personnel administration, seemed a fitting post. Normally a dead end for an ambitious officer, this time fate was on Nimitz's side: finally in 1938, Congress appropriated $1 billion for a two-ocean fleet. Nimitz had to oversee a rapid expansion of personnel, especially reservists and a subtle—sometimes less than subtle—battle with the newer Bureau of Aeronautics. He did it without incident and also got on well with FDR, who took a personal interest in "his" Navy commanders. Nimitz must have fed Roosevelt's voracious appetite for good men, loyal men and their personalities, because in early 1941, FDR offered him a command second only to the CNO, then called commander in chief, U.S. fleet, or CINCUS.

Incredibly, faced with the choice of fleet command or a position near FDR's elbow, Nimitz chose to sit at his desk. He instead recommended for the job the much more sea-capable Rear Admiral Husband E. Kimmel, a close friend. Kimmel was jumped over thirty-one officers more senior. (Had the even younger Nimitz accepted, it would have been fifty!)

On February 1, 1941, Kimmel became not only CINCUS but also "CINCPAC," commander of the newly named Pacific Fleet. Ten months later, Nimitz's decision proved the right one. On Sunday, December 7, 1941, he and his wife were at home listening to a CBS broadcast of the New York Philharmonic when the news came of the Japanese attack. "I won't be back till God knows when," he told her. Eight days later, FDR appointed a Board of Inquiry into the Pearl Harbor disaster; removed Kimmel; separated CINCUS from CINCPAC; and appointed Admiral Ernest J. King as CINCUS, making the post supreme commander over all U.S. naval operations. He then selected Nimitz for CINCPAC. Roosevelt's message was simple: "Tell Nimitz to get the hell out to Pearl and stay there till the war is won." Nimitz, a good man for taking orders, complied. It does not detract from Nimitz's later reputation to say that he had a shrewd sense for politics and an even shrewder understanding of character. These talents enabled him to gain the maximum from the war-fighting egos of Halsey, Spruance, Mitscher and others. He was also able to manage an otherwise impossible sharing of authority with the largest ego of the war, Douglas MacArthur. All of these talents came together in the series of wise judgments and decisions during his first year that resulted in the successes of Midway and Coral Sea.

THE PACIFIC WAR BEGAN with a string of humiliations for the Allied navies. After the rapid fall of Wake Island, Singapore and the Philippines, the Royal Navy lost two prize ships. In February the combined force of U.S., British, Australian and Dutch ships was defeated by a Japanese strike force in the Battle of the Java Sea. In April the Pearl Harbor task force of five carriers under Admiral Nagumo attacked the

British Far Eastern Fleet in the Bay of Bengal, sinking a carrier, two cruisers and a number of destroyers.

Many Americans were understandably discouraged, but the new CINCUS was a fighter and insisted on going on the offensive immediately.

FLEET ADMIRAL ERNEST J. KING: MADE FOR WAR

Among the American high command of World War II, the name of Ernest J. King is least remembered today. Unlike Chester Nimitz, his subordinate, King was memorialized with only a small destroyer. His hometown, Loraine, Ohio, honors him with a plaque. Yet King was arguably the most powerful naval figure in U.S. history, and he commanded the greatest Navy the world has ever seen: 87,000 vessels, 24,000 aircraft, and 3 million officers and sailors, including half a million Marines.

King was not likeable. A tall, taciturn man, profane when he spoke, he was contemptuous of Congress, hated civilian control except for the commander in chief and relished the rod of discipline. Hard drinking and womanizing rounded him out. King was an officer of undoubtable skill, yet so fiercely was he disliked that his ambition to become CNO was laughed at as he neared retirement age.

Born in 1878 of a Scottish father and English mother who died young, King went to Annapolis, where he impressed his contemporaries with his egotism, arrogance, violent temper and intellect (fourth in the Class of 1901). Later he was to say, "I can forgive anything except for three things I will not tolerate—stupidity, laziness and carelessness." He found all three in the peacetime Navy. As he rose up through the ranks, he made war on such habits a habit itself. In 1909 King condemned "the clinging to things that are old because they are old." This was a man headed for a career of collisions.

At age 54, after a career of modest success, Rear Admiral King had a decade to reach CNO before compulsory retirement. He struck out for an untried post—the new Bureau of Aeronautics, widely shunned by battleship-heavy naval traditionalists. There he made enemies by proposing that the swift carriers (30 knots plus) be detached from the slower battleships and cruisers (21 knots). King reviled both his fellow officers and his civilian masters for underfunding the Navy and refusing to change tactics.

Not surprisingly, in 1939 Franklin Roosevelt picked the smooth and politic Harold "Betty" Stark over King as CNO. King thought he was finished. But as it turned out, Stark's promotion was the luckiest stroke of King's career.

With Pearl Harbor still years away, the Navy's first job in the Atlantic, as Roosevelt saw it, was to prevent German U-boats from starving the British as they prepared against an invasion following the fall of France. FDR did not know King well, but he knew of him from Stark, who greatly admired his professional abilities. Nearing retirement and without many friends, King was ideal for Roosevelt's secret war in the Atlantic, one that he admitted might get him impeached. He needed a man easily expendable yet daring enough to do the job.

King was appointed head of the Atlantic squadron, renamed the Patrol Force, in November 1940. What he found was an ill-prepared, underequipped flotilla, many of its best units already transferred to the Pacific to deter Japan. His command ship, the pre-1914 battleship *Texas*, contained a single plan in its top-secret safe: for war with Mexico.

FDR gave King four stars, transferred ships to him from the Pacific Fleet, and gave the "Patrol Force" a grander title, the "Atlantic Fleet," early in 1941. After a brutal review, King made clear to his command that he would not accept lack of equipment as an excuse. He was blunt: "We were really in the war in the Atlantic."

On November 23, 1941, King celebrated his 63rd birthday. Retirement was only a year away and the top job still looked distant. A fortnight later, the Japanese solved the problem for him at Pearl Harbor. Roosevelt knew of only one man ruthless enough to meet the emergency and revived the title of commander in chief, U.S. naval forces, for King. When asked by a reporter why he was picked, King replied with words that could serve well as his epitaph: "When the shooting starts, they call for the sons-of-bitches."

King took full command. His abbreviated title, CINCUS, he thought was demoralizing, so he changed it to COMINCH, for commander in chief. He demanded of Roosevelt that he not have to appear regularly before Congress, that he be given direct command of the independent naval bureaus, that he report directly to the President. He got what he demanded.

King and George Marshall, joined by General H. H. "Hap" Arnold of the Air Corps, were now the Joint Chiefs, while Admiral Leahy served as a kind of chairman. (Among his duties was to make sure the right papers actually got to FDR through the White House's notorious disorganization.) Roosevelt exercised his usual charm over King, winking at him during meetings for approval or disapproval. Harry Hopkins, who knew FDR's real views, waved away complaints about Roosevelt's new system with the observation that "he has got in King, Marshall and Arnold three people who really like to fight."

To get King's full measure, we need to see him in three contexts. The first was in his overall strategic stance. His strategic concept, initially set forth with brilliant clarity in a one-page memo (he would not accept anything longer himself) on March 5, 1942, proposed to hold Hawaii, support Australasia and drive northwestward from the New Hebrides. Echoing Nelson, King made clear what he expected in his command. "The best method," he wrote, "is to fight him [the Japanese] where he is to be found, seek him out rather than to . . . await his coming." There would be no rewards for caution and no medals for commanders who lost ships.

The Pacific theater of war was always foremost in King's mind. After a struggle over whether the Pacific would be supplied only after Europe—the official Europe-first strategy—King got modified language that would allow the Combined Chiefs of Staff to "consider" Pacific operations; it meant for King that he would take the offensive in the Pacific unless the other chiefs actively blocked him. The British felt, with some justification, that King neglected the Atlantic; King was indeed prepared to be more than rough with them. Old sea dogs like Sir Dudley Pound and, after 1943, Admiral of the Fleet Andrew B. Cunningham, often locked horns with King. Cunningham described him as "a man of immense capacity and ability, quite ruthless in his methods." Another officer, George Russell, described one encounter: "Cunningham got insistent and started pounding on the table. King stood up and said, 'Britannia may have ruled the waves for three hundred years, but she doesn't anymore. There's the door.'"

The second context in which King should be seen was with subordinates. Early on, King learned to adjust his imperious nature to sobering realities. When, for example, an exasperated Nimitz simply issued the command for his carriers to attack towards Midway over King's orders, King did not resist it. Although King regarded Nimitz as a bureaucrat, a "trimmer" who refused to roll heads, the COMINCH cooperated with him, aware that war could not be micro-managed from Washington.

Third, last, and most important, we must see King as a fiercely independent Navy man, willing to go to war against anyone who might direct the Navy—including the British and the Europe-first strategy, George Marshall and Douglas MacArthur, Secretary of the Navy Frank Knox and his ambitious deputy (later secretary) James Forrestal and the press. He would conceal naval losses from planners lest the information leak to the "enemy"—and he didn't mean the Japanese or the Germans. Regarding press policy, he once said, "Tell them nothing. When it's over, tell them who won."

He resisted any sort of joint operations, insisting that the Navy alone could manage amphibious operations. He ignored or overrode civilian authority and clashed repeatedly with Knox and Forrestal over war production, though he knew nothing whatsoever about it. He opposed adoption of the invaluable "Higgins Boat" because it didn't come from the Navy. (When the Navy finally got Higgins's excellent boat, King never forgave either Higgins or Senator Harry Truman, whose investigation into the Bureau of Ships had made it happen.) A traditionalist in naval construction, King's idea of a budget was to decide the numbers and kinds of ships then expect his civilian "masters"—the SECNAV or FDR—to provide it. And this admiral who so hated the Navy's resistance to change evoked from FDR the classic lament: "To change anything in the na-a-vy is like punching a featherbed!"

One area where King notoriously insisted upon change—and got it—was the color and style of the naval uniform. In 1943, he settled on what was called "King Gray." It was ugly, the Navy hated it and, outside of Washington, no one wore it, preferring khakis and the traditional dress blues or whites. But King just didn't like anything that resembled the Army (khakis) or the British (dress uniforms).

A fighter and a fighter only, when the war eventually wound down, King floundered, clashing with new Navy Secretary James Vincent Forrestal. As June 1944 approached, King was also beset by family problems. He had an ailing, estranged wife, an alcoholic daughter, a rift with another daughter, and a third felled by appendicitis. Yet June was King's professional triumph. The Allies launched two huge amphibious invasions—the Marianas and Normandy—simultaneously. After Normandy there was an emotional tour of the beachhead and a well-lubricated party hosted by Churchill afterward. For the first and only time during the war, King got drunk.

June 1944 was his personal high point. In the waning days of war King had more blowups: with FDR, the British and MacArthur (on whether the Philippines or Formosa should be the route of advance; MacArthur won). There was one more controversy in the Pacific. King's favorite commander, "Bull" Halsey, ignored his meteorologists and drove his fleet twice into killer typhoons that wrecked numerous ships and cost hundreds of lives. (My father, commanding a small ship in Halsey's fleet, later recalled that the wind reached 138 knots. "Although the Bureau of Ships says the maximum safe roll for this ship is about 37 degrees," he said, "we rolled 45 degrees, and pitched so much that we couldn't stay in our bunks. . . . The list was 70 degrees, so bad that the lubricating oil pumps in the engines wouldn't pick up the oil, and they couldn't use the engines.") The ensuing investigation, coming soon after Halsey's famous blunder in the Philippine Sea (recounted below), should have ended his career. But King always had a soft spot—and a hard defense—for real fighters. He blocked any reprimand. In the hour of the Navy's great triumph over Japan there would be no sensational dismissals.

Though King had not had much to do with Roosevelt in the last year of the war, FDR's death removed one of his few supporters, and certainly his most important one. The COMINCH was aware of his steady loss of influence as Truman found his way as president. King had little to say about the decision to use the A-bomb. "Well, it's all over," King said at last. "I wonder what I'm going to do tomorrow . . . they won't need me."

He was right. The war over, James Forrestal repudiated King's flag selection board recommendations. On November 12, 1945, three months after the war's end, King took a last shot, forcing Forrestal to forward to Truman a resignation letter that recommended Nimitz as his successor over Forrestal's opposition. King later liked to suggest his letter had made the difference in Nimitz's nomination as CNO, but it did not and must have struck Forrestal as a crude attempt to take credit for a done deal. Forrestal rejected King's desired retirement date and kicked him out a month early, in December 1945. He suffered a severe stroke two years later, recovered, then declined until his death in 1956.

It does not matter that Ernest J. King cannot be called a "nice" man; he was the right man for the job. His life stands as a monument to the Navy's continuing ability to find special men for the ultimate emergency. His strategic and engineering gifts were at the service of a personality insufferable in peacetime. If not for war, he would have retired a man unfulfilled, his own worst enemy. But the war did come and King's bad temper was harnessed to the supreme task. He lashed friend and foe alike without mercy, and he measured both himself and his subordinates on an inhuman standard of discipline. Free of foresight and hindsight when it came to the Navy, he directed every formidable resource—not least Ernest King—to the winning of the war. And he did it. Once done, he had no other purpose. He could himself conceive of no greater praise.

IN THE EARLY PORTION of the war, with America still underpowered at sea thanks in part to the Pearl Harbor raid, King's fighting spirit was especially valuable. Placed in a position where some commanders would have simply reacted to events and tried to shore up strength, King instead pushed forward with his one diminished weapon. The U.S. Navy

(along with Japan) led the world in developing sea-based aviation between the wars. With the regular Navy dominated by the battleship
culture, the aviation revolution came through the Naval Reserve. The
backbone of naval aviation in World War I was an organization of
wealthy Ivy-Leaguers called The First Yale Unit. It was incorporated
into the Navy in 1916. Its alumni—Truby Davison, Robert Lovett and
James Forrestal—were instrumental as civilians in pushing the development of carriers and naval aircraft during the 1930s. After Pearl Harbor it was to this same eastern establishment that the Navy turned.
Ronald Spector points out that among aviators on active duty in the
first year of the Pacific war there were almost no named of hispanic,
slavic, Polish, Jewish, Italian or Asian descent. "They were almost exclusively white males of northern European descent," wrote Spector.

Yet these elitists made a difference that was felt early in the war effort. In early 1942, what remained of the Pacific Fleet launched a string
of carrier raids against Japanese facilities in the Gilberts, in the Marshalls, on Wake Island and in New Guinea. Militarily this put the
Japanese under some pressure, but more importantly gave Roosevelt
the morale-boosting image of fighting back.

The first real American success in naval battle against the Japanese
came from the successful code-breaking effort that would prove so
valuable throughout the war. When Nimitz learned that the Japanese
were planning an attack on Port Moresby, New Guinea, he dispatched
Lexington and *Yorktown* under the command of Rear Admiral Frank
Fletcher to intercept them as they entered the Coral Sea.

The result was the first carrier air battle in history. American aircraft
sank the carrier *Shoho* and severely damaged *Shokaku* while the Japanese destroyed *Lexington*. The Japanese were forced to withdraw and
cancel the Port Moresby invasion. It gave the United States its first Pacific victory and the undying gratitude of all Australians.

The next major victory would be of even greater magnitude, and
historians today almost uniformly speak of it as the great turning point
in the war.

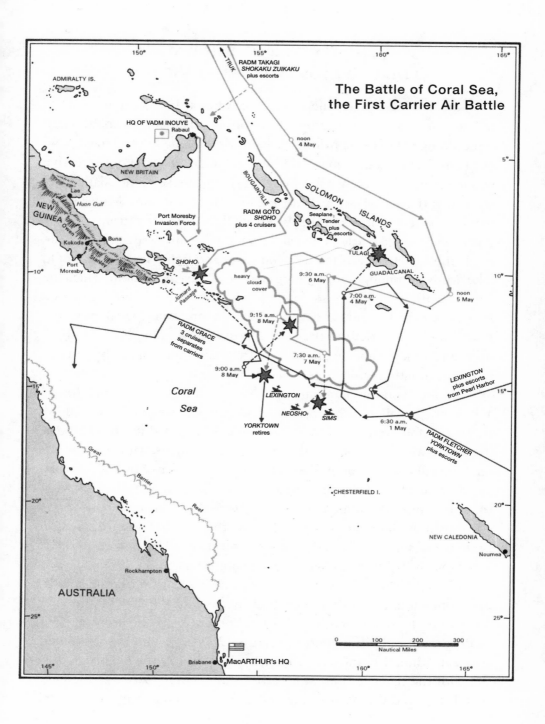

The Battle of Coral Sea,
the First Carrier Air Battle

ADMIRALTY IS.

RADM TAKAGI
SHOKAKU ZIUKAKU
plus escorts

TRUK

noon
4 May

HQ OF VADM INOUYE
Rabaul

NEW BRITAIN

BOUGAINVILLE

SOLOMON
ISLANDS

NEW
GUINEA

Lae
Huon Gulf

RADM GOTO
SHOHO
plus 4 cruisers

Seaplane
Tender
plus
escorts

Owen

Kokoda
Buna

Port Moresby
Invasion Force

TULAGI

GUADALCANAL

Stanley
Mtns.

Port
Moresby

SHOHO

heavy
cloud
cover

9:30 a.m.
6 May

noon
5 May

7:00 a.m.
4 May

Jomard
Passage

9:15 a.m.
8 May

RADM CRACE
3 cruisers
separates
from carriers

7:30 a.m.
7 May

LEXINGTON
plus escorts
from Pearl Harbor

Coral

Sea

9:00 a.m.
8 May

LEXINGTON

YORKTOWN
retires

NEOSHO

SIMS

6:30 a.m.
1 May

RADM FLETCHER
YORKTOWN
plus escorts

Great

Barrier

CHESTERFIELD I.

Reef

NEW CALEDONIA

Noumea

Rockhampton

AUSTRALIA

0   100   200   300
Nautical Miles

Brisbane

MacARTHUR's HQ

THE BATTLE OF MIDWAY:
THE CRYPTOS' SMASHING VICTORY

On June 4, 1942, the Japanese warlord, Admiral Isoroku Yamamoto (a fellow alumnus of Caius College-Cambridge), launched a coordinated three-pronged attack on Midway Island with the largest and most powerful naval armada ever marshaled in the Pacific Ocean. One objective was to extend the defense perimeter of the Japanese home islands; another was the U.S. fleet in Pearl Harbor. By threatening Midway, Yamamoto hoped to draw out the American fleet from Hawaii and destroy it in a decisive sea battle in which he could bring his battleships to bear.

If the U.S. fleet was loath to come out and fight, Yamamoto would take Midway unopposed, gaining a forward sea base from which he could reinforce a Japanese foothold in the Aleutians and threaten Alaska and the Hawaiian Islands. Sooner or later, the U.S. fleet would have come out to defend these U.S. possessions. Then he would fall upon and sink it, capture Hawaii and force their big but flabby country to the negotiating table.

Despite opposition from the Naval General Staff in Tokyo, Yamamoto prevailed with his bold plan to start with air attacks on Midway on June 4, followed by its seizure on June 6. Included in his scheme of maneuver was a diversionary thrust into the Aleutians, with an air attack on the small U.S. outpost at Dutch Harbor and seizure of two of the westernmost islands in the chain, Kiska and Attu. To do it all he had a fleet of some 160 ships, including four carriers, *Soryu*, *Hiryu*, *Akagi* and *Kaga*.

Yamamoto failed for a simple reason: the U.S. had intercepted and broken his supposedly secure communications. His order of battle, timetable and objectives had all been compromised.

Admiral Nimitz reinforced Midway's defenses with Marine antiaircraft artillery and land-based air, and sent two task forces to intercept Yamamoto. Rear Admiral Raymond A. Spruance led one task force out of Pearl Harbor built around the carriers *Enterprise* and *Hornet*, joined by Rear Admiral Frank Jack Fletcher, the victor of the Coral Sea battle, with the damaged but still battle-ready carrier *Yorktown*. Fletcher was designated the officer in overall tactical command of the 76 total ships and 233 aircraft of the two task forces, and the stage was set for one of the most decisive battles in naval history.

Before the battle started, both sides sent out search planes, but with different intentions. The Japanese commanders sent their planes out per established routine, not expecting them to report much. The American commanders knew the Japanese fleet was out there, and just wanted to know exactly where.

As scheduled, the Japanese carrier air strikes on Midway started well before dawn on the morning of June 4 with the launch of 108 airplanes off all four flattops, in three waves of 36 each. A Midway-based seaplane spotted and reported a Japanese carrier's location at about 5:30 and the incoming Japanese planes were confirmed by radar.

The naval commandant of Midway, Commander Cyril T. Simard, an experienced naval aviator, had been handpicked to command the remote island, 1,135 miles northwest of Hawaii. He knew the Japanese were coming because Admiral Nimitz had told him so during a recent visit to the six-mile-diameter outpost. Nimitz had asked Simard for a list of what more they needed to stop a Japanese assault. When he got it, he then asked if he sent them everything on their list, were they certain they could stop the Japanese? Their reply was a confident "yes, sir."

Nimitz was good to his word. Simard's fledgling Air Force soon grew to include 6 Navy Avenger torpedo-bombers and 32 Catalina seaplanes; 7 Marine Wildcat and 20 Brewster Buffalo fighters, 11 Vindicator and 16 Dauntless dive-bombers; and 4 Army B-26 Marauder and 19 B-17 Flying Fortress bombers, refitted to carry torpedoes. Midway's airfield ran out of ramp space.

The troops on Midway thought they were going to take on the Japanese alone, a Wake Island scenario. Only Simard and his immediate subordinates knew that Fletcher's carriers were in the area. As far as the young pilots, grunts and sailors knew, it was going to be an us-*versus*-them fight to the finish.

When the air-raid sirens wailed that morning, Simard launched his Air Force. All available planes were airborne by 6:15, leaving Midway to fend for itself.

Led by the Marine fighter squadron in their Buffaloes and Wildcats, the American planes spotted and dove into a formation of "Vals," Aichi dive-bombers, and "Kates," Nakajima torpedo-bombers. Protected by Zeroes, the Japanese bombers survived and pressed onward, making bombing and strafing runs on Midway, where they met with the thick clouds of vicious and accurate antiaircraft fire that indicated unexpectedly formidable defenses.

Meanwhile, at 9:00 a.m. Torpedo Squadron Eight launched off *Hornet* in fifteen sluggardly and ill-handling Devastators. They were old and obsolete. In order to drop their antique MK-13 torpedoes, the pilots had to fly low and slow on a straight heading toward the enemy ships. Their fighter cover had not arrived on time; nevertheless, led by their skipper, they attacked in a tight but vulnerable tactical formation skimming the waves. Every Devastator in the squadron was picked off one-by-one before reaching an enemy ship. Only one pilot survived, Ensign George Gay, who, after being wounded and shot down, found himself miraculously alone and alive in the water, where he clung to his rubber seat cushion and observed the rest of the day's battle.

Yorktown and *Enterprise* also launched their doomed Devastators, again with no fighter protection. Torpedo Squadron Three off *Yorktown* lost all thirteen planes, and Torpedo Six off *Enterprise* lost ten of fourteen. The Devastators scored no hits on the enemy ships, but they had drawn the Japanese air cover down to sea level and opened the skies for the Dauntless dive-bombers to accomplish their mission.

The dive-bombers made the Devastators' sacrifice worthwhile. By virtue of an earlier order from Admiral Spruance, *Enterprise* had launched a strike force under Commander Clarence W. McClusky consisting of 10 Wildcats, 14 Devastators and 33 Dauntlesses. Simultaneously, *Hornet* had launched an almost identical force of 10 Wildcats, 15 Devastators and 35 Dauntlesses, the latter models all carrying 1,000-pound bombs. *Hornet*'s force was led by Commander Stanhope Ring, flying a Devastator. With 117 fresh planes in the air and the Japanese planes out of fuel and ammo, anything could happen. It did.

At one point, in the confusion of battle, a Japanese reconnaissance plane spotted and reported the presence of an American carrier. When a stunned Admiral Yamamoto learned of this, he issued a fateful order.

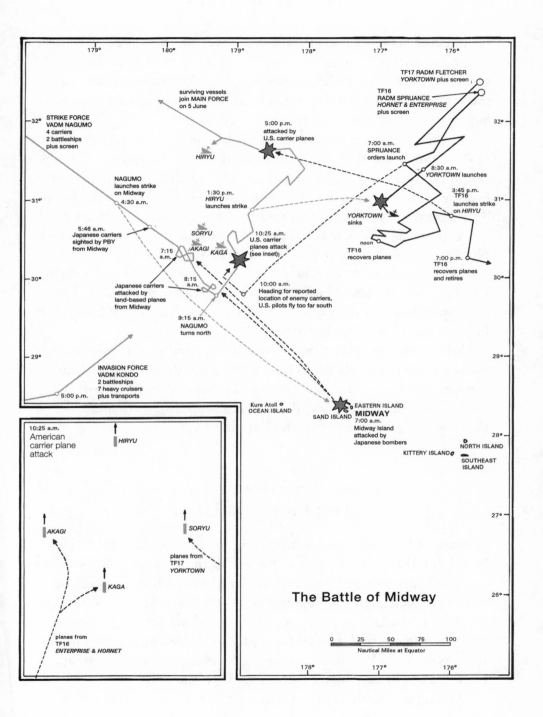

The Battle of Midway

179° 180° 179° 178° 177° 176°

32°

TF17 RADM FLETCHER
YORKTOWN plus screen

TF16
RADM SPRUANCE
HORNET & ENTERPRISE
plus screen

STRIKE FORCE
VADM NAGUMO
4 carriers
2 battleships
plus screen

surviving vessels
join MAIN FORCE
on 5 June

5:00 p.m.
attacked by
U.S. carrier planes

7:00 a.m.
SPRUANCE
orders launch

8:30 a.m.
YORKTOWN launches

HIRYU

NAGUMO
launches strike
on Midway
4:30 a.m.

1:30 p.m.
HIRYU
launches strike

3:45 p.m.
TF16
launches strike
on *HIRYU*

5:46 a.m.
Japanese carriers
sighted by PBY
from Midway

SORYU

AKAGI *KAGA*

10:25 a.m.
U.S. carrier
planes attack
(see inset)

YORKTOWN
sinks

7:15
a.m.

noon

TF16
recovers planes

7:00 a.m.
TF16
recovers planes
and retires

Japanese carriers
attacked by
land-based planes
from Midway

8:15
a.m.

10:00 a.m.
Heading for reported
location of enemy carriers,
U.S. pilots fly too far south

9:15 a.m.
NAGUMO
turns north

INVASION FORCE
VADM KONDO
2 battleships
7 heavy cruisers
plus transports

5:00 p.m.

Kure Atoll
OCEAN ISLAND

SAND ISLAND

EASTERN ISLAND
MIDWAY
7:00 a.m.
Midway Island
attacked by
Japanese bombers

NORTH ISLAND

KITTERY ISLAND

SOUTHEAST
ISLAND

32°

31°

31°

30°

30°

29°

29°

28°

27°

26°

10:25 a.m.
American
carrier plane
attack

HIRYU

AKAGI

SORYU

planes from
TF17
YORKTOWN

KAGA

planes from
TF16
ENTERPRISE & HORNET

The Battle of Midway

0   25   50   75   100
Nautical Miles at Equator

178°   177°   176°

He directed his recovered aircraft, which were in the process of refueling and rearming, to attack the enemy carrier instead of striking Midway once more. This meant harried aircrews had to respot the deck for the incoming planes to download hard bombs and upload torpedoes before they proceeded against the new target.

At this critical juncture, between 10:20 and 10:25, the two strike forces from *Enterprise* and *Hornet* rolled in on Yamamoto's carriers. Within minutes, *Kaga* and *Akagi* were floundering. Ensign Gay, still floating between them, saw both take repeated hits, the planes on their decks going up in flames, and the two flattops burning fiercely from stem to stern. (We know because the next day Gay was rescued, plucked out of the water by a Catalina crew.)

Yorktown launched an hour later and they came upon *Soryu* trying to launch her planes. Thirteen *Yorktown* bombers pounded her with five direct hits, causing her more damage than that inflicted upon the luckless *Kaga* and *Akagi* combined.

With three enemy carriers burning out of control by 11:00 a.m., Admiral Fletcher sent planes to look for the fourth, *Hiryu*, but without success. Around 1:30 p.m., *Hiryu* made her presence known when *Yorktown*'s radar picked up a flight of incoming enemy fighters. It was the beginning of the end for The Fighting Lady.

USS *Yorktown:*
The Fighting Lady

Named for the battle that decided the outcome of the Revolutionary War, USS *Yorktown* (CV-5) was known in the fleet as The Fighting Lady. Initially an East Coast ship, *Yorktown* was built at Newport News and christened there on September 30, 1937, by Eleanor Roosevelt. *Yorktown* embarked on her successful shakedown cruise in the Caribbean in 1938, sparred with German subs in the Atlantic in the opening months of World War II, then sailed to San Diego to become Rear Admiral Fletcher's flagship on December 30, 1941.

During the Battle of the Coral Sea on May 8, 1942, *Yorktown*, under the command of Captain Elliott Buckmaster, dodged eight torpedoes but took one bomb that penetrated below the flight deck, causing 66 casualties. Nevertheless, she continued to make steam, and launch and recover her planes. After the battle, she headed for Pearl Harbor for repairs that experts said would take three months in the yard to mend. In what is one of many great stories of American technical ingenuity, Buckmaster and his crew, laboring side by side with dry-dock workers around the clock, instead got her back into fighting shape within days.

The hard work of the repair crews was critical, because *Yorktown* would be needed in the upcoming Battle of Midway. With Jack Fletcher and his staff still aboard, *Yorktown* departed Pearl on May 30 to rendezvous with Spruance near Midway. Yamamoto's fleet was due to arrive within hours.

Hiryu, under the command of the strong-minded Admiral Yamaguchi, was separated from her trio of doomed sister ships when the Americans attacked. Yamaguchi was still determined to fight on, regardless of changed odds or the tragic turn of events. After successfully refueling and rearming his airplanes, he ordered them launched to seek out an American aircraft carrier and destroy it.

Around 1:30 p.m., *Yorktown*'s radar detected the attackers. Refueling operations for the fighters were halted before their tanks were topped off, and they were launched to intercept the flight. The crew furiously prepared to receive the attack by securing spaces, draining gas lines, pushing a large 8,000-gallon auxiliary fuel tank overboard and breaking out their firefighting equipment, as they had often done in training.

Outnumbered Wildcats flew into the teeth of the oncoming formation of nearly forty Japanese fighters and bombers. A whirling dogfight ensued, but some Japanese bombers leaked through and continued onward toward *Yorktown*. By then, she was at flank speed, her escorts making full steam to stay in formation and protect her. When seven Japanese planes appeared, they were greeted with clouds of flak and streams of tracers, but onward they pressed, scoring three direct hits. Two of those enemy planes were splashed, and the third was hit, crashing out of control into *Yorktown*'s starboard side.

But the damage had been done. Bomb shards sieved compartments, causing terrible casualties and starting fires on the hangar deck, where stored aircraft went up in flames. The crew fought valiantly against the fires, but could not put them all out. Blasts and concussions had blown out boiler fires, and the *Yorktown* lost power, slowed and finally went dead in the water. Admiral Fletcher was forced to shift his flag to the heavy cruiser *Astoria* (CA-34).

Meanwhile *Yorktown's* resourceful 'black gang' was able to relight the boilers, make steam and get underway again. With her fires almost under control, Captain Buckmaster ordered flight operations to resume. Incredibly, *Yorktown* was able to launch a modest flight of a dozen or so fighters, all low on gas, but ready to fight yet another enemy flight that had launched from *Hiryu*.

With *Yorktown* underway at an astonishing twenty knots, her fighters engaged the attackers in a smaller replay of the first attack; this time it was Japanese torpedo planes armed with anti-ship torpedoes that got through.

When two torpedoes penetrated her port side midships, *Yorktown* began to list in that direction. Her rudder hopelessly jammed, she started to run in a circle until she went dead in the water for good. With no power to pump water, and her list increasing with each passing minute, Captain Buckmaster ordered all hands to lay up to the flight deck and don life vests. When the list exceeded 25 degrees, The Fighting Lady seemed ready to roll over, and Buckmaster gave the order that all captains pray they will never have to give: "Abandon ship!"

The men carefully lowered their wounded over the side into life rafts, and struck out for their escort ships waiting nearby with rescue boats already in the water. Captain Buckmaster made a final solo inspection tour of his ship and then lowered himself over the stern.

The exhausted skipper was picked up by the ill-fated destroyer *Hammann* (DD-412) and ferried to *Astoria* to report to Admiral Fletcher, who by this time had seen to it that the diehard *Hiryu* would sink before sunset. Planes from *Yorktown* that had been recovered aboard *Enterprise* helped in this, avenging their Fighting Lady's fate.

Once aboard *Astoria*, Buckmaster viewed his stricken ship through binoculars—she was still afloat! It was decided to attempt to salvage

Yorktown if she made it through the night. During the night, a lone machine gun rattled off a string of tracers from the abandoned *Yorktown*. Someone was still alive aboard The Fighting Lady. Her lone attendant, the destroyer *Hughes*, found two survivors, one of whom passed away a short time later.

The next morning Fletcher ordered five destroyers to form a protective anti-submarine screen around *Yorktown*, and the salvage party, led by Buckmaster himself, went aboard. The fleet tug *Viero* took her under tow against the tide to keep her from rolling. *Hammann*, the sixth destroyer, came alongside, secured to *Yorktown* with lines and put over water hoses to fight fires and electric cables to provide power to the salvage pumps.

Degree by degree, *Yorktown*'s list began to lessen. By that afternoon, she looked like she might survive.

Then tragedy struck. One of Yamamoto's tardy submarines, *I-168*, had finally caught up with his stricken fleet. It penetrated the destroyers' screen under the debris-ladened water and, at about 3:30 P.M., while the salvage operation was still in full swing, lookouts sighted a deadly salvo of four torpedoes knifing through the water, headed for *Hammann* and *Yorktown*. *Hammann* went to general quarters. Still secured to *Yorktown*, she was unable to maneuver. One torpedo missed, passing astern of *Yorktown*, but two found home in her helpless hull. *Hammann* took the fourth and it broke her back. She jackknifed and sank within minutes, only to have all her depth charges explode on her way to the bottom, killing the survivors in the water.

The arduous salvage work had come to naught. Alone and without power, The Fighting Lady's fate was sealed. A brokenhearted Captain Buckmaster called off the operation. Yet *Yorktown* refused to sink beneath the waves. She stayed afloat through yet another night and into the dawn of the next morning. At 5:30 she finally started to go down. Then, as though to seek respite, she rolled and revealed her starboard side as if turning over to go into a well-deserved sleep. The watching bluejackets, many with tear-streaked faces, heard her issue a loud gush of air—to many it sounded like a tired sigh—followed by a soul-wrenching groan. Her tribulations over at last, *Yorktown* sank with her battle flags flying at 7:01 a.m. in the Pacific morning light of June 7, 1942.

The great ship lay quietly resting in her watery grave for over half a century. Then on May 19, 1998, a National Geographic Society deep-dive team led by the famous explorer Dr. Robert Ballard, Cdr. USNR, paid her a visit. They found her nestled within a mountain range in inky blackness at a depth of 16,650 feet, sitting proudly upright in remarkably good shape.

FOR THE AMERICANS, it was the end of a great ship, for the Japanese the end of any hope for victory in the war. The Battle of Midway was unique, a naval first that signaled a change in doctrine that was total, complete and, until the rise of nuclear submarines, unchallengeable. John Paul Jones's day was over at last. Battleships, whether powered by wind, steam or oil-fueled turbines, were no longer the most fearsome ships afloat. The carriers were the proud couriers of a message that transformed naval warfare: ships cannot survive on the surface of the sea without air superiority, and fleets built around air power can command any sea and from it project power into any land mass.

To Yamamoto, engulfed in the fog of war, the message was less clear. He knew he had lost the battle, but believed that he had sunk three American carriers and a destroyer. In fact he had sunk just *Yorktown* and the destroyer *Hammann*. He claimed his fleet had splashed 179 American airplanes, but it was 147.

Yamamoto's own losses were certain. He had lost all four of his aircraft carriers and a heavy cruiser; two destroyers were significantly damaged and an oiler, destroyer and battleship lightly damaged, all by bombs and aerial torpedoes. Moreover, he had lost more than twice as many aircraft as the Americans: 332, with 280 of those going down aboard his four carriers. With them went the cream of Japan's naval aviators, an unreplaceable asset.

The dean of American naval historians, Admiral Samuel Eliot Morison, always said that Midway was a "victory of intelligence." Indeed, all the heroics had been made possible because Admiral Nimitz was reading Admiral Yamamoto's mail before the battle, courtesy of brilliant intelligence work. Commander Joseph J. Rochefort, a cryptologist, and Lieutenant Commander Edwin T. Layton, Nimitz's fleet intelligence officer, had deciphered the Japanese secret code known as "Hypo," and their dogged efforts had given Nimitz an incalculable advantage.

When Yamamoto finally understood the extent of the disaster that had befallen him and his fleet, he withdrew. Much like Lee after Gettysburg, he continued to fight but never again went on the offensive.

The U.S. Navy now took up the offensive in earnest, in accordance with War Plan Orange. The stalwart Midway garrison was reinforced with a sizeable new and unsullied Marine detachment from the United States. Thus bolstered, Midway remained a sentinel that guarded the northern approaches to Hawaii for the remainder of the war.

THE BATTLE FOR GUADALCANAL: FILLING IRONBOTTOM SOUND

Midway was a tremendous victory for America. But while the outcome of the war may have become clearer thanks to excellent intelligence and decisive action, the work that remained to be done was no less difficult.

Within the South Pacific's Solomon Islands chain is Guadalcanal. Off this remote, now legendary, island, is a well-named sea-lane called Ironbottom Sound. It is the watery graveyard for over a hundred Japanese and Allied battleships, cruisers, destroyers, smaller combatants and transports that went to rest there during the Guadalcanal campaign. Both navies had the same missions, to land reinforcements and supplies to its forces ashore locked in brutal combat, and to prevent the enemy from doing the same. The result was six months of continuous close naval combat, engaging every type of surface ship, submarine, carriers and land-based aircraft. By day American air superiority ruled but by night the Japanese Navy came down "the slot" with regularity, landed reinforcements and bombarded the Marines ashore.

In the wake of the Midway victory, Admiral King wanted to capitalize upon the Navy's success by taking the fight to the enemy. In knowledge that the Japanese wanted to expand further south under

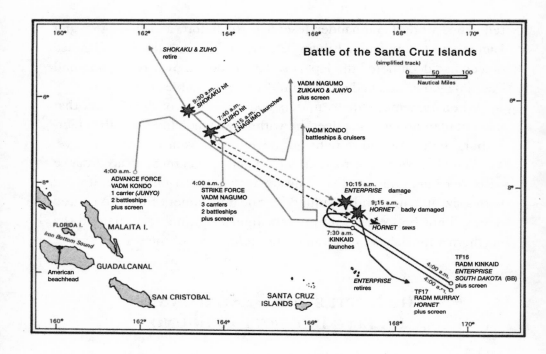

Battle of the Santa Cruz Islands
(simplified track)

0 50 100
Nautical Miles

SHOKAKU & ZUHO retire

9:30 a.m. *SHOKAKU* hit

7:40 a.m. *ZUIHO* hit

7:15 a.m. I,NAGUMO launches

VADM NAGUMO *ZUIKAKO & JUNYO* plus screen

VADM KONDO battleships & cruisers

4:00 a.m. ADVANCE FORCE VADM KONDO 1 carrier (*JUNYO*) 2 battleships plus screen

4:00 a.m. STRIKE FORCE VADM NAGUMO 3 carriers 2 battleships plus screen

10:15 a.m. *ENTERPRISE* damage

9:15 a.m. *HORNET* badly damaged

HORNET SINKS

7:30 a.m. KINKAID launches

FLORIDA I.

Iron Bottom Sound

MALAITA I.

American beachhead

GUADALCANAL

SAN CRISTOBAL

SANTA CRUZ ISLANDS

ENTERPRISE retires

4:00 a.m.

4:00 a.m.

TF16 RADM KINKAID *ENTERPRISE* *SOUTH DAKOTA* (BB) plus screen

TF17 RADM MURRAY *HORNET* plus screen

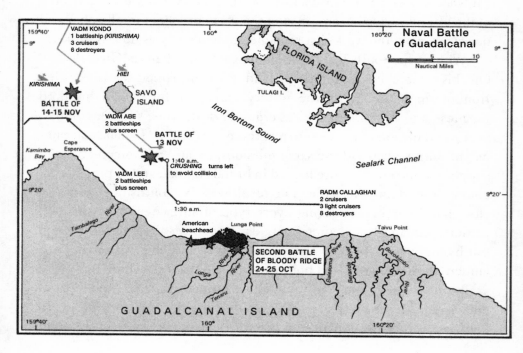

Naval Battle of Guadalcanal

0 5 10
Nautical Miles

VADM KONDO 1 battleship (*KIRISHIMA*) 3 cruisers 6 destroyers

HIEI

KIRISHIMA

SAVO ISLAND

FLORIDA ISLAND

TULAGI I.

Iron Bottom Sound

BATTLE OF 14-15 NOV

VADM ABE 2 battleships plus screen

BATTLE OF 13 NOV

1:40 a.m. *CRUSHING* turns left to avoid collision

Sealark Channel

Kamimbo Bay

Cape Esperance

VADM LEE 2 battleships plus screen

1:30 a.m.

RADM CALLAGHAN 2 cruisers 3 light cruisers 8 destroyers

Tambalego River

American beachhead

Lunga Point

Taivu Point

Tenaru

Lunga River

SECOND BATTLE OF BLOODY RIDGE 24-25 OCT

Balesuma River

Beranda river

Bokokimbo River

GUADALCANAL ISLAND

the cover of land-based air and because the Japanese were building an airfield on Guadalcanal, it was selected as the anvil upon which to test the Imperial Navy's mettle.

The campaign lasted from August 7, 1942, when the First Marine Division under Major General Alexander Vandegrift began landing on the island, until February 7, 1943, when the Imperial Navy withdrew what was left of the Japanese Imperial Army. In the first defeat of the Japanese Army in the war, three out of every four of their soldiers who landed on Guadalcanal perished from combat, disease or malnutrition. Thousands of others drowned aboard sunk transports. Even today in Japan, Japanese veterans remember those terrible casualty figures. They call Guadalcanal "The Island of Death," and view its fall as the beginning of the end of their empire.

Out of these furious, chaotic engagements bitter lessons were learned. First was that the Navy needed more aggressive risk-taking admirals like Halsey who could and would fight. Second, admirals had to learn how to support a land campaign; they could no longer just leave logistics up to their supply corps officers. Third, the fleet had to learn how to fight at night. Fourth, there were glaring failures of some American weapons, particularly the nearly useless Navy-manufactured torpedoes.

The naval combat began with the battle of Savo Island when the Japanese tried to interdict the Marine landing on Guadalcanal during the night of August 8–9. Slipping by the busy invasion force's lax sea pickets, a Japanese naval striking force under Vice Admiral Gunichi Mikawa capitalized on the elements of speed, surprise and the concentration of combat power. Mikawa inflicted the most crushing defeat on the U.S. Navy since Pearl Harbor. Four allied cruisers were lost in less than thirty minutes with 1,024 dead and 709 wounded: Australia's *Canberra*, and America's *Astoria*, *Quincy* and *Vincennes*. The Japanese gunfire was far more accurate and their torpedoes far superior to the Americans'. Nevertheless, Mikawa did not want to press his luck, and promptly withdrew his two light and five heavy cruisers virtually unscathed, still under the cover of darkness. As a result, the Marine landing continued to a successful conclusion with the seizure of the yet uncompleted airfield.

Gunichi Mikawa's incomplete success was still a total disaster for the U.S. Navy. It had been made possible in part by technological factors. The Americans were overconfident about their technological edge in "TBS"—Talk-Between-Ships—radio. The Japanese, on the other hand, relied on intensive night training, rapid line-of-sight communication blinker lights, and vigilant, eagle-eyed lookouts equipped with Zeiss binoculars. Moreover, American ships were filled with combustible materials, be it the captain's gig, the wardroom piano or the wood-and-fabric float plane with topped-off fuel tank inside a canvas hanger on the fantail—they all made fine kindling to start a roaring conflagration in the midst of battle, forcing a beleaguered crew to fight both the fire and the enemy.

There was a more important advantage. With devastating effect near Savo Island, the Japanese had employed their oxygen-breathing Long Lance torpedo. It carried a 1,345-pound warhead and could run toward a target eight miles away at a staggering 50 knots. The U.S. Navy's cruisers did not even have torpedo tubes, because the flawed tactical thinking after World War I was that future naval battles would not be fought within torpedo range. The torpedoes aboard the U.S. destroyers, designed and produced by the Naval Torpedo Factory, simply did not work. There were serious design flaws known for years but never fixed because of bureaucratic inertia, as well as serious quality control problems typical of government-owned and -operated manufacturing facilities.

Nightly battles ensued through August, September and October of 1942 in the Eastern Solomons, Santa Isabel, Lunga Point, Cape Esperance and San Cristobal. The Japanese Navy continued to outfight the Americans. On October 26, America lost another carrier, *Hornet*, off Santa Cruz Island.

AIRMAN FIRST CLASS ALVIN KERNAN: A VOICE FROM THE GUN TURRET

Among the thousands of young sailors leaping the sixty feet into the sea from the burning decks of *Hornet* was 18-year-old third-class ordnanceman Alvin Kernan. In the eleven months since Pearl Harbor, Kernan had been in combat almost constantly. As he bobbed in the waves worrying about sharks underneath him and Zeros above him, it was quite a change from his bucolic life of little more than a year before. Growing up on a remote farm in Wyoming, Kernan joined the Navy out of boredom when he graduated from high school. In March 1941, after boot camp in San Diego and training in aviation ordnance (guns and bombs), he was assigned to the carrier *Enterprise* out of Pearl Harbor. The bars and bordellos of San Diego and then the beauty of the Hawaiian Islands were an awesome experience for the teenaged Kernan. "Unaware of what it meant to be a sailor in Honolulu, I tried to make a date with one of the beautiful (local) girls, only to learn that her father would rather see her date one of the lepers from Molokai than a sailor."

By good luck *Enterprise* and the other carriers were out of Pearl Harbor when the Japanese attacked. The day after the attack he returned to Pearl to stare in awed silence at the still-burning battleships and smoldering aircraft. He saw his first action soon thereafter in the raids on the Marshall Islands. Returning to Pearl, he was transferred to *Hornet* to augment the crew for a top-secret operation. Seeing the decks loaded with army bombers he realized immediately that they were going into the attack against the Japanese home islands. On April 18, 1942 Col. James Doolittle (assisted by Alvin Kernan) led a force of army B-25 bombers, not designed for carrier operation, on a one-way attack against Japan. Most recovered safely in China.

After launching the raid, *Hornet* and the rest of Rear Admiral Raymond Spruance's Task Force Sixteen were sent in strictest radio silence to join the other two remaining Pacific Fleet carriers off Midway on June 4. The code-breakers at Pearl Harbor had intercepted the Japanese battle plans to seize the island of Midway in order to prevent another humiliating raid like Doolittle's.

Hornet was immediately in the thick of the fighting, and Kernan's squadron, Torpedo 6, lost ten out of fourteen aircraft. Despite the fact that modern historians only learned in the last decade of the successful breaking of the Japanese code by the Pacific Fleet, Kernan and his shipmates around the scuttlebutt all knew that the Japanese code had

Airman 1st Class Alvin Kernan, on the left, with the pilot and crew of his TBF Avenger.

been broken. That they were on their way to intercept the Japanese fleet "was widely known among the enlisted men before the battle."

Kernan describes the end of the first day of the Battle of Midway as the returning pilots waited to be debriefed: "Our own strike group and the Japanese sighted each other on the way to their targets, but each passed the other by without engaging. I hoped they didn't wave, but they may have." Kernan, like many men, admired and envied the pilots: "These were heroes dressed in the khaki flight suits, carrying pistols and knives over their yellow Mae Wests, and describing with quick hands and excited voices how they had gone into the dives, released their bombs, and seen the Japanese flight decks open up in flames just below them. The slaves who carried the equipment of the Greek warriors at Salamis . . . could not have felt more envious or less heroic than I."

After the battle, *Hornet* returned to Pearl, and Kernan's squadron was stood down to transition from the slow, obsolete Douglas Devastators that had been decimated at Midway to new Grumman TBF

Avengers. Kernan qualified as a gunner in the Avenger and his squadron was assigned to the new carrier *Nassau,* and later to the second *Lexington.* For the next two years, flying with the Third and Fifth Fleets, he saw almost constant action and had many hair-raising brushes with the Grim Reaper, including a bad catapult shot that crashed his Avenger into the sea next to the carrier: "The ship above us went tearing by, all I saw was Cletus Powell leaning out of a porthole in the parachute loft where I had just lost seventy-five dollars to him, which I did not have, at blackjack, yelling, 'Kernan you don't have to pay! Get out, get out, get out for God's sake!'" On another mission his Avenger was hit by Japanese machine-gun fire which severed the flight-control cables. They were able to splice the cable just in time to land back aboard.

"War's cruelty and randomness, its indifference to human life and the speed with which it erases existence, forces anyone who thinks to realize that war is not an aberration, only a speeded-up version of how it always is," Kernan wrote. "Death lived on an aircraft carrier operating in war-time conditions. One day a plane would crash taking off . . . a thoughtless step backward on the flight and hangar decks where the planes were returning led to decapitation and gory dismemberment by propeller." Indeed, death was a constant companion in this campaign: "April 25th, Collura, Powell to whom I still owed my blackjack losings, and Stewart were hit in a dive and went in and exploded; April 27th, Campbell, the commanding officer, Loughridge, my close friend, and Zahn were hit and disintegrated in the air. Death had by then become familiar and almost unremarkable, but it still was difficult to accept that someone that you knew and had played cards with in a normal way only a few hours earlier was now gone forever. . . ."

Kernan's words reveal the contradictions of the war to the men who fought it, full of both the optimism of boundless hope and the despair of personal loss. "My eyes moved from one face to another of men who are as alive to me now as they ever were," he recalled, "but whose bones are washing around the bottom of the sea, tangled in the wreckage of their planes, between Okinawa and Taiwan, near islands with such romantic names as Ishigaki, Miyako and Kerama-Retto."

Kernan's war came to an end when the bomb was dropped on Nagasaki and Hiroshima and "each of us felt those bombs had saved our lives, not lives in general, but our own felt, breathing lives." He went ashore at Nagasaki and saw the devastation, "grateful and unashamed."

HEAVY NAVAL FIGHTING CONTINUED around Guadalcanal in what was becoming a battle of attrition and the most crucial naval arena of the war. Ashore, a maddening and prolonged stalemate developed between exhausted and malaria-ridden American and Japanese troops. It was an apprehensive time. Self-appointed military analysts predicted the Guadalcanal campaign would end in failure because the Navy was allegedly unable to resupply and reinforce the troops already ashore or safely haul them off the beach. Some of them went so far as to say that the Navy, fearing further losses in ships and lives, had simply abandoned the troops.

Needless to say, it was not so. Both sides were taking a pounding in the slot, each trying desperately to strike the decisive blow. In November, Rear Admiral Hiroaki Abe took a pair of old battleships, ten destroyers and a heavy cruiser against Rear Admiral Daniel J. Callaghan with eight destroyers and five cruisers. Thanks to intelligence reports, Callaghan knew Abe was on the way. But both admirals made tactical errors and results were inconclusive: one battleship, two destroyers and 500 sailors lost for the Japanese; four destroyers and two cruisers for the Americans, including *Juneau* with five brothers, the Sullivans, in the greatest family tragedy of the war.

Although fighting in the slot would continue until December 1942, the nights of November 13 and 14 would see the deadlock at last broken by the two radar-equipped battleships, *Washington* and *South Dakota*, both new and fast, and four destroyers of Task Force Sixty-four, commanded by Rear Admiral Willis Lee. His opponent was Vice Admiral Nobutake Kondo and his "Volunteer Bombardment Force," consisting of the old, but still dangerous, battleship *Kirishima*, two heavy cruisers, *Atago* and *Takao*, two light cruisers, *Sendai* and *Nagara*, and nine destroyers.

The night of November 13 was warm, dark and humid. At about 10:00 P.M. the battle began when *Washington*'s radar spotted *Shikinami*, a destroyer leading Kondo's main force. At the same time, Japanese lookouts spotted Lee's force, and mistakenly reported them as destroyers backed up by cruisers.

When *Shikinami* came within range, *Washington* opened fire, and the night erupted with 16-inch-cannon flashes and thunderous reports. *South Dakota* steamed up and opened, too, and Kondo broke off under fire to try to regroup.

Aggressively, Lee ordered his four destroyers into the thick of things, but Japanese gunnery proved accurate. The destroyer *Preston* took some terrible hits, rolled on her side, and started to sink. *Gwin* too, began to take devastating hits. Meanwhile a sister ship, *Walke*, launched her torpedoes with no effect and then took a hit that cut her in half; she sank within minutes, taking half her crew. Lee's fourth destroyer, *Benham*, took many hits, and a torpedo, too, but remained afloat. Within ten minutes, all of Task Force Sixty-four's destroyers were out of action, two on the bottom of the sound.

It was then that the battleship *South Dakota*, a jinxed ship in the bluejackets' eyes, went dead in the water, leaving Admiral Lee aboard *Washington* in command of only one surviving combatant, his flagship. He did not lose his head. *Washington*'s skipper maneuvered behind Lee's burning destroyers so the battleship would not be silhouetted to Admiral Kondo's accurate gunners. Survival rafts were lowered, and Lee ordered the barely floating *Gwin* and *Benham* to pick up survivors.

Around midnight, Kondo's force detected and spotlighted the stricken *South Dakota*. They started pounding her with torpedoes and guns, but thanks to her crew, her armor plate, and her watertight compartmentation, she did not succumb. Naval historians agree that *South Dakota* was the most heavily armored battleship ever built, on a pound-for-pound basis. They disagree on the number of major-caliber hits she took that night. Some accounts go as high as 42, others as low as 26— and these from 14-inch guns. The huge shells could not penetrate *South Dakota*'s Class B armor plate, but could cut up her radar, communications cables and other exterior rigging. It was the most severe surface-to-surface pounding of any battleship in U.S. Navy history. Yet *South Dakota* went on to serve for the remainder of the war and was among the first battleships to deliver shore bombardment on the Japanese mainland by firing at the Kamaishi Steelworks on Honshu, July 14, 1945.

In little more than two and one-half hours, Lee saw five of his six remaining ships knocked out by Kondo's firepower. But he also saw by the Japanese searchlights that *Washington* was facing *Kirishima*, her position revealed by her own lights. Kondo thought that *South Dakota* was the only battleship he had to worry about; Lee and *Washington* were about to surprise him.

Lee ordered all operable searchlights turned on *Kirishima*, and *Washington* opened fire with her 16-inchers at about 8,000 yards—point-blank range—with huge flat-trajectory guns throwing 2,800-pound shells. *Kirishima* returned fire with her 14-inch guns, and the slugfest was on, the first battleship-versus-battleship engagement of the war.

Within a few furious minutes, three of *Kirishima*'s gun turrets had taken skull-numbing hits, and her rudder had become stuck. She was uncontrollable, running in circles. The heavy cruisers *Atago* and *Takao* came to her aid, but were soon subjected to *Washington*'s rapid, accurate fire. They made smoke and drew off, both severely damaged, while *Kirishima* was scuttled, the first battleship to succumb to an American battlewagon since the Spanish-American War.

Seeing this astounding reversal, Admiral Kondo ordered all his surviving ships, except for a few that were picking up survivors, to converge in an attack upon *Washington*. Trying to comply, his captains came in piecemeal, and *Washington* sank *Ayanami*, a destroyer, before shooing away the rest of Kondo's tin cans. The great showdown engagement was over.

History's longest naval battle had been one of mutual attrition with the ever-increasing loss of aircraft, transports and major surface combatants. The Marines ashore Guadalcanal defeated the Japanese Army, forcing their withdrawal, and the U.S. Navy exacted such a toll on the Imperial Navy that further advances were out of the question. Guadalcanal's Henderson Field continued to be used as the jumping-off point for American air operations, including the mission that shot down, in April 1943, Admiral Yamamoto in his airplane near Bougainville.

After Guadalcanal the full weight of American production, technology and training began to fall upon the Japanese. But even more surprising to them, in the words of Walter Boyne, "was the similar increase in American ferocity and combativeness." American strategy became the "use of massive quantities of heavy weapons by increasingly professional warriors exercising a newly learned savagery."

One of the places the new strategy would be showcased was in the narrow channel separating England and German-held France in the Atlantic Ocean, just about on the other side of the world.

THE NAVAL BATTLE OF NORMANDY/OPERATION NEPTUNE

From the beginning of the Second World War the leaders of the American Army, led by General George Marshall, pushed for an invasion of mainland Europe at the earliest possible time, a move also demanded by the hard-pressed Russians. At the second Washington Conference in June 1942, Marshall asked for an invasion in northern France later that year. Churchill, along with the leaders of the U.S. Navy and Army Air Corps, opposed an invasion at such an early date. The British leader feared a repeat of the carnage of World War I, while the Navy and General Douglas MacArthur adamantly opposed diverting further resources from the Pacific war. FDR adroitly played these enormous egos off each other in order to keep the decision in his own hands. The president's sympathies lay with Churchill and the Navy, favoring gradual strangulation rather than decisive battle while the Russians ground down the Germans. Roosevelt and Churchill agreed on a joint invasion of North Africa instead, the enormously successful operation Torch. Three amphibious landings were made, 35,000 troops under George Patton near Casablanca, 39,000 near Oran, Algeria, and 33,000 near Algiers. The Vichy French forces resisted and in a battle off Casablanca on November 8, 1942, the much superior American force led by the battleship *Massachusetts* sank a French cruiser and five destroyers.

Marshall continued to press for an invasion to take place in 1943, and the British, MacArthur and the U.S. Navy continued to oppose it adamantly, carrying the day once again at the Casablanca Conference in January 1943.

Russian success finally forced the issue. In November 1943, the Allies assured Stalin that there would be an invasion of France in 1944. The experience of D-Day itself soon made it clear that if FDR had acquiesced to Marshall and invaded in 1942 or 1943, before Hitler had lost his Air Force and half of his Army, the German counterattack would have been crushing. Had he waited any longer, the Russians would probably have occupied all of Germany and possibly France. This balancing act was perhaps FDR's greatest feat of leadership during the war.

To prepare for Operation Neptune, as the invasion of Normandy was dubbed, the U.S. Navy set up an enormous training center in the south of England under Rear Admiral John Hall. Here thousands of young sailors had to be trained in the complex tasks of getting the invasion force safely ashore from transports, while providing the gunfire and other support required. Naval gunfire spotters were taught the necessary fire-control procedures; underwater demolition teams were trained in breaching extensive beach obstacles, and most important of all the landing crews learned how to bring their flatbottom landing craft through the dangerous obstacles in heavy seas and avoid broaching the keel-less boats and drowning their occupants.

Overall naval command of the invasion was given to Admiral Sir Bertram H. Ramsay, RN. Rear Admiral Alan G. Kirk, USN, was given command of operations on Utah and Omaha beaches. Kirk's firsthand experience of earlier landings in the Mediterranean led him to recommend a substantial pre-invasion naval bombardment on the landing beaches. Ramsay did not agree and vetoed the idea, counting instead on aerial bombing. As a result bitterly earned American experience was wasted and the kind of naval gunfire that had forced the Japanese to give up contesting landings at the beachhead in the last two years of the Pacific war did not take place.

Ironically, it was precisely the prospect of that devastating naval gunfire that convinced Field Marshall Heinz Guderian that General Irwin Rommel's determination to destroy the invasion on the beaches, and commit reserves immediately to do so, would be suicidal. As a result the German defense strategy was a compromise. Infantry was committed forward to attempt to halt the invasion on the beaches, but armor was held back out of the range of naval gunfire.

General Omar Bradley also expressed misgivings about the inadequate naval gunfire to be included in the landing, but he and Field Marshall Sir Bernard Montgomery acquiesced to plans put forward by their staff that shifted the burden of bombardment suppression to the Eighth Air Force. (The Navy itself gave in since whatever additional gunfire was to be included would have to come from Pacific operations.)

Naval gunfire in World War II was far more precise and accurate than aerial bombardment in the best of times. It did, however, require spotting by forward teams or aerial observers. The weather at Normandy did not make that practical until daylight of the actual invasion day. Because of the decision not to tip off the landing location by extensive naval gunfire preparation, the three battleships, nine cruisers and thirty-nine destroyers did not begin their barrage until 5:50 on the morning of the invasion. The old battleships *Texas* and *Arkansas* were assigned to support Omaha Beach. According to Robert Love they had "ten 14-inch, twelve 12-inch and twelve 5-inch guns and pumped 600 shells on to the coastal battery atop Pointe du Hoc in an all-out attempt to ease the way for the Ranger Battalions . . . [headed] for the 100-foot high sheer cliffs."

When the brief bombardment of the shoreline had to be lifted to enable the landing of the force, the German gun emplacements and pillboxes remained relatively unscathed on the steep bluffs above the high-water line and exacted a terrible price.

Naval operations during the Normandy invasion should nonetheless be seen as incredibly successful. The Navy, despite the enormous operations going on in the Pacific, provided 5,333 amphibious craft, battleships, cruisers and destroyers to deliver the invasion force and provide fire support. At Utah Beach, 20,000 troops and 1,700 motorized vehicles were able to land successfully in the first fifteen hours, with the Fourth Division attaining nearly all of its objectives by nightfall.

Elsewhere the story was different. Omaha Beach was very nearly a catastrophe. German defenses had every inch of it pre-sighted, with enormous firepower embedded on the crests and bluffs over the beach. The first U.S. wave was decimated by accurate fire before it reached shore and the surviving soldiers met hails of lead as soon as they debarked. Many wounded men drowned in the surf, unable to reach the beach.

In his book *D-Day*, historian Stephen Ambrose tells the story of the invasion from the often horrific perspective of the participants. Sergeant Ben McKinney recalled "I was so sea-sick I didn't care if a bullet hit me between the eyes. . . . rifle and machine-gun fire hitting like falling rain. . . . it looked as if all the first wave were dead on the beach." The lieutenant leading the assault team on one boat at Omaha was killed as the ramp went down. Sergeant Harry Bare took over: "I tried to get my men off the boat. We waded to the sand and threw ourselves down. My radioman had his head blown off three yards from me. The beach was covered with bodies. Men with no legs, no arms—God it was awful. . . . there were only six out of my boat alive . . . ." Of the 20,000 tons of weapons and ammunition planned to be landed on Omaha Beach only 100 actually made it; of the first wave of men at Omaha half were killed or wounded; and of 4,900 casualties on D-Day, 2,400 were at Omaha.

The British on Gold and Sword Beaches, and the Canadians on Juno fought fiercely, suffering at Sword and Juno percentage losses as grievous as those at Omaha.

The most valuable naval fire support to the invasion was not the few heavy guns of the battleships or cruisers but the direct fire of thirty-three American and British destroyers and six destroyer escorts, all of whom escorted the landing craft as close to the beach as their drafts would allow, then stayed throughout the day, providing direct fire.

In an analysis done for the Naval Historical Foundation, William

Kirkland reports, for example, that "eight ships of DESRON 18, plus *Emmons* and three British destroyers, backed up the heroic efforts of the soldiers of the First and Twenty-ninth Divisions, and had a large share in starting on the road to victory." Kirkland's valuable report also includes dozens of the individual actions by courageous ship captains that enabled the soldiers ashore to get off the beach: "At 0617 British Landing Craft converted to fire bombardment rockets commenced firing, drenching the area just inland from the beaches. Fire from this beach was temporarily silenced and the entire area covered with heavy smoke and dust. Troops landed and proceeded up the beach into the smoke."

The Navy has never received a large share of the credit for Normandy—public sympathies lay with the men on the sand. But the destroyers paid a heavy price for the assistance they rendered. *Corey* was sunk by a mine off Utah Beach; *Rich* was sunk by a mine on June 8 with the loss of eighty-nine lives; and *Glennan* and *Meredith* were heavily damaged by mines, *Meredith* breaking up and sinking the next day. (On June 10, *Glennan* was sunk by a German shore battery.) The ammunition expended by the destroyers at Omaha says it all: *Cormack* expended 1,127 rounds, *McCook* 975, *Emmons* 767 and *Thompson* 638.

The value of heavy naval guns was proven in the days immediately following the landing, when the weather cleared and aerial spotters were able to direct accurate fire as far as fifteen miles inland. That massed fire, thrown inland twenty-four hours a day, in addition to the aerial bombardment of the Army Air Corps, effectively prevented Rommel from massing the counterattack that was the critical element of his defense strategy. As a result the Allied forces moved steadily forward and within a week a solid defensive front was in place.

The Army had won a great battle. The beach was secure and total victory in Europe was less than a year away.

The landing at the Normandy beaches would have been impossible had it not been for another kind of ship less glamorous than the destroyers: the thousands of specially designed landing craft that could carry significant numbers of troops and equipment at a relatively high speed from the transports to the beaches, go over obstacles without hanging up or knocking off the propellers or rudders, go right up onto the beach so their occupants could exit with alacrity, and then immediately extricate themselves from the beach to prevent clogging and enable a continuing stream of boats to land. That the Allies had these boats in ample numbers is thanks to a single unusual man.

ANDREW JACKSON HIGGINS AND HIS BOATS

Dwight Eisenhower told his biographer that Andrew Higgins was "the man who won the war for us." Most Americans do not know his name. Andrew Higgins was larger than life, a visionary entrepreneur with a genius for design and production. His Higgins Industries, a small specialty manufacturer of workboats in the late 1930s grew to over 20,000 employees and eight plants during the war, ultimately providing Allied forces with 20,094 vessels.

While Higgins Industries built a variety of ships to satisfy the war effort, including PT boats and 170-foot freight supply vessels, the boats that won Eisenhower's praise were the small amphibious landing craft designed specifically to put troops and their equipment ashore on unprepared beaches. Collectively called Higgins boats, these were the LCPs, LCPLs, LCVPs, and LCMs that permitted D-Day forces to land in France and Marines to take beachheads throughout the Pacific. Higgins Industries excelled at designing these small reliable craft, producing them rapidly in the quantities necessary for victory and providing the crew training that ensured their proper employment.

While Higgins was a natural businessman looking to broaden the market for his boats, maximization of sales and profits was not his only goal. His priorities lay with the marines, soldiers and sailors who rode his boats into combat. Unusual for a businessman, he talked of *lowering* profits. It was not fair, he once said, that he should make $28 million when many other Americans had their sons getting shot at. At the same time he urged that other defense contracts be negotiated downward, since defense firms were receiving profits far out of line with their risks. This seems to have been a genuine sentiment on his part, as well as a way of needling his competitors and winning the public's regard.

He was a strong, passionate leader. He fought unionization until it was inevitable, then embraced the union and became their best employer, but one who insisted on their active support. His drive produced extraordinary achievements. In May 1941, the Navy, desperate for a tank landing craft, asked him to begin drawing up plans for one. They hoped that a preliminary design could be reviewed during a visit three days hence. To their disbelief, he replied that instead of plans, they would find a workable boat upon their arrival. His men completed the job in sixty-one hours.

But the biggest challenge facing Higgins was not in design or production, where he had control. It was in dealing with the Navy's ship-acquisition office—BuShips—and its bureaucrats. Andrew Higgins's battle with bureaucracy provides a revealing glimpse of what happens when highly individualistic entrepreneurs must cooperate with rigidly hierarchical organizations.

While it was the forest business that brought 20-year-old Andrew Higgins from his Nebraska home to Alabama in 1906, small boats soon became a part of his timber operations with the purchase of a modest fleet of schooners and brigantines to import logs and deliver finished lumber to market. By the 1920s, Higgins was producing his own barges and push boats and in 1930 he formed Higgins Industries to manufacture workboats for trappers, lumbermen and oilmen. As timber stocks dwindled, boatbuilding became his primary business. His family of workboats eventually evolved into Eureka, a maneuverable shallow-draft model, capable of navigating over logs and other obstructions by virtue of the design and the sturdiness of its bow and hull, and its propeller protected by a skeg, a keel running below it. By 1937 customers included regional and foreign markets, as well as the Coast Guard, Army Corps of Engineers and Biological Survey Agency. All were impressed with his boats' speed, ruggedness and handling, as well as their ability to operate safely in both extreme shallows and the open.

Higgins was no expert on naval warfare but he heard Marine Corps pleas for a boat that could land troops and equipment on unprepared beaches and believed his experience designing for the Gulf Coast uniquely qualified him to provide these types of vessels. But what was obvious to Higgins was not obvious to BuShips. It is not at all surprising that the Navy would view someone like Higgins with suspicion. It naturally and always prefers the familiarity of established suppliers to unknown innovators who nine times out of ten cannot deliver what they promise. One thus might suppose that Higgins's best course of action was to win over the Navy buyer by demonstrating an understanding of the requirements, showing competence, providing more than is asked for, and giving it earlier and cheaper. But that would be wrong.

At every stage of the process, BuShips sought to defeat Higgins's efforts. First they gave the requirement for amphibious craft a low priority. Then they selected only established Northeastern boatbuilders to provide candidates. When those entrants failed they pursued their own unsatisfactory designs. When Higgins' boats did get into trials, their superiority over other designs was ignored. The Navy forced Higgins to invest large amounts of his own capital in order to compete in the design process, then threatened his survival by ordering smaller numbers than promised and ordering late. Through it all, Higgins faced a wall of bureaucratic secrecy and deception. Only his persistence, the increasing reality of the war and, finally, hearings by Senator Harry Truman's investigating committee eventually prevailed over BuShips obstructionism.

There were many reasons for BuShips's aversion to Higgins. One simple one was that no one makes admiral commanding or building "boats." Tiny landing craft had a hard time competing for attention with the glamorous carriers and battleships in an organization where even destroyers were called "small boys." Higgins also lacked the history (the devil you know . . .) of the Northeast's boatbuilders. The Navy still reflected a bit of Yankee stiffness toward unpolished southerners who expressed themselves in colorful style—"I don't wait for opportunity to knock. I send out a welcoming committee to drag the old harlot in," Higgins was fond of saying.

If the entrepreneur has creativity on his side, the bureaucrat has control on his, over contracts, testing, requirements, schedules and, ultimately, money—money that the entrepreneur needs to survive. What made Higgins such a threat to the bureaucracy was the direct relationship the Marines developed with him. It was BuShips' role to represent the Marines, but here was Higgins working directly with the Marines, offering them exactly what they wanted and not focusing particularly on when or how much he would get paid. BuShips had no control over someone like that—someone who viewed the Marines as the customer rather than BuShips—and without control, where was BuShips? The problem is endemic in every bureaucracy, public and private, in every age and every society. The very stability and predictability of process for which bureaucracies are created becomes inevitably its absolute value. The process is more important than the end product.

Fortunately, Higgins was a problem solver. It is a rare and valuable trait. Forty years later I could not have done my job as SECNAV had it not been for the people like Higgins who emerged from the thickets of bureaucracy determined to make the right things happen. You cannot advertise for them, but when there is a leader like James Forrestal, willing to take on the bureaucracy himself, the doers emerge, either by word of mouth—they all seem to know one another—or are found by trolling for them in the fleet and shore establishments. One by one they surface and become essential to every constructive thing accomplished. So it was with Higgins during WWII.

Higgins's eventual success with BuShips was not the end of his problems. Bureaucracy has many paths to vengeance. After the war, in an action attesting to Clare Boothe Luce's observation that in Washington "no good deed goes unpunished," the Justice Department announced it was investigating Higgins Industries for submitting false claims. In February 1947 the federal grand jury concluded there was no basis for prosecution. While awaiting that finding, Higgins sent around his reaction to the charges. He concluded, "The mistakes of the military leaders are excused or forgotten no matter how costly in terms of wealth, material or human lives; but the people that create or build to make victory possible and after victory exert their every effort to maintain the economy of our country are 'war profiteers' to be subjected

to suspicion, to be investigated, to be harassed—their business destroyed—yes—and their character and honor smirched! WHAT PRICE OR
CREDIT PATRIOTISM."

The new company would persevere. With the coming of the Korean War, BuShips again turned to Higgins, and by the end of 1951 his
government boat contracts were increasing rapidly. Higgins died at 65
in 1952 a rich man and, far more important, one who could claim a patriotism of the highest order.

WHILE HIGGINS'S SHIPS WERE PROVING their worth on the Normandy coast, a great battle was taking place, one of the last of the Pacific war.

With the decision tentatively taken in July 1944 at the Honolulu
Conference to liberate the Philippines rather than invading Formosa,
plans solidified around a major invasion of the island of Leyte. On
October 20, the Seventh Fleet (widely known in the Navy as
"MacArthur's Navy") under Vice Admiral Thomas Kincaid, landed the
Sixth Army on Leyte Island against heavy opposition with the support
and protection of Halsey's Third Fleet. The Japanese high command
decided it must throw everything into a counterattack to prevent the
loss of the Philippines.

Three Japanese task forces were formed: "Northern Force" with
four carriers, three cruisers, two hybrid battleship carriers and eight destroyers; "Center Force," with the super-battleships *Musashi* and *Yamato* (72,000 tons apiece!), three battleships, twelve cruisers and fifteen
destroyers; and "Southern Force," with two battleships, four cruisers
and eleven destroyers. Halsey's Third Fleet had four carrier task
forces, six new battleships, eight heavy cruisers and numerous "small
boys." Kincaid had six old battleships, sixteen small escort carriers and
eight cruisers. The naval battle of Guadalcanal is undoubtedly the
most sustained and most furious naval battle in history, but it extended
over six months. The actions in the Battle of Leyte Gulf were the
largest single naval battle ever fought in history.

THE BATTLE OF LEYTE GULF: "THE WORLD WONDERS"

The battle began on October 23 in the Palawan Passage, when the submarines *Darter* and *Dace* attacked Admiral Kurita's Center Force making its way toward the Sibuyan Sea. These attacks sank two of Kurita's heavy cruisers, including his flagship *Atago,* and heavily damaged a third. On the 24th, Third Fleet aircraft attacked the Center Force traveling through the Sibuyan Sea, sinking *Musashi* and a destroyer and disabling a cruiser. With no Japanese air cover, it took four hours of pounding with bombs and torpedoes finally to sink the super-battleship.

After nightfall, the Southern Force attacked through the Surigao Strait. At first it encountered only PT boats and destroyers, though the destroyers nonetheless succeeded in sinking a battleship and two Japanese destroyers. Continuing through the strait the attacking force encountered the Seventh Fleet battle line consisting of six old battleships—*California, Maryland, Mississippi, Pennsylvania, Tennessee* and *West Virginia*—and the destroyers of Squadron 54. Lieutenant James Holloway, later to be CNO, then gunnery officer on the destroyer *Bennion,* remembered the action:

> From my battlestation in the Director, I had a view of the whole scene, from the panorama of the two fleets to a closeup of the Japanese ships through the high-powered lenses of the Mark-37 Director. As our destroyers started the run to the south, we were immediately taken under fire. It was an eerie experience to be rushing through dark towards the enemy at a relative speed of 50 knots, not firing our guns or hearing the enemy fall of shot around us. The awesome evidence of the Japanese gunfire were the towering columns of water from the splashes of their 14- and 16-inch shells, some close enough to wet our weatherdecks. Star shells hung overhead and the gun flashes from the Japanese line illuminated the horizon ahead.
>
> About the time our division made its final turn to run in for the torpedo attack, our battleships and cruisers opened up with

their main batteries, and it was a comforting sight. Directly over our heads stretched a procession of tracers from our battle line converging on the head of the Japanese column. I recall being surprised at the apparent slowness of the projectiles. They almost hung in the sky, taking fifteen to twenty seconds in their trajectory before reaching their target. It was a spectacular display. Through the Director optics, I could clearly see the bursting explosions of our battleships' and cruisers' shells as they hit the Japanese ships, which were now enveloped in flames. . . . We started launching our five torpedoes at a range of about 7,000 yards. . . .

As we retired to the north in formation at 30 knots, still max black smoke, explosions erupted close off our port beam. It was one of our destroyers, *Albert W. Grant* being hit by large-caliber shells during the retirement.

Grant was the only American ship lost in the action. The Japanese had lost *Yamashiro* and two cruisers and retired at daybreak.

The Northern Force remained. In the late afternoon of October 24, Halsey's aircraft had first spotted Admiral Ozawa's force decoying off Luzon in the hope of drawing the Third Fleet away from the protection of the American beachhead. Halsey took the bait, taking the entire Third Fleet north in pursuit and leaving the San Bernardino Strait unprotected.

While this was going on Admiral Nimitz sent to Admiral Halsey his famous message: "Where Is, Repeat, Where Is, Task Force 34, The World Wonders!" Halsey immediately reversed course with his fast battleships, leaving his carriers to continue pursuit of the Northern Force.

Before Halsey arrived, the Japanese Center Force, by now having regrouped, proceeded unopposed through the Strait and caught the task force of six small escort carriers under Rear Admiral Clifton Sprague without protection. Under heavy fire from the Japanese force, Sprague launched all his aircraft against them in attack while he attempted to retreat with his very slow jeep carriers. Aircraft from the other two escort carrier groups to the south also supported him. Two of Sprague's accompanying destroyers and a smaller destroyer escort (DE) were sunk, but they took with them three Japanese cruisers. With the carriers now unprotected, the Japanese moved in, sinking the jeep carrier *Gambier Bay*. Then, in a bizarre move never yet sufficiently explained, the Center Force under Admiral Kurita retired through the San Bernardino Strait.

Halsey had made a terrible mistake, but the Third Fleet was there for the last action of the battle. Halsey's carriers under Vice Admiral Marc Mitscher caught and sank all four enemy carriers of the Northern Force—*Chitosi, Chiyoda, Zuiho* and *Zuikaku*—and a destroyer, while Halsey's force sank a destroyer and a cruiser, ending the battle. The Japanese Navy had lost four carriers, three battleships, eight cruisers and eight destroyers and would never again pose a serious naval threat. The desperate gamble of the Imperial Japanese Navy to risk all in

The Battle of Leyte Gulf

hopes of a Mahanian decisive victory had failed, and in failing deci-
sively it ceased to exist as an effective force. The losses of ships, sailors
and especially aviators, could not be replaced.

The confusions at Leyte highlighted the conflicts in approach
among the key decision makers. King refused to allow MacArthur
overall command but couldn't prevent MacArthur's control of Seventh
Fleet. Marshall refused to allow MacArthur to be subordinated to
Nimitz, denying him the theater command, hence they muddled
through. With the Philippines being secured, the Marianas, Palaus and
Ulithi taken as bases, the noose was now tight around Japan. The question remained over Plan Orange's endgame—to strangle or to invade.

LCSs: The Mighty Midgets

Whatever the decision, much of the dirtiest remaining naval work
would have to be done aboard a powerful new type of American ship
that had made its debut in the Philippine campaign. As the Navy
moved westward across the Pacific Ocean it became clear that greater
close-in fire support was needed to support amphibious troops as they
landed on the shores of Japanese-controlled islands.

Naval bombardment ceased, by necessity, as American troops approached, allowing Japanese defenders to come out of their shelters
and caves and open fire. In late 1943, troop-carrying ships called LCIs
(Landing Craft Infantry), which carried 20 mm guns and were armed
with three additional 40 mm guns on an experimental basis, were introduced in an effort to reduce casualties. After heavy losses were sustained in the assault on Tarawa, the Navy concluded it needed an
urgent program to put greater firepower on more than 200 LCIs. The
LCS (Landing Craft Support) was the result.

This ship was optimized for the fire-support mission. It had a shallow draft and a flat bottom for operation in shallow waters. Its twin propellers and rudders were protected by skegs and it had two huge
Danforth anchors on the stern so that it could drop them offshore,

The Battle of Leyte Gulf

BABUYAN ISLANDS

Cape Engaño

Aparri
Airfield

Tuguegaro
Airfield

Palanan Point

LUZON

Baler
Airfield

**POLILLO
ISLANDS**

★ Manila
Cavite

Lamon Bay

Lucena
Batangas

Naga
Airfield

Lagazpi
Airfield

MINDORO

Battle of
The Sibuyan Sea

Sibuyan Sea

MASBATE

Visayan Sea

PANAY

SAMAR

*GAMBIER
BAY*

Tacloban

U.S.
BEACHHEAD

LEYTE

U.S.
TRANSPORT
FLEET

Leyte Gulf

NEGROS

Cebu

Camotes Sea

CEBU

Panay Gulf

BOHOL

Battle of
Surigao Strait

DINAGAT I.

RADM OLDENDORF
surface fleet

ST LO

Philippine Sea

ZUIHO
ZUIKAKU   *CHIYODA*

VADM OZAWA

CHITOSE   8:00 a.m.
                   U.S. carrier planes
AKITSUKI   hit OZAWA's force

midnight 25 Oct

10:55 a.m.
HALSEY in *NEW JERSEY*
turns south with
TF34 and one carrier group

8:22 a.m.
HALSEY receives
help call from KINKAID

6:45 a.m.
HALSEY launches air strike

midnight 24 Oct

TF38 (3 carrier groups)
and TF34 (RADM LEE)
**VADM HALSEY
THIRD FLEET**

midnight 24 Oct
KURITA emerges from
San Bernardino Strait

6:45 a.m.
KURITA turns east
and opens fire

8:00 a.m.
YAMATO turns away from
U.S. destroyer attack

TAFFY 3
RADM C. SPRAGUE
6 escort carriers

TAFFY 2
RADM STUMP
5 escort carriers

**VADM HALSEY
THIRD FLEET**

San Bernardino Strait

Airfield

0   20   40   60   80   100
Nautical Miles

steam in with the landing force with guns blazing—if necessary until grounding on the beach—and then kedge itself off with the stern anchors. It was designed with open deck space to accommodate single- and twin-gun mounts for 3-inch 20-mm and 40-mm guns and ten Mk7 rocket launchers. The ship also had four 50-caliber machine guns mounted two to a side. The result was more firepower per ton than any other ship in the war. Powered with eight GM diesels giving a top speed of 18 knots, the LCSs had a length of 158 feet 6 inches, a beam of 23 feet, 3 inches and draft of just 6 feet 6 inches. These ships were rushed into production, and 130 of them were built in just nine months in 1944 and early 1945.

By October 1944, the first LCSs were ready to enter the war. A number of them were sent to New Guinea and then on to the Philippines and Borneo. Later-arriving LCSs were assigned to participate in the invasions of Iwo Jima and Okinawa. At Iwo Jima, 12 LCSs participated in the first assault on February 19. They led the way, going in towards the beach in front of the troop carriers, barraging the shore with anti-personnel rockets and 20 mm and 40 mm fire. At about 100 yards from the beach, the landing craft passed the LCSs and headed for the shore. The LCSs then fired their rockets over the heads of the troops and raked the shoreline with more 20 mm and 40 mm fire. After the troops had landed, the LCSs continued to operate close-in, providing gunfire support until they ran out of ammunition. LCSs even participated in the final assault on Mount Suribachi, providing direct gunfire support. Some of the LCS crews actually witnessed the now-famous raising of the American flag.

On April 1, 1945, the conquest of Okinawa began, and LCSs were at the front of the assault wave. After the initial landing, the LCSs and destroyers were assigned to radar picket duty. The "divine wind" kamikaze attacks, first used against the Philippine invasion, were now to reach their height. Losses of radar-picket ships were very high. Of the 148 ships assigned to this duty, 119 of them were hit by Japanese fighter planes or kamikazes. Of the 119 ships that were hit, 43 were sunk or so badly damaged that they had to be scrapped.

Okinawa was within striking range from the southern Japanese is-

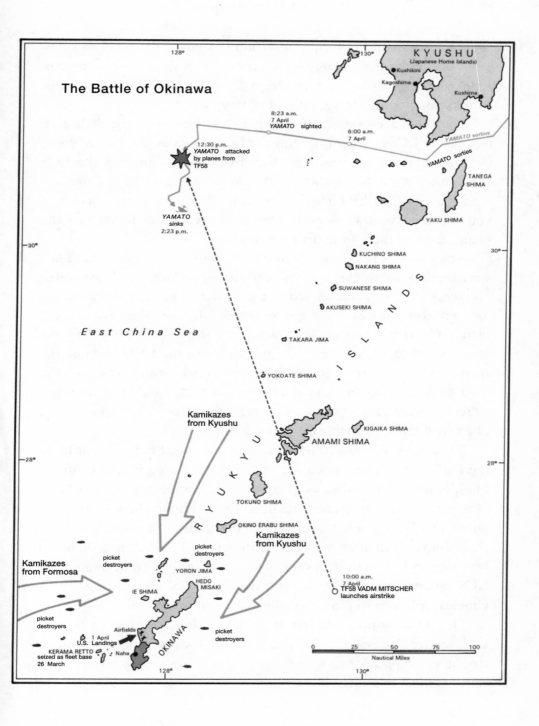

The Battle of Okinawa

KYUSHU
(Japanese Home Islands)

Kushikini
Kagoshima
Kushima

8:23 a.m.
7 April
YAMATO sighted

6:00 a.m.
7 April

YAMATO sorties

YAMATO sorties

12:30 p.m.
YAMATO attacked
by planes from
TF58

TANEGA
SHIMA

YAKU SHIMA

YAMATO
sinks
2:23 p.m.

30°

30°

KUCHINO SHIMA

NAKANG SHIMA

SUWANESE SHIMA

AKUSEKI SHIMA

East China Sea

TAKARA JIMA

ISLANDS

YOKOATE SHIMA

KIGAIKA SHIMA

Kamikazes
from Kyushu

AMAMI SHIMA

28°

28°

TOKUNO SHIMA

OKINO ERABU SHIMA

Kamikazes
from Kyushu

RYUKYU

picket
destroyers

picket
destroyers

YORON JIMA

10:00 a.m.
7 April
TF58 VADM MITSCHER
launches airstrike

Kamikazes
from Formosa

picket
destroyers

IE SHIMA

HEDO
MISAKI

picket
destroyers

U.S. Landings
1 April
Airfields

OKINAWA

KERAMA RETTO
seized as fleet base
26 March

Naha

128°

130°

0   25   50   75   100
Nautical Miles

land of Kyushu and from Formosa, and the Japanese launched thousands of kamikaze raids targeted against the U.S. fleet. With more than 1,300 ships to strike, the Japanese launched wave after wave of kamikazes, often in large groups of fifty or more.

The kamikazes were seeking larger ships, but they nevertheless attacked the LCSs with a fury, and the LCSs gave as good as they got. But the enemy had advantages. Earl Blanton, a sailor from the LCS 118, remembered the kamikazes: "When the Japs gang up and they are suicidal, you don't have much chance, for no matter how good a shot you are, you have to shoot everything apart except the propellers of the planes to keep them from diving into you."

The toll was heavy on the men serving radar picket duty. They were on duty for weeks at a time with kamikaze attacks always possible, day or night. Okinawa had sixteen radar picket duty stations. On just one day, May 3, the ships on station 10 shot down twenty five planes. On May 4, fifty planes attacked the ships on station 1. Two destroyers and one LSM were hit by kamikazes; the LSM and one destroyer sank. The strain on the men was overwhelming. They were at their battle stations for days at a time. According to Blanton, the men were ". . . gaunt, red-eyed and stinking—they were scared. They were filled with terror, despair, rage and exhaustion."

The LCSs played a vital role in the final island-hopping battles of the Pacific war. The knowledge of their devastating firepower in the Philippines and Iwo Jima helped persuade a reluctant General Ushijima not to seriously contest the beachhead. Their valiant service was noticed by Halsey and Turner, and by the Japanese as well. The notorious Tokyo Rose often focused her threats on LCSs, calling them out by name and number in several broadcasts. Individual decorations of LCS sailors were numerous, with one Medal of Honor, three Navy Crosses and numerous Silver and Bronze Stars awarded.

One LCS skipper has left in his letters home a good account of such service. He was not the Medal of Honor winner, but in my opinion, he was typically heroic in the dutiful way of so many reservists. In this, I confess to a slight bias.

LIEUTENANT JOHN LEHMAN SR., USNR: AT WAR WITHOUT A PRIVATE SIGNAL

By 1945 the ratio of reserve to regular naval officers on active duty was 70 to 1. After Pearl Harbor it had become obvious that the Naval Academy could not begin to meet the demands for junior officers to man the fleet that would be needed to fight a war in Europe and the Pacific. The Army and Marines met its officer needs by commissioning from the enlisted ranks. During the course of the war more than half of Army and Marine officers had prior enlisted service. In the Navy only 2 percent came from enlisted ranks. The Navy wanted only university men for its officer corps.

Officer candidate schools were established at existing naval training centers, state maritime academies and certain other facilities. Special programs were also set up to train college and university students on their campuses. The graduates of these many institutions were normally given ninety days of intense naval discipline and training before being commissioned ensigns in the U.S. Naval Reserve. To the Academy ring knockers and the salty chiefs these were the "90 Day Wonders."

A typical example was John Lehman Sr. When war broke out he was a young executive with Bendix Avionics Company in Philadelphia. At 30 years old, married with one young child and another on the way, he was not eligible for the draft. Nor was he eligible for a commission through OCS, being overage. And because he was in what was categorized as a critical job for war production, he had no obligation to fight. But after his second child and first son, John Jr., was born in September 1942, he began to think about going to war.

In 1943 opportunities began to appear because the officer training programs could not fill the significant gap in the middle officer ranks from lieutenant through commander. As a result the Navy opened a selective direct commission program for older and more experienced executives with college degrees. Lehman was accepted for this program, commissioned a lieutenant j.g. and sent to the Navy's OCS at the New York Maritime Academy at Fort Schuyler. After completing the ninety-day course, he was selected for command of one of the new LCSs, *LCS-18*.

Lieutenant John Lehman, Sr., USNR, on the bridge of *LCS-18* off Okinawa,
April 1945. *Lehman Family Collection*

At San Diego, *LCS-18* went through amphibious, fire support, antiaircraft and gunnery training and was ordered to Pearl Harbor. In
March 1945, *LC- 18* proceeded, with Spruance's Fifth Fleet, to the invasion of Okinawa. She was part of the first wave of Admiral Turner's
Task Force Fifty-one.

By April 6 the Japanese counterattack came, with a massive air assault on the American ships. Six hundred ninety-nine Japanese aircraft,
including 355 kamikazes, introduced Task Force Fifty-one to suicide
attacks. On that day alone the Japanese sank four destroyers and two
large cargo ships and severely damaged twelve others, including four
more destroyers so badly hit they had to be scrapped. For three more
months, the task force was to be under virtually continuous air attack.
The only periods of respite were caused by severe weather. On April
10, Lehman wrote home:

We are in a very hot spot, and I am not speaking of the climate. We have been in action, and you can probably guess where. Also, it is not any fun: these Japs play for keeps. I have not been out of my clothes for two weeks, and . . . we keep the gun barrels hot. . . . I haven't set foot on shore in over a month. My last port was Guadalcanal, Purvis Bay. . . . At Guadalcanal the natives come around in their canoes, and will sell you *a* pineapple for $1, or a bunch of little green bananas for the same price . . . or they will trade you a string of beads made of shells for a fifteen pound can of corned beef. I thought we were the ones who traded beads to the poor ignorant savages!

Another crew member described the daily pressure, "The kamikaze attacks came both day and night and there was no rest for the weary crews. The planes came in high; they also came in low over the water to avoid radar. They attacked and it was over. Either you got him or he got you."

Every day, when the weather was good, the stresses were the same. In a combat action report dated April 18, 1942, Lehman mentioned that the gunner on the .50-caliber machine gun forward on the port side sent continuous fire into a kamikaze from the beginning of his dive until the plane crashed about 100 yards from the LCS's port bow. No other guns scored any hits and the entire action consumed less than thirty seconds.

Lehman was so impressed by the gunnery that he told the sailor who had so coolly tracked the kamikaze that he was putting the man up for a commendation for bravery under fire.

The young sailor said, "Captain, I don't deserve it. I was so scared that my knees buckled under me, and it was just luck that as I went down and the muzzle went up, the sight just happened to stay on him!"

On May 18 Lehman wrote home again: "There have been quite a few times lately when I have felt that someone must have been praying for me, and very efficaciously. I have done quite a lot of praying myself since I have been out here. I say without any shame whatever, that I have been scared stiff several times out here. We shot down two planes that suicide dived on us, and believe me there is nothing more scaring than to see one of them diving on you, and coming right through all the shells that you are throwing at him."

The sailor got his medal.

USS WILLIAM D. PORTER: "DON'T SHOOT WE'RE REPUBLICANS"

After a brief period at Kerama Retto to repair damage from the infamous typhoon of June 5, *LCS-18* steamed out of the harbor to join the destroyer *William D. Porter* on radar picket station 10. As the *LCS-18* approached the rendezvous with *Porter* she signaled the now traditional greeting to *Porter:* "Don't shoot we are Republicans." *Porter* was one of the best-known ships in the Pacific Fleet; she had earned the greeting in November 1943.

Porter was named after Commodore William David "Dirty Bill" Porter, the oldest son of the famous Commodore David Porter of *Essex* fame in the War of 1812. "Dirty Bill," as you might suspect, had a rakish reputation but distinguished himself in command of a later *Essex.* The ship named for him, DD579, was launched on September 27, 1942, at Orange, Texas, and commissioned on July 6, 1943. Next to baseball players, sailors are the most superstitious Americans. Almost immediately after her commissioning, *Porter* came to be known as a jinxed ship. When arriving at her first home port in Norfolk, Virginia, she collided with another destroyer while coming into the pier. Being one of the newest ships in the squadron, however, she was assigned to escort the newly commissioned battleship *Iowa* on a top-secret mission along with two other new destroyers. Once at sea and traveling across the Atlantic at flank speed it was learned that *Iowa* was carrying President Roosevelt, Secretary of State Hull and Fleet Admiral King on the way to meet with Churchill and Stalin at the Cairo and Teheran conferences.

By November 14 the weather had cleared and President Roosevelt requested that the ships engage in a weapons exercise with aerial target practice and simulated torpedo runs. Weather balloons were set loose and all of the guns on the battleship and destroyers blazed away until none were left. It was then time for the destroyers to make a simulated torpedo attack on *Iowa*. As *Porter* made her pass at *Iowa* she went through the simulated firing at a range of 6,000 yards—and lo and behold one torpedo left the tube toward *Iowa*.

Still maintaining radio silence, *Porter* attempted frantically to get *Iowa*'s attention by signal light. Failing that, she broke radio silence, calling for an immediate hard turn to starboard. Disbelieving at first, *Iowa* (in fact more maneuverable even than the destroyers) eventually made the hard turn to starboard. The President was notified and wheeled to the rail so he could see the torpedo. His Secret Service bodyguard drew his pistol. The torpedo exploded in the wake turbulence 1,000 yards away and made a lively display for the president.

The captain and officers were sent ashore with their careers ended, and *William D. Porter* found herself assigned to patrolling the Aleutian Islands. By now at every formation she joined or port she entered she was universally greeted with the signal, "Don't shoot we are Republicans."

After a refit in San Francisco she arrived in the Philippines in the autumn of 1944 and was in almost continuous action in shore bombardment and antiaircraft and was given credit for shooting down numerous Japanese aircraft. In late March she was assigned to the Okinawa invasion force and was soon on radar picket duty.

The morning of July 10 was quiet with a low cloud cover, which usually meant no kamikazes. Suddenly out of the clouds dove a "Val" dive-bomber. The Vals were made entirely of wood and fabric and were usually not visible on radar. They were slow but still capable of carrying a large bomb. The Val went for *Porter* but missed, hitting the sea not far from *Porter* and sinking almost immediately without an explosion. Yet somehow *Porter* managed to be directly over the top of the sunken Val when its bomb exploded underneath it. The explosion broke the back of the ship, splitting its seams and rupturing its steam lines. Engine rooms were flooded and the boilers extinguished. *Porter* started to sink fast by the stern.

LCS-18 immediately came to her assistance and, hanging mattresses over the rail, secured fast to *Porter* while sending firefighting parties over to assist in the attempt to save the ship. It soon became apparent that it could not be saved.

Directing his ship's efforts from the bridge, skipper Lehman suddenly observed his ship's cook, Steward's Mate McNair Johnson, leap over the rail and wade down into the sinking ship, entering a half-submerged hatch. He was never seen returning. In the furious efforts to get the last survivors off and to cast loose before the ship went down, Lehman assumed that the cook had been lost. Three hours after the explosion, the order to abandon *Porter* was given, and twelve minutes after that she heeled over to starboard and sank by the stern. Her crew suffered not a single fatal injury.

Steaming back to Kerama Retto loaded with survivors, Lehman held a ship's muster and found to his relief that Johnson was in fact aboard. He called him to the bridge and commended him for his bravery, telling him that he intended to put him in for a decoration. The young sailor replied "Gee, Captain, I don't deserve any medal. Three months ago we lost the last can opener on the ship and I've been opening cans with a fire axe ever since. I went down to their galley to retrieve their can opener before she sank. I cut it a little close since I had to swim underwater to get out, but here is the can opener!"

THE BATTLE FOR OKINAWA: THE FURY OF THE DIVINE WIND

The action described thus far was but a long prelude to the planned invasion of Japan. That began only 325 miles from the southernmost home island of Japan, Kyushu, in the Ryukyus Islands. The largest of these, Okinawa, sixty miles long and from two to eighteen miles wide, was chosen as the first step in the invasion. The Okinawa assault was on the scale of Normandy, with four army and two Marine divisions totaling 150,000 men being put ashore from a 1,300-ship armada (including forty aircraft carriers and eighteen battleships) on Easter Sunday, 1945.

The island was defended by 100,000 troops and auxiliaries of the Japanese Thirty-second Army deeply entrenched in a brilliantly designed system of tunnel redoubts. Learning from the earlier island invasions of the war, Japanese commander Lieutenant General Mitsuru Ushijima concentrated his forces in the mountainous southern third of the island and did not attempt to concentrate force at the water's edge. Admiral Raymond Spruance was in overall command with Vice Admiral Richmond Kelly Turner commanding the expeditionary force. The landing force was designated the Tenth Army and was commanded by Lieutenant General Simon Bolivar Buckner Jr. with more than 183,000 soldiers and Marines.

Little serious resistance was encountered during the first three days of the landing and the northern two-thirds of the island was secured with little difficulty. The serious fighting began on April 4 when the Americans encountered Ushijima's Machinato Line. Three months later the island was declared secured. The army and Marines had suffered 68,000 casualties, with more than 8,000 killed, one of them General Buckner. The Japanese army had fought virtually to the last man.

More horrifying, however, were the casualties among the civilian population, with estimates of between 100,000 and 200,000 killed. The Japanese army used Japan's civilians mercilessly, often sending massed refugees toward American lines at night to draw fire and clear mines. Thousands more died from the air and naval bombardment. Because the Japanese commanders had exhorted the entire population to fight to the death, there were mass suicides by civilians from the southern cliffs of the island.

Colonel Haromishi Yahara was the chief Japanese strategist. Unlike all of the senior commanders, he did not commit hara-kiri and was captured when the island was taken. His full account is authoritative: "The Japanese believed that, as in every other war, they would win this one, even at the cost of millions of lives." Okinawa's defenders fought for every inch of ground. Toward the end of the battle, General Ushijima issued his final order to his soldiers: "Every man in these fortifications will follow his superior officer's order and fight to the end for the sake of the motherland. . . . Do not suffer the shame of being taken prisoner. You will live for eternity."

The Okinawa experience left no doubt about the intention of the emperor and his high command to resist an invasion of the Japanese homeland to the last human being. There would be no surrender. The most decisive result of the battle was to convince wavering American leaders that, as one historian noted, "with such suicidal dedication on the part of the Japanese military and civilians alike, the planned invasion of Japan by twenty-two U.S. divisions would produce hundreds of thousands of American and millions of Japanese casualties. Use of the atomic bomb seemed a far more humane alternative to such carnage."

While the brutal land battle took place, the naval battle raged for eleven weeks just offshore. On June 21, the day Okinawa was declared secured, the last massed kamikaze raid on the Okinawa Task Force took place, sinking one amphib and damaging four others. The Navy had lost 4,900 men killed and nearly the same number wounded. They had significantly more killed than the Marine Corps ashore, and suffered more casualties in that one battle than in all previous wars combined. The Battle of Leyte Gulf had been the end of the Japanese fleet and the beginning of the kamikaze strategy. The eleven weeks of air attacks at Okinawa included 6,000 Japanese aircraft and 3,000 kamikazes. Thirty-six U.S. Navy ships were sunk and 243 separate ships and craft seriously damaged.

On July 8, with Okinawa at last secure, John Lehman Sr. wrote home:

I am very well, and also am enjoying the cool Pacific evenings. We finally got out of our hot spot and are now in a rear area for rest and repairs. I am living the life of Reilly. Ice cream every day, movies every night. Shore liberty consists of a place on the beach where they have some tables and serve canned beer from 1300 to 1700, whiskey from 1500 to 1700. The beer is ten cents a can, whiskey twenty cents a shot, with ice. No soda, no ginger ale, no nothing. Also canned peanuts. At 1700 they pour (the sailors) back onto the Liberty boat which runs out to the anchorage, where they hoist (them) aboard your ship. There is also a ball field a basketball court and four or five horseshoe pits. A place for a real wild time, especially the nightlife. . . .

V-J Day

The war in the Atlantic ended on May 8. German U-boats had remained in action to the very end, but had ceased being a significant threat by mid-1943. In August 1944, the Allies landed in southern France to modest German resistance. The Axis navies were no longer a real factor and the bulk of the Royal Navy was shifted to the Pacific in March 1945.

Even thus reinforced, however, victory in the Pacific might have been months or even years away but for the bomb. The suicidal determination of the Japanese at Okinawa undoubtedly swung the balance in Washington for use of the atomic bomb. On July 16, the first atomic device was exploded in New Mexico, and on August 6 the B-29 *Enola Gay* dropped one of only two atomic bombs then built, on the city of Hiroshima, killing more than 70,000 people. Three days later the second bomb was dropped on Nagasaki, killing more than 20,000 people. On August 14, Japan surrendered, but with the fleet still in full-scale action, there was uncertainty when Nimitz ordered a stop to all combat operations. "Bull" Halsey instructed the Third Fleet as follows: "Hostilities have ceased but if approached by any Japanese aircraft, shoot them down in friendly fashion."

On August 29 the Third Fleet entered Tokyo Bay. Among the less imposing of the victorious armada were the small formation of battle-scarred and somewhat rusty LCSs, including *LCS-18*, fresh from Okinawa. As LCSs steamed slowly in file to their assigned anchorage further down the bay, well below the big boys, they cut across the path of a spanking new cruiser that was slowly looking for its own anchorage. The cruiser blasted its horn and immediately signaled to the lead LCS, demanding the private signal of the commanding officer. Only Annapolis graduates had private signals, which were their lineal number on the list of the Regular Navy. Reserve officers had no private signals. Virtually all of the LCS skippers were ninety-day wonders from civilian universities. While some went Regular Navy after the war and made careers, most were anxious to return to civilian life. And, like the Air Force's system of rotation home after twenty-five combat missions, the Navy had developed a system of points for reserve officers that involved time in combat, decorations, etc. Fifty-nine points were needed to obtain release from active duty. In response to the angry signal from the skipper of the cruiser, no doubt an Academy ring-knocker, the LCS skipper signaled back, "Commanding Officer has no private signal but does have fifty-nine points."

On September 2, by direction of President Truman the Japanese surrender documents were signed aboard his favorite ship, *Missouri*, which had dropped anchor at the exact spot where Commodore Perry had anchored almost a century before, and the war was at an end.

THUS ENDED THE GREATEST naval war in history. The United States Navy was in total command of the seas and held in awe by the world. While a major demobilization began immediately, the victory had a permanent effect on the global outlook of the American people, and a transforming impact on every sailor who served.

No sooner had the surrender been signed, however, than the Navy's leaders were first to recognize that a new kind of war was commencing.

VIII

THE COLD WAR

As the Second World War came to an end, the Cold War began. The Allied conferences at Yalta and Potsdam effectively divided the world into spheres of influence. The evidence is very thin that Stalin ever considered anything else than a resumption of the Marxist-Leninist struggle with capitalism when the Allied war effort was over. No matter what the western democracies had done, the Iron Curtain would have come down on Eastern Europe.

The question—*What else could have been done?*—is far more interesting when applied to Mao Tse-Tung and the Chinese communists, and to Ho Chi Minh and the Vietnamese communists. Without doubt, both were committed Marxist-Leninists, but one is tempted to believe that a more imaginative American diplomacy might have produced a far less destructive course in Southeast Asia.

Policy views in the United States were divided at WWII's end. Many in the Truman administration were optimistic that Stalin, despite his rhetorical truculence, would actually prove defensive and benign. Others, notably James Forrestal and George Marshall, were far more skeptical and fearful of Soviet intentions. The differences in the administration were reflected in public opinion; an anticommunist consensus did not emerge fully until the Korean War. Even when Stalin in February 1946 effectively issued a declaration of Cold War in a speech reaffirming the inevitability of war with capitalism and announcing the first of three five-year plans to prepare for it, many in the administration and the media still hoped for the best.

Not long after Stalin's bellicose speech, Winston Churchill responded with his famous "Iron Curtain" speech given at Fulton, Missouri. The Cold War had begun, and Stalin soon began testing the de facto boundaries of the spheres of influence. The year 1946 saw Soviet moves to occupy Iranian oil fields in Azerbaijan, to force Turkey into sharing control of the Dardanelles, and to support actively the communist insurgency in Greece. Because of the deep divisions within the Truman administration, the American response was confused, though occasionally vigorous as in Iran and Turkey.

In 1947, the Rio Pact was signed, establishing a regional security organization for the Americas, and in 1948 the Marshall Plan was approved to help stabilize rapidly the economic and military strength of the western European nations. The most historic of all Cold War initiatives, the North Atlantic Treaty Organization, was established in 1949 and was subsequently followed with a pact between Australia, New Zealand and the United States in 1951; the Southeast Asia Treaty Organization in 1954; and eventually the Central Treaty Organization with Iran, Pakistan and Turkey in 1957.

The lines of the Cold War were drawn, and through the first five years of it, James Vincent Forrestal would be the leading advocate of a tough military approach to the aggressive challenges of the Soviet Union.

James V. Forrestal: Cold War Architect and Naval Martyr

As the Cold War recedes into history, its heroes and villains begin to slip into the shadows. Government institutions do not change as rapidly, however; today we take for granted the existence of the National Security Council and the Department of Defense. Yet both are not only artifacts of the Cold War, but of one man in particular: James Vincent Forrestal.

Forrestal's early death and the eminence of his contemporaries have made of him an almost forgotten figure. He was not an easy man to understand even by contemporaries who knew him well. Yet the record brims with his achievements even where he did not entirely succeed. He was truly the man who tried to do too much. The effort killed him.

Forrestal was born to a comfortable Irish-American family in 1892. His father was a successful builder in Matteawan, New York, which later merged with the adjoining town, Fishkill Falls, to become Beacon. Forrestal's father, a local Democratic Party leader, was an early supporter of an upcoming Dutchess County politician, Franklin Roosevelt, who once stayed in the Forrestal house and who ended every campaign in his political career with a final speech at Beacon.

Beacon proved too small for Forrestal, a handsome boy of obvious intellectual talent. James was intended by his mother for the priesthood but he had no such leanings. Another departure from his mother's wishes gave him his character-laden face. Forrestal became quite fond of boxing, and twice had his nose broken; he apparently liked the rough, ominous appearance it gave him because he never had it fixed. A beautifully tailored man, the combination of sophisticated dress and flattened Irish nose implied a man at home in many worlds.

After one year at Dartmouth, he transferred to Princeton University, where he was editor of the paper and boxing champion. In the years when a college degree was possessed only by the very few, Forrestal epitomized the observation that more than a college degree, the college experience, including its manifold contacts, was the key to success. Having completed four years, he left Princeton in 1915 without a degree because of a dispute with his English teacher. He never looked back.

Forrestal volunteered for the Naval Air Corps and earned his wings at Pensacola, but too late to see action in World War I. With the help of his Princeton friends he got a job at the Dillon, Read investment bank as a bond salesman and quickly prospered. With newfound wealth, Forrestal became a charter member of the Gatsby set. He abandoned the Catholicism of his youth and joined the sexually hyperactive pleasure-seekers on Long Island. But he was never really "of" this group and retained throughout his life a curious detachment which made him both participant and critic of America's high-rolling WASP society. And Forrestal was different.

The social lionesses of the day, for example, reported that he often carried books to their parties. It was an affectation, but he also read the books, preferring history and philosophy. At first swearing off marriage, he wed Josephine Ogden suddenly on October 13, 1926. Ogden, then a *Vogue* columnist, came from a sedate family, was something of a social climber, but possessed an irreverent wit and great style. They made a dramatic couple for a while, not least because of their publicly "open" marriage which allowed each partner adventure. When the charm wore off, Forrestal stayed with his increasingly alcoholic and erratic "Josie" and their two boys. Not much of a family man, he was self-absorbed, self-reliant and very much a loner. His dashing style and guarded personality made him of great interest to several novelists, a few of whom—John Dos Passos and John O'Hara, for example—put him barely disguised into their stories.

Forrestal and many of his acquaintances during this time became the class that Franklin Roosevelt attacked until he and the nation needed them in 1940. But Forrestal, again comfortable playing two roles, was a Roosevelt sympathizer. Through luck and skill, he retained his fortune after 1929. Worth over $5 million at the age of 40 in 1932, he could do whatever he wanted. Luckily for America, this proved to be public service.

While Forrestal owes his reputation to the post-World War II period, he was arguably the key civilian in organizing the logistics of the U.S. Navy to fight the war. Soon after Pearl Harbor he was called to Washington. He served as one of FDR's prized assistants for only two months, but, as one of the half-dozen men who actually carried out the President's wishes, he had a large impact. (He apparently worked out a clandestine operation to counter Nazi influence in Latin America, meeting in the process the young Nelson Rockefeller.) Seeing his chance to do real war work, Forrestal secured appointment as the undersecretary of the Navy under Frank Knox, a Theodore Roosevelt Republican.

Another naval aviator, Robert Lovett, Forrestal's close friend and a distinguished operator in his own right, well described America's defense establishment in 1940 when he wrote to Forrestal, "There is so much dead wood at the War Department that it constitutes a positive fire hazard." To the Navy, Forrestal rapidly brought efficiency and speed. The fleet swelled from 1,099 vessels to over 80,000 during his tenure, including eight new battleships and ninety-five new aircraft carriers. Forrestal's background in finance and his intimate knowledge of American industry made him a genius in turning America into the famous "arsenal of democracy."

Forrestal also gained a good deal of experience in what he called the human frictions. After Knox died on April 28, 1944, Forrestal became secretary of the Navy. CNO Admiral Ernest J. King was a maverick from the old Navy and shared with his colleagues a contempt for civilian authority. (King's daughter described her father as "the most even-tempered man in the Navy—he is always in a rage.") King said of Forrestal, "I didn't like him, and he didn't like me." Because Forrestal was ruthless as well, this made for some colorful contests. King fought hard against the wartime Joint Chiefs of Staff organization, and FDR himself had to intervene time and again to bridle the Navy's assertion of supremacy. In these disputes, Forrestal championed civilian control but also the Navy; after all, as secretary of the Navy, he was both a leader of the service and a cabinet member required to think beyond partisanship. Like every secretary of the Navy worth his salt, Forrestal became both ally and adversary of the admirals club.

Nonetheless Forrestal was by the end of the war a true devotee of the service. "He looks Navy," said one observer, "and is Navy . . . tough and elegant together."

Busy though he was, Forrestal's hyperactive mind soon began to fix on a larger strategic problem, that of relations with America's wartime ally, the Soviet Union. Forrestal's readings of Marx had persuaded him that "Soviet Russia" (the popular phrase of the time) would be an implacable opponent of American democracy. He was unhappy with FDR's personal diplomacy and disillusioned by Yalta. In one of his wartime speeches as SECNAV, Forrestal had declared that "the only insurance of peace" was to keep "the means to wage war . . . in the hands of those nations that hate war." The Soviets, ideologically committed to class warfare, were in his view determined on conflict as a principle of policy. The only way to handle them was to assemble a preponderance of force on the U.S. side.

These ideas were not widely held in Washington in 1943–45. After Roosevelt's death a sharp debate had broken out over U.S.-Soviet relations. Forrestal led those who argued that the U.S.S.R. would never behave like a normal state; its ideology seemed to remind him of a fanatical religion that might be resisted but not tamed. In early 1946, a series of aggressive Soviet actions and speeches swung the inside debate in Forrestal's direction. On February 12, George Kennan, a Soviet expert in the U.S. diplomatic corps, sent his famous "Long Telegram" expounding on Moscow's combination of aggressive ideology and Russian expansionism. Forrestal himself had actually commissioned a study on this subject by a staff assistant, later called the Willet report, but this had been regarded as much too simplistic. Forrestal had Kennan brought home to re-write the study incorporating the containment ideas in Kennan's famous cable. The result was the famous "X" article, which Forrestal arranged to be published anonymously in *Foreign Affairs*. It became the blueprint for America's cold war strategy for the next forty years.

Once the Soviet danger was understood, it followed for Forrestal that the rapid and chaotic demobilization of the U.S. forces was a mistake. For a short time, he and others believed that the U.S. nuclear monopoly would provide a deterrent; the crises over Greece, Turkey and Iran, and Secretary of State Byrnes's unsuccessful attempts to use the bomb as leverage, soon convinced him otherwise.

There then occurred a conflation of several ideas in Forrestal's mind that made him the foremost crusader for real change in Washington. The Soviet challenge was global and implacable; the U.S. had to lead in frustrating Moscow's designs; Washington could do so only if it assembled a coherent view of the problem and offered a coordinated strategic response. This had to be done at an institutional level, not only in the mind of the president, as FDR preferred to operate. The British wartime model of a coordinated military chiefs of staff organization superintended by a civilian-dominated strategic planning group appealed to Forrestal as a solution. He began to advocate a unified strategic approach at the cabinet level.

Unfortunately, Forrestal also found himself caught up in a different kind of unified approach, the drive by the Army and its air corps to create a single Defense Department that, in addition to creating an Air Force independent of the Army, would dethrone the Navy and give the U.S. what it had never had, a single-headed general staff system along the German model. That model had everything to commend it except victory. It invariably yoked strategy and tactics to a single rigid concept that, if mistaken, produced disaster. In 1946–47 that concept was nuclear war waged by the long-range bomber, downplaying the role of the Navy and virtually eliminating the Marines.

In the ensuing vicious battles for a fast-declining military budget, the Marines, heroes of the Pacific war, barely retained their independence; the Navy lost its cabinet department and became one of three coequal services; and the Army's future role was ambiguous. Forrestal fought hard for the Navy, to the point of antagonizing Truman, and managed to prevent the formulation of a general staff (there was no chairman of the Joint Chiefs at the outset). A key achievement in his mind was precisely the cabinet-level strategy body he had sought, the National Security Council. The newly created post of secretary of defense, the civilian in charge of the vast combined military organization, was also described in the legislation (the National Security Act of 1947) as the president's principal national security advisor. Forrestal was named as its first incumbent. But the bitter and prolonged power struggle had taken a terrible toll. After four years of making war, he was plunged into three years of desperate political infighting. As he gradually won the struggle his enemies became determined to destroy him.

By late 1948 he was burned out and did not know it. Those who have served in responsible positions in the national-security arena know that this can happen easily enough. The body accustoms itself to the punishing hours, the mind to the numbing routine. You can convince yourself that all is well. But sense of proportion, sense of humor and judgment ebb slowly away. And suddenly it is too late.

Forrestal's critical misjudgment lay not in his decision to become secretary of defense, though others thought that his Navy background would make him too partisan a leader. His misreading was not of the post, but of the President.

Truman admired Forrestal, but did not like him and did not like the Navy. The elegant Princetonian fit too well into Truman's "fancy Dan" conception of the Navy. Forrestal, on the other hand, did not care for Truman's poker playing or his friends. (On the one occasion when Forrestal, seeking to cultivate Truman, hosted a poker game, he got bored early and absented himself for most of the game. Truman, as usual, lost; Clark Clifford, as usual, paid the loss; and Forrestal's substitute, a naval aide, surprised his boss the next day by presenting him with several hundred dollars.) Forrestal knew that Truman's direct interest in national-security affairs was sporadic, his knowledge often spotty; he also knew of the President's desire to get the right people to do it for him. So Forrestal assumed that Truman would admire the bright new tool he had designed to coordinate high strategy, but somehow not reach for it himself. When it became clear that the President wanted to run the show from the White House, Forrestal was suddenly face to face with a double failure: he had responsibility but not much authority in a job he did not really want; simultaneously, he could not create the coordinated high strategy essential, in his view, to win the contest with the Soviet Union, because those around Truman, like Clark Clifford, were much more optimistic about Soviet intentions.

Forrestal was soon beset by another group of powerful adversaries. He was the first accurately to warn that the United States would soon become a net importer of oil and that our vital interests were engaged in the Persian Gulf. He established a permanent naval force based in Bahrain that remains to this day. But he vocally opposed the creation of the State of Israel. Motivated primarily by his fears for the Middle East oil supplies and that U.S. troops would be needed to rescue the Jews, Forrestal tried to place these considerations of the national interest at the center of the debate. In these views he kept good company; Dean Acheson, Marshall and many others opposed Truman's often erratic foreign policies. But Forrestal's colleagues kept quiet and encouraged him to carry on the debate long after it was obvious that the President was committed to the Zionists. Forrestal thereby made of himself a convenient target without having much influence over the inner counsels.

Forrestal's poor judgment in taking on such a role led to his vilification in the popular, pro-Zionist press and a lingering view that he was anti-Semitic. He was not, and a good deal less given to anti-Jewish gibes than, say, Truman himself. But the damage to his reputation during the Palestine question would be amplified into assaults on his role as the secretary of defense. And to make it much worse, the same deadly, creeping fatigue that was robbing his judgment on policy issues also made him thin-skinned. He began to take gutter journalists such as Drew Pearson seriously; scenting blood, they redoubled their pursuit with appalling personal attacks (now proved false) on Forrestal, his wife and even his children. Other opponents moved in for the kill. When I was a member of the Nixon White House staff I came to know the dean of White House reporters, John Osborne of *The New Republic*, who covered the Pentagon in Forrestal's day. Osborne told me that the topmost leaders of the Air Force regularly passed internal documents embarrassing to Forrestal directly to Osborne.

After Truman's reelection in 1948, the first DOD budget finished Forrestal. Despite Truman's insistence that it not exceed $15 billion, Forrestal worked up "professional" estimates that a minimum of $29 billion would be needed and then had to get them down to $16.9 billion in the face of the White House's growing exasperation. He and his small staff, overwhelmed by detail and frustrated by the refusal of the Joint Chiefs to agree on anything except the need for more money, waged guerrilla war with each of the services, Congress and the White House simultaneously. Having endured so much to protect the Navy in the bitter unification struggle, Forrestal was deeply hurt when even the admirals club turned on him. And throughout, he refused to trim his anti-Stalin warnings to the prevailing political winds. Truman decided to fire him.

On March 28, 1949, the day Forrestal left office, Truman gave him a surprise party with the full cabinet and Joint Chiefs in attendance. It was a genuine outpouring of affection. But it could not help, and before the afternoon was out, unable to face his departure from high office, Forrestal cracked. Three days later he had to be taken to Bethesda Naval Hospital. The official diagnosis was that he suffered from a version of combat fatigue. Forrestal seemed to respond to treatment, and he began meeting with a Catholic chaplain. Then, early on Sunday morning, May 22, 1949, he was found dead on the ground below an open pantry window of his sixteenth-floor suite. He had just finished copying portions of a Sophoclean poem wherein the hero Ajax contemplates suicide.

While it probably was indeed a suicide, there were some very odd circumstances that have left lingering suspicions to the present day. There were many who hoped, and others who feared, that a recovered Forrestal would someday return to power. He was viewed by the KGB as the most anti-Soviet of American figures. Conspiracy theorists base their case on some strange facts: when admitted to Bethesda, Forrestal was not put in the usual VIP suite on the first floor, but in an unused suite on the sixteenth-floor tower. All of the windows had bars bolted to the outside of the building but the bars on the pantry window were inexplicably removed before Forrestal's admission. Forrestal had hospital corpsmen assigned to be with him in shifts around the clock. The night Forrestal died the corpsman did not show up.

Truman showed the level of his respect for Forrestal by declaring three days of national mourning, stating "this able and devoted public servant was as truly a casualty of war as if he had died on the firing line."

Buried in Arlington with high honors, Forrestal was a popular and well-respected public servant. His close friend and adviser Robert Strausz-Hupé remembers him as an innately kind man, disdainful of politicians and possessed of a wry sense of humor. Not much of a manipulator, according to Strausz-Hupé, he "did miraculous work in a short time." Forrestal understood the Soviet threat early and founded the national-security organization that allowed the United States to fight and win a forty-year "twilight struggle."

In 1954, Forrestal's strategic vision was fittingly memorialized with the first new supercarrier, named USS *Forrestal.* It was to be followed by others.

NEW SECRETARY OF DEFENSE Louis Johnson, whom Forrestal had thought incapable of the post, immediately cancelled one of Forrestal's prime strategic initiatives, the building of *United States,* which was to be the first of a new class of supercarriers. He then ordered the immediate retirement of all but five of the Navy's existing carriers. Such stupidity helped to bring on the Korean War, and Johnson's forced resignation.

KOREA: TRUMAN'S WAR

The primal causes of the Korean War can be found in the end of World War II. At Yalta, Roosevelt had agreed to a Soviet-Chinese-American trusteeship for Korea, but it was never concluded. At war's end Russian troops occupied the northern industrialized half of the peninsula, and the U.S. Army hastily agreed to the 38th parallel as a line below which American forces would occupy. There was no thought of permanence, still less of the defensibility of this arbitrary line on a map of a destitute country smaller than the state of Utah.

A hurried Allied agreement was signed on August 15, 1945, and Korea, the "Land of the Morning Calm," an autonomous society since 661 A.D., was bisected in defiance of logic. North of the 38th parallel in the industrial half of the country, Japanese troops surrendered to the Russians; south of the parallel in the agrarian half, they raised their hands to the Americans. In Korea, the Iron Curtain could have come down without war, as it did in Europe, were it not for blunders in Washington.

After the communist victory in China in 1949, Mao came to view South Korea as a potential American base for retaking the mainland. He strongly supported Kim Il Sung's efforts to persuade Stalin to back Kim's invasion of the South.

When Louis Johnson slashed defense radically, ordering the retirement of all but five aircraft carriers, Stalin began to doubt that the U.S. would interfere. The muddled Truman administration then proceeded to leave Stalin no other possible conclusion.

In June, 1949, all U.S. combat troops were withdrawn from South Korea and then on January 12, 1950, in a speech that in retrospect seems incredible, Marshall's successor as secretary of state, Dean Acheson, omitted South Korea from his description of the U.S.'s defensive perimeter in Asia. The exclusion was explicitly confirmed later in the spring in hearings before the senate. Six months later, in the early morning hours of June 25, 1950, a spearhead of 150 Soviet-built T-34 tanks rumbled across the 38th parallel, followed by six divisions of infantry, totaling about 130,000 troops in all. North Korea, with full Soviet support, had invaded South Korea.

The North Korean army was well trained and equipped by the Soviets. The army had 25,000 hardcore veterans of the Chinese Communists' Manchurian campaign. With 180 Soviet-built airplanes, including the sturdy Yak-9 fighter, their air force was formidable when compared to the fledgling South Korean air force. The North Koreans also had over 100,000 trained reserves. Facing this onslaught was the Republic of Korea (ROK) army, if it could be called one, lacking tanks, artillery, anti-aircraft guns, armored personnel carriers and close-air support. Although there were eight divisions of infantry totaling about 100,000 men, they were in reality a poorly trained and ill-equipped constabulary force. Both the North and the South had only minuscule navies, mainly patrol craft and small gunboats.

The first North Korean objective was Seoul, the South's capital. If they could seize the small city that lay just south of the 38th parallel, their mission to unify the whole peninsula would swiftly follow.

Before the U.N. had time to deem it a "police action," Truman ordered MacArthur, who was headquartered in downtown Tokyo as the de facto viceroy of Japan, to shore up the ROKs with the naval and air forces at his disposal. MacArthur acted quickly, but even with air support, Seoul fell, and the North Koreans continued in their attack southward against feeble ROK resistance. Seeing the ROK army disintegrating in flight, Truman authorized the use of U.S. ground troops to stem the tide, but the ROKs continued to be driven down the peninsula into a small pocket of resistance know as the "Pusan Perimeter," just outside the port city of Pusan.

A masterstroke was needed to rescue South Korea. MacArthur would place the onus of the massive operation he envisioned on a depleted Navy.

Thanks to the power of Forrestal, the Navy had held its own as all of the services were cut back after World War II. But when Forrestal was replaced by Johnson, the Navy became the special target of deep cuts, resulting in the resignation of SECNAV John Sullivan and the firing of the CNO, Louis Denfeld. Both were replaced with more compliant men. By 1950, when South Korea was fighting for survival, the U.S. Navy had only eleven carriers able to deploy and only one available in the Pacific.

Fortunately, the relatively small Seventh Fleet was ready for action, owing to the leadership of Vice Admiral Arthur D. Struble. But the veteran of twenty-two amphibious operations during World War II, including Normandy, had only one carrier, *Valley Forge,* carrying one squadron of the new F-9F Panther jet fighters; another eighty prop-driven aircraft, including the new but untested AD Skyraiders; and the old battle-tested F-4U Corsairs.

Struble threw everything he had into the battle. His destroyers escorted evacuation ships carrying American civilians out of the area and ammunition ships back in. *Valley Forge* launched deep strikes into the North to cut the supply lines of the advancing North Korean army by concentrating on airfields and rail facilities. Her planes cratered runways, blew apart hangars, revetments, fuel farms, warehouses and parked aircraft. Ammo dumps were a favorite of pilots because of the spectacular secondary explosions. Their bombs, rockets and cannon fire also wrecked rail yards, repair sheds and roundhouses. They razed highway bridges and rail trestles and destroyed trains by the hundreds. The only targets that frustrated them were the railroad tunnels.

In the early days of the war, the Navy made tremendous contributions. During the counteroffensive air campaign in the North, the cruiser *Juneau,* named for the cruiser lost with the five Sullivan Brothers at Guadalcanal, had the honor of firing the first shore bombardment of the war. And when the ROKs, now reinforced with the U.S. Army Twenty-fourth and Twenty-fifth Infantry divisions and the First Cavalry Division, were surrounded on three sides at Pusan with their backs to the sea, amphibious ships off-loaded reinforcing troops and thousand of tons of desperately needed supplies. When the Marines arrived in Pusan, there were no airfields in friendly hands and they depended on the air support from the carriers offshore, which turned out to be quite effective, and Air Force fighters at extreme range from their bases in Japan.

To keep the defensive perimeter from caving in, three more flattops had arrived to support *Valley Forge:* the fast carrier *Philippine Sea* and the escort carriers *Badoeng Strait* and *Sicily.* They launched Skyraiders carrying 2,000-pound bombs and Corsairs carrying four 500-pound bombs or four napalm bombs, air-to-ground rockets, and 20-mm cannon. Eager naval aviators, both Navy and Marine, earthquaked enemy positions outside the perimeter so effectively that when asked which American weapon they feared the most, North Korean captives replied: "The blue airplanes."

CINCPAC Admiral Arthur W. Radford and CNO Forrest Sherman promised soon to reinforce the Seventh Fleet with three heavy carriers hastily being reactivated. Meantime, Struble was to support MacArthur, who had been put in command of all United Nations forces marshalling in the region. MacArthur soon conceived his sagacious counterstroke: an amphibious envelopment of the port city of Inchon on South Korea's west coast, adjacent to the capitol of Seoul.

THE INCHON LANDING

The strong-minded commander of the Seventh Fleet's Amphibious Force was Rear Admiral James Doyle, a veteran of both Guadalcanal and Tulagi. Doyle opposed landing at Inchon and correctly noted that such a plan violated every known principle of amphibious warfare:

"MacArthur wanted to send ships up the narrow Flying Fish Channel leading to Inchon, a passage guarded by Wolmi Do Island's heavy guns, and to disembark his assault troops in an area of thirty-foot tidal range onto docks situated in the middle of a city known to contain an enemy garrison."

The veteran First Marine Division of Guadalcanal fame was tasked to make the landing, but its commanding general, the revered, soft-spoken, intellectually inclined Major General O.P. Smith also had his doubts about the undertaking. No shrinking violet, he had commanded a regiment at Cape Gloucester and had participated in the Peleliu and Okinawa operations. Smith sided with Doyle and recommended a more suitable landing site about thirty miles south of Inchon. In the back of Smith's mind was the fact that the requisite high tide needed to get his troops ashore at Inchon occurred only four days a month. A look at the tide tables for the fall of 1950 revealed that those tides would come on or around September 15, October 11 and November 3. Both Smith and Doyle knew the North Koreans could read the tide tables, too, and make their defensive plans accordingly.

The JCS directed that a complete copy of the Inchon operation plan be provided to them for review. MacArthur ignored them, submitting only a sketchy concept. Although well aware of the concept's flaws, the anxious chiefs folded and reluctantly gave their unanimous approval on August 28, 1950, despite their grave reservations about the unusual thirty-two-foot tidal reach at Inchon—the second highest in the world—and the fifteen-foot high stone wall above the rocky beachhead.

The Navy carried out a two-day bombardment and then launched the landing force, with four carrier airwings providing close air support.

Amazingly, the landing went off without a hitch. The First Marine Division under the imperturbable Smith took Inchon on September 15, 1950, liberated Seoul by the 27th, seized the major airfield at Kimpo, and then helped the U.S. Army cut off and rout the overextended North Korean army. Everyone breathed a sigh of relief. Bull Halsey, retired on Fishers Island, New York, fired off a hyperbolic telegram to MacArthur, further inflating his already considerable ego

by declaring that, "The Inchon landing is the most masterly and strategic stroke in all history."

MacArthur's gamble had paid off, and it looked like his deep and
surprising envelopment had shortened, if not won, the war and saved
countless U.N. casualties. The troops might even be home by Christmas. Inchon paid dividends in other ways, too. After the Second World
War, the need for an active-duty amphibious force was questioned by
many, including Truman, who tried to do away with the Marine Corps
in 1948. The Inchon Landing gave the Corps a new lease on life. Up
until that time, shortsighted, "atomic age" strategic thinking saw amphibious doctrine as passé. To marshal troop-carrying ships, supporting
forces and supplies in a small amphibious objective area would present
too lucrative a target for a single atom bomb. Inchon made strategists
take another look.

Meanwhile, basking in accolades from around the world, the
supremely confident MacArthur wanted to capitalize on his brilliant
success by swinging clear around the peninsula and landing the First
Division on North Korea's east coast at Wonsan. Truman and the U.N.
agreed that he could go north of the 38th parallel, and he did so on October 1, 1950. Ignominiously dubbed "Operation Yoyo" by its reluctant
participants, it proved to be as disastrous as Inchon was successful.
Russian sea mines, laid under the supervision of Russian mine-warfare
experts, were the problem. The fields contained some 3,000 mines of
various types, and two of the three U.S. minesweepers dispatched from
Hawaii by Admiral Radford met with tragedy.

Operation Yoyo was put on hold until the mines could be taken
care of. The U.S. Navy had lost sea control for the first time since
World War II. When O.P. Smith's Inchon veterans finally made a non-
tactical landing in Wonsan nearly two weeks later, on October 26, it had
already been captured by South Korean troops and a Bob Hope USO
show was in progress.

The Korean War—and the Cold War—rapidly changed when on
Thanksgiving night, 1950, Lieutenant General Walton H. Walker's
Eighth Army encountered a huge force along the Chongchon river.
The Army was Chinese.

The Chinese routed the Eighth Army and drove inexorably south, aided by President Harry Truman, who forbade sorties north of the Yalu in fear of provoking the Soviets. Chafing at these restrictions, Navy and Air Force pilots—who violated the line whenever they could get away with it—nonetheless amassed a stunning seven-to-one kill ratio in air-to-air combat, with a total of 839 confirmed Soviet MiGs shot down by war's end (most by Air Force F-86s). In the air above the Yalu, American pilots were engaging Russian pilots and jets head on. The Cold War was not very cold at all.

Alas, the pilots' heroics in shooting down planes and knocking down the bridges across the Yalu did not slow the massive Chinese counter-offensive. Manchurian weather froze the Yalu solid, allowing easy access to North Korea by Chinese infantrymen, who, in their padded winter uniforms, moved by night.

Meanwhile, an epic battle took place at the Chosin Reservoir involving the First Marine Division, which had become completely surrounded by an entire Chinese army. Led by O.P. Smith, the Marines broke out of the encirclement and fought a harrowing rear-guard action, mauling seven Chinese divisions in the process with help from more "blue airplanes" off the carriers *Philippine Sea, Valley Forge, Leyte Gulf* and *Princeton,* and Air Force heavy and medium bombers.

Aboard the ships, the tired crews struggled with the additional burden of constantly de-icing their equipment in order to sustain ongoing flight operations. This teamwork led to the Marine, U.S. Army and ROK evacuation off the docks of the east coast port city of Hungnam where Admiral Doyle was waiting with 76 cargo ships and transports. To help Doyle pull off this huge evacuation of 100,000 troops, 100,000 refugees and 17,000 pieces of equipment, the Seventh Fleet stood off with the battleship *Missouri,* two heavy cruisers, eight destroyers and three rocket-firing ships pounding the encircling communists.

Then, with the war going badly, Truman fired MacArthur. On April 11, 1951, after eleven months of the war. Matthew Ridgway replaced the American Caesar.

It was the beginning of a new kind of war for the Navy. In consultations with Ridgway, Admiral Turner Joy ruddered the Navy into support of a reinvigorated land campaign. Joy began laying siege to communist coastal ports and bombarding coastal installations. More navy-blue airplanes and haze-gray gun turrets interdicted North Korean truck traffic, broke up their troop formations, silenced their numerous shore batteries and made their observation posts uninhabitable. To further squeeze the North Koreans, civilian fishermen were denied access to offshore fishing beds, thereby cutting off a major source of the North's traditional food supply.

By June 1951, the enthusiasm of Chinese and North Korean leaders was waning. The Chinese, in particular, were losing men, material and equipment at a terrific rate; ultimately about 200,000 men were killed, most by air attack. The Chinese and North Korean leadership decided to sit down at the truce talks at Panmunjom and try to salvage their losing position.

Thereafter, the Korean War became static, with little maneuvering for either tactical or strategic advantage on the ground. Politics and diplomacy came to the forefront, and both sides essentially stood down to let talks continue toward an armistice that was finally agreed to on July 27, 1953. After thirty-seven months the war ended, and the Seventh Fleet's bluejackets rested, her big guns fell silent and her blue airplanes launched no more into North Korean skies.

THE KOREAN WAR had a lasting impact on the Navy. It was fought with the reactivated ships and aircraft of WWII, and manned by reactivated sailors and aviators from that war. The success of the latter established the Naval Reserve as a fundamental element of naval power in the Cold War.

The one entirely new naval weapon used in the war was the jet fighter. The intense use of the F-9F Panther and the F-2H Banshee in three years of combat added a new dimension to the power an aircraft carrier could project. The anti-navalism that had gained ascendancy in Washington prior to Korea had been totally discredited by events. The

"Dirty Bill," the oldest son of David Porter famous captain of *Essex* had a sporty reputation. The World War II destroyer named for him had worse luck. *U.S. Naval Historical Center*

Destroyer *William D. Porter* sinking after Kamikaze attack off Okinawa July 10, 1945. *LCS-18* is secured to the port quarter, taking off survivors—and their can-opener. *Official U.S. Navy Photograph*

A Japanese Zero Kamikaze about to hit the carrier *White Plains* off Okinawa. *U.S. Naval Institute*

Carrier-based F-9F Panthers on the attack going "feet dry" over Korea. *U.S. Naval Institute*

Secretary of the Navy and first Secretary of Defense James V. Forrestal, tough and elegant. *U.S. Naval Institute*

Admiral Rickover in his prime, and in his rarely worn uniform. *U.S. Naval Institute*

There were unusual challenges in MacArthur's landing at Inchon, like this fifteen foot wall and the second highest tides in the world. *U.S. Naval Institute*

USS *Parche*. Her sailors earned many medals for bravery on mysterious missions. *Courtesy John Dale USS* Parche *Association*

Captain Grace Hopper dragging the navy into the digital age. *U.S. Naval Institute*

James E. Williams, BM1, USN, receives the Medal of Honor from President Lyndon B. Johnson at the White House, May 14, 1968. *U.S. Naval Historical Center*

One of the "Black Ponies"—OV-10 Broncos—attacking a Viet Cong bunker with Zuni rockets in the Mekong Delta, South Vietnam. *Official U.S. Navy Photograph*

A-6 Intruders inbound to North Vietnam from Yankee Station. Their motto was "We go deeper, stay longer, and deliver a bigger load." *Official U.S. Navy Photograph*

PBR on patrol in the Mekong Delta, South Vietnam. *U.S. Naval Institute*

Admiral James L. Holloway III wearing medals and ribbons from four wars. *U.S. Naval Institute*

The high-tech Tomahawk cruise missile heads to Baghdad with an accuracy of ten feet, launched from the forty-seven-year-old *Wisconsin* during Desert Storm. *Official U.S. Navy Photograph*

Marine on patrol in Beirut, 1983. *U.S. Naval Institute*

AH-1J Cobras. They were invaluable in supporting the marines and rangers in Grenada. *U.S. Naval Institute*

Navy would now get its supercarriers and remain at the forefront of deterrence for the next four decades of the Cold War.

The basic rules of the war would nonetheless be defined by atomic and nuclear power. While the Korean War proved that the atomic bomb had not revolutionized all of warfare, atomic technology would soon revolutionize undersea warfare.

James Forrestal as secretary of defense, and Chester Nimitz as chief of naval operations became early advocates for the adaption of nuclear power to submarines. Nimitz began the program for development of a nuclear submarine in the last days of his tenure. One of the first engineering officers assigned by BuShips to the Oak Ridge, Tennessee, laboratory of the Atomic Energy Commission to work on this top-secret project was Hyman Rickover.

ADMIRAL HYMAN G. RICKOVER: NUCLEAR HIGH PRIEST

The Navy has often benefited from the services of single-minded men, those who found a special purpose and pursued it to the end against all opposition. Such a man was Hyman George Rickover, who deservedly laid claim to the title "Father of the Nuclear Navy." But "Rick," as he was known within the service, did not stop at his objective, the safe and efficient employment of nuclear power in warships. He went on and built a political base that enabled almost complete independence from the Navy. He asserted almost total control over Navy personnel policy and over the decades created an elite corps of nuclear officers who performed magnificently—but owed allegiance to Rickover. He did much good but he stayed too long. And thereby hangs a tale that begins with the steam Navy of the 1920s and ends in Ronald Reagan's White House sixty years later.

There are many legends about Hyman Rickover, and the admiral did little to clear them up. Sources agree that he was born in a small Polish village, but his Navy file says in 1900, his Chicago public school

file 1898. His parents were Jewish immigrants, the father a tailor and
Hyman their only child. He gained admittance to the Naval Academy
Class of 1922, partly through the intervention of Chicago's so-called
Jewish Congressman, the Democrat Adolph Sabath.

There has been much political attention to the issue of Rickover's
Jewish background and its effect on his career. Commentators have
been tempted to ascribe Rickover's later troubles to anti-Semitism, but
the evidence is rather slim. Rickover was among seventeen professing
Jews in a class of 955, by far the largest contingent of Jews in the history of the academy to that point. No doubt the dislike of Jews that
pervaded some segments of the American population afflicted many
officers as well. But Rickover was no Uriah Philips Levy. He rarely
complained of anti-Semitism and went out of his way to distance himself from Judaism, becoming an Episcopalian and opening a long quarrel with his parents by formally writing them that he no longer
considered himself Jewish. When the Navy failed to promote Rickover
to admiral, New York senator Jacob Javits, himself Jewish, put it accurately: "It's more a Billy Mitchell case than a Dreyfus case."

This Billy Mitchell case was long in developing but there were
early signs that Rickover would not be a typical academy graduate. He
was a "nerd": his work was his life, he detested the social and protocol
side of the Navy, and took little pleasure in the arts of navigation and
warfare. He was fascinated by the technology of propulsion—the engine room and its associated machinery—that gave a ship life on the
ocean. After service on various destroyers and the battleship *Nevada*,
he earned a master's degree in electrical engineering from Columbia
and in 1937 became an EDO—"engineering duty only," later engineering duty officer. Rickover served briefly on the submarine *Finch* at
a time when such service was considered undesirable. This apparently
unremarkable sailor would do much to make sure that submariners in
the U.S. Navy would never again be regarded as average.

Like the great naval leaders of World War II, Rickover was rescued
by events. The advent of nuclear power and then the Cold War turned
Rickover from unknown EDO into one of the most celebrated and
controversial figures of his time. Despite Forrestal's best efforts, the

unification of the services came with a loss of the Navy's influence at the cabinet level. The triumphant carriers and battleships of WWII were now overshadowed by strategic bombers. The Navy knew that it had to carve a role for itself in the nuclear era. Contrary to Rickover mythology, his assignments to the Oak Ridge Laboratory and later the newly founded Atomic Energy Commission enjoyed the full support of the Navy brass. The famous "dual hat" arrangement, whereby Rickover served as the safety officer of the AEC while simultaneously in charge of nuclear-reactor systems at the Navy, was wholly the product of his patron, Vice Admiral Earle W. Mills, head of BuShips. CNO Nimitz, in turn, had jumpstarted the effort by making sure that one of his last acts before retiring was to provide for the development of a nuclear submarine.

Still, it was Rickover with his "discipline of technology" approach who pulled it all off. While the Navy debated whether it should use scarce funds to develop a nuclear weapon or nuclear propulsion, Rickover, the one-time submariner, saw that a nuclear reactor would turn a submarine into a true submersible. Once freed of the necessity to use diesel engines, the nuclear-powered submarine suddenly became a far more capable warship, able to exploit both its newfound speed and concealment. This strategic insight was not Rickover's alone, but he, and perhaps no other, could engineer it to reality.

Radical technologies, Rickover would say, required conservative engineering. He was fully aware of the dangers of nuclear power and determined to contain them safely. To do so, he created a unique system, built around a creed of excellence, monastic living and a singular focus on the "job." In the pre-computer age, he invented a fail-safe system built on human redundancies. These humans would themselves be very special men, cloned as closely as he could clone them to his own impossible standards of fitness, devotion to duty and austere living. He personally interviewed each new candidate for his program, selecting almost solely high-performing math and science majors from Annapolis and NROTC. Selectees were then sent away to his nuclear-power school, which he designed, staffed and supervised. It was a nuclear monastery.

The engineering specialist had been let loose to engineer a new Navy, and this is exactly what he did. The results were not what the Navy expected, but by 1951–52, Rickover had done what he had been assigned to do. The revolutionary submarine *Nautilus* was well on the way to completion. The Navy organization dominated both the AEC on the one side and the prime contractor, the Electric Boat division of General Electric, on the other side. Rickover had established the highest personnel standards and written the manuals with zero tolerance for error and slack. But the Navy was already tiring of Rickover's methods. In Rickover they had a man who did not go out of his way to befriend naval colleagues.

Thus it came about that Rickover was twice passed over for promotion, normally the prelude to retirement. But Rickover did not want to retire. He persuaded himself that he was indispensable to the new nuclear Navy and he then persuaded both Congress and the media of the same thing. This was a winning combination. His supporters in Congress withheld confirmation of all promotions to admiral until the Navy submitted Rickover's nomination to rear admiral. Rickover was promoted. The same procedure was repeated for promotions to two, three and four stars. After he reached mandatory retirement age every president from Eisenhower to Carter gave him two-year extensions. He had a mighty instrument with which to smite his enemies. Congress liked to stick it to the brass and the press loved a military man out of step with his colleagues.

It was the beginning of a long guerrilla war—between Rickover's Navy and the "other" Navy. On the one side, a lean, profane little man who worked for years in relative anonymity out of a converted ladies' restroom, and regaled the Congress with true stories of stupidity, waste and mismanagement while seeming to perform ever-increasing miracles with submarines that traveled to the North Pole or circumnavigated the world underwater. On the other side—according to the media—were the be-medalled ranks of the high-living admirals, with their ever-increasing demands for money, muddled jargon and self-protective excuses for delays or blunders. For every snub that they had ever given him over his long career, Rickover exacted revenge by obtaining the honors the Navy valued most: the Congressional Gold Medal, ranking him with Admirals Richard E. Byrd and Ernest J. King; promotion to rear admiral, vice admiral, then full admiral, four stars for a uniform that he almost never wore. Indeed only once, under direct order of Secretary of the Navy John Warner, did Rickover don his full admiral's uniform—when Rickover Hall was dedicated at the Naval Academy on March 29, 1974. It did not fit him well. Then again, neither did the admirals' club.

Rickover had disdain for the Navy and many in the Navy had disdain for him. Many CNOs tried to contain, harness or remove Rickover; all failed. Arleigh Burke, an early supporter, concluded that Rickover's often whimsical requirements and fierce distrust of contractors would cripple the then-revolutionary Polaris Missile Project; Burke did it on time and on budget, largely excluding Rickover. Meanwhile Rickover's favorite projects, the unfortunate *Thresher* (which sank with the loss of all hands in 1963) and later *Triton*, were vessels designed primarily around his new reactor power plants rather than their military utility. Navy Secretary Paul Nitze tried to retire him with Lyndon Johnson's approval, only to be thwarted when Rickover himself appeared at the meeting with his congressional supporters. Elmo Zumwalt tried to retire him, finding it extremely difficult to uphold Navy morale in the face of severe officer shortages, partly because too many good men could no longer stomach Rickover's egotistical rages and rules. He too failed.

And then there was the contracting mess. Admiral Rickover believed that no one should make a profit in national defense. He recognized but never admitted that government-run shipyards were far more costly than private yards but his answer to that was to run them himself when he could. Through endless design changes and brutal contracts he drove the private yards to distraction. Ironically, his efforts, noble in intention, often had the effect opposite to the one Rickover desired. By the collapse of vital shipbuilding in bitter legal disputes, and by driving the extreme over-engineering necessary for nuclear power into the design of all Navy ships, Rickover helped to create a gold-plated fleet with too few ships at the very moment when the United States badly needed large numbers of new ships.

The ships, like Rickover himself, had to be perfect. "Why not the best?" was the motto of a man who inspired loyalty with his singular devotion to his work twelve hours a day or more, seven days in a week that was always too short. He disdained riches and the material things that other men of power coveted. But his system bred skilled officers who too often allowed their admiration for Rickover's self-sacrifice to overshadow his other excesses. He personally interviewed every candidate for his Navy, and to feed his personnel needs he gradually acquired control of all Navy personnel policy. In a memo shortly after I became SECNAV, he informed me that he controlled the "selection, qualification and training of operating personnel." He required all of his nuclear commanding officers to write him a personal letter every week. It came to foster a "them-us" in the Navy between the "nukes" and everyone else.

After my years in government and involvement with the Navy I came into office convinced of Rickover's greatness and deeply admiring of what he had done for the Navy and the nation—and also determined to retire him. (I have told that story in detail in another book, *Command of the Seas*.) At 81 (or 83) he had stayed too long, but not long enough in his own mind. He had become a huge obstacle to the rebuilding of Navy morale and to building the 600-ship Navy.

On November 13, 1981, the admiral was finally retired. He was given an office for life by the Congress. In it over his desk he hung two pictures, one of Benedict Arnold and one of me.

When he died in 1986, I was reminded of what Rickover's first wife, Ruth Masters, a scholar in her own right, had once said of him: "Someday, I hope the Navy will have officers who will understand odd officers with odd talents." Rickover had been an odd officer with odd talent. He had indeed been understood and had achieved a deserved greatness by helping to build the nuclear Navy that became the strongest pillar in America's wall of deterrence. But his career was also a warning for the Navy: the system should not forever be dominated by odd officers and odd talents. The Navy and the country were fortunate to have had Hyman Rickover but not fortunate to have had him for so long.

SUBMARINERS:
THE VALOR AND VICTORIES
OF THE SILENT SERVICE

During the Cold War the contributions of Rickover's creations were so immense they would require several books to recount (and, in fact, several good ones have been written recently). Going into the sea in submarines has always been particularly hazardous, and it takes special bravery to choose it as one's vocation.

The first submarine to sink an enemy warship while submerged, the Confederate submarine *H.L. Hunley*, killed more Confederates than Yankees. *Hunley* sank twice during training cruises. In its first accidental sinking, five crew members out of nine died—later a second sinking killed all nine aboard, including H.L. Hunley, one of its inventors. Even in the final engagement, the entire crew of *Hunley* perished. Its target, USS *Housatonic*, lost five. (*H.L. Hunley* was discovered in Charleston Harbor and recovered in the summer of 2000).

Though the sinking of *Squalus* has received attention recently, and in the summer of 2000 the sinking of the Russian submarine *Kursk* in the Barents Sea reminded the world that submarines are dangerous even in peacetime, few people realize the sacrifices of this, the most silent of services. *Squalus* was just the most famous of a list of boats lost before World War II in peacetime accidents and collisions. Forgotten today, *F-1*, *F-4*, *O-5*, *H-1*, *S-51*, *O-9* were all submarines that sank with some or all of their crew, between 1915 and 1941. While naval service on the surface or in the air is dangerous even in peacetime, submariners have always gone in harm's way during daily operations.

In World War II, 52 American submarines out of 263 never came back. Immediately after Pearl Harbor these men took the war to the enemy's home territory long before any other naval units were capable of offensive operations. They carried out the function that privateers carried out in the Revolution and the War of 1812, that of commerce raiding, while also exacting a heavy toll on the warships of the Imperial Japanese Navy. According to the organization of Submarine Veterans of World War Two, during the 1,347 days of the war, 465 skippers took 263 boats and 16,000 men out on 1,736 patrols, collectively spending 79,838 days at sea, and operating about half of their time in enemy territory. The results were astounding. They sank 1,178 merchant ships and 214 naval vessels. A force of 2 percent of the U.S. Navy accounted for 55 percent of Japan's maritime losses.

The men of *Tang, Wahoo, Trigger, Dace* and others—named after fish, and not all ferocious fish, at that—performed incredible feats of bravery. Men like Howard Gilmore, skipper of *Growler;* wounded on the bridge, the sub under attack, he ordered his men to "take her down," sacrificing his life. Capt. John P. Cromwell, a wolf-pack commander, privy to ULTRA secrets and upcoming invasion plans, chose to go down with his sinking *Sculpin* rather than risk revealing his secrets under torture.

V-J Day did not bring to an end the submariners' war. They were plunged into Cold War operations almost at once. In World War II the warriors of the "silent service" got much less publicity than their exploits warranted. In the Cold War, submarine operations went on far longer and involved more sensitive and demanding missions. In addition to antisubmarine and antiship responsibilities, the submariners took on two of the most critical missions in defense preparedness: operating the sea-based nuclear deterrent of *Polaris, Poseidon* and *Trident* submarines and their ballistic missiles, and gathering intelligence. The missile boats have been widely publicized, as indeed their mission of deterrence required. The intelligence operations, which were at least as important as the strategic missiles in winning the Cold War, remained one of our best-kept secrets.

While there were isolated leaks to the press, most notably from congressional critics, the public only became aware of the nature of these perilous and invaluable operations toward the end of the Cold War. The first real attention to the undersea Cold War came in Tom

Clancy's 1984 bestseller, *The Hunt for Red October.* The book did a useful service in finally revealing in fictional form some of the daring operations of U.S. nuclear submarines against their Soviet counterparts during the forty years of the Cold War. (I joked to Clancy that if he were a sailor he would have to be court-martialed for revealing so much.) While the dashing destroyermen and flashy aviators got the glamour, the nukes, in their fast attack boats, were winning the highest decorations for bravery. But not one hint of what they were up to could be talked about.

In 1998 another book hit the bestseller lists, *Blind Man's Bluff,* by Sherry Sontag and Christopher Drew. Because it covers the period of my service in government, it would be inappropriate for me to confirm or deny anything recounted by them.

According to Sontag and Drew, after the Soviet Union exploded its first nuclear bomb, U.S. subs routinely began to retrieve dispersed fragments of tested Soviet inter-continental ballistic missiles (ICBM) from the ocean floor. Some subs actually got in among the Soviet ships, filmed the missile tests and collected the telemetry. By 1969, the Soviets began deploying lethal "Yankee" missile submarines into the Atlantic, bringing most American cities under the threat of nuclear attack. Using technically difficult and highly stressful tactics, American attack subs learned to trail Soviet missile subs as soon as they entered the Atlantic and to stay with them for their entire cruises.

For many years, say the authors, the Soviets never knew this was going on. Trailing operations had to be done so close to the Soviet subs that U.S. sub crews could hear everything through sonar. "A quick clank was automatically recorded as a toilet lid being slammed and every time a sonarman heard the rushing of air over their headsets [sanitary tanks being blown] . . . they reported, quite formally, 'Conn. Sonar. We just got s——on.' "

In 1970, the Navy put forward the daring idea of tapping underwater cables carrying Soviet military communications. Submarines were modified to do the job. Success came in 1971, inaugurating one of the most brilliant sustained intelligence operations of the Cold War.

In the midst of these successes, however, Soviet behavior began suddenly to change. Russian subs started to act as if they knew they were being trailed. Suddenly, the tap in the Sea of Okhotsk was located and the canister publicly displayed in Moscow. More ominously, the Soviets launched a new generation of attack and missile submarines that were almost as quiet as American subs—using technology that was exactly the same. Then one day the wife of a retired Navy warrant officer, John Walker, called the FBI to reveal one of the greatest Soviet espionage successes of the Cold War. The Walker spy ring, together with a traitor named Ronald Pelton, had revealed to the Soviets the cable tapping, the trailing and the sub design secrets that had given America its priceless edge.

There were unexpected benefits to even this intelligence failure, however. The Soviets shifted their naval strategy from one of challenging the West around the world by means of a 1,700-ship blue-water Navy to a defensive "bastion strategy," pulling back into the northern seas and under the polar ice cap to protect their missile subs. The entire underwater great game was a critical battleground in the Cold War.

THE SUCCESSES OF THE SUBMARINES during the Cold War remind us that the culture and values of the Navy should always be set by the warriors who actually go into harm's way, the leaders aloft and alow who have won the nation's wars. Nevertheless, the Navy has also drawn greatness from the innovators and reformers who never left the beach. One of these was the leader of the digital revolution in the United States Navy.

REAR ADMIRAL GRACE HOPPER: NAVAL REFORMER

In 1944, newly commissioned Lieutenant (J.G.) Grace Hopper reported to the Navy's Bureau of Ordnance Computation Project at Harvard's Cruft Laboratories. This first assignment proved fortuitous, both for her and the Navy. Since graduating from Vassar in 1928, Grace Hopper's career had centered on the study and teaching of mathematics. She graduated Phi Beta Kappa from Vassar and was hired onto their faculty at a time when math departments accepted few women instructors. She received a master's degree from Yale in 1930 and a doctorate in 1934, a rare accomplishment for anyone in those days. (Between 1862 and 1934, a total of only 1,279 doctorates were granted in the U.S.)

By 1943, wanting to do her part in the war, she left her Vassar professorship for the Navy reserves. Upon arriving at Cruft Labs, her first assignment was working on the programming of the new Mark I, America's first programmable digital computer. She was the third programmer assigned to the project. "It was fifty-one feet long, eight feet high, eight feet deep," she recalled of the Mark I, "and it had seventy-two words of storage and could perform three additions a second." At the time, the Mark I was conceived as a machine that might crank out quick solutions to laborious tactical problems, such as running the computations needed to determine how best to lay a minefield. It was the beginning of an effort that has transformed naval warfare and given the U.S. Navy a vast technological superiority over its adversaries in the Cold War.

While turning to the immediate task of learning to program the Mark I, Hopper began developing a vision of computers and society that would define the rest of her life. It was a vision in three parts. First was the task of continued development of the digital computer; second was creating an interface that would permit the nontechnical public to use these machines; finally there was the necessity to teach this large population of potential users that technology was not a mysterious foe, but rather a "machine that assisted the power of the brain rather than the muscle."

Hopper set about devising procedures for using these first machines and, at the same time, expanding their capabilities. Back then the few handmade computers were programmed sequentially in a numeric binary code that was neither intuitive nor tolerant of human error. One solution she and her team came up with was to save and share successful programs to use them over again without rewriting them each time. She collected these subroutines in a catalog that could then be reused without repeating each tedious process—and each invitation for error.

At war's end, Hopper, now 40, could not transfer into the regular Navy. She remained active in the Reserves, however, as a research fellow working on the Mark I, II and III.

A true visionary, Hopper had already conceptualized how a much wider audience could use computers if they were both programmer-friendly and application-friendly. In 1949, in pursuit of this vision, she left a safe position at Harvard to join the Eckert-Mauchly Computer Corporation and take on the challenge of designing computers for general business use. Eckert-Mauchly, developers of the UNIVAC, by 1955 had become part of the Sperry Corporation. In 1952, Hopper became the systems engineer and director of automatic programming for the UNIVAC Division, a job she would hold for twelve years. It was with UNIVAC that Hopper developed a program that would translate symbolic programming language into machine language, so that the programmer need no longer be conversant with basic binary code.

By 1957, Hopper and her staff had gone a step further by creating a program called FLOW-MATIC which enabled one command to set off a sequence of commands in machine code. It was designed for typical business tasks like automatic billing and payroll calculation. Using FLOW-MATIC, Hopper was able to make the UNIVAC I and II recognize twenty simple statements in English. This streamlined programming eliminated time-consuming steps and made computers more accessible to operators with no knowledge of the computer's physical characteristics. When she recommended the obvious next step, however, that an entire programming language be developed using English, she was told it wouldn't work. Her arguments began taking hold, nonetheless, and she headed a combined effort that eventually led to COBOL—a Common Business-Oriented Language—which would do for business what IBM's FORTRAN would do for scientists.

While at Sperry, Hopper remained active in the Naval Reserve until her first retirement in 1966. Only seven months later, however, she was asked to return to active duty to direct the standardization of COBOL in the Navy. She requested military leave from Sperry, and remained on military leave from them until her retirement in 1971. "I seem to do a lot of retiring," she once said.

I first met Grace when Bob Conn, the comptroller of the Navy, proposed a total reform of Navy information and accounting systems. There were at the time seventeen different incompatible computing systems in the Navy procurement, supply, logistics and accounting activities. He said only one human being alive could design a plan to modernize and rationalize the Navy's information technology: Grace Hopper. It took her six years but she did it. And while she was doing it she kept chastising me and the admirals for our (in her view) Luddite attitude towards technology. She gave me the first desktop computer ever to grace the SECNAV office. More importantly, she was a constant goad to the fleet: Why weren't carrier squadrons using available desktops for strike planning and surface ships for navigation? The sensible, and often difficult to answer, questions of her energetic mind came continuously. And she got results and made converts who fundamentally changed the Navy.

In 1983 I took her over to the Oval Office so that President Reagan could personally present her with a promotion to the rank of commodore. In 1985 she was appointed to rear admiral. She continued to serve in the Navy until 1986, working out of her office at the Navy Yard in Washington. She retired at 71 as the Navy's oldest active duty officer. During that time, she received increasing recognition as a spokesperson for the usefulness of computers, giving lectures—up to two hundred days out of the year—to university students, businessmen and military personnel. In 1969 the Data Processing Management Association had named her "Man of the Year." It was "before we had all this hoopla," Hopper said of the award, "all this silly women this and that stuff. When I was made the man of the year, I was the man of the year." Many other awards would follow.

With all of her accomplishments, Hopper considered herself first and last a naval officer, not a "techie," and it was this close focus on actual naval operations that made her work have such an impact. Her work with computers helped to solve real tactical naval problems: strike planning, ship maneuvering, logistics, etc. More than any other person she kept the culture of the Navy focused on exploiting the digital revolution. The ever-widening lead in technology over the Soviets that came from this focus hastened the end of the Cold War.

AFTER KOREA, the Navy was fully engaged in the many dimensions of Cold War deterrence. Regular carrier deployments to trouble spots around the world, and constant presence in the Western Pacific, Mediterranean and Middle East kept crises like Lebanon, Quemoy and Matsu from getting out of control. The Cuban blockade and missile crisis in 1962 brought the Navy very close to hot war.

The Navy during this period was heavily engaged in taking on an entirely new Cold War mission: the operation of submarine-based strategic ballistic missiles. The first Polaris missile was launched from *George Washington* on July 20, 1960, and *Washington*'s first Polaris patrol began November 15, 1960.

Events were simultaneously moving the Navy and the country to a new hot phase of the Cold War in Indochina. On August 2 and August 5, 1964, the American destroyers *Maddox* and *Turner Joy* were apparently attacked by North Vietnamese torpedo boats under circumstances that remain uncertain and controversial.

VIETNAM:
BROWN WATER AND ALPHA STRIKES

It will be many decades before a wholly comprehensive and objective history of the origins of the Vietnam War can be written, and such a history will certainly not be attempted here. Almost nothing that happened in Vietnam has been left uncontested by pundits over the years. But whatever their political baggage, historians must agree that the war began with France's attempt to reacquire control over her Indochinese colonies seized by the Japanese during World War II. The political and military situation on the East-Asian mainland was far different and far more complex than in postwar Europe. But the inescapable fact was that both Stalin and Mao wished to add all of the nations of Southeast Asia to the socialist camp.

The string of American decisions leading to support France against Vietnamese independence, and eventually to displace France in the war, came simply and directly from the consensus in the American government that communist expansion must be contained. Unfortunately, there was never a consensus in the U.S. government throughout that long war for how it should be fought. Today there is little consensus on its lessons.

The most extensive American naval operations in the war were strategic and interdiction bombing in the North and close air support in the South from aircraft carriers, and riverine warfare in the South. Ironically the most effective application of naval superiority, tight blockade and mining of enemy waters, was prohibited for political reasons throughout the war until its final months, when as long predicted by the Navy it proved to be decisive and effective.

In all of America's wars, seapower has played a key role. So too in America's longest war. Although the major strategic issues of sea control and air superiority were never in doubt, the war was not confined to those traditional realms of 20th-century warfare. From the Mekong Delta to the Red River Delta, and from the DMZ to the PRC's border, the geography and hydrography of Vietnam presented unusual and difficult tactical challenges to the Navy. The naval battles of the Vietnam War were fought on that nation's rivers, and in the air above them.

Vietnam occupies a relatively narrow strip of coastline beside the Gulf of Tonkin and the South China Sea, and is tipped by the Camau Peninsula in the south. Hundreds of small islands are found off this long misty shore, and inland there are thousands of nautical miles of rivers and canals, which serve as the rural populace's principal transportation network. Offshore waters are shallow, making for wide tidal flats, swamps and marshlands, thereby pushing the fleet's gun line well offshore in many places. Operations in these tidewaters are further complicated by the heavy monsoon rains, which often bring flooding and unpredictable inshore currents.

The terrain and tropical weather necessitated a shift of the Navy's tactical thinking from blue water to brown with emphasis on littoral control to block the infiltration of war materials from North to South Vietnam. This was no easy task because of the thousands of junks, sampans, fishing boats and assorted watercraft that plied these waters on a daily basis as they had done for centuries.

To deal with the North Vietnamese infiltration, the Navy began a two-tiered sea and air blockade of the South only in December 1965. The Seventh Fleet set up surveillance centers in port cities along the South Vietnamese coast from Danang down to Vung Tau to enforce the offshore blockade known as Operation Market Time, and the inshore blockade known as Operation Game Warden.

Radar picket ships formed the backbone of offshore surveillance. They were converted destroyer escorts (DERs) that could stay on station for prolonged periods. The DERs were reinforced by Coast Guard squadrons of WPBs and Swift-model patrol boats. Seaplane tenders enabled P-5 Marlin seaplanes to provide aerial surveillance, along with shore-based P-2 Neptune and P-3A Orion patrol planes. A lightly armed but very mobile junk force patrolled the transitional waters between the picket line and the shoreline, manned by volunteer crews of South Vietnamese sailors assisted by U.S. Navy advisors.

Rivers and canals are the highways and byways of the Mekong Delta and had to be controlled much as the mighty Mississippi and other rivers such as the James, the Cumberland, and the Tennessee had to be controlled during the American Civil War. To gain control of these crucial waterways in the 1860s, the U.S. Navy had successfully employed steam ferries converted to gunboats and armored monitors. This historical lesson was not lost on French military strategists.

In the late 1940s, the U.S. Navy gave the French Navy many of its surplus amphibious assault landing craft left over from World War II. The French converted them into riverine warfare vessels and deployed them against the Vietnamese communists. Aimed at supporting ground forces deployed to control the labyrinth of waterways in both the Red River and Mekong Deltas, their hand-me-down flotillas known as *Dinassauts* performed well. After France's withdrawal in 1954, the fledgling South Vietnamese Navy inherited many of these vessels and embraced the American-inspired tactical concept, but changed the *colons'* name of the flotilla. Now known as a River Assault Group—or RAG—each flotilla was usually comprised of about twelve vessels. It might include, for example, six troop carriers, four river patrol craft, a *Monitor* fire-support vessel, and a *Commandament* command-and-control vessel.

The ships named above—*Monitor* and *Commandament*—were both built on LCM-6, "Higgins boat" hulls. Originally, the LCM-6, designed for ferrying tanks from ship to shoreline, had a full-load displacement of seventy-five tons, more than enough to carry several World War II tanks. Twin Cummings diesels driving two propellers powered both *Monitor* and *Commandament*. The LCM-6 front landing ramps had been removed during conversion and bows added, increasing their overall length to sixty feet. Under eighteen feet in width, both versions had shallow bottoms and could easily navigate most of the rivers in the Mekong Delta, particularly at high tide. With flat bottoms and propellers protected by skegs, they had no fear of grounding.

Commandament was armed almost as heavily as the *Monitor* was, except she had no 81-mm mortar. Instead, the mortar position was covered with an elevated steel deck, serving as a helicopter-landing platform. *Monitor* was a throwback to the Civil War in both name and design. With her boxy man-of-war outline and spoon-shaped bow, she served as the primary firepower provider of the flotilla's tactical formation. Besides her .50-caliber machine gun and 81-mm mortar, she bristled with more heavy-duty armament: one 40-mm and two 20-mm gun mounts.

Thus the South Vietnamese RAGs, along with their U.S. Navy advisors, became the direct descendants of Civil War gunboats manned by Joseph Kelly and William Cushing. Despite the relatively old age of the hulls involved, the RAGs again validated the tactical concept of using shallow-draft combatants to control inland waterways over a century later. Alas, not a few also suffered the same fate as *Commodore Jones*.

Seeing the success of the RAGs, the U.S. Navy went full circle, and again began to build and deploy its own gunboat fleet into the Mekong Delta in 1967 to support U.S. Army troops operating there. The Navy expanded the tactical concept by providing YRBM mother-ships—for Yard Repair Berthing and Messing—to the flotillas where they could tie up in midstream. The YRBMs provided repairs, maintenance and replenishment, and the crews could shower, sleep, relax and eat aboard them.

The American flotillas consisted of Armored Troop Carriers (ATCs), Command and Control Boats (CCBs) and the proven *Monitors*, all built on sturdy old and reliable LCM-6 hulls. The American *Monitors* had even more firepower than the French/Vietnamese models in the form of flamethrowers, 20-mm Oerlikon and 40-mm Bofors rapid-fire cannons, backed up by venerable 105-mm howitzers. All of the American vessels were distinctive in their appearance from the Vietnamese because they were equipped with newly developed bar-armor screens that gave them protection against rocket-propelled grenades.

Other special naval craft proved useful in the Vietnam War. One such was the mini-ATC, designed to land forces behind enemy lines. These ships were driven at speeds up to 28 knots by gas turbines. Their aluminum hulls were protected by ceramic armor and drew no more than one foot of water. Another was the PBR. The initials stood for Patrol Boat River, but to the four-man crew of brown-water sailors who manned the little combatant, the initials stood for either Proud Brave and Reliable or Pabst Blue Ribbon. The PBR looked like a shrunken World War II torpedo boat. About thirty feet long with ten-foot beam, they were lightly built of aluminum and fiberglass. Well armed, they mounted a Mark-18, 40-mm grenade launcher, a twin .50-caliber machine gun turret forward and a single .50-caliber aft, and M-60 machine guns midship.

The PBRs were the cavalry of the riverine force. Powered by two General Motors diesel engines producing 220 horsepower each, these miniature men-of-war had a top speed of twenty-five to thirty knots depending on weight and fuel load. The twin diesels drove Jacuzzi jet pumps through submerged propulsion nozzles. With no propellers to foul, the PBRs were able to lurk in extremely shallow waters, drawing less than two feet. When Viet Cong prey entered their sights, they could accelerate and overtake a motorized sampan in seconds.

To support their brown-water riverine forces operating in the Mekong Delta, the Navy needed close air support in the form of helicopter gunships. But at the time, none were available. The solution was as old as the naval service: "cumshaw." (The old Navy term means obtaining things outside official channels.) The Army was then in one of its ongoing doctrinal fights with the Air Force and was desperate to keep as many fixed-wing airplanes on its olive-drab flight line as possible. The Navy traded P-2 Neptunes to the Army for Huey gunships, and in July 1966, the first Navy detachment of Seawolves arrived in country.

Over the months, more detachments took station aboard converted LSTs anchored in the major rivers of the Mekong Delta. By April 1967, the Seawolf squadron was officially born in the form of HAL-3, Helicopter Attack Light, and its duties included SEAL support, convoy protection, coastal surveillance, and covert-agent and sniper-team insertions. They flew the first operational-model Huey, woefully underpowered for its mission.

Despite the Seawolves' best efforts, more capability than could be provided by helicopters in terms of speed, loiter time and ordnance load was needed. In early January 1969, Light Attack Squadron Four (VAL-4) was commissioned and deployed to Vietnam. Known as the "Black Ponies," the new squadron flew the combat-tested Rockwell OV-10A Broncos. In order to expedite the squadron's establishment in country, the Navy borrowed eighteen Broncos from the Marine Corps and sent a detachment to Binh Thuy and Vung Tau, with both being operational by mid-April 1969.

The Bronco is an all-purpose, twin-turboprop observation aircraft specifically designed for the Vietnam War, with good close-air-support capability. Manned with a tandem-seated crew of two, the sturdy twin-boomed and high-tailed bird carried both 7.62-mm and 20-mm machineguns, 5-inch Zuni folding-fin rockets, and flares. During the Vietnam War, the Black Ponies' duties included routine patrol, air cover, observation, forward air control and artillery/naval-gunfire spotting. They specialized in busting bunkers, sinking enemy watercraft and blowing away .51-caliber gun sites in support of riverine operations. They were good dive-bombers. I flew several WWII-style close-air-support missions with them before their final standown in mid-April 1972.

During their brief years in active combat operations, both HAL-3 and VAL-4 won numerous unit citations. Their personnel were among the most highly decorated to come out of the conflict, despite their relatively late arrival.

As in the Civil War, the riverine operations were very effective and severely curtailed communist ability to operate in the South, particularly the Mekong Delta. Market Time, however, like the British blockade of America in the Revolution, was never completely successful in preventing the regular infiltration of supplies from the North into the long coastline of the South. Most supplies went in through the Cambodian port of Sihanoukville.

It was not for lack of trying. The day-to-day life aboard the Navy's PBRs, and the routine heroism involved in such duty, is well illustrated by the story of one of the River War's most decorated sailors.

BO'SUN'S MATE JAMES ELLIOT WILLIAMS: A VOICE FROM THE PBRS

"Damn, Williams, you've got a big neck," the tall Texan said, while snapping the clasp of the sky-blue suspension ribbon he had draped around the South Carolinian's neck. When the Texan finally secured the clasp, he centered the rare medal below the throat of the bald, stocky, round-faced sailor who stood at attention before him.

Dressed in his crackerjack whites complete with black scarf, Boatswain Mate First Class James Elliot Williams received the Congressional Medal of Honor from President Johnson on May 14, 1968 with embarrassed humility, a living brown-water legend who had survived a harrowing eleven months of combat duty in South Vietnam. This was the last in a long list of valor medals won by the 37-year-old father of five.

From the first crews of the Continental Navy to the present day, of all the ratings and specialties necessary to operate a warship, it is that of boatswain—or "bo'sun"—that is the heart of the seagoing Navy. For this role, the Scots-Irish Williams came straight from central casting. The son of a policeman, Williams grew up in Darlington County, South Carolina, graduated from high school and forged a consent letter from his parents that allowed him to join the Navy at age 16 in 1947. Before serving in the Korean War, he married his neighbor's daughter and childhood girlfriend, Elaine Weaver, in 1949.

By the time he arrived in Vietnam in April 1966, Williams was a gravel-voiced salt with the nickname earned by all bo'suns: Boats. He was assigned to River Section 531, operating PBRs in the Mekong Delta in the vicinity of My Tho. From the outset, he was known as a serious, hardworking, no-nonsense leader who was determined to do his duty to its fullest. Assigned *PBR #105*, he christened her *Elaine* in honor of his wife and set about turning her into a mini-dreadnought.

In order to carry more ammunition, Williams lightened his boat by cutting away excess fiberglass, drilling holes in metal supports, and getting rid of anything that did not directly relate to combat effectiveness. He removed all *Elaine*'s armor except that protecting her engines. He used styrofoam instead of metal chests to store rations. He kept the twin 220-horsepower engines tuned to perfection and prided himself on having the fastest boat in the section.

Like most PBR sailors, he was on patrol about eighty hours a week, mostly at night when the Viet Cong were most active. While on patrol, his ammunition canisters were always cracked, ready to be easily opened, and his machine guns were charged and ready to fire in a heartbeat. If no enemy were encountered during the course of a patrol—which was usually the case—Williams test-fired all his weapons on the way back to the base to keep them in good working order. Al-

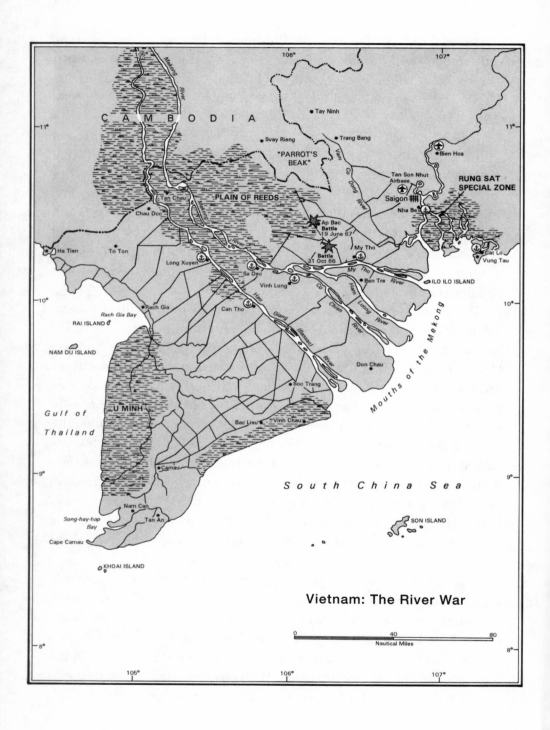

Vietnam: The River War

though this meant the weapons would have to be cleaned before the next patrol, it was a confidence builder for his men and improved their ability to deliver fire rapidly on target.

Williams' Medal of Honor action took place on October 31, 1966. It is known in the annals of PBR battles as the "Halloween Massacre."

It was just another muggy monsoon day in Vietnam, *Elaine* on a routine patrol, her twin Jacuzzi-turbine thrusters burbling quietly in the Mekong River's mocha-brown water. She and *PBR #99*, also under Williams's tactical command, were scouting for contraband-laden sampans. It seemed like an easy R&R outing until they rounded a bend and spotted two boats cutting through the water, obviously trying to evade them. Williams went after them. Drawing closer, the fugitives began firing at the PBR and Williams realized the boats held North Vietnamese regulars, a rarity in the Mekong Delta in 1966.

Williams's bluejackets returned fire with their forward twin .50-caliber machine guns as the fleeing pair split and headed toward opposite banks of the river—one to the north and one to the south. They sank the southbound one, but the other slipped up a narrow canal next to a rice paddy. With *Elaine*'s bow too wide to pursue it into the canal, Williams quickly checked his map and saw that he could go further downriver, cut into a canal and intercept the vessel.

The two PBRs raced a short distance down the river and into the narrow canal where they began to take fire from concealed positions on its banks. Returning suppression fire, they sped on at thirty-five knots until they came around a bend—they had stumbled into a large waterborne enemy staging area.

Unable to turn around, Williams continued rushing forward, swerving left and right to run over and sink sampans loaded with NVA soldiers from the 261st and 262nd regiments. He and his brown-water warriors were now entrapped in a wild three-hour battle against overwhelming odds. Instinctively, he obeyed Nelson's dictum: "No captain can do very wrong if he places his ship alongside that of the enemy."

Williams's Medal of Honor citation for conspicuous gallantry and intrepidity at the risk of life above and beyond the call of duty reads in part:

... the U.S. patrol encountered a heavy volume of small-arms fire from enemy forces at close range, occupying well-concealed positions along the riverbank. Maneuvering through this fire, the patrol confronted a numerically superior enemy force aboard two enemy junks and eight sampans augmented by heavy automatic weapons fire from ashore. In the savage battle that ensued, BM1 Williams, with utter disregard for his safety exposed himself to the withering hail of enemy fire to direct counter-fire and inspire the actions of his patrol. Recognizing the overwhelming strength of the enemy force, BM1 Williams deployed his patrol to await the arrival of armed helicopters. In the course of his movement, he discovered an even larger concentration of enemy boats. Not waiting for the arrival of the armed helicopters, he displayed great initiative and boldly led the patrol through the intense enemy fire and damaged or destroyed fifty enemy sampans and seven junks. This phase of action completed, and with the arrival of the armed helicopters, BM1 Williams directed the attack on the remaining enemy force. Now virtually dark, and although BM1 Williams was aware that his boats would become even better targets, he ordered the patrol boats' search lights turned on to better illuminate the area and moved the patrol perilously close to shore to press the attack. Despite a waning supply of ammunition, the patrol successfully engaged the enemy ashore and completed the rout of the enemy force. Under the leadership of BM1 Williams ... the patrol accounted for the destruction or loss of sixty-five enemy boats. ...

In the wake of the battle, Williams found he had been wounded with a small piece of shrapnel embedded in his side. He had not even noticed it before. One of his crewmen took a clean in-and-out wrist shot that touched no bones. Aside from these minor wounds, both PBR crews were unscathed.

Reflecting upon the battle in a June 1999 interview, Williams said, "We had fate on our side that day. Fire came from all directions. But their aim was off that day 'cause they were shootin' and hittin' more of each other than we were. . . . We got through that area and I am trying to hightail it back. We got around the corner and by God! There's another staging area. We had to just fight. There was no way out. I twisted, crisscrossed and turned the patrol boat. I did whatever I could to get them off our backs. We got blasted to hell and back. . . ."

Normally, when a man is recommended for the Medal of Honor he is taken out of the front lines so that, if the award is approved, he might better his chance of receiving it while still alive. But Williams refused to leave his shipmates and continued to take the fight to the enemy. He voluntarily remained in harm's way and within six weeks, Boats was back in the thick of it again, this time adding a Navy Cross to his collection for sinking nine enemy vessels.

Williams finished his tour of duty in Vietnam, retired as a chief boatswain's mate in April 1967 and returned to his home state. He had earned thirty-nine medals in twenty years of honorable service to his country including the Congressional Medal of Honor, the Navy Cross, the Legion of Merit with combat "V", two Silver Stars, the Navy-Marine Corps Life Saving Medal, three Bronze Stars with combat "V", three Purple Hearts, the Navy Commendation Medal and five Navy Good Conduct Medals. Not one to rest on his laurels, he ran for sheriff of Darlington as a Republican in 1969 but lost. President Richard Nixon appointed him a U.S. marshal as consolation, and he rose in the civil service to its highest rank, a GS-18. He always kept his war record in perspective. "Medals," he noted, "don't put food on the table."

Despite the heroics of Williams and PBR captains like him, the Navy's war in Vietnam is remembered primarily as an air war. Here too, the Navy's contribution was great.

YANKEE STATION: THE TONKIN GULF YACHT CLUB

For generations of naval aviators, no name conjures up more pride, heartache and wistful nostalgia than that of Yankee Station. From an objective point of view, Yankee Station was merely an intersection of longitude and latitude in the Tonkin Gulf, 17°30' N by 108°30' E, a place where sea snakes swam, flying fish broke the blue-green water and white gulls fought over the flotsam and jetsam of fresh garbage dumped over the fantails of American ships. Located about 75 miles off the coast of North Vietnam, this stretch of the South China Sea, with the Hainan Island lying to the east, served as the principal naval airpower launching area for over ten years of the Vietnam War.

Offensive air operations started in 1964 when Carrier Task Force Seventy-seven arrived on Yankee Station. This powerful force was built around three carriers: *Ranger* (CVA-61), *Hancock* (CVA-19) and *Coral Sea* (CVA-43), all with airwings with a proven combination of reconnaissance, fighter and strike aircraft. The carriers did not confine themselves to any exact longitude and latitude. In order to launch and recover aircraft, they needed a 35-knot headwind down their flight decks and constantly steamed on various headings to catch the fickle currents of air.

The task force also had the normal cortege of ammunition, refrigeration, resupply and refueling ships that provided everything from napalm bombs to ice cream and turned Yankee Station into a watery piece of America, with movies and card games in the squadron ready rooms and the hangar bay every night. Soon the bluejackets of the task force started to refer to themselves as members of the "Tonkin Gulf Yacht Club."

Despite the task-force's command of the sea area, its awesome offensive power was held back by the Johnson White House. From the outset of operations, the pilots were leashed tight by the infamous "Rules of Engagement." Before striking a target, permission had to be granted from Washington and each mission approved prior to launch. This absurd policy did not allow pilots to attack targets of opportunity. Follow-on attacks were not authorized either, thus strike effectiveness was often minimal. Much of the country was declared a "bomb-free zone," including all villages and any harbor that might have a third-party ship. No fools, the North Vietnamese located their antiaircraft artillery (AAA) and surface-to-air missile (SAM) sites in those bomb-free

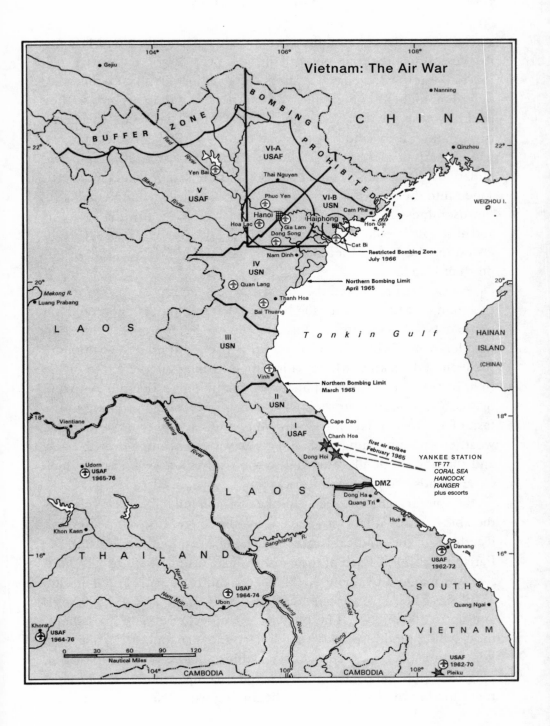

Vietnam: The Air War

zones, stored their ammunition in churches and maintained foreign-flag vessels in all of their ports all of the time.

The war to which naval aviators had to adjust involved being catapulted off night after night into the darkness, at enormous risk, so they could use the greatest technology in the world to bomb "suspected truck parks," ferry landings, pontoon bridges and other useless targets, while nearly everything of military value remained off-limits. Secondary targets were seldom approved, and unused ordnance was jettisoned into the sea. Hostile aircraft had to be visually sighted, negating the usefulness of superior American radar target-acquisition systems and air-to-air missiles. For fear of escalating the war, no attacks were allowed on the North Vietnamese MiGs huddled at Phuc Yen airport north of Hanoi.

As the war progressed the rules became even more constraining, to the point that Lyndon Johnson bragged that the Joint Chiefs could not bomb a North Vietnamese outhouse unless he approved. The commander in chief's obsession with control reached around the world into the cramped cockpits where white-lipped young pilots tried to pickle their bombs onto approved targets, while pulling g's, dodging AAA and SAMs, and looking over their shoulders for MiGs, then turning to the task of an arrested landing aboard ship, often at night and in marginal weather with a pitching deck and green water cascading over the bow and then, worst of all, returning to the ready room to find out which close friends had not made it back.

Despite its dangers, life on Yankee Station fell into a relatively predictable routine that was driven by the target list, the monsoon weather and the political vagaries of Hanoi, Washington and, later, the Paris Peace Talks. Each of the World War II veteran flattops like *Hancock* was manned by about 3,500 officers and men, and carried around 75 planes. The postwar supercarriers like *Ranger* carried 5,500 souls and up to 100 aircraft. The busy little nautical city had repair shops, mess halls, laundries, sickbays, a library and a chapel. All hands were kept up to speed via plain old scuttlebutt, a closed-circuit television system, a published plan of the day and compartment loudspeakers that piped in the latest "gouge," beginning with "Now hear this. . . ."

No one has captured the uniqueness of this strange warfare better than Tom Wolfe in his classic essay in *Esquire:* "The Truest Sport: Jousting with Sam and Charlie."

He wrote:

> There is something eccentric in the way the day begins. A Filipino steward in starched white jacket gently awakens the aviators in their staterooms. Then to breakfast in the wardroom with its starched napkins. Silver and heavy glass wink out of a manly backdrop . . . for here in the wardrooms of *Coral Sea* the Navy has done everything that interior decoration and white mess jackets can do to live up to the idea of Officers & Gentlemen, within the natural limits of going to war on the high seas. Every day they touch the napkins to their mouths, depart this gently stewarded place, and go forth, observing a checklist of written and unwritten rules of good form, to test their mettle, to go forth to battle, to hang their hides out over the skeet shooters of Hanoi-Haiphong . . . thence to return, after no more than two hours . . . to this linenfold club and its crisp starched white servitors.
>
> One thing it is not good to think about is the fact that it would be even thus on the day when, finally, as has already happened to 799 other American aviators, radar-intercept officers, and helicopter crewmen, your hide is blown out of the sky. That day, too, would begin within this same gentlemanly envelope.

Navy fighter pilots, Wolfe noted, stood one chance in four of dying in an accident before their twenty years were up—even without going into combat.

A number of different types of naval aircraft played a major role in the war and launched from Yankee Station, including helos, A-5 Vigilante reconnaissance jets, A-4 Skyhawk fighter bombers, A-6 Intruder night and all-weather strike bombers, F-8 Crusader and F-4 Phantom fighters, A-3 Sky Warriors, A-1 Skyraider prop-driven bombers, E-1 and E-2 Tracer radar controllers and the C2 Greyhound carrier onboard delivery aircraft.

A major workhorse of the decade-long naval air campaign over North Vietnam was the McDonnell Douglas F-4 Phantom with its tandem-seated crew of two and its mean drooped-nose appearance. The rugged, twin-engined, all-weather jet fighter proved to be remarkably versatile and effective in combat. Carrying its heavy payload in a typical mission, the Phantom could bomb a target, then drop its wing tanks and take on a MiG. Despite its large size, the F-4 was agile; with its supersonic speed, it emerged as the leading MiG killer of the war, inflicting 107 confirmed kills.

Aiding the F-4 was the solo-seated McDonnell Douglas A-4 Skyhawk. Affectionately referred to as "the Scooter" by its pilots or "Heinemann's Hot Rod" in honor of its designer, the single-engined Skyhawk jet was smaller, lighter and cheaper to build than the Phantom, and larger numbers of them were found in the fleet. Unique among naval aircraft, the A-4 was so undersized that it did not have folding wings. The A-4 proved to be a reliable, trouble-free and accurate ground-attack bomber, which pilots would "strap on" prior to launch.

The Phantoms and the Skyhawks performed their ground-attack roles well, but the subsonic Grumman A-6 Intruder, a two-seat, night and all-weather bomber that could carry a tremendous payload, eventually overshadowed them both after several difficult years working out the problems with its new technology. In a single pass, this bulbous-nosed, twin-engined jet could drop twenty-eight 500-pound bombs with precision placement, over five times the ordnance than the famed World War II-era B-26. With pilot and bombardier sitting side-by-side in the wide cockpit, and the prominent refueling "donkey-dick" sticking up between them right above the windshield, the odd-looking Intruders' motto was, "We go deeper, stay longer and deliver a bigger load."

Over the course of the campaign, hundreds of naval aviators were lost, starting with the earliest shootdowns in the summer of 1964, when

Everett Alvarez, Jr. had to punch out of his A-4C, becoming the first Navy prisoner of war on August 5.

The problem was not American flying; with the assistance of their Soviet allies, the North Vietnamese had built the most formidable air-defense system in the history of warfare. When the air campaign began, North Vietnam possessed fewer than 1,500 antiaircraft guns, mainly 37-mm and 57-mm with optical sights and a maximum ceiling range of 18,000 feet. Within a year, the number of guns increased to over 5,000. Long-range 85-mm and 100-mm radar-directed guns enabled the North Vietnamese to fire up to an altitude of 45,000 feet.

Surface-to-air missiles were added to back up the AAA batteries. The mainstay was the "flying telephone pole," the Russian-built SA-2, weighing in at a whopping two and one-half tons. With a ceiling of 59,000 feet and Mach 2.5 speed, it was a major player in the air war to the very end. As described by Wolfe:

> The SAMs come up, and the boys go down, one way or the other! The SAMs . . . were aimed and guided by radar. They climbed at about Mach 3, which was likely to be at least three times as fast as your own ship was going when you heard the warning over your radio ("I have a valid launch!"). The SAMs were not fired at random—each had a radar lock on your aircraft or somebody else's. The only way to evade a SAM was to dive for the deck, . . . The SAM's own G forces were so great they couldn't make the loop and come back down . . . The dive brings you down so low, you are now down into the skeet range of that insidiously well-aimed flak! This, as they say, put you between a rock and a hard place.

The SAMs were supplemented with Soviet planes, most notably the supersonic MiG-21s. In the beginning, naval aviators viewed their North Vietnamese counterparts as second stringers with subsonic, Korean War-vintage MiG-15s and MiG-17s dominating. It was dangerous to underestimate the enemy, and as the months passed by, more and more North Vietnamese pilots graduated from crash courses in the PRC and U.S.S.R. Although most had never driven an automobile, these pilots soon knew how to get the most out of their short-winged, lightweight, and highly maneuverable MiGs.

Their first time in action, April 3, 1965, North Vietnamese pilots surprised their opponents, damaged an F-8 Crusader and splashed two F-105s, with no losses of their own. But the People's Air Force was unable to sustain this initial success and soon suffered high losses. They stood down, and retired to China for more training. When they returned to the North Vietnamese skies in April 1966, they were flying not only their workhorse MiG-15s and MiG-17s, but MiG-21s as well. Although they splashed only fifteen U.S. Navy aircraft overall (five in 1967 alone), their mere appearance on radar screens had a profound effect on all hands, particularly those on strike missions. Despite the threat, the MiG sanctuary at the Phuc Yen airport remained untouchable, much to the fury and frustration of the carrier pilots.

As the years passed on Yankee Station, pilots came back on subsequent tours to strike the same targets again and again. Historian Zalin Grant tells the incredible story of a cadre of pilots off *Oriskany* who struck the same North Vietnamese bridge on the same day in 1966, 1967 and 1972. Literally hundreds of aviators and aircraft were lost flying through AAA, SAMs, and MiGs to strike, repeatedly, the Ham Rung, Co Trai and Paul Doumer bridges over the years, only to find them rebuilt within days, if not overnight. The Ham Rung, known as the "Dragon's Jaw," was particularly aggravating. Tons and tons of ordnance struck The Jaw, but to no avail. It stood intact and became "a source of pride for the North Vietnamese, and a symbol of frustration to the Americans."

As the war dragged on, the corrosive cynicism among naval aviators risking their lives under no-win rules of engagement spread throughout the services. Growing racial tension, drug use and a perception that the American media was sympathetic to the enemy created a devil's brew in the Navy. Race riots and near mutinies climbed up the Jacob's ladder to board many ships of the fleet. In two notable instances, on

Constellation and *Kitty Hawk,* underway operations were disrupted by what were called racial incidents but were in fact mutinies.

In April 1972, after all American ground forces had been withdrawn from Vietnam, Hanoi launched an all-out invasion of South Vietnam. In response, President Nixon finally took off all the absurd bombing restrictions inherited from the Johnson administration, and also ordered the mining of the North Vietnamese ports. Morale in the Navy and Air Force soared as jets cheerfully pulverized the NVA military establishment that had been off-limits for a decade. By the end of the summer, the communists were totally defeated in both North and South and secretly offered terms that after the final "Christmas bombing" of Hanoi resulted in the Peace Agreement of 1973.

In the end, some seventeen different attack carriers made 73 cruises and logged over 8,000 days on Yankee Station. During this time, their pilots splashed 59 enemy aircraft, with 4 probables. In the war overall, naval losses were gut-wrenching: 530 fixed-wing aircraft and 13 helicopters lost in hostile action. Operational losses added another 299 fixed-wing and 35 helos. Death from all losses totaled 2,340, including 317 aviators. In 1973 during Operation Homecoming, 144 naval aviators were released from North Vietnamese custody, but 77 missing men were still unaccounted for.

The war was over for the Navy, if not the Vietnamese. The subsequent defeat of the South after the total cutoff of U. S. assistance was a final insult to the ten years of heroism on Yankee Station.

THE EFFECTS OF THE WAR on the Navy were far-reaching. The policy of the Johnson administration to avoid appearing to be actually at war, and to keep the public from knowing the huge costs of the war, meant that normal research, maintenance, training and replacement accounts were used to fund the war, and when it was over, the entire Navy was worn-out and obsolete.

The stresses of the war had coincided with the emergence of the domestic civil rights activism, and in the fleet that meant morale problems. By the end, recruitment and retention of sailors were at historic lows. The Navy urgently needed reforming and renewal, and it needed wholesale modernization and re-equipping. The former began at once under Admirals Elmo Zumwalt and James Holloway, and Secretaries of the Navy John Warner, William Middendorf and Graham Claytor. The latter would have to wait until Ronald Reagan.

The strategic effect of America's defeat in Vietnam during the Cold War is mixed. On the one hand, if leaders like Lee Kuan Yew are to be believed, the American confrontation of Russian—and Chinese—supported communism gave the struggling Southeast Asian nations of Thailand, Malaysia, Singapore and Indonesia—the so-called "dominoes"—time and motivation to build their economies, join together and become the "Asia Tigers."

On the other hand, American defeat inflicted wounds on American society, civilian and military, that have still not healed, and encouraged and emboldened the Soviet Union to redouble pressure on the West with the Brezhnev Doctrine, supporting insurgencies throughout the Third World.

The Cold War would last another fifteen years.

IX

THE 600-SHIP
NAVY AND COLD
WAR VICTORY

THE FALL OF SAIGON in 1975 and loss of the Vietnam War, combined with the shame and disillusionment surrounding the Watergate scandal, brought to power a congressional majority highly critical of the military and the presidency. It meant trouble for American national security. Public ridicule and congressional and judicial investigations of the armed services gave joy and encouragement to America's enemies around the world. The Soviet Union renewed its adventurism and its support of insurgency in Latin America. The Middle East fell into turmoil.

The replacement of President Nixon with Gerald Ford did not alter these trends. Defense budgets were deeply cut and the intelligence agencies were subjected to years of debilitating investigations. The U.S. Navy was also a target. Between 1969 and 1979 the fleet was cut from 950 ships to 479, even as the Soviets were pursuing a blue-water strategy and building their fleet towards a 1,700-ship goal.

President Ford was defeated in 1976 by Jimmy Carter, who brought in an administration heavily staffed by veterans of the anti-defense activism of the preceding decade. Once in office they took a new look at defense policy and concluded that the Navy and Marine Corps were no longer as important to national security as had previously been thought. Senior officials like Paul Warnke argued that the United States should begin taking unilateral measures of disarmament—with the confidence that the Soviets would follow suit. The new Carter defense policy viewed offensive naval operations as a wasteful diversion of resources. Strategists reasoned that defeat of the Soviets at sea would not cripple the Soviet war effort, while an attack on Soviet naval or air facilities might threaten escalation in the early stages of a struggle. Any serious attempt at defending Norway and maintaining an aggressive defense of the northern flank of NATO was abandoned; the U.S. Navy was restricted to operations south of the Greenland-Iceland-U.K. line, so that it would not be seen as threatening to the Soviets.

Carter's first plans called for a reduction to only 6 aircraft carriers, but the administration settled on a Navy of 450 ships and 12 aircraft carriers. The era of the large nuclear carrier was declared over. Any replacements would be small conventional carriers.

In 1978, in keeping with these trends, CNO Admiral James Holloway was ordered to drop the use of the term "maritime superiority." The orders had been conveyed not by the president or by the secretary of defense but by their staffs. Mindful that he was responsible to the principals and not to their "gofers," Holloway continued to argue forcefully against the kind of downgrading and cuts that were underway. He was not the average, docile peacetime chief.

ADMIRAL JAMES L. HOLLOWAY III:
COMBAT LEADER IN FOUR WARS

In 1998, James L. Holloway III was elected into the National Wrestling Hall of Fame at Stillwater, Oklahoma. In his years at the Naval Academy he was on the varsity intercollegiate wrestling team and was never once pinned in his entire career. That resolute spirit remained intact through mortal combat with the Japanese, Communist Chinese and North Vietnamese in three wars, and the Soviet Navy and Washington disarmers in the Cold War.

A "Navy junior," born in Charleston, South Carolina, on February 23, 1922, Holloway is the son of Admiral James Lemuel Holloway Jr., one of the naval leaders of World War II. At age 17, James III entered the Naval Academy, graduating with the first war-accelerated, three-year class of 1942.

Aboard the new destroyer *Bennion* during WWII, Holloway participated in operations that seized the key islands of Saipan, Tinian and Peleliu. He saw major action in the Battle of Leyte Gulf, where *Bennion* played a leading role in sinking the Japanese destroyer *Asaguma*, and torpedoing the battleship *Yamashiro* during the Battle of Surigao Straits, the last naval battle on the high seas in which aircraft played no role.

Shortly after the battle, Holloway received orders to flight school. When saying farewell, his skipper, Commander Josh Cooper, asked him to reconsider, to remain a career surface line officer. In response, Holloway said, "Captain, in the past week as a destroyer gunnery officer, we've silenced three shore batteries, shot down two Zeros, battled a Japanese cruiser, sunk a destroyer by gunfire and scored a torpedo hit to help sink a Japanese battleship. What is there left to do?"

For his actions in WWII, Holloway received the Bronze Star with Combat "V" and a Navy Commendation award for meritorious service, the first of forty some decorations he would earn in his naval career.

Holloway proved as heroic a Navy flier as he was a Navy sailor, leading many successful flights against heavy opposition in Korea off the carrier *Boxer*. Even after the Korean War, Holloway was never out of the cockpit for long, and in 1958, he assumed command of Attack Squadron 83 aboard the carrier *Essex*, tasked to cover the often-forgotten Marine battalion landing in Beirut on July 14, 1958, to help stabilize the government of that troublesome country.

Back ashore in 1962, Holloway continued to strive for distinction, becoming one of the first aviators to survive Hyman Rickover's famous interviews and go to nuclear-power school. From July 17, 1965, to July 11, 1967, Captain Holloway commanded the first nuclear-powered carrier, *Enterprise*, which was also the longest (1,123 feet), the tallest (250 feet) and, with its eight nuclear reactor engines and four propellers, the mightiest warship in the world. "Big E" transited to the Pacific in November 1965 and became the first nuclear-powered ship to engage in combat when it launched strikes against the Viet Cong on December 2, 1965. During two tours off the coast of Vietnam, Holloway launched more than 16,000 sorties against the North Vietnamese.

As the commander of the Sixth Fleet's Carrier Striking Force in 1970, Rear Admiral Holloway was deployed in the Eastern Mediterranean, where his team provided constant air cover over Jordan in response to the Syrian-backed PLO invasion. Taking command of the Seventh Fleet in 1972, Vice Admiral Holloway played a major role in the final days of the Vietnam War. As a part of the intense joint-service effort to bring about a cease-fire, he directed the precision mining of all North Vietnam ports and the massive campaign of carrier air strikes against North Vietnam that helped end hostilities in 1973.

In 1974 Holloway was appointed chief of naval operations, and it was in this role that I first got to know him. He came to the job during a difficult time. The Soviets, led by Admiral Gorshkov and massive expenditures, sought naval supremacy; the U.S. Navy was shrinking. Watergate had paralyzed the Nixon administration, and the turmoil created by Admiral Zumwalt's bold reforms had alienated many of the Navy's traditional supporters.

Perhaps Holloway's greatest contribution during this period was in the senior policy arena. Henry Kissinger and President Ford had come to admire his policy instincts and his intellectual strengths, and Holloway persuaded them to initiate a major new study of naval requirements by the National Security Council. Led by the new defense secretary, Donald Rumsfeld, the six-month study produced a rigorous and compelling document, concluding with the need for a complete rebuilding of the Navy with the goal of maritime supremacy. It became the basis for the 600-ship Navy built during the Reagan years.

With the election of President Carter, Holloway found himself in an administration whose staff was dominated by veterans of the antiwar left and whose senior officials, with notable exceptions like Zbigniew Brzezinski and Graham Claytor, were anti-navalists. The NSC study of 1976 was rejected, and the Navy subjected to even more severe cutbacks.

But Holloway never trimmed his sails to these prevailing winds, as some of his JCS colleagues did. He remained a calm, powerful and very inconvenient voice of dissent until he was duly retired in 1978.

By that time he had become in Navy parlance my "sea-daddy." Before becoming CNO, he had encouraged me to complete my flight training as an A-6 bombardier and to stay fully committed to the Naval Reserve. More important, he was an inspiration to me, a role model of what a leader should be. The success of the 600-ship Navy in the Reagan years owes more to Holloway than to any other person.

THE *NIMITZ* CLASS

The end of the 1970s was a difficult time for Holloway and like-minded people. When the Carter administration launched its new national security policy emphasizing human rights and de-emphasizing the role of the Navy, it also adopted the argument that smaller, cheaper carriers were better and dropped the *Nimitz*-class design, sending to Congress in 1978 a proposal for a much smaller oil-burning carrier called the CVV class. It was 55,000 tons compared to the *Nimitz*'s 95,000. As a kind of hobby, I spent a good deal of my time in 1978, 1979 and 1980 working with Senators Henry "Scoop" Jackson and John Tower to kill the CVV and replace it with another *Nimitz*-class carrier. At last, in 1979, we managed to get this included in the final defense bill that was passed.

The *Nimitz*-class carrier became a symbol and battleground for two opposing visions of American power. Many in the administration saw in the carrier a dangerous increase in U.S. military power. In an unprecedented move, President Carter vetoed the entire defense bill to kill the aircraft carrier.

While the real issue was political, the debate centered on small vs. large, and is worth discussing.

A smaller carrier is less expensive, meaning more carriers for a given dollar amount and fewer eggs in each basket. But compared to the large nuclear carrier, small carriers lack the speed and endurance of the big deck; the poor seakeeping qualities of smaller carriers curtail flight operations as much as 30 percent of the time. Smaller deck areas limit aircraft in performance as well as in numbers. A ten-year review of carrier landing accidents showed the smaller decks with nearly double the accident rate of the *Nimitz* class. Moreover, the reduced volume on smaller ships limits weapons mix and storage capability. Since volume increases by the cube while surface increases only by the square, bigger is better for carriers just as it is for supertankers. A smaller ship is ultimately harder to sustain and needs far more under-way replenishment and hence additional replenishment ships.

Nor does smallness of size diminish detectability. In today's world of satellite technology and sophisticated reconnaissance systems, a 10,000-ton or even 5,000-ton vessel runs the same risk of detection as a 90,000-ton carrier. But both are equally effective in utilizing deception to evade targeting.

On the contrary, size provides strength, and strength the greatest security of all. Some of the war-fighting features that make the *Nimitz* class the least vulnerable ship in any fleet include high-tensile-strength steel armoring of the flight and lower decks, magazine protection from high- and low-angle attack missiles and torpedoes, and multiple provisions for torpedo protection including more than two thousand watertight, shock-resistant compartments with the necessary power and pumps for dewatering flooded compartments; protective fire-fighting and flooding systems; chemical, biological and radiation protection; and unlimited range at top speed.

All weapons are vulnerable, though ships much less than immovable land targets. Large-deck carriers are the least vulnerable and most survivable ships we have, along with battleships. It is one thing to hit a carrier with a missile; it is another to damage it sufficiently to prevent it from launching aircraft; and, as the battles of WWII have demonstrated, it is quite another order of magnitude to sink it.

To prevent this from happening, the larger carrier can bring into play a far greater array of defenses than its smaller cousin. No ship but the large carrier can dominate the airspace within five hundred to eight hundred miles.

When Carter's primary response to the hostage crisis, still going in

Teheran, was to place two aircraft carriers on station in the Gulf of Oman, we could add urgent reality to our other strong arguments. By late-spring 1980, the CVN-71 carrier was overwhelmingly approved and included in the bill that Carter signed. It fell to me a year later as the new Navy secretary to negotiate a contract for the construction of the ship. I had the pleasure of naming her *Theodore Roosevelt* and appointing my wife, Barbara, to christen her.

Barbara and I have remained involved with the ship ever since. I logged the first helicopter landing made aboard her just before she was launched in 1984. In an added twist of fate, after leaving as secretary of the Navy, my new reserve assignment was as an A-6 bombardier with Attack Squadron 36, one of the squadrons aboard *Theodore Roosevelt*. Since commissioning, she has served in Desert Storm, and in numerous deployments to the Balkans.

THE FALKLANDS WAR: THE SPECIAL RELATIONSHIP

My years as secretary of the Navy gave me a chance to see my opinions about large combatants like *Theodore Roosevelt* proven in action. It was not the U.S. Navy but our oldest friend who had to bear the brunt of lessons learned the hard way.

On March 31, 1982, at 6:30 p.m. Washington time, President Reagan called the president of Argentina, General Galtieri, to warn him not to seize a nearby British crown colony, the Falkland Islands. The invasion had already been launched. Within two days, Argentine Marines overwhelmed the few Royal Marines defending the colony, suffering several dead but, under orders, harming none of the British. As rejoicing broke out in Buenos Aires, an outraged Prime Minister Margaret Thatcher in London brushed aside the hesitations of her ministers and ordered the Royal Navy to recapture the Falklands Islands forthwith.

Thus two civilized societies made war over a remote, cold and boggy territory near the Antarctic Circle, home to only 1,200 Britons and 600,000 sheep. The year 1982 had marked a century and a half of British rule over the Falklands, based on a claim of discovery in 1592 and continuous British settlement since 1832. The Argentines argued, however, that the Malvinas, as they called them, had been part of the Spanish patrimony passed to Argentina with her independence in 1816.

In 1981 Mrs. Thatcher's Conservative government announced its commitment to the Trident missile and submarine strategic deterrent, and a consequent major reduction in conventional naval forces, including elimination of the Royal Marines, a 20 percent reduction of surface combatants, and the sale of the new *Invincible*-class VTOL (vertical takeoff and landing) cruisers. Shorn of all aircraft, the Royal Navy was to become a coast guard.

In a politically courageous act, the Conservative First Lord of the Admiralty, Keith Speed, spoke out against these cuts. He was promptly fired by Mrs. Thatcher, who then abolished the historic office itself to ensure no more naval apostasy.

As has happened so often in history, naval disarmament produced an irresistible temptation.

Fortunately for Britain, when the Falklands were seized, the order to sell and scrap the ships had not yet been carried out. Even more fortunately, the Royal Navy had retained its high level of professionalism. And unlike the diminished American merchant marine, London could call upon extensive private maritime assets. Fifty-eight ships were pressed into service, including the luxury liner *Queen Elizabeth II*. Only three weeks after Mrs. Thatcher's order was given, the British war fleet, a hundred strong and carrying 28,000 men, assembled near the Falklands.

Argentina had become the leader among Latin American nations in taking active, concerted measures to confront Soviet, Cuban and Nicaraguan subversion in Central America. Any perception that the United States was tilting toward the United Kingdom would undermine this dimension of our Central American policy. Secretary of State Alexander Haig undertook a skillful shuttle diplomacy attempting to mediate, but it was too late.

On April 30, the United States declared its own sanctions against Argentina. Argentina immediately informed us of their cancellation of active support of our policy in Central America.

In the Pentagon there had been a massive de facto tilt toward Britain from the very first day. It was the inescapable result of the "special relationship." None of the senior officials in the Pentagon cared about the territorial issue. Indeed, there was strong sympathy for the active role that Argentina had lately played in organizing action against Soviet and Cuban subversion in our hemisphere. Moreover, in the Navy Department at least, there were bonds among aviators with their Argentine counterparts, some of the few pilots in the world who operated a conventional aircraft carrier. Most of these Argentineans were trained at Pensacola, Florida, and at Kingsville, Texas. I had flown with several at Kingsville, and they were all warmly regarded.

Nevertheless, the depth and breadth of cultural, social and historic ties between the United States and the United Kingdom were overwhelming.

The creation of the Joint NATO Supreme Allied Command Atlantic in the postwar period added a new dimension of common command and full integration of wartime planning, doctrine and logistics. Through this framework, the two navies developed a substantial integration of doctrine, weaponry, operations and logistics. Perhaps even more important, it provided a system of very active exchange of personnel between the two navies, building bonds of friendship and familiarity.

This common framework proved decisive in the Falklands War. Because there was a system in place for sharing communications and intelligence, and liaison offices existed to handle the sale, loan and other transfer of weapons and equipment, there were no hard decisions to be made in the first days of the crisis.

Requests through these channels for things like Sidewinder missiles began to flow in April. At first, before the British task force arrived at the Falklands, the requests were handled routinely, without reference to higher authority. As the requests began to involve more substantial logistical assistance, communications equipment, and intelligence, we kept the secretary of defense informed, and he then required us to submit a daily report to his deputy, Frank Carlucci. There was little doubt where Weinberger's sympathies lay, but because of the deep divisions within the administration we did not want to raise the level of consideration of increasing the flow of assistance to the Royal Navy. We made sure that "Cap" Weinberger knew at every step what we were proposing to provide. It is highly unlikely that Jeane Kirkpatrick or anyone at the State Department or the White House understood at first the extent of the assistance we were providing, especially in communications and intelligence. We had for instance sent two tankers to Ascension Island without which the Task Force could not have made it to the Falklands.

Shortly after I became secretary of the Navy, the British Defence Ministry invited me to make an official visit to the United Kingdom. The date was set long in advance—May 3, 1982—and my itinerary included the usual official meetings and visits to Royal Navy ships and facilities. On May 2, however, the Falklands War got off to a dramatic start when a British submarine, HMS *Conqueror,* sank the Argentine heavy cruiser *General Belgrano* using fifty-five-year-old Mark 8 torpedoes. Although the Argentines had an aircraft carrier, the sinking of *General Belgrano* and the loss of 308 sailors of her 1,000-man crew shocked the Argentine Navy into passivity. They played no significant role for the remainder of the three-week campaign.

The bloody inauguration of the war at sea put a different cast on my reception. On my first day of discussions at Whitehall with ministry and Royal Navy officials I was perplexed to find that many of the civilian members of the ministry seemed to be resentful of what they perceived as reluctance by the U.S. government to give full support and assistance to the United Kingdom. Jeane Kirkpatrick and, surprisingly, Al Haig came in for some considerable criticism. The Royal Navy itself, by contrast, could not have been more grateful and appreciative. I concluded that the Royal Navy had not fully shared with their ministers everything that was going on.

In the historic paneled rooms of the Admiralty Board in Whitehall we had a vigorous discussion of what was happening in the Falklands and what the United States ought to be doing about it. It was hard for me to keep my mind on the subject at hand as I looked around the room at the large half-moon cutout of the table at the end, done to accommodate the vast potbelly of one very rotund first lord of the admiralty. Around this table Nelson had given his report to the Admiralty Board on the total defeat of the French Navy at the Battle of the Nile; and his survivors, the reports of the victory at Trafalgar. It was here that the First Lord of the Admiralty Winston Churchill planned the ill-fated Dardanelles campaign and (according to legend) where, to an admiral's protest that he violated naval tradition, he retorted, "Naval tradition? Bah! Rum, sodomy and the lash—that is naval tradition." Still operating on the wall looking down on the Admiralty Board is the famous wind-driven compass showing the wind relative to the coast of France—essential for tactical planning in the days when the threat was from France and success required gaining the windward position.

The afternoon of May 4 we received word that the Argentines had exacted their revenge for *Belgrano* by sinking HMS *Sheffield*, a destroyer, with a French Exocet antiship cruise missile fired from a French-built Super Étendard fighter. The British were now face-to-face with the limitations of their fleet and the consequences of their budget-cutting. The Royal Navy had deployed a large surface task force eight thousand miles from home without effective protection against air attack. They had retired their large aircraft carriers as obsolete, depriving the fleet of airborne early-warning systems.

That evening the government hosted an official dinner in my honor at Lancaster House. It was an emotional time—news of the dead arrived during dinner. In my toast I expressed the deep commitment of sympathy and support of the U.S. Navy for the Royal Navy. Of course, I could not speak publicly of the actual extent of what we were doing. Across from me sat one of the most senior officials in the Defence Ministry. It was obvious from his attitude and conversation that he did not know what was being done, and his remarks reflected a bitterness toward what he clearly believed to be an ally deserting Britain in her time of need. He was rude. Uriah Levy might have challenged him to a duel. I was satisfied when, weeks later, he learned the truth and resumed his cordiality.

That night, the war moved into its crucial phase and I returned to Washington. The admiralty had calculated that the fleet would be in more danger from the Argentine Air Force than from the Navy. If the Port Stanley airfield in the islands were lengthened to accommodate the agile Argentine Skyhawks and other effective, if dated, aircraft in the Argentine inventory, then the whole operation would be endangered.

Fearing the worst, the British had attempted to put the airfield out of action. A squadron of Vulcans, obsolete strategic bombers, flew from England to Ascension Island on April 28. Then, on May 1, one of the Vulcans, fueled en route by ten tankers, dropped twenty-one 1,000-pound bombs on target. It was the longest-range bombing raid in history. The airfield was damaged but not disabled, so later that day, all twenty Sea Harriers based on the VTOL cruisers *Invincible* and *Hermes* raided it again, despite heavy antiaircraft fire. The airfield still was not destroyed. Luckily for the Royal Navy, however, the Argentines never did lengthen the runway to take jets. So the fleet faced the single sorties of fuel-short daredevil Argentine pilots flying at maximum range from the mainland rather than from the islands. The Argentines performed brilliantly and inflicted great damage, but they paid a heavy price.

Ninety-one Argentine planes were lost to gunfire and to the Harrier jumpjets. But six major British ships were lost, and ten others were damaged. All told, it was estimated that if all the bombs accurately dropped by the Argentine pilots, some flying as low as twenty feet above the waves, had actually exploded, a quarter to a third of the British fleet would have found the bottom.

On May 21 the British landed on the main islands. They met variable resistance. Bad weather, air attacks and a helicopter shortage impeded their advance. Nonetheless, three and a half weeks later, Argentine defenses had dissolved into chaos, and the Royal Marines took Port Stanley. All told, 1,000 men had died and over 1,700 were wounded.

A POLITICAL RECKONING in Argentina was not long in coming. On June 17, General Galtieri and the junta resigned, mystified to the end why the United States had not stopped the British. They were arrested later as Argentina lurched into a more democratic phase of its history. In London, Prime Minister Thatcher accepted the accolades of a triumphant Britain. A grateful Parliament voted large sums to improve conditions in the Falklands. The prewar Thatcher naval reduction that precipitated Keith Speed's demise was quietly withdrawn and the three VTOL carriers taken off the auction block.

Unlike the Lebanon War or the Vietnam War, with their extraordinary press coverage, London took no chances with the media. Deception was used as a tool of war to fool the Argentines about the extent of British losses and even the timing of its invasion. In fact, the Defence Ministry convinced more than one analyst and pundit that there would *not* be an invasion—just a blockade. The Argentines, for their part, believed their own propaganda, including the oft-repeated story that Prince Andrew, the queen's second son, had been killed. Truth during the Falklands was undoubtedly a casualty, but the complaints of the journalists were silenced by the roar of victory.

For a brief period following the war, it appeared that another truth might also be a casualty: the real naval lessons of the conflict. Armchair strategists in Washington who for years advocated small, lightly armed ships now declared that because small, lightly armed ships could be sunk by one Exocet, therefore large, armored ships, such as carriers, were a waste of money. In fact, the opposite was true.

We in the Navy did not want to chance losing any lessons from this first truly naval war since the 1940s, so before it was over we assembled a team of our best experts to gather the facts and find the useful lessons for the U.S. Navy. Contradicting the armchair strategists, our team de-

termined that, next to the quality of personnel, the most important factor in the Falklands was intelligence. Because of the quality and timeliness of intelligence available to the Royal Navy from the United
States, the U.K. forces had available to them far better information
about the location, training and intentions of the Argentine forces than
the Argentines had about the British; in fact the Argentines were frequently in the dark. Some of the most senior British officials have gone
so far as to say that without the substantial U.S. intelligence assistance
given, the British would have been defeated. I agree.

The other lesson—clearly stated—is that relying exclusively on
smaller, cheaper, less well-armed combatants can be a false economy.
They are more vulnerable, as demonstrated by the loss of the four
Royal Navy combatants. If any of the sixteen successful attacks against
British ships had instead hit the battleship *New Jersey*, it could not have
done sufficient damage to prevent continuing operations of the ship.
The Exocet missile that sank *Sheffield* would not have been able to
penetrate the armor anywhere on a battleship. Unlike many of its critics, the Navy retains its institutional memory of World War II, when it
lost a ship a day at Okinawa.

JOHN LEHMAN:
THE DRIVE FOR MARITIME SUPREMACY

As I have already entered this story, it would be useless for me either
to pretend to a kind of dispassionate narrative or to hide behind the
skirts of modesty and try to exclude myself from the story of those
events in which I participated. The reader is forewarned.

As the descendant of a privateersman and the son of a naval veteran
of the great Pacific war, I was predisposed to the Navy. While I never
considered a career in the Navy, from my childhood I had always
wanted to be a naval aviator and I joined the Naval Reserve as soon as
I was able. My academic interests and my undergraduate and graduate
degrees all were focused on foreign affairs and national security policy.

The role of sea power in history fascinated me. It was my five years working for Henry Kissinger on the National Security Council, however, that made me a true navalist, like Kissinger himself.

Because of Kissinger and President Ford's concern for the serious decline of the Navy after Vietnam, he had commissioned a top-priority NSC study of our naval force structure. For two years I participated in this; it resulted in a National Security Decision Memorandum that called for rebuilding the Navy. It was the thinking, reading and debating that I (and others more senior) did during this study that formed the intellectual basis for the program that Ronald Reagan adopted as part of his campaign platform, and after his election, which I had the honor of carrying out for him.

I experienced the effect of the Carter years on the Navy firsthand, flying as a reserve A-6 bombardier with the fleet airwing at Oceana Naval Air Station, Virginia, supporting the deployed aircraft carriers. From 1976 until 1980, pay for all of the services was frozen during a period that saw annual inflation grow to nearly 20 percent. In addition, the fleet was cut almost in half, and sailors were thus subjected to much more family separation to meet crisis deployments, particularly in the Mediterranean and Persian Gulf. Enlisted retention by 1979 had dropped to the lowest level ever recorded. The Navy nearly had to resort to press gangs. Recruits were accepted who were illiterate, convicted felons, drug users and worse. Yet still the fleet was manned at only 91 percent and four ships could not sail on schedule for lack of minimum crew. The CNO, Admiral Thomas Hayward, testified to Congress that we had a one-and-one-half–ocean Navy for a three-ocean commitment.

Even more disturbing was the collapse of self-confidence in the naval officer corps itself. There was a fragmentation into narrow parochialism between aviators, submariners, etc., squabbling among themselves for the shrinking budget and paying little attention to the larger issues: mission, purpose and strategy.

As a presidential appointee in the Ford years, I had resigned when President Carter was elected and started a consulting company, while continuing my flying duties as a naval reservist. As the Navy sank to an alarming state during the Carter years I shared the sailors' frustration and anger. I became determined to do something about it.

During my years with Kissinger I had developed strong friendships with Senators John Tower and Henry "Scoop" Jackson and with George Bush. These men, and Reagan's future national security advisor, Richard Allen, were leading what had become a strong bipartisan opposition on national security affairs. I was able to help. During Bush's primary campaign for the presidency he raised to a high degree of visibility the need for rebuilding the Navy, and when President Reagan eventually got the nomination and Bush became his vice-presidential nominee, they adopted as one of their main campaign issues the need for maritime superiority and a 600-ship Navy.

After the election I expressed my strong interest in becoming secretary of the Navy for the purpose of carrying out the intended naval renaissance. President Reagan appointed me to the job, and his choice for defense secretary, Caspar Weinberger, gave me free rein and support to get it done.

Having bachelor's, master's and doctoral degrees in international relations and national security affairs, twelve years in the Naval Reserve and eight years with Kissinger there was not another job in the government for which I could have been better prepared or more enthusiastically committed. With strong supporters in the House and Senate, a strong president and secretary of defense, and a building plan that had been refined for six years, we launched from a ready deck.

Our first priority was to re-establish the morale and self-confidence of the naval service. A huge step was taken by the president: his submission of a major pay increase with special bonuses and other major improvements to quality of life for Navy families. But most important was renewing a sense of mission and eliteness. We needed to get the word out throughout the fleet that sailors had an elite and a historic mission to make the Soviets understand that if they went to war we would sink them. Sailors had to believe that they were part of a winning team. For my first six months in office I preached that message to the fleet and testified to it before Congress and in the media. The response to these efforts—and more importantly President Reagan's constant reassertion of respect for the military—was almost instantaneous: recruiting and retention went from all-time lows to all-time highs in less than six months. We were on our way to solving the people problem. The next priority was to re-establish a winning strategy.

My first day in office, February 5, 1981, I established the Navy Policy Board, made up of the most senior Navy and Marine civilians and flag officers. We met weekly to settle important policy issues, the first of which was the need for a clear strategy of maritime superiority fully integrated with actual war plans. Some commentators were shocked that an administration would actually use the word superiority—it had become politically incorrect because it was thought to be provocative to the Soviets. But the Reagan administration was not breaking new ground. Such rhetoric had foolishly been dropped in the years of malaise following Vietnam. Since the time of Theodore Roosevelt it had been naval and national orthodoxy that the United States *must* have a Navy superior not only to any other Navy but also to any potential combination of naval adversaries.

I told Congress over and over again that "clear maritime superiority must be acquired," that it was "a security imperative." Some disagreed. Even the phrase "maritime superiority" became the subject of astonishing controversy. The entrenched anti-naval orthodoxy of the 2,000-strong Office of the Secretary of Defense (OSD) bureaucracy was most responsible for this. If one could describe that bureaucratic consensus, it would be a genuine belief that Central Europe was the only theater of importance, that the U.S. Army and Air Force were insufficiently funded to defend it, and that the Navy was of no use whatsoever.

No one who has not served in the five-sided building would believe the strength of bureaucratic inertia. In my entire six years as secretary I was never once able to get cleared an official statement that included the words "maritime superiority," despite the fact that the President and the Secretary of Defense repeatedly affirmed it. The OSD staff would not budge. I of course simply ignored the OSD bureaucracy and continued to use the phrase without clearance.

For example, in December 1982, President Reagan was to make a major policy speech in California and the White House staff asked my assistance in preparing it. I submitted some draft material to the OSD for clearance and they removed every reference to maritime superiority. I therefore had to go down and see Cap Weinberger personally to get his reassurance that he had not changed his strategic views. Then I sent my draft directly to the White House. The President gave the speech with resounding success on December 28, 1982. It read in part:

> . . . although the Soviet Union is historically a land power, virtually self-sufficient in mineral and energy resources and land-linked to Europe and the vast stretches of Asia, it has created a powerful blue-ocean Navy that cannot be justified by any legitimate defense need. It is a Navy built for offensive action, to cut free-world supply lines and render impossible the support by sea of free-world allies.
>
> By contrast the United States is a naval power by necessity, critically dependent on the trans-oceanic import of vital strategic materials. Over 90 percent of our commerce between continents moves in ships. Freedom to use the seas is our nation's lifeblood. For that reason our Navy is designed to keep the sea-lanes open worldwide—a far greater task than closing those sea-lanes at strategic choke points. Maritime superiority for us is a necessity. We must be able in time of emergency to venture in harm's way, controlling air, surface and subsurface areas to assure access to all the oceans of the world. Failure to do so will leave the credibility of our conventional defense forces in doubt.
>
> We are . . . building a 600-ship fleet, including fifteen carrier battle groups.

That, in short, was our strategy. To accomplish it we needed to obtain from Congress a building program capable of producing 600 ships. The first priority if the Soviets attacked would be to establish early control of the sea bridge of the North Atlantic and then carry the offensive to the vulnerable northern approaches of the Soviet Union through the Norwegian Sea. Another high priority would be to establish immediate control of the Mediterranean to defend NATO's southern flank and to carry the fight to the enemy through its southern flank. Additional critical tasks would be to insure control of the Persian Gulf and its strategic oil supplies, the Indian Ocean and its vital sea-lanes, and the strategic straits of Sunda and Malacca in Southeast Asia; assure the successful defense of Japan and our allies in Southeast Asia; and to maintain control of the North Pacific, to protect Alaska and its vital oil supply, as well as carry the fight to the Soviet Union's thinly guarded eastern flanks.

Equally important to these sea-control tasks were the maintenance of the sea-based nuclear deterrent with the *Trident* and *Poseidon* submarines and ballistic missiles. And all of the above would have to be done simultaneously, not sequentially.

Derived from all these tasks, the full program that we sent to Congress included 15 carrier battle groups; 4 battleship battle groups; 250 frigates, destroyers and cruisers; 100 attack submarines; and 40 strategic submarines and amphibious ships sufficient to lift two full Marine amphibious brigades. A strong consensus emerged behind this program. By the time that I left the Navy Department in April 1987, we had 594 ships in commission and 30 under construction. We were able to achieve this ambitious building program by bringing in competition and multiple sources for building ships, aircraft and missiles. George Sawyer, my assistant secretary of the Navy for shipbuilding, completely reformed the contracting procedures and management of Navy shipbuilding and repair. As a result, over the six years we were able for the first time in history to achieve overall cost *underruns* of nearly $8 billion in shipbuilding.

As important as the strategy and building program were to reversing our fortunes in the Cold War, the most important thing we could do was to deploy and operate the Navy in a way that would leave the Soviet Union with no doubt as to our seriousness of intent and our ability to defeat them if they were to risk war. We began at once by changing the nature of the annual NATO naval exercises, for many years defensive in nature.

The northern flank of NATO, Norway, Denmark and neutral Sweden, were the most exposed to Soviet military power and the most difficult to defend. Because of the defensive mindset that had dominated naval planning, for many years navies were prohibited from sending aircraft carriers into the Norwegian Sea for exercises. This prohibition was immediately dropped and in the annual NATO naval exercise in the autumn of 1981, we sent three aircraft carriers, along with two British "jumpjet" carriers into the Norwegian Sea practicing not only amphibious landings to defend Norway but offensive air strikes from aircraft carriers based in the Norwegian fjords into the vulnerable Soviet military targets on the Kola Peninsula. The Soviets were impressed. We repeated these exercises every year and did similar fleet exercises in the Northwest Pacific as well. I personally took part and made sure I met with the press in Norway or the U.K. to draw attention to our changed strategy. We were very much in the Soviets' face, with the intention of forcing a major reassessment by them and hopefully a real crisis of self-confidence in their military high command.

By 1984 there was a fundamental shift in Soviet naval strategy. Instead of deploying their attack subs aggressively to both coasts of the United States, and conducting fleet exercises training to interdict the Atlantic sea bridge, they pulled their nuclear strategic-missile submarines under the polar ice cap and used their fleet for defending those boats rather than practicing attacking NATO.

The Soviets were back on their heels.

THE *IOWA*-CLASS BATTLESHIPS: TIMELESS DREADNOUGHTS

If working in government is combat of sorts, it is a war not without some satisfying victories. For me, one such is the *Iowa*-class battleships. Four of these battlewagons were built, *Iowa*, *Wisconsin*, *Missouri*, and *New Jersey*. The first two remain on the Navy's rolls in mothballs; the latter two are floating museums in Pearl Harbor and Camden, New Jersey. These ships were the ultimate achievement of the class of ship that dominated naval planning from the 1890s until World War II. Until they were built, though, the design philosophy of the battleship was big guns and thick armor at the expense of speed.

With the passage of the Navy Expansion Act in May 1938, the mold was broken and plans were laid for a new kind of battleship, one that would be the fastest ship the world had ever seen. This would become the *Iowa* class.

The newest class designed up to that point had been the *South Dakota*, of 35,000 tons. These ships had a top speed of 27 knots. The Navy's Bureau of Construction and Repair pressed ahead for something new under the enthusiastic leadership of Captain Alan Chantry. His direction was for a ship that could fit through the Panama Canal and draw no more than 36 feet fully loaded; carry armor able to withstand a 2,200-pound 16-inch shell, and above all, in Paul Jones's words, sail fast so it could go in harm's way.

The design of the *Iowa* class was completed by the end of 1938 by the Brooklyn Naval Shipyard. The first pair, BB-61 and BB-62, were authorized in 1938, the second in 1939 and the last pair, BB-65 and BB-66, in 1940. Each vessel would cost about $125 million to build. *New Jersey* (BB-62) was built in the Philadelphia Navy Yard and launched December 7, 1942. *Missouri* (BB-63) was built at the New York Navy Yard, and *Wisconsin* (BB-64) in the Philadelphia Navy Yard. Only the first four were commissioned, with *Illinois* canceled immediately after WWII when 21 percent complete and *Kentucky* in 1950 when 73 percent complete. By the summer of 1944, *Iowa* and *New Jersey* had proven so valuable to the war effort that Admiral King (an aviator) ordered the preparation of plans for the improved *Iowa* class.

Iowa was commissioned on February 22, 1943, followed by *New Jersey* on May 23, 1943. The designers and builders had succeeded in producing one of the classic warship designs of all time. Aesthetically the ships were exceedingly graceful, and their performance surpassed expectations in every respect. While specified to have a top speed of 32 knots, I have personally been aboard *Iowa* when she made 37 knots on sea trials. She can also make 24 knots on just two of her four turbine engines. In addition to this extraordinary speed she turned out to be incredibly maneuverable, handling like a destroyer but with a turning radius even smaller. Huge rapid-fire guns and virtual impregnable armor made these formidable warships. The armament was indeed awesome. Each carried three turrets containing three 16-inch .50-caliber guns. In addition they carried ten twin 5-inch/.38-caliber dual-purpose guns, twenty quadruple 40-mm rapid-fire guns and fifty single 20-mm rapid-fire guns. This power enabled them to put 800 tons of accurate munitions on a target in thirty minutes.

As commissioned, the *Iowa* class had a length of 887 feet 3 inches and a beam of 108 feet 2 inches (1 foot, 10 inches less than the Panama Canal locks) and a maximum draft of 37 feet 9 inches with a full load displacement of 57,540 tons. Each carried a crew of 151 to 173 officers and 2,500 to 2,800 enlisted personnel.

After shakedown *Iowa* operated for a while in the Atlantic, keeping distant watch on the German battleship *Terpitz*. In November 1944, she was selected to carry President Roosevelt to and from the Cairo and Teheran Conferences. During the upkeep period a square bathtub with handrails was installed in the flag stateroom for President Roosevelt's use, the only one aboard a fighting ship in the Navy. (I had several occasions to take advantage of the use of that bathtub while aboard *Iowa* in the 1980s. In 1985 I had the honor of bathing both in Roosevelt's bathtub on *Iowa* and Mao Tse-tung's bathtub—much bigger—in Dalien, China. Alas, no pictures survive.)

All four of the ships served admirably during WWII, most notably *Missouri*, which accepted the Japanese surrender. She, *Wisconsin* and *Iowa* were particularly useful in pulverizing facilities in Northern Japan beyond the range of the Marianas-based B-29s. All four saw almost continuous action during the Okinawa campaign. Yet after the war all the ships but *Missouri* were decommissioned, the victims of cost cutting. Only President Truman's special interest in *Missouri* kept her in continued service.

In Korea, however, *Missouri*'s big guns were so valuable that the American commanders now demanded the reactivation of all three of her sister ships. It took five months for *New Jersey* to be recommissioned, eight for *Wisconsin* and fourteen for *Iowa*. During the entire war it was calculated that the four battleships had fired a total of 20,424 16-inch projectiles.

In February 1955, with President Truman no longer in office, *Missouri* was decommissioned and the three remaining battleships were modified to carry nine Mark 23 atomic shells designed for their 16-inch guns. Each had a yield of 20 kilotons (equal to the Hiroshima bomb). Not long after, the ships were decommissioned, *New Jersey* in August 1957, followed by *Iowa* in February 1958 and *Wisconsin* in March 1958. For the first time since 1895, the U.S. Navy was left without an active battleship.

The four ships lay in mothballs until 1967. Given the targets along the north and south coasts of Vietnam, the battleship was an obvious primary weapons system. With jet aircraft costing $2 million each and being lost at the average of one a day attacking targets mostly within range of the battleships' guns, the argument to use them was very strong. But air-power zealots within the U.S. Navy and the U.S. Air Force were able to block activation. Finally a compromise was reached and, after a little over ten years in mothballs, *New Jersey* was recommissioned on April 6, 1968, at a cost of $21 million. By September 29, 1968, she was providing direct fire off the demilitarized zone off the Vietnam coast and was invaluable in destroying bunkers, trenches, fortifications, ammo dumps and logistics centers. Suddenly in September 1969, Secretary of Defense Melvin Laird ordered *New Jersey* deactivated. Senator John Warner, who served as undersecretary of the Navy at the time, later said that "[*New Jersey*] was so effective that we were ordered to take it out of active service because its belligerency and its antagonism was impeding the progress of the peace talks at that time."

As they lay in mothballs during the 1970s there were repeated attempts by Pentagon anti-navalists to strike the battleships from the rolls and have them scrapped. CNO Admiral Elmo Zumwalt barely stopped one such order by appealing directly to the secretary of defense in 1973. After Zumwalt retired, another push was made to scrap them; this time it was blocked by Zumwalt's successor, Admiral James Holloway.

When I presented my first Navy budget in February 1981, reactivation of all four battleships and the funding for the first of these, *New Jersey*, had a high priority. After considerable discussion the authorization was approved, with a firm price of $326 million for *New Jersey*'s reactivation. The remaining three battleships were included in subsequent years' budgets, and *New Jersey* was recommissioned on December 28, 1982, *Iowa* on April 28, 1984, *Missouri* on May 10, 1986, and *Wisconsin* on October 22, 1988, all within or under their budgets. All four were to see adventurous service during the following decade.

The recommissioned ships were not the same; their armaments had been much modernized. While they retained the three 16-inch .50-caliber gun turrets, they now had six twin 5-inch 38s, four quad Harpoon surface-to-surface missile launchers, eight quad Tomahawk cruise-missile launchers and four 20-mm gatling gun missile defenses, as well as much improved communication, electronics and enough automation to reduce the crew by almost half to 1,400 officers and men. And these were young ships. Originally designed for a 35-year service life, *Iowa* had only 12.7 years of service, *New Jersey* 13.7, *Missouri* 10.1 and *Wisconsin* 11.3.

New Jersey's Pacific shakedown cruise ended in a round-the-world tour. While conducting exercises in the Gulf of Siam in July 1983, she was ordered to head for Central America because of the tense Nicaraguan situation. After two months of patrolling off Nicaragua she had achieved her desired effect and in September was ordered to proceed off Lebanon to support the Marines that had been placed between the warring factions. There she fired her guns in anger for the first time in fifteen years, eliminating ten Syrian artillery batteries that had been shelling civilian areas in Beirut. Sadly, there would soon be even greater reason for *New Jersey*'s guns to fire, but they would remain silent.

BEIRUT: TRAGIC DEFEAT

As of this writing, the United States and its NATO allies have deployed some 100,000 troops in the Balkans in peacekeeping operations. This culminates nearly a decade of frequent armed intervention into the affairs of failed states such as Somalia, Haiti and the former Yugoslavia. Overall, Washington and the other Western capitals can count remarkably few casualties. They can also count remarkably few successes.

Lest we grow overconfident in our superpowerdom—and our good luck—we should look in good times to history for examples of how things can go very wrong. No better example will be found than Lebanon, the preeminent failed state of the 1980s. It contained—and still contains—all of the ingredients that we face elsewhere: an artificially rigged political system based on religious and ethnic differences that cannot accommodate change; more-powerful neighbors anxious to change it in their interests; and a whole set of international slogans such as sovereignty and constitutionalism mouthed by everyone, but taken seriously only by the United States.

In the autumn of 1982, after a massacre of Palestinian refugees by Christian militia, President Reagan sent in 1,200 Marines, who took up positions within Beirut airport. Their mission was defined as "presence," but they were viewed by the Syrians and various muslim factions as being in de facto support of the Lebanese government. The situation steadily deteriorated over the following year.

On Sunday morning, October 23, 1983, at about 6:30, a large yellow Mercedes Benz stake-bed truck crashed through the wire barricade guarding the Marine headquarters building that housed virtually all the troops. Following the restrictive rules of engagement provided by their commanders, the sentries had no chance to load and fire their weapons. The subsequent detonation of a gigantic 18,000-pound equivalent bomb destroyed the building, killing 241 Marines, many in their sleep.

What happened next confirmed the Washington rule that just when you think things cannot get worse, they do. It did not take long to establish that the Syrians and the Iranians, who had run a terrorist training base in the ancient town of Baalbek, were partners in the bombing. The President wanted to retaliate and the means were again at hand: *New Jersey* had aboard it the new Tomahawk cruise missile, which was targeted to take out the Syrian defense ministry in Damascus where the attack on our Marines was planned; she could also deliver a good raking of the Syrian positions in the mountains with her 16-inchers. But the Joint Chiefs wanted out of the entire enterprise; they dithered. The vast joint bureaucracy went into molasses mode. It was not until December 3 when the Syrians fired SA-7 missiles at the daily F-14 photo reconnaissance flights, ordered after the disaster, that the President, still angry over the Marine casualties, demanded action. The plan provided to the President was a warmed-over Vietnam Alpha strike, specifically rejecting the use of *New Jersey*.

Instead of using *New Jersey* to destroy the antiaircraft and missile sites in the hills or to blast a key radar site while the aircraft devastated Baalbek, the battleship sat silent as pilots risked aircraft and lives for piddling targets.

An A-6 and an A-7 were downed by missile fire, killing one pilot, Lt. Mark Lang. His bombardier, Lt. Bobby Goodman, survived; he was taken to Damascus and later released ostentatiously into the custody of the Reverend Jesse Jackson after the U.S. government, in the person of special negotiator Don Rumsfeld, indicated we would not bargain for him.

On December 14, after another firing on an F-14, *New Jersey*'s guns destroyed six anti-aircraft sites. Then on February 8, 1984, as the Marines left Beirut, the Syrians rained 5,000 shells on the Christian-held areas of West Beirut, killing dozens of civilians. The *New Jersey* was then unleashed. With the aid of army radar, she halted Syrian fire. Eight of the Syrian batteries were destroyed, though the Syrians claimed before an obliging CBS camera that only civilians and goats had been killed.

The American mission in Lebanon—ill-conceived and badly executed—was over. Lebanon was eventually ceded to Syrian control and the Israeli border is still a mess.

To MAKE OUR FAILURE in Lebanon even more complete, the most obvious lesson of the conflict was unlearned. All of the *Iowa*-class battleships had proven valuable, *New Jersey* especially so. Yet, when the Cold War was over, it was announced that *Iowa* and *New Jersey* would be decommissioned.

Missouri and *Wisconsin* would also have gone into mothballs but for Saddam Hussein, who in 1990 invaded Kuwait. *Missouri* and *Wisconsin* were sent to the Persian Gulf, where both provided enormous and accurate firepower pulverizing Iraqi positions along the coast. Along with other ships, they also launched the first Tomahawk onslaught against Baghdad at the start of Desert Storm. Their naval gunfire was so effective that on Fallacy Island, once the battleship's silhouette was seen on the horizon, hundreds of Iraqi soldiers surrendered to *Missouri*'s reconnaissance drone rather than face her guns. During the war both ships delivered over 2.1 million tons of ordnance, the equivalent of 542 A-6 strikes. Of the sixty-eight targets that received battle damage assessments, 68 percent received damage ranging from heavy to total annihilation.

After the war the sultan of Oman was so impressed with the ships that he offered to pay the entire cost of keeping both active as long as one of them was kept in the Gulf for nine months each year. Once again the anti-navalist faction in the Pentagon won out. The last two battleships were decommissioned, with *Wisconsin* hauling down her colors on September 30, 1991, and *Missouri* on March 31, 1992. Fortunately, great care was taken in deactivating these ships. The Navy spent $16.9 million on preserving the fighting capabilities of *Iowa* and $19.4 million on *Wisconsin*. While *Missouri* has returned to her status as a museum, now on Battleship Row in Pearl Harbor, and *New Jersey* has become a museum for the first time in Camden, New Jersey, Congress has directed that *Iowa* and *Wisconsin* remain on the Navy List at least until 2007. These magnificent ships may well sail in harm's way once again.

Tripoli:
Return of the Berber Pirates

American failure in Beirut would be partially redeemed by success against a pirate in Tripoli.

Moammar Gadhafi is a living monument to the weakness and indecision of the West. On more than one occasion, this foremost practitioner of state-sponsored terrorism has been vulnerable to overthrow, only to be spared by European or American vacillation. When Washington finally was driven by his outrages to strike, it offered a case study of how difficult it had become to deal with the obvious.

Gadhafi ascended to power in 1969 under peculiar circumstances. As Libya's economic prospects brightened, its political system disintegrated. The Americans and the British, both of whom retained military bases in Libya, had helped King Idris I onto the throne when Libya gained independence in 1951. As Idris aged, however, he and his heir fell into a bitter quarrel. When Dick Allen and I were sent to Libya by Henry Kissinger in April 1969, Tripoli was full of rumors about expected coups against the king. Both the monarch and the crown prince were preparing to depose each other, but when a coup was launched on September 1, it turned out to be that of the unknown, British-trained Gadhafi. With the old king infirm, ineffective and conveniently out of the country, the coup succeeded.

Libya's new master lost little time announcing that he was a disciple of Egyptian president Gamal Abdel Nasser. Gadhafi, a devout Muslim and fierce anti-Marxist, was by no means a Soviet puppet. Yet, like Nasser, his anti-Western proclivities propelled him to seek Soviet assistance.

We of the West have a hard time dealing with terrorism, perhaps because we do not really understand the terrorist's aims. He knows that he cannot win an open test of strength. His objective instead is to paralyze our will to act—to pit our regard for individual life against our instinct for self-defense. So every terrorist action has a political purpose—to get us to change our policy to save innocent lives. Democratic leaders here and abroad have found it very difficult to resist this pressure, especially when it is amplified by sensational TV coverage, even if it means that other innocent lives may be put at risk later.

Gadhafi first used terrorism as part of the effort to force the United States and Western Europe to reduce their support for Israel—an effort that began with airline hijackings. Beyond the Arab-Israeli conflict, Gadhafi also sought to make of himself a world power through terrorism. By the early 1970s, as Western Europe reeled under the Munich massacre, airline hijackings, murders and mayhem, Gadhafi's oil money was financing a terrorist internationale: the PLO, the IRA, the Red Brigades, the Japanese Red Army, even the Moro Muslim guerrillas in the Philippines. The Soviet Union and its Eastern European allies were happy to provide arms and training to these various "freedom fighters" in exchange for desperately needed hard cash. The result was a horrifying paradox: In purchasing Libya's oil, the West was financing Gadhafi's attacks on the West.

The United States itself was mercifully free of many incidents on its own territory, although Americans abroad were often targets. When Iran's Ayatollah Khomeini turned to open terrorism, however, the issue transformed American politics. America's inability to come to grips with state-sponsored terrorism helped to seal the doom of President Jimmy Carter's bid for reelection. The Reagan administration hoped to do better.

Gadhafi had made himself a target not just because he blatantly supported terrorism but also because he had expanded his operations into outright international aggression.

Against international law, Libya had laid claim to the entire Gulf of Sidra (or Sirte), a large indentation in the North African coastline that was flanked by Libyan territory but was far deeper than the twelve-mile limit. This normally would have been treated like the dozens of other unlawful claims that we do not recognize. But the Gulf of Sidra was the only place in the Mediterranean that was free of any major sea-lanes or airways—for decades the U.S. Sixth Fleet had depended on it for periodic live-fire exercises. Gadhafi's new prohibition gave the Sixth Fleet a training problem. The chief of naval operations, Admiral Holloway, strongly recommended that the Sixth Fleet continue its exercises and be prepared to defend itself. The Carter administration, however, received firm intelligence that Gadhafi was prepared to fight. (There was indeed strong evidence that in 1979 at least one of his MiG fighters actually fired a missile at an Air Force EC-135 aircraft.) The Carter administration had no desire for any such confrontation with Gadhafi, and the Navy was prohibited from deploying any of its ships or aircraft below the 32°30' N latitude line—the "line of death," as Gadhafi called it—thus bowing to the master terrorist's power play.

With Reagan in office, the Navy put forward a new request to resume operations in the Gulf of Sidra below this so-called line of death. Approval was swiftly given, and the Sixth Fleet proceeded with its plans for a major exercise in that area. In August 1981 the fleet crossed the "line of death," and the Libyan Air Force, now grown to several hundred late-model MiGs, SU-22s and Mirages, rose to meet it. Gadhafi had bought far more aircraft than he had pilots able to fly them, and there were Syrian, North Korean, North Vietnamese and East German "volunteers" manning his force. In the first few days of the exercise Libyan aircraft attempted to get into firing positions on U.S fighters protecting the fleet. In every case they were unable. The high-tech F-14 Tomcats, with two-hundred-mile radars, were able to maneuver into firing position long before the Libyans ever saw them. Very often the Libyans first noticed the F-14s when they were just a few feet off their wings. Finally, in circumstances that are still unclear today, two SU-22s were suspected of firing on a flight of two F-14s launched from *Nimitz*. The outcome never was in doubt. The F-14s had had the Libyan planes locked up in their fire-control radars since the SU-22s were on the runway in their takeoff roll sixty miles away. The Tomcats splashed them each with a single missile.

But this was not the end of America's involvement with Gadhafi.

On June 14, 1985, TWA flight 847 was seized, forced to Beirut, then flown to Algeria and, before our antiterrorist units could act, returned to Beirut. The pattern proved familiar. The terrorists found an American—in this case, Navy diver Robert Stethem—and murdered him. Their courage fortified, the killers then demanded that Israel release Shiite prisoners taken from Lebanon as part of the Israeli withdrawal. There were dramatic scenes of helpless Americans held at gunpoint. Finally, though no overt American pressure was proved, a deal was reached to release the Shiites.

This incident angered the Reagan White House. It was followed in October by a similar incident, but this time with a better ending. On October 3, 1985, the *Achille Lauro* cruise ship departed Genoa, Italy, for the Middle East. Careless security let four Arab gunmen board the boat despite Latin American passports and lack of luggage. Their original mission was probably to infiltrate Israel on one of the ship's port calls, but a steward discovered them oiling their guns while moored in Alexandria, Egypt.

The pirates then seized control of the ship and forced it to sail for Syria, but the Syrian government refused to receive them, and the Israeli government rejected the terrorists' demand for the release of fifty Palestinian prisoners. True to form, the terrorists then murdered an American. This time, Leon Klinghoffer, a New Yorker confined to a wheelchair, was the victim.

Upon their return to Alexandria, the terrorists were set free under terms negotiated by their leader, the particularly vicious Palestinian Abu Abbas, with the support of the Egyptian government. The Italian and West German ambassadors, but not the United States, agreed formally to these arrangements, which were to send the terrorists to freedom.

But when the White House confirmed on Thursday, October 10, that the terrorists, despite Cairo's claims, were still in Egypt, an operation began that will always redound to the credit of the President's national security advisor Bud McFarlane and his deputy John Poindexter. They orchestrated a daring plan to intercept the terrorists and force them to land at a NATO air base in Italy. The instrument would be the Sixth Fleet, commanded by Admiral Frank Kelso. Kelso also had experienced with me the extreme frustration of seeing the bloated chain of command bring on tragedy and paralysis in Beirut, and he had learned the lessons well. He turned the operation over to his battle group commander, Rear Admiral Dave Jeremiah, who did the job flawlessly. He launched six F-14 interceptors, two A-6 tankers and two E-2C radar aircraft from the carrier *Saratoga*. They had to fly five hundred miles in pitch darkness to the point where they hoped to intercept the terrorists preparing to fly to Tunisia on an Egyptian aircraft.

The Egypt Air 737 from Al Maza Air Base took off for Algiers at 10:10 p.m. Cairo time, only ten minutes after the President made his final decision to intercept. While intelligence had provided the type of the aircraft and its side number, there were more than sixty airliners in the air over the eastern Mediterranean at the time. Thanks to the quality of the radars aboard the E-2Cs and F-14s, the number of potential targets was narrowed, but visual inspection had to be made of four different aircraft before the correct side number was found. In each case the F-14s had to fly silently right up next to the unsuspecting aircraft and read the side number with a flashlight. One of those aircraft inspected turned out to be the American C-141 carrying General Steiner and his commandos, who had been ordered to Akrotiri, Cyprus, in hopes of apprehending the pirates in the event of the successful interception and who were now returning to Sigonella, Italy. While the aircraft was in the air, intelligence learned that Abu Abbas, the mastermind of the plot, was himself aboard the Egyptian airliner, along with some Egyptian commandos.

When the F-14s found the right airliner, there was a problem of communications in that they were equipped only with military UHF radios, and the airliner had a civilian VHF radio. They communicated instead through one of the E-2C planes, more than a hundred miles away (the E-2C had both types of radio). One of the controllers aboard the E-2C spoke to the Egyptian pilot, pretending he was one of the F-14 pilots. After making initial contact, the F-14s suddenly turned on all their lights, and the Egyptian crew discovered, to their amazement, that they were surrounded by four F-14s. The initial reluctance of the Egyptian Air pilot to change course to Sigonella was soon overcome by threats of dire consequences. He changed course and was escorted some four hundred miles to Sigonella by the F-14s. On approach to Sigonella, the Italians denied the Egyptian plane landing permission, and only when he declared an emergency was he given permission to land. The E-2C controllers had ordered him to make a left turn off the runway over to the American side of the base, but at the last minute the Italian tower reversed instructions as to which runway to use, so when he turned left, it was onto the Italian side of the field rather than the American side. General Steiner and his commandos landed directly behind the Egyptian airliner and followed it off the runway. They immediately surrounded the aircraft and sought to take custody of the pirates. Italian *carabinieri*, however, arrived and surrounded the airliner and the Americans. A tense standoff followed until General Steiner agreed to turn the pirates over to the Italians. In the meantime, once the F-14s saw the aircraft safely on the ground, they returned the five hundred miles back and trapped aboard *Saratoga*. The terrorists were eventually released by the Italians.

On November 23, an Egyptian flight was hijacked after leaving Athens; this time a U.S. Air Force civilian was murdered. Sixty passengers were killed when the Egyptians botched the rescue. The next day a U.S. military shopping mall in Frankfurt, Germany, was bombed, wounding twenty-three Americans. A month later, on December 27, the Rome and Vienna airports were struck. Five Americans, including an 11-year-old girl, were among the dead; over a hundred people were wounded.

Clear evidence of Gadhafi's complicity in these attacks finally persuaded Washington to do what it should have done years before. Economic links were broken; the fifteen hundred Americans in Libya were ordered to leave immediately; and Libya's actions were described by executive order as an "unusual and extraordinary threat to the national security and foreign policy of the United States." Libyan assets were frozen ($2.5 billion worth), and at last the President declared that Gadhafi must end support and training camps for terrorism.

Gadhafi had reached an advanced stage of delusion with respect to American intentions. Choosing to interpret the European reaction as a rebuff to Washington, he pursued fresh terrorist plans. Once more, these were covered by "dialogues."

This time Washington would not be put off. In March, the Sixth Fleet prepared again to cross the "line of death." The exercises began just north of 32°30' but did not cross it; their purpose was to give our F-14s and F-18s a good idea of Libya's air force. Hundreds of their MiGs and Mirages attempted intercepts, but there was no shooting.

In the second week of March, just after these events but before the crossing of the "line of death," I flew out to the Mediterranean to meet with Admiral Frank Kelso to discuss upcoming operations, and visit the fleet and see firsthand how ready the men were. Kelso was settled in aboard *Coronado*, an amphibious assault ship, which had been modified to serve as his flagship. After the Beirut fiasco Admiral Watkins and I had decided that the commander of the fleet belonged at sea, not on land. Kelso reviewed the plans and the rules of engagement. The fleet was ready.

There were some light moments. As we departed, the bo'sun piped us over the side, and the traditional two bells rang through the ship, "*Ding, ding*, Navy departing, *ding, ding*, Sixth Fleet departing." We went down the ladder and through a double row of side boys in full dress. There was a delay in the arrival of the admiral's barge, so we stood on the float by the side boys, awaiting its arrival. I noticed there were swarms of fish, each about a foot long, all around the flagship, so while we waited I asked the admiral what kind of fish they were. Frank did not know and asked his aide, who also did not know. Frank then asked if anybody among the dozen or so officers standing there knew what kind of fish they were. All shook their heads in the negative. Then one of the young side boys said in a very nervous voice, "Excuse me, sir, but I know what kind of fish they are." The admiral said, "Well, sailor, tell the secretary what kind of fish they are." The young sailor, still at attention, said, "Sir, they are called shiteaters, sir."

Aboard the carrier *Coral Sea*, whose keel was laid when I was two years old, everyone was spring-loaded for their next visit down to Libya. *Coral Sea*, *Saratoga* and *America* were all loaded to the gunnels with every kind of missile and ammunition, and each had ninety days of spare parts. Here was the payoff from the 600-ship Navy and the Reagan buildup. What was especially satisfying to me was to see the tremendous change in tactical thinking that "Strike U" had brought about in each of the three air wings. The lessons of Beirut had been applied.

In the third week of March, the fleet assembled for the third time for a massive exercise in the Gulf of Sidra. This was to be the full challenge below the "line of death." There were finally enough ships to satisfy even the most cautious planner. Kelso had under his command the three aircraft carriers; two Aegis cruisers, *Ticonderoga* and *Yorktown;* and 122 other American ships. On March 22. the first ships and aircraft crossed below 32°30', and Gadhafi's response was immediate. During the earlier exercises there had been more than 160 attempts by the Libyan Air Force, now grown to more than 500 MiGs, Mirages and Sukhois, to intercept American aircraft or ships. Not a single sortie ever got into a firing position on an American aircraft, thanks to the superb coordination of our Aegis cruisers, E-2C radar aircraft, F-14 interceptors, and F-18 strike fighters. Only one Libyan aircraft, a MiG-25, ever got a visual sighting on a U.S. ship, and he was under escort by F-14s when he did so.

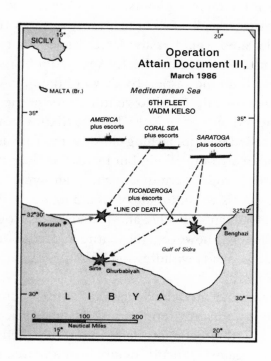

Gadhafi's air force was intimidated. He ordered all his aircraft away from the fleet. Not one took to the air over water. But as soon as the first F-14s were within range of the Soviet-built long-range surface-to-air missiles Qaddafi gave the order to fire, and a pair of SA-5s were launched. I reviewed the printouts from the *Aegis* cruisers following the engagements, and there on the computer paper is the trace of the SA-5s locked up in the *Aegis* cruisers' fire-control radar, streaking toward the U.S. aircraft, which were immediately warned. Our planes were able to counter the missiles. These highly deadly supersonic weapons exploded harmlessly at high altitude.

Jim Watkins and I were sitting in the Navy Command Center in the Pentagon when we heard Kelso give the order to attack the SA-5 missile site. We then heard the A-7 pilots report, "Missiles away." Within a few minutes Kelso reported that the missile sites were off the air. They had been hit by the Harm antiradiation missile that for years had been the target of military reformers in Congress who claimed it wouldn't work. In the following hours, three Libyan fast missile boats attempted to engage the fleet. These were the ships that armchair strategists had declared would easily defeat large aircraft carriers and surface combatants. In each case the Libyan patrol boats were easily destroyed by A-6s from the carrier. By dawn of the following day, not one Libyan ship or aircraft dared to venture outside the twelve-mile limit, and not one did until after Kelso left the Sixth Fleet.

Kelso's plan called for approaching closer to the Libyan coast, staying outside of the twelve-mile limit, but increasing the pressure to the point where Gadhafi would have to launch his air force. It was Kelso's expectation that a massive turkey shoot would follow, perhaps dealing a mortal blow to Gadhafi's prestige and leadership. To our consternation and astonishment, however, the entire exercise was called off early, and the huge armada withdrew on March 27. Internal Pentagon politics had prevailed.

While Kelso had executed the operation flawlessly, its fullest effect was frustrated by premature termination. Gadhafi seized upon the withdrawal of the Sixth Fleet to proclaim victory. He then began a new round of terrorism against civilians. Beginning on March 27, the intelligence community received evidence of almost daily new orders for the initiation of terrorist attacks on American and other Western targets by Qaddafi's "people's bureaus." Because of good intelligence, nearly every one was thwarted, but on April 5, the La Belle disco in West Berlin, favored by American soldiers, was bombed, killing two Americans and wounding more than fifty others. On April 8, a TWA flight from Rome had a midair explosion that took four American lives, including that of one little girl.

Following the Berlin bombing, for whatever reason, a flood of leaks from the White House, the State Department and the Defense Department filled the media with stories that the President was now really going to clobber Gadhafi and that a retaliatory strike against him was imminent. It was, as a journalist remarked, the least-secret operation in history. It was all true; Oliver North's working group was selecting targets. Five were finally settled on, two in Benghazi—a commando/terrorist training camp and the military airfield—and three in Tripoli: a terrorist/commando naval training base, the former Wheelus Air Force Base, and the prime target, the Azziziya barracks compound in Tripoli, which housed the command center for Libyan intelligence and which also contained one of five residences that Gadhafi used. (The attitude in the Pentagon was that if the Libyan leader proved to be a casualty of the raid, so much the better.) These were all difficult targets, located in built-up areas where the danger of civilian damage was great.

The raid could have been executed by the twenty A-6 aircraft aboard *America* and *Coral Sea,* supported by an additional forty F-18 and A-7 light attack aircraft from the same ships, but it was decided that in order to send the strongest possible message to Gadhafi, Air Force F-111s should be added to the strike force. Kelso welcomed the inclusion of eighteen additional bombers to his force. If he was to have but one raid on Libya, as Washington decreed, it should be the heaviest he could mount. Once more our European allies were put on the spot in testing their will to confront terrorism. All but the steadfast British failed utterly. The French in particular refused to allow even overflight of their territory by our Air Force.

The stream of leaks beginning on April 6 about the imminent raid greatly distressed the fleet. It had the effect of putting the formidable Libyan air defense on full alert status. But as days chased days without any raid, the fleet began to see the Libyan defenses relax, despite the media. At 1:30 a.m. on April 15, when the raid was launched, the city lights were still on in Tripoli.

By coincidence, the air force unit chosen for the strike was the same tactical fighter wing of F-111s at Lakenheath RAF Base in England to which I had been assigned for two years as a reservist while attending Cambridge University. Because of the political cowardice of our allies, they had to fly twenty-seven hundred miles around Gibraltar, refueling four times in the seven-hour flight. In perfect coordination, *America* and *Coral Sea* launched a large, integrated support package for the Air Force F-111s, consisting of EA-6B jammers, EA-3 intelligence aircraft, EA-2C radar aircraft, A-7 and F-18 antiradar missile shooters to suppress the antiaircraft missiles and guns, and F-14 and F-18 fighter cover.

Without any voice communications, the three sections of six F-111s rendezvoused with their Navy support aircraft within three seconds of the appointed time and launched into the target area. Simultaneously, the A-6s from *America* and *Coral Sea* picked up a separate support package from the two carriers and launched into their target area around Benghazi, 450 miles to the east.

Six minutes before the first F-111 hit its target, Navy jammers and antiradiation-missile shooters began their suppression of Libyan defenses. The air defenses around Libya and Benghazi are among the most sophisticated and thickest in the world, operated under the direction of 3,000 Soviet air defense technicians. Using the Navy EA-6 jammers, which could jam ten different bands simultaneously, and the Air Force EF-111 jammers, the Libyan early-warning-surveillance and fire-control radars were rendered inoperable. The F-18s and A-7s were able to fire Shrike and Harm missiles down the throats of any SAM sites that came up operational.

The F-111s went "feet dry" west of Tripoli and flew into the desert well south of Tripoli, then turned north to attack their targets from landward. The 111s assigned to the Azziziya barracks put their bombs on target. Apparently Gadhafi had gone to his underground command center and escaped harm. An aboveground headquarters was destroyed and his family injured from the blast. An adopted daughter was killed. The 111s assigned to hit the air base put their bombs precisely on the target and destroyed a great many Russian-built Ilyushin jet transports and helicopters. The F-111s assigned to the commando training site in the port city of Sidi Bilal, near Tripoli, put their bombs generally on the target as well. One F-111 dropped its bombs nearly on the French embassy, damaging it badly. This caused the most civilian casualties; its target, narrowly missed, had been the Libyan External Security building, a reputed headquarters for terrorist operations. Because of malfunctions in their bombing systems and the stringent rules to avoid collateral damage, four of the 111s did not drop their bombs. One

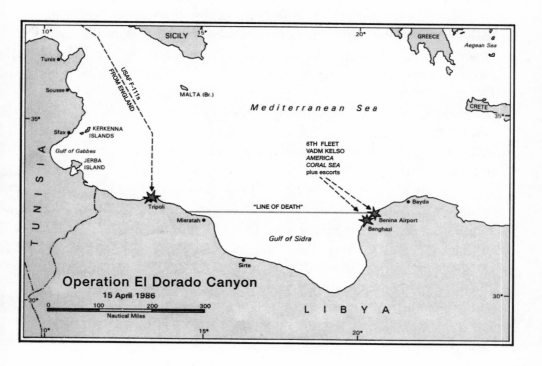

Operation El Dorado Canyon
15 April 1986

F-111 did not return and was presumed to have flown into the water just offshore while exiting the area. The first F-111 hit the target at exactly 2:00 a.m., and the last one cleared the beach at 2:11 A.M. Tripoli time.

Simultaneously, 450 miles to the east, the Navy began its attack on the Benghazi complex. At 1:54 A.M. Tripoli time, the suppression aircraft, the jammers, and the Shrike and Harm shooters launched their attack at the defenses, in exactly the same way as was done against the Tripoli defenses. At 2:00 A.M. the first section of A-6s, led by VA-55 skipper Rob Weber (a former flight instructor of mine at Kingsville) crossed the beach at 200 feet and 500 knots. Eight A-6s hit the Benghazi air base and destroyed more than 20 MiGs, utility aircraft and helicopters. Six A-6s put their bombs precisely on a target that looked on radar exactly like the commando training base but was in fact a civilian building. Thirteen minutes later the last A-6 was clear of the beach. All returned safely to *America* and *Coral Sea*.

After clearing the beach, the F-111s immediately rendezvoused with their tankers to begin the long seven-hour flight back to England. When one was reported missing, the Navy commenced a search-and-rescue operation that lasted into the next day, with no result. The huge Libyan Air Force, supplemented by aviators from Communist bloc nations and Syria, was so intimidated by their experiences with the F-14s and F-18s in the earlier fleet exercises that they refused to take off to defend against the American attackers. Not a single Libyan aircraft rose in opposition.

From a military standpoint the Libyan operation would stand as a model for decades to come. It was a flawless joint Navy Soliders Air Force operation. Gadhafi got the message and terrorist attacks on Americans ceased after the Pan Am Lockerbie bombing. Other terrorist sponsors, Syria, Iraq and Iran, went to ground, and Americans abroad were to enjoy nearly a decade of security as a result. Gadhafi remains unwilling to risk direct confrontation with the United States to this day, although he has resumed financial support of terrorist organizations.

GRENADA:
THE LAST FIREFIGHT OF THE COLD WAR

Nearly simultaneous with the tragic crisis in Lebanon, the United States launched an operation in the Caribbean, this one almost totally successful. On the island of Grenada, Americans were rescued, a would-be communist government defeated, Castro given a black eye and Moscow embarrassed, all at modest cost in lives and treasure.

How these important issues came to be played out on tiny Grenada is a story worthy of Graham Greene. The island was discovered by Columbus in 1498, settled by the French, then captured by the British in 1783. Located in the Grenadines, the most southerly of the Windward Islands in the Eastern Caribbean, Grenada itself is a volcanic dot on the map, about eighty-six nautical miles off the coast of Venezuela.

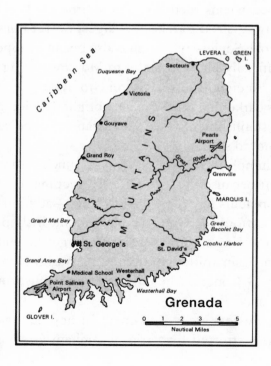

The island is only 133 square miles: about twenty-one miles long and just over twelve miles wide at its broadest point. The 110,000 residents, granted independence by London in 1974, lived blissfully free of international politics, earning a modest living through farming.

The first prime minister, Sir Eric Gairy, ruled by the stars. His profound interest in astrology and high-handed ways soon cost him popular support, and in March 1979, Maurice Bishop, head of the New Jewel Movement, seized the government. The Carter administration, thinking of Bishop as a democratic reformer, recognized him, only to discover that Bishop preferred Cuba as an ally.

This immediately touched the most sensitive nerve in U.S. policy. Ever since the Cuban missile crisis, American presidents had been burdened by the threat of the Soviets acting through Cuba.

Bishop had some vague ideas of social reform but very definite ideas about staying in power. Over the next four years, he obtained over $33 million in aid from Cuba and equipment for an army of 10,000 men. He also began construction of a new airport at Port Salinas with a 10,000-foot runway, sized to take the largest Soviet bombers. The familiar features of a Soviet-style regime also began to appear. Finally, in 1983 Bishop officially pledged fealty to Moscow during an awestruck interview with Foreign Minister Andrei Gromyko.

During this darkening time, the only bright development on the island was the establishment of an American-run medical school with some eight hundred students.

Bishop's triumph in meeting Gromyko quickly turned sour. The Soviets—in part because they were busily keeping up with American military developments like the 600-ship Navy—advised him that they could no longer afford the Grenada experiment: Bishop should mend relations with the United States instead and get his money from the U.S.-Caribbean Basin Initiative. Invited to Washington by the Black Caucus of the U.S. Congress, he unveiled a new constitution and plans for a free election.

At this, the Soviets grew frightened; Bishop had taken his orders too well. He was arrested by a trio of Graham Greene characters—

"General" Hudson Austin and the Coards, Bernard and Phyllis—in a tense atmosphere. Freed by a mob, he sought to reclaim the government; he was killed on October 19, 1982, after a massacre perpetrated by soldiers loyal to the new group. On October 21, even the Cubans denounced the violence.

These events alarmed Washington enough for the President to order the USS *Independence* carrier battle group and a Marine Amphibious Unit (MAU) to divert from their planned course, the relief of the forces in Beirut, and to head towards the Caribbean. Secretary Weinberger issued the order to Cinclant Commander Wes McDonald to invade Grenada on October 22. Then on October 23 came news of the Marine catastrophe at the Beirut airport. That same day President Reagan comfirmed Operation Urgent Fury. Its main purpose was to rescue the thousand Americans at the medical school to prevent another Iran-style hostage-taking episode, and in the course of this, to restore order and democracy to the island.

McDonald decided that Vice Admiral Joseph Metcalf, commander of the Second Fleet, should be commander of Navy-Marine Task Force 120, already on its way. It made sense. *Independence* and its 85 planes, as well as the 2,000-strong Marine Amphibious Unit, were self-contained by design with everything needed to take the island. There was a legitimate concern, however, that the force was just too small to take such a large island against what could be determined resistance.

The Pentagon decided that more was needed, and that the additional forces should be drawn from the elite units of the Air Force and Army. Metcalf was therefore ordered to add these additional forces to his plans. Major General Norman Schwarzkopf (then commander of the Twenty-fourth Infantry Division) was added to his staff. He was to advise on the operations of the Army Rangers, the Eighty-second Airborne Division, the Air Force's C-130s to carry them, and the special operations Delta Force. These 15,000 troops were to be joined by 300 soldiers and police drawn from six of the neighbors.

The Grenadan People's Revolutionary Army ostensibly numbered one thousand, backed by a dubious militia of several thousand more.

Six-hundred-thirty-six military-trained and armed Cuban construction workers were concentrated at the Salinas airport site. There were another forty-three professional Cuban soldiers in advisory roles.

The plan used to assault this force began with the insertion of special units to seize the critical points while the main Marine forces, fully equipped to attack the Salinas airfield (which is located right on the beach) were instead sent against the lightly held and insignificant Pearls airfield at the far north of the island. The Eighty-second was assigned to make a textbook parachute assault on the Salinas airfield, where most of the Cuban strength was concentrated. Without armor they were immediately pinned down, and it took another five days to secure the field.

The U.S. Army and Air Force are trained and equipped to operate together in land warfare. The U.S. Navy and Marines are trained and equipped for sea-based warfare, which requires different radio frequencies, weapons and procedures. When a conflict requires the capabilities of both land and sea services, they can operate very well together, but it requires attention to communications equipment and above all time to train together. On Grenada, because of the last-minute decision to add land forces, they did not have that time.

The operation was of course a success, and the freed American students rejoiced publicly in front of the astonished skeptics of the TV networks.

Along with the inevitable mistakes came some incredible heroics. The mission and nature of the U.S. Navy has changed quite a bit since the days of Nicholas Biddle and John Paul Jones, but the story of one flier in the Navy-Marine force attacking Grenada demonstrates the timeliness of the spirit of sailing into harm's way.

TIM HOWARD:
BATTLE WITH THE CUBANS AND THE DOCTORS

On D-Day, Tuesday, October 25, at 5:36 a.m., some 400 Marines of the 22nd MAU from the USS *Guam* (LPH-9) made synchronized landings via two waves of helicopters on the northern portion of Grenada. Their mission was to seize Pearls Airport, the only functioning air facility on the island. Simultaneously, Army Rangers, flying from Barbados, parachuted into the Cuban-engineered airfield at Point Salinas on the southeastern tip of the island. Their mission was to seize the yet-unopened field and clear it for follow-on airborne forces that would soon land in air force transports from the U.S.

The 22nd MAU was a doctrinally balanced, air-ground task force commanded by Colonel James P. Faulkner. The Marine force consisted of the colonel's command and control element; an infantry battalion landing team reinforced with tanks, artillery and amphibious assault tractors; a combat service support group; and a composite helicopter squadron.

Lieutenant Colonel Granville "Granny" R. Amos, a well-known and respected pilot from Vietnam days, commanded the composite squadron. His outfit had a variety of helicopters, including heavy-lift CH-53 Sea Stallions, medium-lift CH-46 Sea Knights, UH-1 Hueys and light-attack AH-1 Huey Sea Cobras. The Sea Cobras had a crew of two, and were armed with 2.75-inch rockets, TOW antitank missiles and a chin-mounted 20-mm cannon capable of firing 650 rounds per minute. One such Sea Cobra was manned by a pilot, Captain Timothy B. Howard, and his copilot, Captain Jeb F. Seagle.

Howard, a graduate of the University of North Carolina, Wilmington, had completed Navy flight school at Pensacola, Florida, and had some 400 hours of flight time in both the front and back seats of the Sea Cobra. From Florida, he was married, with a baby girl. A friendly, talkative and outgoing officer, his call sign was "TB." His copilot, Jeb, also married, hailed from Lincoln, North Carolina.

On the afternoon of D-Day, Paul Scoon, the legal governor general of Grenada, and the SEALs protecting him, needed help. They were under siege in the governor's mansion, surrounded by rebellious Grenadian soldiers in Soviet-built BTR-60 armored personnel carriers. (Eight years later I took tea in this mansion with other mourners as President Bush's personal representative at Scoon's funeral.)

Before a relief force could get organized and be on its way, Admiral Metcalf ordered Sea Cobras, with their precision-guided TOW mis-

siles, to take immediate action in the area. Captains Howard and Seagle were to be in real combat for the first time in their lives.

The two eager Marine aviators lifted off *Guam*, an amphibious assault ship specifically designed to support helicopter operations. Their
mission was to attack Fort Frederick, an historic old battlement atop a
prominent hill, which looked down from the east upon Grenada's capital, the charming little 18th-century seaport town of St. George's. Built
during the British colonial era, the fort was located approximately one
kilometer south of the governor's residence, also on high ground.

Within a few minutes of being airborne, Captains Howard and Seagle discussed their attack options and determined they had only one:
high, straight and dead ahead from the south up the valley. Fear of hitting neighborhood houses with errant shots was the deciding factor.

Howard successfully made four passes on the target, Seagle hosing
it down with 20-mm cannon fire and slamming two TOW antitank missiles into its tall, surrounding walls.

Coming in at about 1,200-feet altitude for their fifth pass on the
same constrained and prolonged attack heading, their Sea Cobra took
multiple AAA hits on the starboard side.

The hits were catastrophic. Both turbo-shaft engines were put out
of action. The gunship plummeted, its main rotors turning dangerously
slowly—around 75 rotations per minute. (According to the manuals,
controlled flight is impossible below 80 RPM.) Other rounds sieved
the cockpit, wounding both Howard and Seagle.

Howard saw his copilot had been knocked out in the front seat, his
head bobbing unconsciously against his gun sight. Howard yelled at
him to take control of the aircraft, but to no avail. He then sorted out
his own wounds. He felt shrapnel in his neck, and saw his right leg had
suffered a compound fracture. Some four inches of the femur was
sticking out of the skin above the knee, so he could not use the pedals.
His right forearm was severed, the hand held only by about an inch of
skin, the forearm bones and muscles literally blown away.

Despite his condition, Howard did not give up the ship. He resolved to keep on flying the doomed Sea Cobra, one of its engines now
afire. With remarkable sangfroid, he wrapped his left leg around the

cyclic control stick, brought in all the collective pitch he could muster with his left arm and got the helicopter into a controlled autorotation, a procedure where the power derived from the falling aircraft is used to spin the rotor blades to generate a counterforce.

As a reserve aviator, I had become qualified to fly this model of the Cobra, and trained in it regularly while I was SECNAV. Power-out autorotations have to be practiced all the time. I found the maneuver to be among the most demanding in all of flying—with all my limbs functioning.

Howard was prepared to die, but to his surprise, the violently shuddering Sea Cobra slammed hard into the ground, bounced and remained upright. Its landing skids groaned and straddled abnormally wide under the huge strain, but held together. The shaking gunship's tail rotor furrowed the ground and shed itself from the tail boom. Miraculously, the ship did not roll over—incredible airmanship—but its engine cover flew off, and all of its windows blew out.

With the Sea Cobra's engine starting to blaze rapidly, Seagle regained consciousness, got out and ran to a point on the ground where he could encourage Howard to get out of the smoke-filled cockpit. With great effort, Howard unstrapped himself from his armored seat, rolled over the side and dropped to the hard-packed playing field, further aggravating his broken leg. His communications cord was still attached to his flight helmet when he dropped, causing his head to jerk violently upward like it was garroted, compounding his pain.

Enemy fire rattled in from near the fort. Seagle shouted, "Tim, let's get the hell out of here." He grabbed the back of Howard's flight vest and, with Tim pushing backward with his good left arm and leg, dragged him across about eighty yards of the field to a point where Howard could go no further.

There with Seagle exhorting Howard to continue onward, they had a confrontation. At one point, with both of them in shock, Howard threatened to shoot himself so Jeb would not have to worry about him. Seagle then decided to go for help, but Tim suspected his copilot just wanted to draw fire to himself, and away from Howard's exposed position. With this suspicion in mind, Tim struggled to sit upright, waved his good left hand at the soldiers to attract his share of the fire, and then lay back on the grass.

Reaching for their side arms, the two strong-willed comrades suddenly realized they had only one .38-caliber pistol between them. Seagle had lost his in the confusion.

Believing his wounds were mortal, and realizing he could not properly aim and fire with his left hand, Howard beseeched and then ordered Seagle to take the pistol, leave Howard and save himself.

Seagle finally relented, and reluctantly taking the pistol, said he would get help and return.

After Seagle set off, Howard, still bleeding, continued to take fire. Rounds crackled around him, one hitting so close to his head it threw dirt into his eyes. Angry that they would shoot at an obviously wounded man, Tim waved his good left hand in a defiant single-digit salute before his wounds and the gunfire forced him to lay back on the grass once more.

Ignoring them, Howard watched the flames completely consume his once-proud Cobra, its nose facing directly toward him. The flames caused the remaining 2.75-inch rockets to start cooking off randomly, like huge bottle rockets, that roared low past his prostrate form. They were so close he could feel their heat and smell their burning propellant, as they spiraled away and exploded out of control. He was relieved to see that the shots from the 20-mm cannon, pointed starboard, caused the Fort Frederick soldiers' shots to dwindle.

When the Sea Cobra had expended its rounds and rockets, however, the harassing fire resumed. At last the soldiers, wearing East German Vopo-style helmets and carrying AK-47 assault rifles, came down from the fort, headed for Howard. But help was on the way.

Another Sea Cobra, flying protection overhead, engaged the Grenadians just in time. It was Howard's squadron mates, Captain John P. "Pat" Giguere and First Lieutenant Jeffery R. Scharver, who started launching more 2.75 rockets and engaged an AA gun on the beach that was shooting at them. The Grenadians did not bother Howard a bit. (Unbeknownst to Howard, his brave copilot, Jeb Seagle, had been captured about this time and was being paraded around by rebel Grenadian soldiers.)

A CH-46 Sea Knight appeared in the sky, wreathed in blackish-gray smoke. Under cover of Giguere's rocket and cannon fire, it landed on the field in a hail of small-arms fire, some rounds just punching holes in the Sea Knight's thin aluminum skin, others fouling up its stabilization system. A seasoned Vietnam veteran, Gunnery Sergeant Kelly M. Neidigh, M-16 rifle in hand, hopped off the chopper to half-carry, half-drag Howard to the relative safety of the idling CH-46.

Navy doctors aboard *Guam* saved Howard, but not his right forearm. Ironically, the heat of the Soviet round that hit him had helped cauterize his wound, and in so doing probably saved Howard's life.

The men in Giguere's escorting Sea Cobra were not so lucky. The gunship was hit by a devastating burst of AA. Pat Giguere, hit in the chest, and Jeff Scharver, hit in the head, fell out of the balmy tropical sky, and disappeared quietly into the calm, lapis-blue waters of St. George's Harbor. Giguere's wife had a baby boy three months later.

Jeb Seagle had been murdered in cold blood. After he was shot in the stomach a rebel soldier carried his body to a run-down funeral parlor. The funeral director could take no more bodies; he already had ten from Grenadians executing their own people. The rebels, getting cold feet, dumped Seagle's body down on the beach. It was later found, stripped of its boots. Captain Seagle was posthumously awarded a Purple Heart for his wounds and the Navy Cross for his actions in assisting Captain Howard.

Tim Howard was flown from *Guam* to the Naval Hospital at Camp Lejeune, North Carolina, for recovery and processing for discharge for medical disability. Some weeks after his arrival, I visited the hospital to talk to the wounded veterans of the battle. I walked into Tim Howard's room and found him doing one-armed pull-ups on a bar over his hospital bed. I introduced myself and I asked him about his wounds. He told me briefly, as if they were of little consequence. He then became nervous and said, "Please don't take this personally, Mr. Secretary, but I am going to sue you."

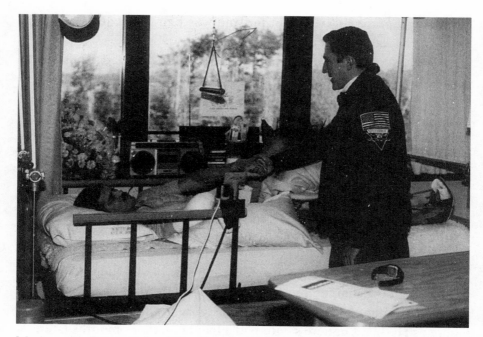

My introduction to Cobra Pilot Captain Tim Howard USMC. He told me with the utmost courtesy of his plans to sue me. *U.S. Navy Photo*

Surprised, I asked why. He said that the Navy doctors had found him medically unfit for service because of his lost forearm and shattered leg and that he must be discharged from the Marine Corps. A lawyer had told him there was no appeal; his only recourse was to sue the secretary of the Navy. He was adamant: "I know that with an artificial arm I am just as good as any Marine, and I will *not* be thrown out of the Corps—Sir!"

I told him that I would look into it. It might not be necessary to sue me. When I returned to the Pentagon, I discussed the matter with General P.X. Kelley, the Marine commandant. He knew all about the captain, and together we decided to overrule the system and continue Howard as a career Marine.

After a tour in the Pentagon, while he recovered full use of his limbs, including a new artificial one, he was assigned to command the first Marine "Pioneer" drone squadron. This he did brilliantly, and the system is now an integral part of Marine doctrine. He has been successively promoted to his current rank of colonel without the benefit of trial lawyers.

DURING THE BATTLE there were unfortunate tactical errors born of lack of interoperability between land and sea forces. Navy air bombed a mental hospital by mistake, some members of the Eighty-second were wounded by similar errors, the Eighty-second and the Marines lost contact, SEAL teams were trapped or lost. There was the apocryphal story that an Army major used a credit card at a pay phone to call the Pentagon in order to reach the ships offshore.

When it was all over, 19 Americans were dead, 116 wounded. The Cubans lost 29 killed, 59 wounded and the rest captured. Forty-nine Grenadan troops lost their lives, 358 were wounded, and remarkably only 24 civilians were killed. The U.S. also captured a huge hoard of intelligence data which laid out beyond any doubt the ambitious plans once entertained by the Soviets and Cubans for making trouble throughout the Caribbean.

The operation was a success, but the military analysis of it a failure. Soldiers and civilians alike felt they proved the need for more jointness and less service specialization. What is needed is more joint operational training for missions where each specialization is really needed, not a forced jointness, one that compels commanders to add units just so every service can be part of the show.

THE END OF THE COLD WAR

Grenada was perhaps the last true Cold War conflict, though the Middle East would continue to prove problematic even without Soviet interference. Yet Grenada grew more out of the end of the Cold War than it did its zealous prosecution. Many Soviet leaders may have still had the will to fight—but they no longer had the means to compete.

The purpose of the grand Reagan strategy—of which the 600-ship Navy and maritime supremacy were an important part—was to instill in Soviet decision-makers the realization that American weakness in the 1970s was an aberration; they could never achieve the military advantage they had pursued in the preceding decade. Their vast military building program was like their vast, centrally controlled economy, an abject failure. Their support of Castro and revolution in Latin America and Africa had failed; their support of terrorists in the Middle East had failed; their attempt to destabilize NATO had failed; their attempt to achieve strategic nuclear superiority had failed; and their attempt to achieve maritime supremacy had failed utterly.

I left the Reagan administration in 1987 to return to private life knowing that the objectives of maritime supremacy had been achieved. I did not dream, however, that the grand strategy of which it was an element would bring about the actual collapse of the Soviet empire a few years later. Exactly how much had the 600-ship Navy contributed to that victory? Of course, no one can say. But we can say with certainty that without it the Cold War would not have ended when or in the way it did.

EPILOGUE

THE END OF THE COLD WAR BROUGHT to a close a distinctive naval era. The era of the 600-ship Navy, like that of the War of 1812 and the Second World War, was a naval Golden Age. There had been a real enemy, an uncomplicated and uncompromising strategy to win, and a tide of public support that carried the strategy through to victory.

It was a great privilege to lead the U.S. Navy in this era, and the temptation to stay in what was to me easily the best job in Washington was equally great. President Reagan wanted me to stay and told me so, and Vice President Bush had expressed to me his interest in having me serve in his administration if he were elected. But I was mindful of the fates of the two men who had served as secretaries of the Navy in its previous golden years. William Jones was a forceful and effective leader of the Navy in the War of 1812. He had been masterful in forging the strategy of concentration of firepower, commerce raiding, and combined operations. He had put great emphasis on development of the Marine Corps and he had funded the first steam warship, *Fulton*. He left the office just before the end of the war, in December 1814, and lived happily ever after.

James Forrestal, on the other hand, Navy secretary in the last years of WWII, left the job to become the first secretary of defense. He stayed too long. At the center of the battle, and having accumulated too many enemies by his success, he was driven to a nervous breakdown and then suicide. Having accomplished what I had set out to do I decided to follow Jones's example rather than Forrestal's and resigned in April 1987.

NAVAL POWER BEYOND
THE COLD WAR: DESERT STORM

The new world order began with a bang. Saddam Hussein had ended his war with Iran and had long coveted the oil fields of Kuwait. With his experienced Army, the fourth largest in the world, and freed from the constraints of his former Soviet benefactors, he believed that he could dominate the Persian Gulf. He did not believe America would oppose him.

On August 2, 1991, completely surprising American intelligence, Saddam entered Kuwait. There was little American force available to stop him. One aircraft carrier, *Independence*, with its battle group, was on station in the Indian Ocean supplementing the small permanent naval force in the Gulf and a British patrol. Saddam should have seized the Saudi port of Dahran, the main entry for the U.S. and Allied forces later on. But his Army lacked mobility and, more important, the fully prepared *Independence* battle group blocked his path. Iraqi armor driving down the main road leading toward the Saudi Gulf coast would have offered a fine turkey shoot for the carrier airwing. Saddam instead stopped and waited to strengthen his forces. While he waited, prepositioning ships were launched from Diego Garcia on August 8, arriving at Dahran on August 15. The division-sized Marine Expeditionary Brigade flew in from California and there married up with the prepositioned equipment. They immediately took a blocking position along the Kuwaiti border. The Eighty-Second Airborne Division, which had arrived in Saudi Arabia the day before, also took their equipment from the ships.

The carrier *Eisenhower* arrived from the Mediterranean through the Suez Canal; a third battle group with *Saratoga* arrived; and Secretary of Defense Richard B. Cheney went to Saudi Arabia and got permission to deploy an additional 160,000 troops. Naval power was deployed in both the Red Sea and the Gulf, sealing a devastating blockade on import-dependent Iraq. Naval aircraft could cover the military bases in western Iraq that were difficult to reach from Saudi Arabia.

For the remainder of the year the Bush administration carried out two major efforts. Secretary of State James Baker did a masterful job in assembling an international coalition to oppose Saddam, while the Pentagon transferred forces from Europe and the United States until the combined force of was more than half a million.

The war itself began with the launch of a Tomahawk cruise missile from the cruiser *San Jacinto* at 1:30 a.m. on January 17, 1992. Lieutenant General Charles Horner, USAF, commanded the air war and did a brilliant job of integrating U.S. Air Force, Navy, Marine and allied aircraft to best advantage. The Navy launched some 500 Tomahawk cruise missiles—which have a range of 1,000 miles and an accuracy of ten feet—from the battleships, cruisers and submarines in the Gulf and the Red Sea. Six aircraft carriers provided essential deep precision strikes with A-6 Intruders, and air superiority fighters with F-14s and F-18s. They were of course outnumbered by the Allied Air Forces operating from the thirty-five bases in Saudi Arabia.

Meanwhile a massive sealift continued. The heavy investment by the Reagan administration in fast deployment ships and mothballed merchant ships paid off. Ninety-five percent of the needed equipment and supplies for the Air Force and the Army came by sea some 14,000 miles from the United States.

As the battle unfolded the battleships and carrier aircraft pulverized the coastal defenses while Marine forces trained and assembled for a massive amphibious assault. The sea was cleared of mines and nearly 150 fast Iraqi torpedo and missile boats (within weeks of the first shots 140 of these boats had been sunk by the U.S. and allied navies, finally putting to rest the old chestnut of military reformers that patrol boats could easily defeat large capital ships). The amphibious armada that was assembled, combined with the Air Force's destruction of Iraq's communications, tied down Iraqi mobile reserves who expected an attack from the sea.

On February 24 General Norman Schwarzkopf launched his now famous left hook attack, outflanking Iraqi defenses. In 100 hours the war was over, with a dazzling demonstration of American and Allied technology. There were fewer than 146 Americans killed in action, 242 in accidents and 458 wounded. The Army and the Air Force have rightly gotten the lion's share of credit for the victory, but the Navy played a critical role.

Naval Decline

Desert Storm made use of the military and naval power rebuilt during the Reagan administration for the Cold War. The inevitable post–Cold War disarmament had already begun before Desert Storm but had not yet taken effect. It resumed immediately after the conflict. By the end of the Clinton administration ten years later, American naval forces had been reduced by about 40 percent overall and the fleet had been cut from 592 to 317. The decline of the Navy was greater than numbers suggest. In the 1980s the Navy had an aura of glamour, of eliteness that was both a result and a contributor to its success. Stephen Decatur, Thomas MacDonough, James Forrestal and Ernest King were not paragons of humility. Their Cold War successors continued the tradition. The men of the Cold War, myself included, relished the idea of "going at the enemy." When President Reagan gave us that opportunity, we had the sense that we were carrying out a responsibility as important as that of our storied predecessors. When the Soviet Union collapsed, we felt we had done our duty.

There were those who felt differently. Just as the anti-naval onslaught of the Truman years followed the glory of V-J Day, so the "Tailhook Affair" followed Cold War victory. Allegations of sexual harassment at the 1991 convention of the Tailhook Association drove nearly an entire generation of naval aviators—almost 300 sailors—from the Navy. This event ushered in the beginning of a long cultural war within the military and especially the Navy.

The effort was described in 1993 by the assistant secretary of the Navy Barbara Pope: "We are in the process of weeding out the white male as norm. We are about changing the culture." Social re-engineering came to dominate Navy recruitment, training and promotions. Has political correctness made the Navy weaker? To suggest that it has not is, in the words of military strategist Edward Luttwak, "a grotesque, puritanical hypocrisy." Some would say that this price is worth paying; a historical tour of the costs of weakness would say otherwise.

Anti-navalists have always criticized the Navy for being tradition-bound and resistant to change. While tradition has often been used as an excuse for complacency, the American naval tradition has been one of reform and greatness. This tradition I have seen all my life: visiting Andalusia, the historic Biddle family home on the Delaware; gazing on the model of *Fair American* built as a trophy for its captor, the Royal Navy captain who sent my fourth-great grandfather to prison in England; dining in Nelson's cabin on *Victory;* listening to my father's tales of kamikazes and the stories told to him by his grandfather of naval battle during the Civil War—these have been wonderful, romantic traditions for me.

But when I sought to become secretary of the Navy it was not because I wanted to dine in Decatur's house, occupy Forrestal's office and make my father proud. It was because I wanted to play my own part in a tradition that was still alive; to reawaken the Navy's spirit of innovation and leadership, end its postwar defeatism, and draw on its past to provide direction for the future.

It is that tradition which I have tried to elaborate in this book. I hope it will serve to draw the reader into deeper soundings and perhaps to spark the interest of some future builders of American naval tradition.

BIBLIOGRAPHY

THIS BOOK IS BASED ON A COMBINATION of secondary and primary sources. Research on the lesser known naval persons like George Lehman, Joseph Kelly and others consisted almost entirely of the latter, conducted in archives and record offices in the United States and England. Similarly, the lesser known ship classes like the *Commodore* class gunboats and *LCS*s required considerable digging.

I was somewhat surprised to find that, among the many secondary sources dealing with American naval power, there is much inconsistency regarding details and even dates of important events and battles among authoritative naval sources. This is partly a reflection of the primary sources, which themselves differ, often depending on which side they were on and how long after the fact events are being recounted. In all cases I have depended on the view of the Naval History Center in Washington, D.C., as the final arbiter of such disagreements and on Jack Sweetman and his authoritative chronology, *American Naval History*, for dating.

GENERAL

Beach, Edward L., *The United States Navy*, Naval Institute, Annapolis, 1986.

Cooper, J. Fenimore, *Naval History of the United States, Vols. I & II*, Lee and Blanchard, Philadelphia, 1839.

Hagan, Kenneth J., *The People's Navy*, Free Press, New York, 1991.

Howard, Stephen, *To Shining Sea: A History of the United States Navy 1775–1991*, Random House, New York, 1991.

Isenberg, Michael T., *Shield of the Republic*, St. Martin's, New York, 1993.

Keegan, John, *The Price of Admiralty*, Viking, New York, 1989.

Love, Robert W., *History of the U.S. Navy, 1775–1941, Vols. I & II*, Stackpole, Harrisburg, 1992.

Nortzen, Len, *Guns at Sea*, Galahad Books, New York, 1976

Mack, William P. and Royal W. Connell, *Naval Ceremonies, Customs and Traditions, 5th Edition*, Naval Institute, Annapolis, 1980.

Miller, Nathan, *The U.S. Navy: A History*, Morrow, New York, 1997.

Morison, Samuel Eliot, *History of the American People*, Oxford University Press, New York, 1965

Padfield, Peter, *Maritime Supremacy*, Overlook Press, Woodstock, 1999.

Pocock, Tom, *Battle for Empire*, Michael O'Mara Books, London, 1998.

Sweetman, Jack, *American Naval History, 2nd Edition*, Naval Institute, Annapolis, 1991.

Spector, Ronald H., *At War At Sea*, Viking, New York 2001.

Sprout, Harold and Margaret Sprout, *The Rise of American Naval Powers 1776–1918*, Princeton University Press, Princeton, 1939.

Tute, Warren, *The True Glory: The Story of the Royal Navy Over 1000 Years*, Harper & Row, New York, 1983.

CHAPTER I
THE REVOLUTIONARY WAR

Bradford, James C., ed, *Command Under Sail; Makers of the American Naval Tradition 1775–1850*, Naval Institute, Annapolis, 1985.

Bradford, James, C., *The Reincarnation of John Paul Jones: The Navy Discovers its Professional Roots*, Naval Historical Foundation, Washington, 1986.

Brookhiser, Richard, *Founding Father*, The Free Press, New York, 1996.

Cappon, Lester J., ed., *The Adams-Jefferson Letters*, University of North Carolina, Chapel Hill, 1959.

Clark, William Bell, *Captain Dauntless: The Story of Nicholas Biddle of the Continental Navy*, Louisiana State University Press, Baton Rouge, 1949.

Coggins, Jack, *Ships and Seamen of the American Revolution*, Stackpole, Harrisburg, 1969.

Cook, Don, *The Long Fuse: How England Lost the American Colonies 1760-1785*, Atlantic, New York, 1995.

Davis, Burke, *The Campaign that Won America: The Story of Yorktown*, Dial Press, New York, 1970.

Dunn, Mary Maples and Richard S. Dunn, eds., *The Papers of William Penn*, University of Pennsylvania, Philadelphia, 1981.

Eller, Ernest McNeil, *Chesapeake Bay in the American Revolution*, Tidewater Publishers, Centerville, 1981.

Esposito, BrigGen, Vincent J., USA, *The West Point Atlas of American Wars*, Vol. 1, Praeger, New York, 1978.

Fowler, William M., Jr. *Rebels Under Sail: The American Navy during the Revolution*, Charles Scribner's Sons, New York, 1976.

Gardner, Allen W., *A Naval History of the American Revolution*, Russell & Russell, New York, 1913.

Gardner, Robert, ed., *Navies in the American Revolution 1775-1783*, Naval Institute, Annapolis, 1996.

Guttridge, Leonard F. and Jay D. Smith, *The Commodores: The U.S. Navy in the Age of Sail;* Harper & Row, New York, 1984.

Henderson, James, *The Frigates,* Leo Cooper, London, 1994

Johnston, Henry P., *The Yorktown Campaign and the Surrender of Cornwallis, 1781,* Harper, New York, 1881.

Leech, Samuel, *A Voice from the Main Deck,* Naval Institute, Annapolis, 1999.

Mahan, A.T., *The Major Operations of the Navies in the War of American Independence,* Little, Brown, Boston, 1913.

McCullough, David, *John Adams,* Simon & Schuster, New York, 2001.

Miller, Nathan, *Sea of Glory: The Continental Navy Fights for Independence, 1775–1783,* Mackay, New York, 1974.

Miller, Nathan, *Broadsides: The Age of Fighting Sail 1775–1815,* John Wiley & Sons, New York, 2000.

Morgan, William James, *The Pivot Upon Which Everything Turned: French Naval Superiority That Ensured Victory at Yorktown,* Naval Historical Foundation, Washington, 1981.

Morgan, William James, ed., *Naval Documents of the American Revolution,* Naval Historical Center, Washington, 1986.

Rodger N.A.M., *The Wooden World,* Naval Institute, Annapolis, 1986.

Tuchman, Barbara W., *The First Salute,* Knopf, New York, 1988.

Villanueva, Marcel, *The French Contribution to the Founding of the United States,* Vantage Press, New York, 1975.

Wallace, Willard M., *Traitorous Hero: The Life and Fortunes of Benedict Arnold,* Harper, New York, 1954.

Chapter II
The Privateers

Drowne, Solomon, *Journal of a Cruise in the Fall of 1780 in the Private Sloop of War, Hope.* New York, 1872.

Flower, Raymond and Michael Wynn Jones, *Lloyd's Of London,* Hastings House, New York, 1974.

Lauterpacht, H., *Oppenheim's International Law,* Vol. II, Disputes, War, and Neutrality, 7th Ed., Longmans, London, 1955.

MacLay, Edgar S., *A History of American Privateers,* Ayer Co. Publishers, 1977.

Petrie, Donald A., *The Prize Game,* Naval Institute, Annapolis, 1999.

Stivers, Reuben E., *Privateers and Volunteers,* Naval Institute, Annapolis, 1975.

Wildes, Harry Emerson, *William Penn,* Macmillan, New York, 1974.

CHAPTER III
WAR WITH THE BERBER PASHAS AND REVOLUTIONARY FRANCE

Adams, Henry, *History of the United States of America During the First Administration of Thomas Jefferson*, Scribners, New York, 1921.
Albion, Robert Greenhalgh, *Forests and Seapower,* Naval Institute, Annapolis, 2000.
Allen, Gardner W., *Our Navy and the Barbary Corsairs*, Houghton Mifflin, Boston, 1905.
Allen, Gardner W., *Our Naval War with France*, Houghton Mifflin, Boston, 1909.
Adams, John Charles Francis, *The Life and Works of John Adams*, Little, Brown, Boston, 1853.
Callo, Joseph F., *Nelson Speaks*, Naval Institute, Annapolis, 2001.
Fowler, William M., Jr., *Jack Tars and Commodores*, Houghton Mifflin, Boston, 1984.
Howarth, David and Stephen Howarth, *Lord Nelson: The Immortal Memory*, Viking, New York, 1989.
Karsten, Peter, *The Naval Aristocracy*, Free Press, New York, 1972.
Knox, Dudley W., ed, *Naval Documents Related to the United States' Wars With the Barbary Powers*, Naval History Center, Washington, 1939.
Knox, Dudley W., ed., *Naval Documents Related to the Quasi-War Between the United States and France*, Naval Historical Center, Washington, 1935.
Koch, Adrienne and William Peden eds., *The Life and Selected Writings of Thomas Jefferson*, Modern Library, New York, 1993.
Leiner, Frederick C., *Millions for Defense: The Subscription Warships of 1798*, Naval Institute, Annapolis, 2000.
Mahan, Alfred T., *The Life of Nelson*, Little, Brown, Boston, 1847.
Martin, Tyrone G., *A Most Fortunate Ship: A Narrative History of Old Ironsides*, Naval Institute, Annapolis, 1997.
Moony, James L., ed., *The Dictionary of American Naval Fighting Ships*, Naval Historical Center, Washington, 1981.
Pocock, Tom, *Horatio Nelson*, Knopf, New York, 1988.
Wood, Virginia Steele, *Live Oaking: Southern Timber for Tall Ships*, Naval Institute, Annapolis, 1981.

CHAPTER IV
THE WAR OF 1812

Ball, Charles, *Slavery in the United States: A Narrative of the Life of and Adventures of Charles Ball, a Black Man . . .* , Kraus, New York, 1969.
Barney, Mary, *A Biographical Memoir of the Late Commodore Joshua Barney*, Gray & Bowen, Boston, 1836.
Bolster, W. Geffrey, *Black Jacks*, Harvard University Press, Cambridge, 1997.
DeKay, James T., *Chronicles of the Frigate Macedonian 1809–1922*, Norton, New York, 1995.
Fitzpatrick, Donovan and Saul Saphire, *Navy Maverick: Uriah Philips Levy*, Doubleday, New York, 1963.

Gardner, Robert, ed., *The Naval War of 1812*, Chatham, London, 1998.

Kanof, Abram, *Uriah Philips Levy*, American Jewish Historical Society, no. xxxix, 1949.

Leech, Samuel, *A Voice from the Main Deck*, Naval Institute, Annapolis, 1999.

Mahan, Alfred T., *The Influence of Seapower in its Relation to the War of 1812*, Little, Brown, Boston, 1905.

Norton, Louis Arthur, *Joshua Barney: Hero of the Revolution and 1812*, Naval Institute, Annapolis, 2000.

Paine, Ralph D., *Joshua Barney: A Forgotten Hero of Blue Water*, Ayer Company Publishing, North Stratford, 1979.

Pope, Dudley, *Life in Nelson's Navy*, Naval Institute, Annapolis, 1981.

Robotti, Frances Diane and James Vescovi, *The U.S.S. Essex*, Adams Media, Holbrook, 1999.

Roosevelt, Theodore, *The Naval War of 1812*, Naval Institute, Annapolis, 1987.

Roosevelt, Theodore, *The Naval War of 1812 The History of the United States Navy during the Last War with Great Britain to which is appended an Account of the Battle of New Orleans*, Scribner's, New York, 1926.

Zimmerman, James F., *Impressment of American Seamen*, Columbia University, New York, 1925.

Defense of Uriah P. Levy Before the Court of Inquiry Held at Washington City, November and December, 1857, William C. Bryant and Co., New York, 1858.

Chapter V
The Civil War

Anderson, Berne, *By Sea and By River: The Naval History of the Civil War*, Knopf, New York, 1962.

Bates, Samuel P., *History of Pennsylvania Volunteers*, B. Singerly, State Printer, Harrisburg, 1869.

Boyton, Charles B., *History of the Navy During the Rebellion Vols. I & II*, Appleton, New York, 1867.

Coombe, Jack D., *Gunfire Around the Gulf*, Bantam, New York, 1999.

Courtemanche, Regis A., *No Need of Glory: The British Navy in American Waters 1864–1868*, Naval Institute, Annapolis, 1977.

Hearn, Chester G., *Admiral David Glasgow Farragut*, Naval Institute, Annapolis, MD, 1998.

Dalzell, George W., *The Flight from the Flag*, University of North Carolina Press, Chapel Hill, 1940.

Duffy, James P., *Lincoln's Admiral*, John Wiley & Sons, New York, 1997.

Dudley, William S., *Going South: U.S. Navy Officer Resignations & Dismissals on The Eve of the Civil War*, Naval Historical Foundation, Washington, 1981.

Fowler, William M., Jr., *Under Two Flags*, Norton, New York, 1990.

Grant, U.S., *Personal Memoirs*, Jenkins & McCowan, New York, 1894.

Kay, James Tertius, *Monitor*, Pimlico, London, 1999.

Lewis, Charles Lee, *David Glasgow Farragut: Admiral in the Making,* Naval Institute, Annapolis, 1941.

Mahan, Alfred T., *The Gulf and Inland Waters,* Scribner's, New York, 1883.

Marvel, William, *The Monitor Chronicles,* Simon & Schuster, New York, 2000.

Milligan, John D., *Gunboats Down the Mississippi,* Naval Institute, Annapolis, 1965.

Captain Rafael Semmes and the C.S.S. Alabama, Naval Historical Foundation, (Series 2-Number 10), Washington, 1968.

Remini, Robert V., *The Battle of New Orleans,* Viking, New York, 1999.

Ringel, Dennis J., *Life in Mr. Lincoln's Navy,* Naval Institute, Annapolis, 1998.

Robinson Charles M. III, *Shark of the Confederacy,* Charles M. Robinson III, Naval Institute, Annapolis, 1995.

Roske, Ralph J., and Charles Van Doren, *Lincoln's Commando, The Biography of Commander William B. Cushing, U.S. Navy,* Naval Institute, Annapolis, 1957

Semmes, Raphael, *The Confederate Raider Alabama: Selections from Memoirs of Service Afloat During the War Between the States,* Fawcett Publications, Gloucester, 1969.

Schneller, Robert J. Jr., *A Quest for Glory: A Biography of Rear Admiral John A. Dahlgren,* Naval Institute, Annapolis, 1996.

Semmes Papers, Alabama State Department of Archives and History.

Sinclair, Lieutenant Arthur CSN, *Two Years on the Alabama,* Naval Institute, Annapolis, 1989.

Soley, James R., *The Blockade and the Cruisers,* Scribner's, New York, 1885.

Spencer, Warren F., *Raphael Semmes: The Philosophical Marine,* The University of Alabama Press, Tuscaloosa, 1997.

Taylor, John M., *Confederate Raider,* Brassey's, Washington, 1994.

West, Richard S., Jr., *Mr. Lincoln's Navy,* Longman's, New York, 1957.

Civil War Naval Chronology 1861–1865, Compiled by Naval History Division, Navy Department, Washington, DC, 1971.

Official Records of the Union and Confederate Navies in the War of the Rebellion, Washington, DC, Government Printing Office, 1900.

U.S. Navy, *Official Records of the Union and Confederate Navies in the War of the Rebellion,* Government Printing Office, Washington, DC, 1894.

Chapter VI
Manifest Destiny

Alden, John D., *Flush Decks and Fore Pipes,* Naval Institute, Annapolis, 1965.

Bertram, Edith Wallace and Anne Martin Hall, *Ships of the United States Navy and Their Sponsors, 1797–1913,* Privately printed, 1913.

Brown, D.K., *Warrior to Dreadnought,* Chatham, London, 1997.

Burton, David H., *Theodore Roosevelt, Confident Imperialist,* University of Pennsylvania, Philadelphia, 1968.

Cooling, B. Franklin, *Olympia: Herald of Empire,* Naval Institute, Annapolis, 2000.

Friedel, Frank, *The Splendid Little War,* Boston, Little, Brown, 1958.

Hart, Robert A., *The Great White Fleet,* Little, Brown, Boston, 1965.

Hough, Richard, *A Great War at Sea 1914–1918*, Oxford University Press, Oxford, 1986.

Keegan, John, *The First World War*, Knopf, New York, 1998.

Livesey, William E., *Mahan on Seapower*, University of Oklahoma Press, Norman, 1981.

Long, John D., *The New American Navy*, vol. I, The Outlook Company, New York, 1903.

Mahan, A.T., *The Influence of Seapower Upon History 1660–1805* Francis-Hall, Englewood Cliffs, 1980.

Marder, Arthur J., *From the Dreadnought to Scapa Flow*, Oxford, London, 1970.

Mathew, Robert K. *Dreadnaught*, Random House, New York, 1991.

Miller, Edward S., *War Plan Orange: The U.S. Strategy to Defeat Japan, 1897–1945*, Naval Institute, Annapolis, 1991.

Miller, Nathan, *Theodore Roosevelt: A Life*, New York, William Morrow, 1992.

Morgan, Ted, *FDR*, Simon & Schuster, New York, 1985.

Morris, Brayton, *The Age of the Battleship 1890–1922*, Watts, New York, 1965.

O'Gara, Gordon C., *Theodore Roosevelt and the Rise of the Modern Navy*, Princeton University Press, Princeton, 1943.

Puleston, Captain W.D. USN, *Mahan*, Yale University Press, New Haven, 1939.

Sargent, Commander Nathan USN, *Admiral Dewey and the Manila Campaign*, Naval Historical Foundation, Washington, 1947.

Rawson, Edward Kirk, *Twenty Famous Naval Battles*, vol. II, Thomas Y. Crowell and Company, New York, 1899.

Rickover, Hyman G., *How the Battleship* Maine *Was Destroyed*, Naval History Division, Washington, 1976.

Roskill, Stephen, *Naval Policy Between the Wars*, Walker, New York, 1968.

Sims, William S., *The Victory At Sea*, Doubleday, Garden City, 1920.

Taylor, A.J.P., *The First World War*, Hamilton, London, 1963.

Ward, Geoffrey C., *A First Class Temperament: The Emergence of Franklin Roosevelt*, Harper, New York, 1989.

White, Colin, *The End of the Sailing Navy*, Naval Institute, Annapolis, 1981.

Wimmel, Kenneth, *Theodore Roosevelt and the Great White Fleet*, Brassey's, London, 1998.

CHAPTER VII
WORLD WAR II

Ambrose, Stephen E., *D-Day: June 6, 1944*, Simon & Schuster, New York, 1994.

Appleman, Roy E., *Okinawa: The Last Battle*, Barnes & Noble, New York, 1995.

Astor, Gerald, *Operation Iceberg: The Invasion and Conquest of Okinawa*, Fine, New York, 1995.

Baker, A.D., 3rd, *Allied Landing Craft of World War II*, Arms & Armour Press, London, 1985.

Ball, Donald L., *Fighting Amphibs: The LCS (L) In World War II*, Millneck, Williamsburg, 1997.

Belote, James H., and William M. Belote, *Typhoon of Steel: The Battle for Okinawa*, Harper, New York, 1970.

Blair, Clay, Jr., *Silent Victory: The U.S. Submarine War Against Japan*, Lippincott, Philadelphia, 1975.

Boyne, Walter J., *Clash of Titans: World War II at Sea*, Touchstone, New York, 1997.

Buell, Thomas B., *Master of Seapower: A Biography of Fleet Admiral Ernest J. King*, Little, Brown, Boston, 1980.

Butow, Robert J.C., *Japan's Decision to Surrender*, Stanford University Press, Stanford, 1954.

Dyer, George C., *The Amphibians Came to Conquer: The Story of Admiral Richmond Kelly Turner*, Naval History Center, Washington, 1971.

Edmonds, Robin, *The Big Three: Churchill, Roosevelt & Stalin in Peace and War*, Norton, New York, 1991.

Frank, Richard B., *Guadalcanal*, Random House, New York, 1990.

Fuchida, Mitsuo and Okumiya, *Midway: The Battle that Doomed Japan*, Naval Institute, Annapolis, 1955

Fuller, J.F.C., Mag. Gen, *The Second World War: A Strategical and Tactical History*, Duell, Sloan, and Pearce, New York, 1949.

Gardiner, Juliet, *D-Day: Those Who Were There*, Collins & Brown, London, 1994.

Grace, James W., *The Naval Battle of Guadalcanal*, Naval Institute, Annapolis, MD 1999.

Griffith, Samuel B., *The Battle of Guadalcanal*, Ballantine, New York, 1966.

Halsey, William F., and Joseph Bryan III, *Admiral Halsey's Story*, Whittlesey, New York, 1947.

Hough, Frank O., Maj, *The Island War: The United States Marine Corps in the Pacific*, J.B. Lippincott Co, New York, 1947.

Howarth, Steven, *Men of War: Great Naval Leaders of WWII*, Wiedenfeld, London, 1992.

Jeffers, Geoff, Phil Peterson, Ray Balmer and Don Gordon, *LCS (L) Landing Craft Support (Large)*, Turner Publishing, Paducah, 1995.

Keegan, John, *The Battle for History: Refighting World War II*, Hutchinson, London, 1995.

Keegan, John, *The Second World War*, Penguin, London, 1989.

Kernan, Alvin, *Crossing the Line: A Bluejacket's World War II Odyssey*, Naval Institute, Annapolis, 1994.

Larrabee, Eric, *Commander in Chief: Franklin Delano Roosevelt, His Lieutenants and Their War*, Harper, New York, 1987.

Leahy, Admiral William D., *I Was There*, Whittlesey, New York, 1950.

Leighton, Rear Admiral Edward T. USN (Ret.) *And I Was There: Pearl Harbor and Midway—Breaking the Secrets*, Morrow, New York, 1985.

Lundstrom, John B., *The First Team and the Guadalcanal Campaign: Naval Fighter Combat from August to November 1942*, Naval Institute, Annapolis, 1994.

Lundstrom, John B., *The First Team: Pacific Naval Air Power from Pearl Harbor to Midway*, Naval Institute, Annapolis, 1984.

Mason, John, *The Pacific War: An Oral History*, Naval Institute, Annapolis, 1986.

Miller, Nathan, *FDR: An Intimate History*, Doubleday, Garden City, New York, 1983.

Millis, Walter, ed., *The Forrestal Diaries*, Viking, New York, 1951.

McInnis, Edgar, *The War: Third Year*, Oxford University Press, London, 1942.

Morison, Samuel Eliot, *The History of U.S. Naval Operations in World War II, Volumes IX*, 1947-1962, Atlantic Little Brown, Boston, Vols. I-XV.

Potter, E.B., *Nimitz*, Naval Institute, Annapolis, MD, 1976.

Potter, E.B. and Chester W. Nimitz, eds., *Sea Power and Naval History*, Prentice Hall, Englewood Cliffs, 1960.

Rohwer, Jurgen, *The Critical Convoy Battles of March, 1943*, Naval Institute, Annapolis, 1977.

Roskill, Steven, *Churchill and the Admirals*, Morrow, New York, 1977.

Ryan, Cornelius, *The Longest Day*, Wolff, New York, 1959

Sholin, William, *The Sacrificial Lambs*, Mountain View Books, Washington, 1994.

Spector, Ronald H., *Eagle Against the Sun*, Vintage, New York, 1985.

Strahan, Jerry E., *Andrew Jackson Higgins and the Boats that Won World War II*, Louisiana State University Press, Baton Rouge, 1994.

Yahara, Colonel Hiromichi, *The Battle for Okinawa*, Wiley, New York, 1995.

Weigly, Russell F., *The American Way of War: A History of United States Military Strategy and Policy*, Indiana University Press, MacMillan, New York, 1977.

Weinberg, Gerhard L., *A World at Arms: A Global History of World War II*, Cambridge University Press, New York, 1994.

Weintraub, Stanley, *The Last Great Victory*, Dutton, New York, 1995.

Weintraub, Stanley, *Long Day's Journey into War: December 7, 1941*, Dutton, New York, 1991.

Ziegler, Philip, *Mountbatten*, Knopf, New York, 1985.

CHAPTER VIII
THE COLD WAR

Albion, Robert G. and Robert H. Connery, *Forrestal and the Navy*, Columbia University Press, New York, 1962.

Blair, Clay Jr., *The Atomic Submarine and Admiral Rickover*, Holt, New York, 1954.

Cagle, W., VAdm, Malcolm, and Frank A. Manson, *The Sea War in Korea*, Naval Institute, Annapolis, 1957.

Caraley, Demetrios, *The Politics of Military Unification*, Columbia University, New York, 1966.

Chesneau, Roger, *Aircraft Carriers*, Arms & Armour Press, London, 1992.

Coontz, Steven, *Flight of the Intruder*, Naval Institute, Annapolis, 1986.

Cutler, LCDR Thomas J., USN, *Brown Water; Black Berets*, Naval Institute, Annapolis, 1978.

Ebbert, Jean and Marie-Beth Hall, *Crossed Currents: Navy women from WW I to Tailhook*, Brassey's, New York, 1963.

Ferrell, Robert H., ed., *Off the Record: The Private Papers of Harry S. Truman*, Harper, New York, 1980.

Field, James A., Jr., *History of United States Naval Operations: Korea*, Naval History Division, Washington, 1962.

Forrestal, James, *Report of the Secretary of the Navy 1946*, Naval History Division, 1947.

Friedman, Norman, *The Fifty-Year War: Conflict & Strategy in the Cold War*, Naval Institute, Annapolis, 1999.

Gorshkov, Admiral Sergei G., *Red Star Rising at Sea*, Naval Institute, Annapolis, 1974.

Grant, Zalin, *Over the Beach: The Air War in Vietnam*, Norton, New York, 1986.

Hallion, Richard P., *The Naval Air War in Korea*, The Nautical and Aviation Publishing Company, Baltimore, 1986.

Heinl, Robert D. Jr., *Victory at High Tide*, Lippincott, Philadelphia, 1968.

Hoopes, Townsend and Douglas Brinkley, *Driven Patriot*, Naval Institute, Annapolis, 1992.

Kissinger, Henry, *Years of Upheaval*, Little, Brown, Boston, 1982.

Manchester, William, *American Caesar*, Little, Brown, Boston, 1978.

Margiotta, Col. Franklin A. USAF (Ret.) ed., *Brassey's Encyclopedia of Military History and Biography*, Brassey's, Washington/London, 1994.

Marolda, Edward J., and G. Wesley Price III, *A Short History of the United States Navy and the Southeast Asian Conflict 1950–1975*, Naval History Center, Washington, 1984.

Marshall, S.L.A., *The River and the Gauntlet: Defeat of the Eighth Army by the Chinese Communist Forces, November, 1950, in the Battle of the Chongchon River, Korea*, Morrow, New York, 1953.

Mastny, Vojtech, *Russia's Road to the Cold War*, Columbia University Press, New York, 1979.

Mersky, Peter B., and Norman Polmar, *The Naval Air War in Vietnam*, 2nd ed., The Nautical and Aviation Publishing Company, Baltimore, 1986.

Momyer, General William W. USAF (Ret.), *Air Power in Three Wars: World War II, Korea, Vietnam*, U.S. Air Force Academy, Colorado Springs, 1978.

Morroco, John, *The Vietnam Experience, Thunder from Above: Air War, 1941–1968*, Boston Publishing Co., Boston, 1984.

Nixon, Richard M., *The Memoirs of Richard Nixon*, Grosset & Dunlap, New York, 1978.

Polmar, Norman and Thomas B. Allen, *Rickover*, Simon & Schuster, New York, 1982.

Rockwell, Theodore, *The Rickover Effect*, Naval Institute, Annapolis, 1992.

Sebald, William J., *With MacArthur in Japan*, Norton, New York, 1965.

Schreadley, Commander R.L. USN (Ret.), *From the Rivers to the Sea: The United States Navy in Vietnam*, Naval Institute, Annapolis, 1992.

Sontag, Sherry and Christopher Drew, *Blind Man's Bluff*, Public Affairs, New York, 1998.

Strausz-Hupe, Robert, *Protracted Conflict*, Harper, New York, 1963.

Truman, Harry S., *Memoirs*, Doubleday, New York, 1956.

The U.S. Navy: Keeping the Peace, Naval History Division, Washington, 1968.

Voice of America Interviews with Eight American Women of Achievement, USIA, 1985. (Grace Hopper).

Watkins, James and John Lehman, *The Maritime Strategy*, Naval Institute, Annapolis, 1986.

Webb, Willard J. & Ronald L. Cole, *The Chairman of the Joint Chiefs of Staff*, History Division, JCS, Washington, 1989.

Weintraub, Stanley, *MacArthur's War*, Free Press, New York, 2000.

Zumwalt, Elmo R. Jr. *On Watch*, Quadrangle, New York, 1976.

Chapter IX
The 600-Ship Navy and Cold War Victory

Blundy, David and Andrew Lycett, *Qaddafi and the Libyan Revolution*, Little, Brown, Boston, 1987.

Friedman, Norman, *U.S. Battleships*, Naval Institute, Annapolis, 1985.

Grenada Documents: An Overview and Selection, U.S. Department of State, Washington, 1984.

Haig, Alexander M., Jr., *Caveat*, Macmillan, New York, 1983.

Hart, B.H. Liddell, *Strategy, 2nd ed.*, Praeger, New York, 1967.

Lehman, John F., Jr., *Aircraft Carriers*, Sage, Beverly Hills, 1978.

Lehman, John F., Jr, *Command of the Seas*, Scribners, New York, 1988

Lessons of the Falklands, U.S. Department of the Navy, Washington, 1983.

Marolda, Edward J., and Robert J. Schneller, Jr., *Sword and Shield: The United States Navy in the Persian Gulf War*, Naval Historical Center, Washington, 1998.

O'Shaughnessy, Hugh, *Grenada: Revolution, Invasion and Aftermath*, Hamish Hamilton with *The Observer*, London, 1984.

Public Papers of the Presidents of the United States, U.S. Government Printing Office, Washington, 1985.

Report of the Department of Defense Commission on Beirut International Airport Transit Act, October 23, 1983, Long Commission, U.S. Government Printing Office, Washington, December 20, 1983.

Sumral, Robert F., *Iowa Class Battleships*, Naval Institute, Annapolis, 1988.

The Falklands Campaign: The Lessons, Presented to Parliament by the Secretary of State for Defence, Her Majesty's Stationery Office, London, 1982.

Sterling, Claire, *The Terror Network: The Secret War of International Terrorism*, Berkley Books, New York, 1982.

The Sunday Times Insight Team, *War in the Falklands: The Full Story*, Harper & Row, New York, 1982.

Wilson, George C., *Supercarrier: An Inside Account of Life Aboard the World's Most Powerful Ship, the* U.S.S. John F. Kennedy, Macmillan, New York, 1986.

Archives

The Historical Society of Pennsylvania
1300 Locust Street
Philadelphia, PA 19107
http://www.hsp.org/

Department of the Navy Library
Naval Historical Center
805 Kidder Breese Street, S.E.
Washington Navy Yard
Washington, DC 20374
http://www.history.navy.mil/library/

National Archives and Records Administration
700 Pennsylvania Avenue, N.W.
Washington, DC 20408
http://nara.gov/

Order of Cincinnati
Library
Anderson House
Washington, DC

Library of Congress
101 Independence Avenue, S.E.
Washington, DC 20540
http://www.loc.gov/

Germantown Historical Society
5501 Germantown Avenue
Philadelphia, PA 19144
http://www.libertynet.org/ghs/

Pennsylvania Historical & Museum Commission
Pennsylvania State Archives
350 North Street
Harrisburg, PA 17120
http://www.sites.state.pa.us/PA_Exec/Historical_Museum/DAM/overview.htm

Web sites

A wag has described doing research on the Web as "like using a library assembled piece-meal by pack rats and vandalized nightly." That being said, the sites listed below have been quite useful and have links to numerous other Web sites, far more than I could list.

Also, interesting results can be had by entering things like Naval History or Maritime History, etc. into a decent search engine, such as www.google.com—and most Web directory sites, such as Yahoo, can get you to the bigger Navy and maritime sites, and from there, you can follow links . . .

Maritime History on the web
http://www.ils.unc.edu/maritime/home.shtml

Maritime History web sites
http://www.cronab.demon.co.uk/marit.htm. An excellent site, with many separate sections. Out of the United Kingdom, good for U.S. and Royal Navy, but also general naval history.

Hazegray and Underway - Naval History and Photography
http://www.hazegray.org/

Official U.S. Navy History site
http://www.history.navy.mil/

The United States Civil War Center at Louisiana State University
http://www.cwc.lsu.edu/

This is a huge collection of civil war links, by category, one of which is naval, hence an excellent start to begin looking for civil war naval sites.

The online version of Official Records of the Union and Confederate Navies in the War of the Rebellion (1894–1922) and the War of the Rebellion: A Compilation of the Official Records of the Union and Confederate Armies (1880–1901) are available in the Cornell University "Making of America" website: http://cdl.library.cornell.edu/moa/moa_browse.html.

Submarine Veterans of World War Two
http://www.submarinevets.com.

The maritime history 'listserv,' an electronic discussion group or bulletin board devoted to maritime issues.
http://www.marmus.ca/marmus/marhst.html

ACKNOWLEDGEMENTS

I WISH I COULD SAY that I was responsible for the richness of detail, the new material and the accuracy of facts and events throughout the book, but most of that credit goes to a number of professionals, each an expert in his own right, who helped me in research, drafting or advice. They are David Baker, Seth Cropsey, Roger Duter, Samuel Loring Morison, Stephen Lehman, Don Price and Harvey Sicherman. Gloria Adelson was extremely creative in finding and obtaining the prints, photos and illustrations that accompany the text. Mark Geier oversaw the bewildering number of data requests, permissions and multiple drafts.

Those who argue that editing is a lost art have not met Dan Freedberg, my editor at The Free Press. He has greatly improved this book and while we had a fair amount of arm wrestling, he always allowed me to win my share.

Bill Dudley, Director of the Naval Historical Center, and his colleagues Jeffrey Barlow, Michael Crawford and Edward Marolda reviewed the manuscript and provided many corrections and helpful changes. They did not always agree with my interpretation of events, particularly about privateers, but they have improved the text immensely. Any errors of fact that remain—and all of the heresies—are entirely my own.

INDEX